Anonymous

Papers of the American School of Classical Studies at Athens

Vol. IV

Anonymous

Papers of the American School of Classical Studies at Athens
Vol. IV

ISBN/EAN: 9783337180140

Printed in Europe, USA, Canada, Australia, Japan

Cover: Foto ©ninafisch / pixelio.de

More available books at **www.hansebooks.com**

Archæological Institute of America.

PAPERS

OF THE

American School of Classical Studies at Athens.

VOLUME IV.

1885–1886.

Press of
J. S. Cushing & Company,
Boston, Mass.

PREFACE.

THIS fourth volume of the Papers of the American School of Classical Studies at Athens follows the first after an interval of three years. The first volume represented the work of the first year of the School, 1882-1883, and it was hoped that it would be followed by a similar volume for each succeeding year. But as no material for a volume of Papers to represent the second or the third year of the School has come to the Committee of Publication, it has been decided to devote the second and third volumes (belonging to the years 1883-1884 and 1884-1885) to the publication of the reports of Dr. J. R. S. Sterrett's two journeys in Asia Minor, with his large collections of inscriptions, most of which have never been published before. These journeys were made in the summers of 1884 and 1885, to a great extent under the auspices of the School at Athens. A Preliminary Report of the journey of 1884 was published in 1885; and it was at first intended to make this a part of the second volume of Papers, which the Committee then hoped to publish within the same year. But the great importance of that journey, and the large collection of new and valuable inscriptions discovered and copied by Dr. Sterrett in the course of it (of which the Preliminary Report contains only a small portion), have made it necessary to devote a whole volume to the publication of its results. This will form the second volume of Papers of the School. It is now in press, and will, it is hoped, be published in the autumn of the present year.

The results of Dr. Sterrett's journey of 1885, known as "The Wolfe Expedition to Asia Minor," the expense of which was defrayed by the late Miss Catharine L. Wolfe of New York, through the agency of the Managing Committee of the School, fill the third volume of Papers. This will be published in advance of the second, at about the same time with the present volume.

The present volume nominally represents the fourth year of the School, 1885–1886. It is devoted in great part to the paper of the Director of that year, Professor Frederic D. Allen, on Greek Versification in Inscriptions. It contains also the paper of Professor John M. Crow, a student of the first year, on the Athenian Pnyx, which was presented too late to appear in the first volume. This paper is accompanied by a plan of the Pnyx Hill, made in 1883 by Mr. Joseph Thacher Clarke from an actual survey, which is believed to be the first thorough survey ever made of this important site with exact measurements and by the help of proper instruments. The Managing Committee are under great obligation to Mr. Clarke for this valuable plan, and for the technical notes which he has kindly appended to various passages of Mr. Crow's paper on the Pnyx. Two papers on the Theatre of Thoricus by Messrs. Miller and Cushing, giving the results of the exploration of this ruin which was undertaken by the School in 1886, will be found in this volume. The second of these, though it relates chiefly to work done in the autumn of 1886, during the directorship of Professor D'Ooge, is now published in anticipation of the volume for 1886–1887, in order that the full account of the excavations at Thoricus may appear in one volume. The views of the theatre given in Plates III.–VII. are from photographs made by Mr. W. L. Cushing, the author of the second paper.

The volume ends with an article by Mr. J. McKeen Lewis on Attic Vocalism, which will be read with a sad interest. The death of this gifted and enthusiastic young scholar, which occurred April 29, 1887, a few days after his return from Athens, brings deep grief to all who knew him, and disappoints the hopes of many others who knew the promise of his scholarship.

The latest circular giving information about the School at Athens, issued in January, 1888, will be found at the end of the volume.

It is hoped that the publication of three volumes of Papers during the present year will do something to justify the confidence which the friends of our School at Athens have always felt in its success, and to encourage their renewed efforts at this time to secure its permanent establishment.

WILLIAM W. GOODWIN,   *Committee of*
FREDERIC D. ALLEN,   *Publication for*
THOMAS W. LUDLOW,   1885–1886.

February, 1888.

CONTENTS.

		PAGES
1.	THE THEATRE OF THORICUS, Preliminary Report, by WALTER MILLER . . .	1–10
	PLATES OF THE THEATRE, I.–VI.	12–21
2.	THE THEATRE OF THORICUS, Supplementary Report, by WILLIAM L. CUSHING	23–34
3.	ON GREEK VERSIFICATION IN INSCRIPTIONS, by FREDERIC D. ALLEN	35–204
4.	THE ATHENIAN PNYX, by JOHN M. CROW; with a SURVEY and NOTES, by JOSEPH THACHER CLARKE.	205–260
5.	NOTES ON ATTIC VOCALISM, by J. MCKEEN LEWIS .	261–277

THE THEATRE OF THORICUS.

BY

WALTER MILLER.

THE THEATRE OF THORICUS.

PRELIMINARY REPORT.

In the spring of 1886 funds were granted by the Managing Committee of the American School for excavating the theatre in the old Attic deme of Thoricus. We were thus enabled to bring to light a Greek theatre of very peculiar construction.

The work was begun in April by Professor Allen, and was continued by students of the school for about a week. It was taken up by myself on the 5th of May, and carried on until the 2d of June, when the advance of summer interrupted the work. The main features of the structure had been opened to view, but most of the earth in the orchestra and some debris upon the seats still remained to be removed; the inner wall also needed to be more thoroughly uncovered. This was reserved for the autumn. The work was resumed about the first of November, in the directorship of Professor D'Ooge, and was placed under the supervision of Mr. W. L. Cushing. It was finished early in December, and the final Report of Mr. Cushing will be published at the same time with this paper.

A provisional plan of the theatre, which was prepared for this paper with the kind aid of Dr. Wilhelm Dörpfeld, of the German Archæological Institute at Athens, and of Mr. Georg Kawerau, who was in charge of the excavations on the Acropolis, has been replaced by a more exact and complete plan, drawn by Mr. S. B. P. Trowbridge from careful surveys made after the excavations of the past year had been completed. This plan is given in Plate I. (page 12). The other plates are reproduced by the Moss Engraving Company from photographs taken by Mr. Cushing.

TOPOGRAPHY. — The theatre is built between two spurs of a steep, cone-shaped hill, about 146 m. high, the modern name of which is

Βελατοῦρι. It presents another example of the remarkable æsthetic taste which the Greeks displayed in choosing for their public buildings sites that commanded magnificent views. The spectators in this theatre looked out immediately upon the straits and the island of Helena, while they could see Ceos, Cythnus, and Seriphos, in the distance. The Laurian mountains bounded the view on the west, while between these and the islands was a broad expanse of open sea.

Thoricus, one of the more populous of the Attic demes, belonged to the tribe of Acamantis. It was celebrated in fable as the home of Cephalus and Procris, and is named as one of the twelve Attic cities in the time of Cecrops, before the συνοικισμός of Theseus. The name has been preserved in the modern village of Θερικό, which is on the coast, near the harbor of the old city.

Thoricus is seldom mentioned by Greek authors, and what little they say does not throw much light upon its importance and character. Thucydides mentions it once, VIII. 95, 1: αἱ δὲ τῶν Πελοποννησίων νῆες παραπλεύσασαι καὶ περιβαλοῦσαι Σούνιον ὁρμίζονται μεταξὺ Θορικοῦ τε καὶ Πρασιῶν, ὕστερον δὲ ἀφικνοῦνται ἐς Ὀρωπόν. Herodotus also mentions the place once, IV. 99: τὸν γουνὸν τὸν Σουνιακὸν μᾶλλον ἐς τὸν πόντον τὴν ἄκρην ἀνέχοντα τὸν ἀπὸ Θορικοῦ μέχρι Ἀναφλύστου δήμου. In Demosthenes we find the name more frequently. Cf. Or. XXXIX. § 30: Πόθεν τῆν Ἀκαμαντίδος φυλῆς γέγονας καὶ τῶν δήμων Θορίκιος; also, § 7; XI. § 52; XXI. §§ 82 and 121. Xenophon, *Hell.* I. 2, 1, says that in the twenty-second year of the Peloponnesian war (B.C. 410-409) Ἀθηναῖοι Θορικὸν ἐτείχισαν. He speaks of these fortifications again, *de Vect.* IV. 43: ἔστι μὲν γὰρ δήπου περὶ τὰ μέταλλα ἐν τῇ πρὸς μεσημβρίαν θαλάττῃ τεῖχος ἐν Ἀναφλύστῳ, ἔστι δὲ ἐν τῇ πρὸς Ἄρκτον τεῖχος ἐν Θορικῷ· ἀπέχει δὲ ταῦτα ἀπ᾽ ἀλλήλων ἀμφὶ τὰ ἑξήκοντα στάδια.[1] Of this wall extensive remains are found west and northwest of the theatre, among them a well-preserved, massive, square

---

[1] For further mention of Thoricus, cf. Scyl. 57; Nonn. XIII. 187; Hom. *Od.* XI. 321; Schol. Soph. *O. C.* 1595; Etym. Mag. s. v. Θόρικος; Hymn. Cer. 126; for Θορικός in inscriptions, see Ross, *Demen v. Attika;* Pliny mentions Thoricus as if the silver mines of Laurium were there; and, indeed, there are two ancient galleries within a stone's throw of the theatre. Cf. Plin. *Nat. Hist.* XXXVII. 18, 3, and IV. 11.

tower, built in the same manner and of the same material as the wall of the theatre. The whole character of the masonry marks it as a work of the last quarter of the fifth century B.C.

Strabo mentions Thoricus several times,[1] but without giving us any information about it, while Pausanias does not notice the place at all. Dodwell says: "Indeed, it was ruined before the time of Mela, who says,[2] Thoricus et Brauronia, olim urbes, jam tantum nomina."[3]

Modern writers and travellers have given little attention to the ruins of the city. Dodwell[4] visited the place, and made a drawing of the theatre which is utterly untrustworthy. Neither the shape of the structure nor the style of the masonry is accurately represented. His remarks about it are equally far from being correct.

Then came Leake,[5] whose plan is much out of proportion; and the dimensions which he gives could never have been taken from actual measurements. See Plate I., Fig. 1.

What is given by Dr. Lolling in Bädeker's *Griechenland*[6] is faithful, and as good as the concealed state of the theatre permitted when he wrote.

MATERIAL AND FORM.—The material of the fortifications and of the theatre is a blue-gray marble, easily worked and very brittle, which was quarried on the spot. All the parts of the theatre are built of it, excepting a part of the lowest row of seats (from 1 to 2 on the plan), and three battlements at the back part.

The theatre, when seen from above, seems oblong, rounded at one end and square at the other. That this unsymmetrical form was necessitated or even suggested by the nature of the ground seems far from the truth, for the slope of the hill is as well adapted to the usual horseshoe shape of Greek theatres as to the form which this one has. It is true that, owing to the insufficient inclination of the ground, it was necessary to build the heavy retaining wall $A A' A''$, and fill in earth and rubbish, to support the upper rows of seats. But there seems no real reason why both ends of the wall could not

---

[1] IX. pp. 397–399, and X. p. 485.
[2] *De situ orbis*, II. 3 (about 50 A.D.).
[3] Dodwell, *Travels in Greece*, p. 534.
[4] *Ibid.* pp. 534–556.
[5] *Topography of Athens*, II.
[6] pp. 117, 118.

have been rounded. There might indeed have been a small saving of material and labor in the adoption of the present form. But the difference is not enough to counterbalance the sacrifice of beauty and symmetry.

The irregular shape of this theatre remains therefore unexplained. It has been suggested that it was not originally intended for a theatre at all. The difficulty in this is to see what else it could have been. A theatre it is, and as it seems adapted to no other use, we must conclude that its final purpose was also its original purpose.

DESCRIPTION. — 1. Of the scene-structure little was discovered. At a distance of 16.07 m. from the lowest seat we came upon the foundations of what must have been one of the walls of the σκηνή, CCC on the plan. It is 29.60 m. in length, much longer than we should expect it to be; it is not straight, but at the right it bends off toward the outside at an angle of about 35 degrees. What remains must have been entirely underground, as the masonry is exceedingly rough, though strong.

Inside this wall, at a distance of 2.90 m. from it, were found very scanty remains of a second substructure, D on the plan, which would seem to be the scene-wall belonging to the front of the stage, but it is so badly broken and destroyed that it cannot be identified as such.

Connected with the scene-appurtenances in some way may have been the chamber on the southeast corner, VV. It might seem at first to be a later addition to the theatre, owing to the fact that the wall $AA'A''$ is abruptly broken off at B'', from top to bottom, and then hastily reconstructed in a manner far inferior to the general character of the wall.[1] But after the discovery of the wall $BB'B''$, it was evident that the little chamber is as old as any other part; for the wall $BB'B''$, one of the oldest parts, is a prolongation of the back wall of this chamber, EE. This wall $BB'B''$ must originally have been the boundary of the theatre, for on the outer or convex side the facing is smooth, showing that that side was intended to be seen. From this three things are evident: (1) That the chamber did belong to the original design; (2) that the theatre was originally not as large as afterward; and (3) that the building of the chamber was not the cause of the break in the wall.

---

[1] The Rock-cut Chamber is shown in Plate IV., and this break in Plate VII. (Frontispiece).

The chamber is made by cutting down the natural rock to a depth of 3.14 m. at the highest part. The wall EE does not reach the floor in an unbroken line, but at the bottom there are two terraces, extending the entire length of the chamber, 15 m.; the upper one has a width of 0.40 m., and a height of 0.31 m. The lower terrace is larger; it has a width of 0.64 m., and is 0.40 m. high. At the end next to the spectators' seats there is only one such offset; it has otherwise the same dimensions as the lower one, but is only 2.85 m. in length, that being also the width of the chamber.

From the walls in this chamber we learn nothing; for while they may partly rest upon the old foundations, they are undoubtedly of comparatively modern construction; the cross wall, which divides the whole into two small rooms, 2.85 m. × 7.00 m. and 8.00 m. respectively, certainly does not rest on any ancient substructions. The apartment V has what seems to be a doorway, 3.18 m. wide; outside the doorway is built, parallel to the line of the ends of the seats, a short wall, to a distance of only 3.70 m. This prompted me to seek for a parodos here, but no traces of one appeared. I found nothing but the natural rock, forming such an obstacle to a passage as to preclude the possibility of there ever having been a parados here. What was the object of this chamber is by no means clear. It undoubtedly belonged to the original plan of the theatre, and may have served as the green-room, or even as a sanctuary, the terraces being in this case receptacles for votive offerings.

At the west end of the scene-wall I had the good fortune to come upon what I at first took to be a παρασκήνιον, the rectangular building K. But it proved too large for that, its dimensions being 8.70 m. × 6.28 m., and it shows no connection with either of the two walls CC or D. This is the most carefully joined and fitted piece of work discovered at Thoricus, and what there is left of it is but slightly displaced. The material is the same as that of the theatre, but its style is totally different. Near the bottom of my trench is a slight offset of 0.06 m. on the wall (see Plate II., Fig. 3), but near the corner the offset is 0.17 m. wide. Only the stones of the corner are hewn smooth; on the rest each stroke of the chisel is plainly recognizable. This rectangular structure is not nearly so old as the rest of the theatre, but belongs to the early Macedonian period, as is shown by the nice joints in the masonry and the parallel layers, the careful, square corners, and the manner of hewing the stone.

In the debris surrounding this square building was found a clay acroterion of no mean workmanship. It is small, 0.27 m. in height, and has no trace of painting. Does it mean that this was a temple of Dionysus? It may well have been. The acroterion certainly belongs to Macedonian times, and it is altogether likely that it adorned the square building. (See Plate II., Fig. 8.)

This building is just parallel to GG', and between them is a πάροδος 3.21 m. wide. The substructure of the seats along the line GG' is a heavy, roughly finished wall of huge stones. That this was the only πάροδος of the theatre seems probable.

2. Though I made four trenches for the sake of finding some trace of a regular boundary of the orchestra, such as is to be seen at Epidaurus[1] and in the recent excavations at Athens, nothing of the sort was found. Whether the orchestra occupied the whole or only a part of the irregular space between seats and scene-wall is still a problem. (See Plate II., Figs. 4 and 7.)

3. We now turn our attention to the κοῖλον. This is by far the best preserved part of the whole theatre. It is bounded by the high wall $AA'A''$, already mentioned, the object of which was to support the embankment on which the upper tiers of seats rested. Instead of having a horseshoe shape, this wall is almost straight in the middle, for a distance of 17.50 m. It is built of large blocks, which are laid in approximately horizontal layers and generally with perpendicular joints. The workmanship shows the solid, substantial style of the latter half of the fifth century. No care was taken to have the joints of the alternate courses fit one above the other. The entire length of this retaining wall is 118.50 m. The height of the level top of the wall above the present surface of the ground outside varies from 1 m. at A' to 3.70 m. at A''. The wall has a thickness of 1.13 m., and at the point A' is 19.48 m. distant from the lowest seat. (See Plates V. and VI.)

The outside of the wall, though the stones are not hewn smooth, presents an excellent appearance; but inside, where it was covered by the earth and was not seen, it is built up with small, unhewn stones loosely placed together.

It was never any higher than it is at present. The finish of the top layer on the inside shows this. The level is uniform from A to A'',

---

[1] Cf. Πρακτικὰ τῆς Ἑλλ. ἀρχαιολ. Ἑταιρ., 1883.

with but few displacements; from A to B, and from A'' to B''', it descends in regular steps. See Plate II., Fig. 5, which represents the point B''' and the part adjoining it. See also the Frontispiece, Plate VII.

Of the break at this point and of the inferior continuation which supports the ends of the seats above the rock-chamber, we have already spoken (p. 8). This continuation forms a tangent to the produced curve, not a chord of it. At the other corner of the theatre, however, the case is quite different. The wall does not bend in a curve, but makes a slightly obtuse angle at A, and then continues in a straight line to the place where it *intersects* the wall GBB'. Here, at B, the seats resting upon it meet with those lying upon the natural *terrain*. The west side of the theatre has, as will be seen, a heart-shaped form, because of the reëntrant angle.

It might be a question whether this outer wall, $AA'A''$, was not a later addition made for the sake of increasing the seating capacity of the building. The joining of the walls on the west side, at B, favors that view, but on the other side evidence is lacking, on account of the break and the subsequent repairs, at just the critical point.

At the back of the theatre there are two huge stone abutments (Y and Z on the plan), which served as entrances for the spectators. They are built up from the slope of the hill to the top of the wall, so that by taking a few steps uphill one might enter the theatre by a slightly inclined plane. Both are built up against the wall, but are not bonded to it. The western one presents some noticeable peculiarities. It is pierced by an arch (see Plate II., Fig. 1) very similar in style to the pointed arches in the walls of Tiryns.[1] The opening is 0.72 m. from the wall AA', and is 0.80 m. wide. The object of this arch is not clear. At first one is tempted to say that it was made to let out the water that should flow from the hill and collect between the two buttresses. But upon digging down to a depth of 4.00 m. from the top of the wall, this theory had to be abandoned, for the natural rock sloped the wrong way for the water to flow off. The explanation given in Bädeker's *Griechenland*, that the opening was left in order to save material, is hardly tenable. Probably the arch was built simply to afford an easy passage around the outside of the theatre. It is to be observed that this western abutment has a branch, Y', nearly at right angles to Y, 4.15 m. from BB', an

---

[1] See illustrations in Schliemann, *Tiryns*, pp. 184, 320, and 334.

entrance to the entrance. It is a paved, inclined plane, between the two balustrade-like walls. The southern one is well-preserved to a length of 3.20 m. The part Y' is 3.00 m. wide, 0.50 wider than the other part. The existence of this structure made it more difficult to go around the abutment, and furnished a reason for the archway.

The eastern buttress is built of the same massive, polygonal masonry as the other, but has no passage through it. It is 5.50 m. long and 2.50 wide. The whole length of the western buttress is 6.40 m., its width 2.50.

I was greatly surprised to find beside this eastern entrance three soft poros-stone battlements of large proportions. A fourth was afterward found at the other entrance. They are 1.28 m. long; the base of the triangular end measures 0.58 m., and the equal sides 0.48 m. They undoubtedly belong to the theatre, and probably served as a sort of balustrade to the entrance bridges. They are the only poros parts of the theatre. Poros is quarried at Laurium, two and a half miles away, and also at a place about four miles north of Therico, and so was a more expensive material than the marble which they had on the spot. Accordingly, it would have been a more costly finish for the upper parts of those entrances.

The seats are as a whole the best preserved part of the theatre. Remains of thirty-one rows are distinctly preserved, and from the state of preservation it is highly probable that there never were any more. The upper twelve rows rested upon the supporting wall $AA'A''$ and the rubbish between it and $BB'B''$. These rows are destroyed except at the ends, where they rest upon the wall at AB and $A''B''$; here they are still *in situ*, set obliquely to the direction of the wall, and projecting beyond its face to a distance of 0.10 m. (See Plate VII.) It is evident at the first glance that these are seats. The remaining nineteen rows are in general preserved. They are made of similar large slabs, resting upon either the prepared solid rock of the hill or upon rough masonry built to support them, while a few are cut out of the live rock itself. In artistic finish the seats are vastly inferior to those in the theatres at Athens and Epidaurus, while they are much better than the seats of the theatre of Argos. The "magnificence" which Dodwell[1] seems to have seen here has long since vanished. The surface of the seats is not, as at Athens,

---

[1] *Travels*, p. 536.

divided into three parts (seat proper, depression for the feet of the man who sat behind, narrow ledge at the back on the same level as the seat) ;[1] they are simply smooth slabs without any ornamentation.

The dimensions of the seats vary, for no attention was paid to exactness in their construction. Their average height is 0.35 m., and their average width 0.60 m.

The *cavea* is cut into three unequal κερκίδες by two flights of stairs, II and II'. The number of the κερκίδες, though unusually small, is the same as at Argos. Noteworthy also is the lack of any steps at all at the sides. The staircases are furthermore very narrow; their width is but 0.62 m., while those of the Dionysiac theatre at Athens are 0.70 m. and those at Epidaurus are 0.74 wide. Two men cannot pass each other on the staircases at Thoricus. The narrowness is rendered still worse by the fact that they lie so deep; they are let down from 0.58 m. to 0.92 m. below the seats. It is, however, quite possible that these are only the foundations of the steps and that other stones lay on top of them, and they were in reality not so low. But no slight objection to this view is, that in this case the real step is nowhere preserved. (See Plate I., Fig. 2.)

The lowest row of seats is in several ways peculiar. It is farther below the one above than we should expect, and it differs in its dimensions from the other rows. The part between the two κλίμακες is not made of the blue marble, but of a white marble, hewn smooth. I am inclined to the belief that this was a terrace for chairs of honor; but perhaps it is simply a passage along the front. On the sides from G' to II and II' to 3 the material is the same as in the rest of the theatre.

Another peculiar feature, more striking in the front row than elsewhere, is the nearly straight direction of the rows of seats in their central portion. In fact, from 1 to 2, a distance of 23.80 m., is a perfectly straight line.[2] At the sides the irregularity of the theatre is again conspicuous. On the east side the distance from 2 to J, another straight line, is 8.65 m., while on the west the length of the curved line $G'II$ is only 5.15 m. The corner 2 is 5.75 m. from the κλῖμαξ II', but 1 is only 2.65 m. from II.

---

[1] See *Papers of the American School at Athens*, Vol. I. p. 147.

[2] But it is only this row that is exactly straight; the others do curve, if only slightly.

At the eastern extremity the three lowest seats are wanting; in their place is a pedestal (*J* on the plan), and behind it a curved passage-way, which is 1.38 m. wide at the southern end. To make this passage-way, the live rock is cut down to a depth of nearly four feet, leaving on the right a wall 1.14 m. in height and 7.65 m. long. The pedestal is 3.90 m. long and 1.24 m. wide. The facing on the inside is rough-hewn; on the outside it is smoother. The eastern side is well preserved for one layer; but on the western side only the corner-stone is left *in situ*. The object of this construction is obscure. It may have been for a few seats of honor; it may have been for a statue, or a number of statues.

By approximate calculation I find that not more than five thousand spectators could have found room in the theatre, allowing one and a half feet for each. So that in capacity this structure falls far short of the more famous theatres of Athens, Epidaurus, and Piraeus. On the other hand, it is larger than the theatres of Chaeronea and Argos.

NOTE. — The fragment of pottery forming the tail-piece of this paper was found by Mr. Cushing within the theatre. It is a drinking-cup, or cantharus, about four inches high, of a brownish clay, coated uniformly without and within with glazed black, and devoid of decoration.

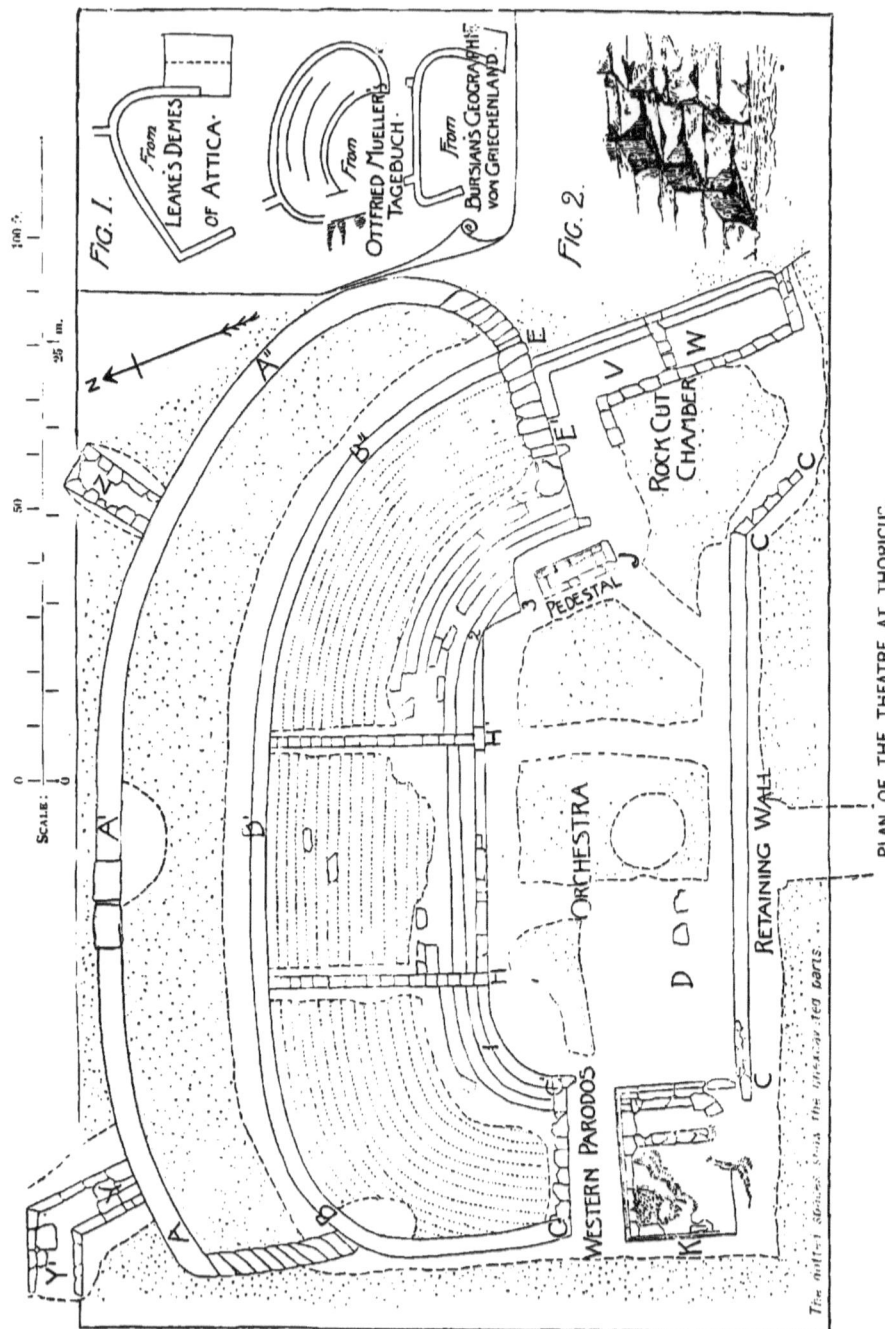

PLAN OF THE THEATRE AT THORICUS.

SECTIONS AND DETAILS OF THE THEATRE AT THORICUS.

PLATE III.

(The Western Wall.) (The Eastern Wall.) (The Rock-Cut Chamber.)

GENERAL VIEW OF THE THEATRE AT THORICUS

PLATE IV

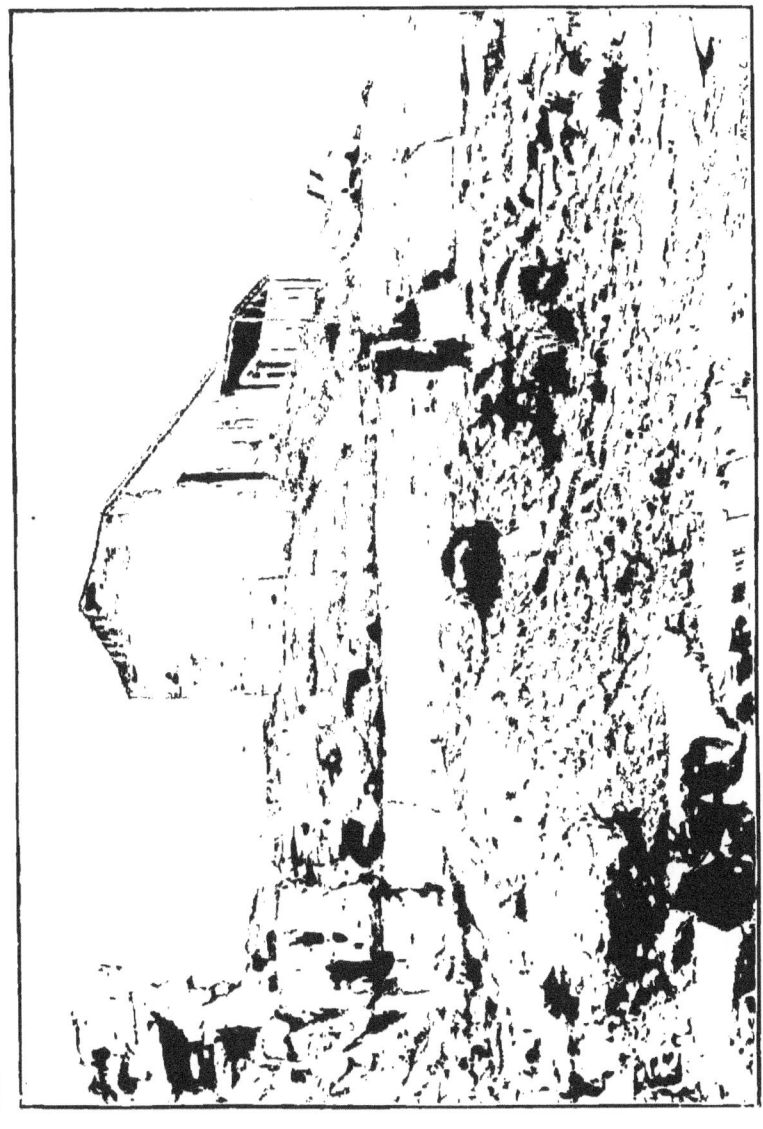

THE ROCK-CUT CHAMBER.
(The Eastern Wall)

PLATE V.

THE UPPER PART OF THE THEATRE AT THORICUS.
(The trench follows the line of the inner wall.)

PLATE VI.

THE LOWER PART OF THE THEATRE AT THORICUS.

THE
THEATRE OF THORICUS.

BY

WILLIAM L. CUSHING.

THE THEATRE OF THORICUS.

SUPPLEMENTARY REPORT.

The following extracts from the reports of archaeologists who have discussed the Theatre of Thoricus, while describing its situation, show the unsettled state of the opinions heretofore held in regard to its peculiarities, and suggest some of the problems which it was the object of the excavations to solve.

For differences in drawings made on the spot by former travellers, see Plate I. Fig. 1.

From Dodwell's *Classical Tour through Greece* (1819), Vol. I., page 534:—

"This place, which was in the tribe Akamantis, retains its ancient name; the port is called Porto Mandri. It was one of the twelve Attic cities in the time of Cecrops, and the birthplace of the lover of Procris. It was probably a place of strength at an early period; and we know that about the twenty-fourth year of the Peloponnesian war Xenophon recommended that it should be fortified and become one of the safeguards of the neighbouring silver mines. In another place he says, the Athenians did fortify it in the ninety-third Olympiad. It is not noticed by Pausanias; indeed it was ruined before the time of Mela, who says, 'Thorikos (*sic!*) et Brauronia, olim urbes; jam tantum nomina.' The present remains are interesting and extensive. The city, which was of an irregular form, was surrounded by a wall with square projecting towers, and apparently about two miles and a half in circuit. The Acropolis was on a pointed hill above the city. The ruins are all of white marble of an inferior kind, veined with gray. It was cut on the spot, as the rocks are of the same materials. The grain is close, but does not sparkle like most of the Grecian marbles.

and is moreover of a brittle and decomposing quality. The walls, though not in the Cyclopian or polygon style, are nevertheless systematically irregular; and the stones, though generally quadrilateral and placed in horizontal layers, are of various dimensions, and their angles seldom rectangular. . . .

"The foot of the Acropolis presents the remains of a curious and magnificent theatre. The seats are preserved, and fifteen layers of blocks of the exterior *Koilon*, in the construction of which some trifling irregularity occurs, but not so much as what is seen in the walls of the city, to which a more remote antiquity may reasonably be ascribed. The form of this theatre is distinguished by the singular circumstance that one of the sides is much longer than the other. A passage seems to have led round the exterior of the *Koilon*. A pointed gate of the Cyclopian or Tirynthian style is attached to this part of the wall, but it is considerably buried. Inscriptions might probably be discovered at Thorikos by a diligent search; but the ruins are overgrown with bushy evergreens, particularly the lentiscus."

From Wordsworth's *Athens and Attica* (1836), page 212 : —

"The view of the ancient theatre at Thoricus affords an agreeable relief to the dismal dreariness of this district. It is a vestige, one of the few which remain, of the pleasures which an Attic village enjoyed in the cheerful seasons of the year. The agreeable landscape which has remained to us of an ancient Italian audience collected on the sloping sides of a rural theatre (Juvenal III. 178), might have been supplied with a Greek counterpart here. The mimicry of the village Dionysia which Aristophanes exhibited in his Acharnians was doubtless a frequent reality in this place. Here also we are reminded of the scene which Virgil has sketched from the antique life of the Attic peasantry : —

> 'The ancient games are ushered on the stage,
> And in crossways and towns the Attic swains
> Strive for the scenic prize, and, cheer'd with wine,
> Leap 'mid the swoll'n, smear'd skins on meadows green.'
>
> (Virgil, *Georg.* II. 381.)

— a scene which no doubt has often enlivened with mirth and laughter the now void and silent sides of this hollow theatre.

"A theatre was an appropriate edifice at Thoricus, for it was in the port of this place that Dionysus, the deity of the Athenian drama, first landed in Attica.

"The outline of this theatre is not of a semicircular form; it is of an irregular curve, nearly resembling the fourth of an ellipse,—the longer axis commencing with the stage, and the seats beginning from the lesser axis, and running in tiers rising above each other concentrically with the curve. They faced the south. The curved outline of the κοῖλον of the theatre formed part of the town wall; this irregular form was perhaps adopted as more defensible than any other.

"In the wall near the theatre is an old postern, surmounted by a pointed arch formed in approaching horizontal courses, in the same manner as the arches in the galleries at Tiryns. . . . The style and massiveness of this postern . . . afford clear evidence of the great antiquity and local importance of Thoricus."

From Fiedler's *Reise durch Griechenland* (1841), page 41 : —

"In this plain of Mandri, extending as far as the range of limestone, stood old Thoricus, one of the twelve oldest cities of Attica, now Theriko. On the lowest declivity of this hill an old theatre of roughly dressed marble blocks is found. It shows little art."

From Vischer's *Erinnerungen und Eindrücke aus Griechenland*, (1856) page 67 : —

"On the south slope of this hill appear extensive ruins of the former prosperity of the district. The most conspicuous are the remains of the theatre, whose periphery wall is fairly well preserved in a very irregular curve, and with two abutments. Of the seats nothing now remains. To the west are the ruins of an ancient square tower, ten feet high. Meagre remains of a stoa are still to be seen. Old Thoricus appears to have spread over a considerable portion of the valley besides."

From Bursian's *Geographie von Griechenland* (1862), Vol. I. page 353 (see Plate I. Fig. 1) : —

"Of the fortifications made in the twenty-third year of the Peloponnesian war remains are still found on the crest of the hills surrounding the plain, especially on the hill to the north of the bay, which served as the Acropolis, on whose western slope a square tower about ten feet high still stands. On the south slope is the theatre, built like the tower of the gray marble of which the hills here consist. The cavea, unique on account of its odd shape, is preserved, though the seats are gone."

From Fergusson's *History of Architecture in all Countries* (1876). Vol. I. page 215: —

"The Pelasgic races soon learned to adopt for their doorways the more pleasing curvilinear form with which they were already familiar from their interiors [of beehive tombs]. The gateway in Thoricus shows its simplest and earliest form."

Compare the actual form, Plate II. Fig. 1.

From the *Archaeologische Zeitung* (1878), page 29, in a report of the meeting of the Archaeological Society in Berlin, Jan., 1878: —

"Herr Peltz spoke of the antiquities to be seen at Thoricus, submitting a sketch of the theatre, the diameter of which was fifty-four metres. He explained its remarkably irregular outline, and referred to the peculiar construction of the outside wall surrounding the tiers of seats, — a construction which occurs also in a square tower on the plain, and which leads to the conclusion that these structures belong to a very high antiquity. The seats, of which only a few traces are preserved, follow the natural slope of the hill. Nothing remains of the stage structure. In the neighborhood of the theatre are scanty remains of an apparently later marble building, consisting of one corner of the foundation and four roughly dressed drums without flutings, eighty-two centimetres in diameter."[1]

From Baedeker's *Griechenland* (1883), page 117: —

"The ruins are in great part at the foot of the mountain-peak on its south side. . . . The most important are the ruins of the theatre. . . . The auditorium faces the south, and has an oval form which is unique of its kind, and was undoubtedly determined by the formation of the ground here.

---

[1] The lime kiln, shown at the right in Plates V. and VI., must be held responsible for the total disappearance of these remains.

"It lies between two spurs of the hill, and is enclosed by a wall of military style, which is composed of marble blocks of different sizes. The seats are formed of broad stone slabs, in great part destroyed. The additions northwest and northeast on the outside of the surrounding wall probably served as foundations for flights of stairs, by means of which the spectators ascended to the top of the wall and thence gained the auditorium.

"The northwest addition is in a fair state of preservation. To save material without loss of strength it is pierced by a low passage-way, the roof of which is made by corbelling.

"Whether the quadrangular chamber, cut into the rock, and opening toward the auditorium before the east end of the main wall, was a side building connected with the stage must remain unsettled."

A. Müller, in *Die Griechischen Bühnenalterthümer* (1886), briefly designates the form of the theatre at Thoricus as " utterly irregular," and refers to the report of Peltz already quoted.

THE work of excavating the Theatre of Thoricus, described by Mr. Miller in his Preliminary Report, was suspended on the second of June, 1886. It was resumed in the autumn of the same year by other members of the American School at Athens. This supplementary work consisted in thoroughly excavating the temple at the west end of the orchestra and the orchestra floor in front of the temple, and in a general examination, by means of a number of shafts, of the various walls entering into the construction of the theatre, with reference to their purposes and limitations. The later excavations served to establish the correctness of most of Mr. Miller's opinions and to settle some questions which were before in doubt, while a few explanations that had been suggested in the absence of necessary evidence were found to be unsatisfactory.

THE MAIN OR OUTER WALL ($A A'A''$. Plate I.). — This wall is built of "rock-faced" or "quarry-faced" ashlar. Its construction is distinguished by the so-called "broken range" work. The abutting joints are of irregular inclination. The bed-joints are "random" or "rambling," a portion of the upper surface of a stone being often cut away in order to make a true bed for the stone of the next course, breaking joints. See the Frontispiece (Plate VII.), and Plate II. Fig. 5. The backing is rubble work, the joints of which were very wide and were filled with mud, which in process of time has crumbled away at exposed surfaces. In respect to careful and artistic workmanship this wall is far in advance of the inner parts of the theatre. Examples of the same construction are found at Ephesus, in the fortifications built by Lysimachus; Messene, founded by Epaminondas; Eleutherae, fortified by Epaminondas; Oeniadae of Acarnania, fortified by Philip; Psophis, near Elis, conquered by Philip; Orchomenos in Boeotia, restored by Philip or Alexander; Plataeae, restored by Alexander; at Mazi, Corinth, and Sikyon; and also at Norba, Cora, Setium, and Terracina in Italy. In none of those walls is there a precise resemblance to the Thoricus walls; but all have irregular abutting joints and a tendency, though in a much less degree than at Thoricus, to the use of rambling bed-joints. The military tower, a few rods to the west of the theatre, furnishes the only other known example of construction which corresponds identically with that of the wall under discussion, though the exposed surfaces of the tower have suffered considerable abrasion, while the stones of the theatre appear unharmed.

No exact conclusion as to age can be drawn from this kind of workmanship. It seems to be a transition from the polygonal to the quadrangular style of masonry, confined to no particular epoch. Its motive is the effort to secure greater solidity by the use of horizontal courses, and at the same time to avoid waste of material, such as is involved in cutting all stones to the same dimensions. We can only say that while broken range work was employed by the Greeks and Italians generally before the second century B.C., the time of its most extensive use seems to have been about the fourth century, judging by those walls of which the builders are known with some certainty.

The similarity of workmanship in the theatre wall and the military tower suggests that both structures were built by the same architect. But assuming that they are of the same age, it cannot be proved that the tower is a remnant of those fortifications mentioned by Xenophon

(*Hellen.* i. 2, 1) as having been built by the Athenians in the Peloponnesian war. Attempts, therefore, to fix the date of the theatre by that allusion in the Hellenica depend upon a defective chain of evidence.

The passage through the west abutment is built with the skill which is characteristic of the general work of the main wall, and the converging sides of the stones which form the arch are trimmed accurately to form a smooth surface. This interior finish, as well as the height of the passage, forbids the conjecture that it was designed merely as a culvert. A plain lintel might have terminated it, but greater sustaining power was secured, and at the same time the comparatively slender buttress, built against but not bonded to the main wall, was strengthened, by adopting the common device of extending successive courses of masonry toward each other until the space was covered at the desired height. The expensive and unstable voussoir arch was discarded here, as it was in all Greek masonry, not subterranean, which is known to us.

THE INNER WALL, $BB'B''$ (see also Plate V.), discovered by Mr. Miller, is made of thin, unhewn slabs laid evenly in clay. Its construction is the same as that of the retaining wall CC, and cannot be said to characterize any particular time or race.

This wall marks the limits of the original theatre, which was subsequently enlarged by means of the outer wall. This proposition, aside from the impossibility of finding a motive for reducing the original dimensions, is established by the following considerations: —

1st. If the theatre had been contracted to a shorter radius, there would have been no need of an inside wall unless the outer one had been demolished.

2d. It is not credible that, if the outer wall were to be rejected, the architect would have allowed so much good material for a new structure to go to waste.

3d. At the west end, where the main wall meets the inner wall at B, no traces have been found of an original continuation of the main wall inside.

THE ORCHESTRA. — No vestiges of a stage structure have been brought to light. The long, straight wall (marked CC in the diagram) was merely for the purpose of retaining the artificial mass of earth forming the orchestra floor, which on its outer side was raised sixteen feet above the natural slope of the hill. Below the wall was found a stone block containing a square hole four inches wide and six inches deep. (Plate II. Fig. 6.) This looks like a socket of some kind, and may have been part of a temporary scene-frame, or of an ordinary railing along the edge of the retaining wall. The floor of the orchestra was formed of red earth well beaten down.

It seems easy to believe that this orchestra was intended for the production of Dionysiac choruses and for other festal celebrations which needed only a dancing floor. The absence, however, of foundations for a stage building in this theatre cannot safely be adduced as negative evidence in favor of the theory of Höpken and Dörpfeld, that actors and chorus in dramatic representations performed on the same floor. For the inference is reasonable that the rustic community of Thoricus, standing alone among their fellow-Greeks in the open violation of almost every law of architecture in the construction of their theatre, could have had little appreciation of the conventional niceties and sobriety of the Greek drama, and hence made no arrangements for its production.

THE TEMPLE. — At the west end of the orchestra and lying parallel with the parodos wall are found the ruined foundations of a small temple, *K*. (See also Plate II. Fig. 3.) At its west end the stylobate is cut in the native rock. The entrance was at the east end, where the lowest of the three steps is *in situ*. In the northwest corner, on a level with the stylobate, a pavement is preserved, formed of pebbles set in mortar. Portions of the cella wall, nearly five feet in height, are still standing on the north and west sides. It is composed of roughly dressed blocks of the inferior white marble found in this locality, and in the details of its construction it exactly resembles the outer wall of the theatre. Parts of the marble cornice and a section of a marble architrave, all Ionic and roughly dressed, were discovered near these foundations (see Plate II. Fig. 2), together with numerous pieces of tiling and antefixae of terra cotta. The outlines of the antefixae are moulded in the form of the honeysuckle, and the same pattern is painted on their outer surface.

The position of the cella wall and the character of the architectural fragments show that this was an Ionic temple *in antis*. Nothing whatever was found on the orchestra floor which could have come from the temple, except a thumb of life size in Pentelic marble.

In a joint of the cella wall was found a bronze coin of Athens. If, as seems probable, it was deposited there during the construction of the wall, an important clue is thus furnished for determining the date of the edifice. Bronze coins were first struck at Athens in the archonship of Kallias (406 B.C.), but these were soon demonetized, probably in 394 B.C. In 350-322 B.C. bronze money began for the first time to be reissued in larger quantities.[1] The latter period corresponds with the conjectured age of the main wall of the theatre (page 28), to which time also belongs the only inscription discovered by the excavations, ΔIONYΣΩI, on the head of a broken stele. (See Plate II. Fig. 8.)

THE ROCK CHAMBER. — (See Plates III. and IV.) It is not possible to prove that this rectangular cut in the natural rock served any purpose connected with the performances of the theatre. On the contrary, the magnitude of the labor involved in hewing out the solid rock so as to form a smooth wall fifty feet long and ten feet high — a work out of all proportion to the general character of the theatre proper — opposes such a theory. The remains of another "chamber" of the same kind are seen at the base of the military tower. Both resemble the artificial workings in the rock city at Athens.

THEORIES AS TO THE CONSTRUCTION OF THE THEATRE. — As one approaches the theatre from Laurium, the spot is seen, at some distance up the valley on the left, where, in the early part of this century, the British Society of Dilettanti excavated a Doric stoa. Here, half buried in alluvium, are numerous unfinished drums; these are without flutings, except in the case of those which formed the top or bottom of a column, where the flutings are merely begun as guide marks. Not far from the stoa, on two low foot-hills, rude remains of an ancient civilization are visible, — roughly hewn stone blocks, and traces of a circular wall of upright slabs. Directly from the plain at this point rises on the northeast a conical hill, the west slope of which is covered with a confusion of walls, mostly of rude and weak construction. The southern slope is thickly strewn with chips of white

---

[1] Head, *Historia Numorum*, page 315.

marble which partially hide numerous graves and a plain sarcophagus. In this desolate field, at the lower edge of the hillside, stand the well-built walls of the theatre and of the watch tower.

The sense of this ancient community's poverty of taste and resources, which impresses the visitor when viewing the ruins in the plain and the crude work of walls and graves on the hillside, is now only deepened by an investigation of the theatre and the irregular and mean workmanship of its interior. The cavea is provided with but two stairways, and these are narrow and misshapen. The seats and the parodos walls are made of unhewn slabs. The original configuration of the hillside has not been so modified as to allow the usual curves in the lines of seats or to make symmetrical terminations in the ends of the rear walls. In the later enlargement the old seats were unchanged, and stone chips instead of masonry were used as foundations for the new seats in the extension. The temple is coarsely finished, and the art remains are very scanty; these consist — besides the stele, the architectural fragments, and the thumb already mentioned — of a lion's claw in marble and a few potsherds of fine workmanship.

Under these circumstances it seems reasonable to attribute the irregularities in the construction of the theatre to the want of means or want of taste under which the remote rural deme of Thoricus labored. The people, desiring to celebrate their vintage festivals in the usual way, selected this natural hollow, at the bottom of which a good deal of filling in was required in order to make a suitable floor for the performance of choruses and buffoons. A retaining wall was built of flat, unhewn stones laid in mud mortar, — the prevailing construction of the walls in other parts of the hill. The least possible work was devoted to correcting irregularities in the natural shape of the hill in making the auditorium. Tiers of seats were made to rise one above another, and some digging and filling in must have been necessary that a rough symmetry might be secured in the succession of parallel lines. But the striking of a true circle was not thought of. The middle section of seats shows almost no curvature, and the two flights of steps which bound it are nearly parallel.

The two end sections were formed in sharp curves, so as to bring the spectators at those points into the most favorable position for viewing the orchestra. At the rear a supporting wall was built, following the line of the topmost seats. At the west end this wall terminated in some coarse slab work. At the east, an ancient perpendicular cut in the solid ledge relieved the builders of considerable labor, and they so arranged the seats that by finishing them in a line with its face they had ready-made the second parodos wall. It thus happened that the curve described by the original rear wall took the form of a sickle, the sharpest part of the curve being at the west end.

At some later time the theatre was enlarged. The existing auditorium was untouched, the plan calling not for reconstruction, but merely for extension. The new tiers were carried up at the same inclination with the old (Plate II. Figs. 4 and 7), set in a bed of small stones,[1] and retained by a high wall. On the construction of this wall much care and labor were spent; but in running his lines the architect was governed solely by the situation of the old theatre as he found it. Hence the inside and outside walls of the cavea are parallel for the greater part of their course, and the peculiar shape of the latter is largely due to the same causes which gave the inside wall its irregular form.

The extremities were finished in an independent and utterly unconventional way. At the eastern end the builder brought the wall around in a sharp curve so as to form a continuation of the old parodos wall along the edge of the rock chamber. At the west end he was obliged, for some reason, to stop his work abruptly, and, being trammelled by no inconvenient laws of symmetry, he simply closed up the space by bending the wall nearly at a right angle so as to meet the old wall. The new theatre, therefore, was mutilated of part of its rear western section.

The auditorium thus increased needed additional means of ingress and egress, the cornice of the rear wall being some fifteen feet above the ground. Hence two inclined planes were constructed, Y and Z, leading to the topmost row of seats. That on the west side crosses a depression between the ledges of the hill, is pierced by the "Tiryns Arch," and continues along an elevated terrace for some distance to

---

[1] The soil which covered the seats and orchestra was mixed with stone chips, which made the work of pick and mattock unusually difficult. Between the two rear walls these small stones form a solid mass.

the west. (See Plate II. Fig. 1.) As the people approached the west end of the theatre from their homes in the plain, some entered by the west parodos; others, whose places were so assigned, ascended by the special terrace and viaduct $Y'Y$; while those who were to use the other rear entrance took the path which skirted the wall, passed under the arch, and so, with little extra effort, found their seats. The formation of the steep, rocky hillside, the raised walk at the west end, and the situation of the necropolis at the rear made no other approach possible. As the tide of theatre-goers always came from the west and went no farther than the second abutment or inclined plane Z, this abutment was not provided with a passage-way underneath.

NOTE. — This fragment was found by the writer within the theatre. It is apparently a portion of an unguent vase. It is about three inches high. The decoration is in glazed black upon a brown ground. The front bears the lower portion of three figures, all clad in the himation or, possibly, in the chiton and chlamys, and advancing in the same direction. The vine-branches pendent before each figure indicate a Dionysiac subject. The back bears no figures.

ON

GREEK VERSIFICATION IN INSCRIPTIONS.

BY

FREDERIC D. ALLEN.

CONTENTS.

		PAGE
INTRODUCTORY REMARKS .		37
I. Metres of the Inscriptions		41
II. Unmetrical Verses		45
III. Structure of the Hexameter		47
IV. Structure of the Pentameter		63
V. Structure of Other Verses		65
VI. Quantity of Vowels		69
VII. Quantity by Position		79
VIII. Contraction and Synizesis		99
IX. Hiatus		105
X. Vowel Shortened before Vowel		107
XI. Crasis, Written and Unwritten		124
XII. Elision		126
XIII. Aphaeresis		157
XIV. N Movable		158
APPENDIX: List of Inscriptions Used		161
A. Kaibel's Inscriptions		162
B. Inscriptions not in Kaibel's Collections		174
POSTSCRIPT .		203

ON

GREEK VERSIFICATION IN INSCRIPTIONS.

In the following pages will be found a collection of examples arranged to illustrate the technical part of Greek versification, as shown in the metrical inscriptions of the Hellenic period. It was my hope, by getting together the extant material of this kind, to enable this inscriptional poetry to be fully utilized in questions relating to the history of versification, to the text-criticism of Greek poets in certain small details, and to Greek pronunciation.

The aid to be derived from this source is, for several reasons, less than we could wish. One reason is the paucity of material from the earlier period. The great mass of the epitaphs and dedications with which we shall have to do are from stones of the fourth, third, and second centuries before our era. Of course, even these are worth observing, as possessing an authenticity beyond that of our oldest manuscripts. But we could well afford to give up a good many of them for a few more brief distichs of Theognis's time or of Sophocles's time.

Another thing is the wide diversity in the quality of the epigrams. They are the compositions of hundreds of men, of all conceivable degrees of culture. From exquisitely turned bits of verse, they range all the way to the absurdest doggerel. Of course, mistakes and crudities are themselves instructive in a way. But if we undertake to apply inscriptional verses as a norm to literary compositions, we must consider the character of the work, and beware of using that as a model which should only serve as a warning.

Instances of clumsy epigrams are Kaibel, n. 26, 48, 96. Here, as often, mere ignorance and helplessness were the factors. But a frequent source of muddlement was the tinkering of old epigrams to adapt them to new uses. For instance, new names might be substituted for the old, as in. n. 1136 (see p. 45) and n. LVI (see p. 47). Or insertions were made. Thus the good people who had Kaibel's n. 60 cut, not content with the pentameter

σώφρων καὶ χρηστὴ πᾶσαν ἔχουσ' ἀρετήν,

and desiring a more specific commendation of the deceased, made it read

σώφρων καὶ χρηστὴ καὶ ἐργάτις πᾶσαν ἔχουσα ἀρετήν.

Other examples hereafter (p. 46). Herwerden has pointed out a less clumsy but hardly less certain case of adaptation in the epitaph n. 53:

οὗ σπάνις ἐστὶ γυναικὶ ἐσθλὴν καὶ σώφρονα φῦναι
τὴν αὐτὴν δοκίμως. τοῖςδ' ἔτυχεν Γλυκέρα:

a sentiment of puzzling ineptitude, until we realize that the too conscientious relatives of the dead lady had put ἐσθλήν in the place of an original καλήν. One epigram of Simonides has been travestied in the beginning of n. 768, and another still worse maltreated in the opening verse of n. XXVI, in which the Simonidean distich (fr. 100 Bgk. = A.P. vii, 253),

εἰ τὸ καλῶς θνήισκειν ἀρετῆς μέρος ἐστὶ μέγιστον,
ἡμῖν ἐκ πάντων τοῦτ' ἀπένειμε Τύχη.

appears in this extraordinary conflation:

εἰ τὸ καλῶς ἐστι θανεῖν κἀμοὶ τοῦτ' ἀπένειμε Τύχη.

In fact this whole epitaph seems to consist of reminiscences, patched together without regard for sense or metre. On the last verse, see p. 47.

Of course these are extreme cases. The bulk of the epigrams with which we shall have to deal are the work of intelligent persons: most are sufficiently correct in language and versification; the minority have small infelicities of one sort or another. Of metrical eccentricities the most frequent cause is the necessity of introducing proper names unsuited to the metre.[1]

---

[1] It is interesting to observe the various devices, legitimate and illegitimate, by which this difficulty of proper names was met. A recalcitrant feminine name like Χαιρεστράτη could be subdued by putting it before a vowel: see the examples

This, then, is the second trouble — the unskilful composition of many of the epigrams. Errors of transmission constitute a third difficulty. For even inscriptions are not absolutely authentic. Between us and the author of an epigram on an Attic stele there do not stand, it is true, a dozen blundering copyists; but there does stand the stonecutter. Now the Greek stonecutter was a very dreadful fellow. He chipped recklessly ahead; if he left out a letter or cut a wrong one he seldom tried to correct it; he transposed the words; he misread his copy, or deliberately tinkered it. Thus he cut ΣΕΤΙΜΩ for σ' ἔτι τιμῶ (n. 48), ΔΕΡΕΤΗΣ for δὲ ἀρετῆς (n. 56), ἕταροι ἐκτέρισαν for ἕταροι κτέρισαν (n. 183); by inserting a redundant τε in

ξυνὸν Ἀθανοδώρου τε καὶ Ἀσωποδώρου τόδε ϝέργον

(n. xcv) he made an already faulty verse atrocious. A luculent case is in n. 58 a RM. The copy had ΗΔΕΘΑΝΕΝ, which was meant to be ἥδ' ἔθανεν, but the graver took it as ἥδε θανεῖν, without reading the context; so he undertook to improve the spelling of the infinitive (it was just at that time when ΕΙ was beginning to replace Ε in such words), and cut ΗΔΕΘΑΝΕΙΝ. On a still worse muddle, in n. 96, see the foot-note on p. 128.

A singular case is that of the paean of Isyllus (n. xcvii₄). The shape in which it stands on the stone cannot be exactly the shape in which it was composed. The aberrations will be pointed out on p. 192: the original in three cases is certain, in another doubtful. Now the noteworthy thing is that these do not look like stonecutters' blunders. Not only is a certain semblance of sense everywhere preserved, but — what is more remarkable — the Ionic metre is nowhere

---

on pp. 117, 118. A similar masculine in -ας or -ης could be put in the vocative, as Εὐθία οὐκ, 38 (cp. 65), or the genitive (see examples on pp. 116–118). Or an uncontracted form could be used, as Δημοφόων, 86; or, on the other hand, contraction or synizesis be resorted to: Πυθίων, 26: compare the examples on p. 104. Sometimes an archaic form helped out; so Ξενοκράτης appears as Ξεινοκράτης, 768 a pref.; and Δαμασαγόρας as Δαμασσαγόρας, 234. A more desperate case like Στρατεία (205) induced neglect of position: see p. 79. Finally, the name is not unfrequently forced in, with absolute violation of natural quantity: Νικίας, Ἀθανοδώρου; see p. 75. A more circumspect poet chose another metre — iambic trimeter, or some combination: on this see p. 44. The device of dividing a proper name between two verses (Simonides, frag. 131 Bgk.) is not found in our inscriptions, but occurs in the later epigram, Kaibel n. 805 a add. = CIG. 5974.

violated. I cannot help suspecting that between the poet and the graver stood a third person — the decipherer, perhaps, of an ill-written manuscript — some one who knew his rhythms, but paid little attention to the context of what he was transcribing.[1]

These examples will serve to show the nature of the uncertainties which beset us, and which, after all, must not be imagined as greater than they really are.[2]

My plan was to include in the examination all known metrical inscriptions of the Hellenic epoch — that is, down to the middle of the second century before our era. Of course it was often hard to draw the line, and it is impossible that I should not have made some mistakes. Where more decisive indicia were lacking, I made it a rule to take in inscriptions which had ι adscript in final syllables and were free from traces of itacism.[3]

---

[1] This person seems to have put τόδε for τοῦδε and αὔξων for αὔξον; the suggestion accordingly obtrudes itself that he was transcribing from a fifth-century manuscript. But I forbear to press conjecture further.

[2] I am moved to lay the more stress on these uncertainties because a distinguished scholar, Hermann Usener, in his just published tract *Altgriechischer Versbau* (Bonn, 1887), has put a number of halting inscriptional verses to a use which seems to me exceedingly questionable. He sees in them survivals of older and freer forms of the hexameter, — antiquities, therefore, not negligences. As proof, for instance, of original independence of the two verse-halves (with syllaba anceps and free anacrusis) he cites the following:

Ἰστιαιεὺς μ' ἀνέθηκεν Κάλλωνος ὕπερ, φίλ' Ἄπολλον	(= CXLI).
Ἰου φαγόρας μ' ἀνέθη]κεν Διὸς γλαυϛώπιδι ϛούρηι	(= 738).
Διογένη[s] ἀνέθηκεν Αἰσχύλου ὓς Κεφ[α]λῆο[s]	(= 760).
ξυνὸν Ἀθανοδώρου τε καὶ Ἀσωποδώρου τόδε ϝέργον	(= XCV).
μνᾶμ' ἐμὶ Πυρ(ρ)ιάδα ὃς οὐκ ἠπ[ί]στατο φεύγειν	(= CXLIV).
. . . . . τόδε σῆμα μήτηρ ἐπέθηκε θανόντι	(= 229 a KM).

Now I am in substantial agreement with Usener's view of the early history of the hexameter, and should gladly welcome any inscriptional confirmation of that view. But it is impossible to assign any such significance to examples like these, where half the irregularities depend simply on the presence of a redundant -ν or τε, and all can be paralleled by similar enormities in other parts of the verse. Nor should we expect in the sixth and fifth centuries to find survivals of our supposed older type of verse. The development of the hexameter was complete long before Solon's time; the archaic period lay further back.

[3] There were cases where a rational decision seemed impossible. So with n. 228 a and b in Kaibel's addenda (published by Wood only in minuscules). These I deemed it safest to omit.

Much of my material lay ready to hand in the collections of Kaibel: *Epigrammata Graeca ex lapidibus conlecta* (Berlin, 1878), and a supplementary article in the *Rheinisches Museum*, vol. xxxiv (1879), pp. 181 flg. It remained to select from these the inscriptions which came within the above epoch, to compare subsequent publications of the same inscriptions where such existed, and to add such other inscriptions as I could find.

Kaibel's inscriptions are cited by his own numbers, *RM* signifying the article in the *Rheinisches Museum*. The rest I have arranged separately, and cite by Roman numerals. The age of the inscriptions is indicated in the citations by small Roman numerals (iii–ii), which signify centuries before the Christian era.[1]

An enumeration of all the inscriptions employed, together with the text of those not in Kaibel's book, will be found in the Appendix, pp. 161 flg.

I.

METRES OF THE INSCRIPTIONS.

Nearly all our metrical inscriptions are epitaphs, dedications, or artists' signatures, and, for reasons which I need not detail, the great mass are composed either in hexameters or in elegiac verse. We count in our collection 117 inscriptions in hexameters only, and 229 in elegiacs; whereby we leave out of account all those (marked in the list *dact.*) which from their fragmentary condition are indeterminate, but count separately those artists' inscriptions which, though standing in connexion with others, yet form a separate epigram.

If we omit a few inscriptions, of which either the subject-matter or the age cannot be determined,[2] the remainder can be thus arranged:

---

[1] These definitions of time are sometimes conjectural, and meant to be only approximate.

[2] Three elegiac fragments which may be either dedications or epitaphs; five inscriptions in Cypriote characters, and three second-hand inscriptions in the Delian inventory (CXLI, CXLII, CXLIII).

		Epitaphs.	Dedications.	Others.
Centuries VI–V	Hex.	20	35	11
	Eleg.	24	31	3
Centuries IV–II	Hex.	21	14	9
	Eleg.	108	56	3

From which we see two things: first, that the preference for the elegiac form over the pure hexameter increased as time went on; and, secondly, that the proportions of elegiacs is a little — but only a little — larger in the sepulchral than in the dedicatory inscriptions.

These figures will, however, look differently if we throw out, as perhaps we ought, all hexameter inscriptions of one verse, since in an epigram of that extent the poet had virtually no choice. The artists' inscriptions, let me observe, which make up most of the third column, are almost entirely monostichs. With this change our table would be

		Epitaphs.	Dedications.	Others.
Centuries VI–V	Hex.	7	19	0
	Eleg.	24	31	3
Centuries IV–II	Hex.	19	12	5
	Eleg.	108	56	3

Whence we see that a part of the difference between earlier and later times may be ascribed to the greater proportion of very brief epigrams in the earlier period.

It is by no means a matter of course, in inscriptional elegiacs, that hexameter and 'pentameter' shall follow each other in regular alternation. We find the following departures from this rule,[1] many of them in epigrams otherwise well constructed.[2]

2 *hex.* + *pent.* Four cases: XXXI (Att. iv), 23 (Att. iv; two verses are unmetrical), 52 (Att. iv), 66 (Att. Mac.).

3 *hex.* + *pent.* Six cases: 844 (Att. iv), 850 (Att. iv–iii), XXIV part (Att. iv–iii), 84 a RM (Att. iii), 67 (Att. iv–ii), CIX (Olymp. *Sparta* iv).

---

[1] I do not, of course, here or elsewhere, count cases where two separate epigrams stand together on one stone. For instance 750, where a dedicatory distich is followed by a hexameter of the artist. Other cases, 8, X, 489, CX, LXXXIII, 759, 1098 a RM, 751, XXVI, 81, XXXVI, 783.

[2] Compare the epigram in Aristot. Mirabil. 133.

Hex. + 3 *pent.* One case: LXXIII (Cypr. Mac.; one verse unmetrical).
2 *hex.* + 3 *pent.* One case: 74 (Att. iv–ii).
Hex. + *pent.* + *hex.* Two cases: 75 (Att. iv–iii), XXXIV (Att. Mac.). Also 34 according to Kaibel, but this is wrong.
Hex. + *pent.* + 2 *hex.* Three cases: 90 (Att. iv), 490 (Theb. Mac.), CXII (Theb. Mac.) not certain.
Hex. + *pent.* + 3 *hex.* One case: $xcvii_3$ (Epid. iii).
Hex. + 2 *pent.* + *hex.* Two cases: XXV (Att. iv), 785 (Cnid. ii).
2 *hex.* + *pent.* + *hex.* One case: XXIV part (Att. iv–iii).
2 *hex.* + *pent.* + 3 *hex.* One case: 96 (Att. iv–ii).
3 *hex.* + *pent.* + 3 *hex.* One case: 95 (Att. iii).

Especially abnormal are the following two cases. — 768 (Xanthus iv) has two hexameters followed by two pentameters, then two regular distichs, and lastly four hexameters. — The incantation-formula 1136 (Att. iii–ii) consists, as cut on the tablet, of 3 hexameters, followed by a pentameter (δεσμοῖς ἀργαλεῖοις σύν θ' Ἑκάτηι χθονίαι) and a half-verse (καὶ Ἐρινύσιν ἠλιθιώναις) standing by itself. But Kaibel is right in taking the words σύν θ' Ἑκάτηι χθονίαι καὶ Ἐρινύσιν ἠλιθιώναις together as a hexameter. The original is evidently muddled; probably it was all in hexameters, and the complement of the half-verse δεσμοῖς ἀργαλείοις has fallen out.

As stragglers of the dactylic class we may enumerate four cases in which a pentameter stands alone:[1]

τάθάναι Φιλλῶ Χαρμυλίδα δεκάτα[ν], CXXIX (Posidonia vi),
Εὔφρων ἐξεποίησ' οὐκ ἀδαὴς Πάριος. 759 (Att. v),
[υ]ἱὸς Πατροκλέος Δαίδαλος εἰργάσατο. LXXXII (Ephesos iv),
εἰμὶ δὲ Παυσανία τοῦ καταπυγοτάτου. 1131 (lamp, v);

and two epitaphs which consist of a dactylic penthemimeres only, and are perhaps reminiscences of poetry rather than poetry:[2]

Ἐγδήλου τόδε σᾶμα. XLIV (Aegina vi),
[Μαν]δροπύλου τόδε σᾶμα. XCIII (Corinth vi).

None of these are included in the tabulations on p. 42.

---

[1] Cp. the epigram of Phormis in Paus. v, 27, 2.
[2] Cp. Δηιόπης τόδε σῆμα, Aristot. Mirabil. 131.

Of non-dactylic metres the least rare is the iambic trimeter. Twenty epigrams are composed in it, as follows:[1]

	Epitaphs.	Dedications.	Artists' inser.	Others.
Centuries VI–V	2	1	5	4
Centuries IV–II	4	2	–	1
Uncertain (Cypriote)	–	1	–	–

Their brevity is noteworthy: thirteen of the twenty are monostichs, and only three (all late) exceed two verses. — The verse, from its nature and associations, had less dignity: it would do for a short inscription of a lighter character, a gift-epigram or an artist's signature, but was seldom chosen for graver monumental uses. A long epitaph in iambic trimeter (like 246 and 258) was not possible before the Macedonian epoch. Perhaps the oldest trimeter inscriptions are the epitaph of Amorgos LVI, and the Spartan inscription C, both bustrophedon. The oldest Attic inscription of this form is the epitaph of Μυρίνη, 11: here the metre was chosen with regard to the form of the name, as also in 246 (Ἀσκληπιόδοτος), and 751 (Κρησίλας).

This repugnance to the trimeter for epitaphs led in three cases to the adoption of a distich of mixed form:

Hexameter + iambic trimeter, 211 (2 distichs) and CXVII (3 distichs);
Dactylo-trochaic heptameter + elegiac pentameter, 187 (2 distichs).

The object in each of these was the introduction of a proper name containing $- \cup -$; Κλειτοφῶν (where, however, Κλειτοφόων was possible; see p. 101), Δαμότιμος, Εὐθύδαμος. All are of the Macedonian period.

More extraordinary combinations are the following. — The maker of 48 sandwiched a single iambic dimeter hypercatalectic among his five hexameters, simply to bring in the name Ἱπποστράτη. — The epitaph 79 consists of two hexameters and two trochaic tetrameters, without visible reason. — In CXVII, an Orphic gold tablet of Sybaris, we have three hexameters + two doggerel verses containing iambic reminiscences, + 1 hexameter. — In CXLIV, an ancient Thessalian

---

[1] Of Cent. VI–V: 11, LVI. — 746. — 1098 a KM (part), 751 (part), 762, 1099, CXXXV. — 1097, C, 1130, CXXXIV. Of Cent. IV–II: 93, 210, 246, 258. — 783, CXI. — XXXVI (part). Cypriote CXXXVII.

epitaph, one hexameter is followed by eight words with distinct poetic coloring, but without definable metre.

In trochaic tetrameters are composed three epigrams: 783 (part), 790, xcvii₁; all of Macedonian time.

In 1133 we have iambic trimeters catalectic, in 1132 catalectic iambic tetrameters, in cxxxvi a verse consisting of two catalectic trochaic dimeters (Φιλτός ἠμι τᾶς καλᾶς ἁ κύλιξ ἁ ποικίλα). All three are vase-inscriptions.

There remain three inscriptions in lyric measures: these are the paean of Isyllus xcvii₄ (Epidaurus iii) in ionics, the short anapaestic dedication of Dodona, 775 a RM, and the inscription on Hiero's helmet 745, in three logaoedic verses[1] (according to Röhl, the last two form a hexameter).

II.

UNMETRICAL VERSES.

1. — HEXAMETERS WITH TOO MANY FEET.

(*a*) *Seven feet.*

χαίρετε οἱ παριόντες. ἐγὼ δὲ Ἀντιστάτης υἱὸς Ἀτάρβου. 22 (Att. v).

χαίρετε δ' οἱ παριόντες. ἐ[γ]ὼ δὲ λιπὼν πατρίδα ἐνθάδε κεῖμαι. 23 (Att. iv).

οἶδα δὲ σοὶ ὅτι καὶ κατὰ γῆς. εἴπερ χρηστοῖς γέρας ἐστίν. 48 (Att. iii).

φιλοῦντα ἀντιφιλοῦσα τὸν ἄνδρα Ὀνήσιμον ἦσθα κρατίστη. 79 (Att. iv–ii).

δήσω ἐγὼ Σωσίκλειαν κα[ὶ] κ[τ]ήματα καὶ μέγα κῦδος. 1136 (Att. iii–ii).

In the last case the trouble seems to lie in the substitution of Σωσίκλειαν for some other name, like Μυρτώ, to which the formula was originally adapted.

(*b*) *Eight feet.*

πρώτηι σοι τιμαί. τίτθη. παρὰ Περσεφόνηι Πλούτωνί τε κεῖνται. 48 (Att. iii).

---

[1] Compare the logaoedic dedicatory inscription of Echembrotus at Thebes, Paus. x, 7, 6 (Bergk Poet. Lyr.⁴ iii, p. 203).

2. — INTERPOLATIONS IN HEXAMETERS.

ξυνὸν 'Αθανοδώρου τε καὶ 'Ασωποδώρου τόδε ϝέργον. XCV (Olymp. *Arg.* v) : τε is redundant.

δεξιὸν ἐ[νν]οίας δεῖ τινα πεφυλαγμένον εὖ μάλα πάντα, CXXVII (Sybaris ii) : δεῖ τινα superfluous.

ἐγὼ ἠμὶ 'Αριστοκρέτης κά μεν ἔστασαν κασίγνητοι, LXXVI (Cypriote) : ἐγὼ is added.

μεμναμένοι εὐϝεργεσίας τάς παι εὖ ποτε ἔϝρεξα, same. Either παι or εὖ is interpolated.

Νικίας με ἀνέθηκεν 'Απόλλωνι υἱὸς Θρασυμήδεος, 778 (Calymna iv-ii) : υἱός is interpolated (Herwerden). Dittenberger, "Απολλον υἱός.

Probable also is the interpolation of χόον in the Cypriote inscription LXXVIII : see Appendix, p. 187.

3. — OTHER UNRHYTHMICAL HEXAMETERS.

[— ∽] ων μ' ἀνέ[θη]κε Ποτειδᾶνι ϝάν[ακτι], LXXXVIII (Corinth vi).
[— ∽ — μ' ἀνέ]θηκε [Ποτει]δᾶνι ϝ[άνακτι], XCI (Corinth vi).

Both should read Ποτειδάϝωνι.

In XXVI (Att. iv), the atrocious epitaph spoken of above (p. 38), occur several unrhythmical verses ; the first being a conflation of a hexameter and a pentameter. See Appendix.

A halting hexameter, lacking two syllables, in the first and second feet, appears to be in the Cypriote inscription LXXVII, if Deecke has rightly reconstructed this.

Irregular quantity of single syllables will be treated in section VI.

4. — UNMETRICAL PENTAMETERS.

Φανο[κ]ρίτη παιδὶ χαριζομένη, 229 a RM (Erythrae vi). Röhl would complete the first half by transposing μήτηρ from the preceding verse.

'Αρχεστράτην ἀνδρὶ ποθεινοτάτην, 51 (Att. iv-ii).

δύσμορος οὐδὲ φίλους γονέας ἐπιδών, 23 (Att. iv). The stonecutter omitted καὶ before γονέας.

σώφρων καὶ χρηστὴ καὶ ἐργάτις πᾶσαν ἔχουσα ἀρετήν, 60 (Att. iv-ii). The spaced words are an interpolation.

γήραι καὶ φροντίδι εὐσεβίας ἕνεκα, XXVI (Att. iv). The first words should read φροντίδι καὶ γήραι.

['Ο]νασο[ς 'Ον]άσ[αν]τος μήπω δϊόμενος, LXXIII (Cypr. Mac). A pentameter with an anacrusis! The restoration seems certain, from the accompanying inscription in Cypriote characters.

The second verse of CXXII (Pharsalos v), in Lolling's restoration, appears as a hybrid hexameter-pentameter:

[— ᴗ γο]ῶσα ὅτ' ἀνώρως ὤλετο ὢν ἀγαθός.

But this is very uncertain.

5. — UNMETRICAL IAMBIC TRIMETERS.

Δημαινέτης εἰμὶ μνῆμα τῆς Λαμψαγόρεω, LVI (Amorgos vi).

The original was adapted to another name, like Λύσωνος.

Χάρης ἔδωκε Εὐπλοίωνί με, CXXXIV (vase v).

Insert δῶρον after ἔδωκε.

III.

STRUCTURE OF THE HEXAMETER.

A. — CAESURAS.

1. — CAESURA OF THE THIRD FOOT.

In thirteen verses the usual gap between the two verse-halves is bridged over by a long word reaching to the middle of the fourth foot:

[— ∞ — ᴗ] τοῦ Εὐθυμάχου Ναυσιστράτου εἰμί, IV (Att. vi).
Εὔθυμος Λοκρὸς Ἀστυκλέος τρὶς Ὀλύμπι' ἐνίκων, 940 a RM (Olymp. *Samos* v).
τὴν μὲν ἀδελφὴν Δηϊκράτης τὴν Γοργίου ἔσχεν, 875 a add. (Olymp. iv).

σῆς ἀρετῆς, Νικοπτολ[έ]μη. χρόνος οὔποτε λ[ύ]σει, 61 (Att. iv–iii).
ἀγγεῖλαι Λακεδαιμονίοις ἐλθόντα τὸ θεῖον, XCVII₅ (Epid. iii).
[πάππου] δ' εἰμὶ Εὐανορίδα, πατρὸς δὲ Νέωνος, 490 (Theb. Mac.).
Δεινομένεος δὲ κασιγνήτη. Φράξον δ' ἄλοχος μ[ὴν], LIV (Del. Nax. vi).
[– ∞ – δ]ὲ χαριζόμεν[ος – – ◡ ◡ – ◡], 936 a RM (Lac. v).
σῆς δ' ἀρετῆς καὶ σωφροσύνης μνημεῖον ἅπασιν, 59 (Att. iv–ii).
τοὺς δὲ τρόποις καὶ σωφροσύνην ἣν εἴχομεν ἡμεῖς, 78 (Att. iv–ii).
εὐνομίαν τε καὶ εἰράναν καὶ πλοῦτον ἀμεμφῆ. XCVII₂ (Epid. iii).
αὐτὰρ ἐμοὶ γένος οὐράνιον· τόδε δ' ἴστε καὶ αὐτοί. 1037 (Petil. ii).
μεμναμένοι εὐϝεργεσίας τάς παι εὖ ποτε ἔϝρεξα, LXXVI (Cypriote).

Röhl's restoration of XLV (Aegina v) gives [ἔ]στασες, but it is
                                               3   4
possible to make [ἔ]στασες. In the Cypriote inscription LXXVIII,
                  4   5
Neubauer reads ϝεθόχω᾽Αλεϝότης, and says that the two words are
                       3   4
united by crasis; but even if the words were certain, it would be
better to assume aphaeresis. See furthermore p. 77.

Of 656 verses in which the third-foot caesura is discernible, 397
have the penthemimeral or 'masculine' caesura, and 259 the trochaic
or 'feminine.' The proportion of masculine caesuras is a little more
than 3 to 2. If, however, we separate the earlier from the later
inscriptions, we shall see that the preponderance of the masculine
caesura is altogether a matter of the later period. (I throw out six
verses in Cypriote characters and three indeterminate second-hand
inscriptions.)

    Cent. VI–V . . . Masc. 60.   Fem. 65.   Ratio 100 : 109.
    Cent. IV–II . . . Masc. 331.   Fem. 191.   Ratio 100 : 58.

The proportion in the first line is entirely normal, but that in the
second line is almost startling, when we reflect that in the hexameter
of literature the feminine caesura has almost everywhere a marked
predominance.

The following statistics are here in point. For a part of them I
am indebted to Seymour (Transactions of the American Philological
Association, vol. xvi, p. 33); the rest are from my own enumerations.

HEXAMETERS.		ELEGIACS.	
	M. F.		M. F.
Homer, average of six books,	100 : 131	Tyrtaeus, 73 distichs . .	100 : 192
Hesiod, Erga, and Theog.,		Mimnermus, 43 dist. . . .	100 : 153
400 vv.	100 : 190	Solon, 105 dist.	100 : 133
Hom. Hymns, i, ii, vii . .	100 : 120	Theognis, 350 dist.	100 : 154
Cyclic poets, 200 vv. . . .	100 : 106	Xenophanes, 31 dist. . . .	100 : 82
Panyassis, 50 vv.	100 : 56	Simonides, epigrams approved	
Antimachus, 50 vv. . . .	100 : 79	by Bergk	100 : 143
Aratus	100 : 100	Ion, 20 dist.	100 : 54
Theocritus, bucolic and popular poems [1]	100 : 104	Plato, epigrams approved by Bergk	100 : 330
Theocritus, 5 epic and court pieces [2]	100 : 281	Callimachus, epigrams approved by Schneider . .	100 : 366
Callimachus, first 4 hymns .	100 : 279 [3]		
Apoll. Rhod., B 1-600 . .	100 : 188		
Nicander, Ther., 600 vv. .	100 : 217		

This brings the case pretty clearly before us. At first there was a distinct, but not excessive, predilection for the trochaic caesura. Then this preference diminished a little. Thence we discern two divergent tendencies. With one set of poets the feminine caesura came again into vogue. They swung back to the Homeric point, and went far beyond it. This fashion prevailed at the Alexandrian court, where he was the best poet who could put the most trochaic endings into the third foot. The other, less numerous, group kept on in the old direction, cultivating the penthemimeres more and more. If we may accept the evidence of very scant remains, Panyassis and Antimachus, Xenophanes and Ion belong here. At any rate, there can be no doubt about Aratus, whose usage contrasts strongly with that of his contemporary Callimachus. Theocritus has two styles, as the table shows. In his folk-poetry he uses the masculine caesura about half the time; in his court compositions he outdoes Callimachus in avoiding it. It is clear how the matter looked to him. The masculine caesura had a familiar, every-day air; the trochaic a loftier ring.

---

[1] Eight strictly bucolic pieces (i, iii, iv, v, vi, viii, ix, xi) with an average ratio of 100 : 96; five popular scenes (ii, vii, x, xiv, xv) showing 100 : 115.

[2] Nrs. xiii, xxii, xxiv, xvi, xvii.

[3] The hymn to Delos, taken by itself, has 100 : 542!

In this light, the usage of the inscriptions appears less surprising. They belong with this more popular vein of poetry. The unliterary poets — the occasional versifiers — of the fourth and succeeding centuries preferred distinctly the penthemimeral form of the hexameter, following a fashion which has left a few, but only a few, traces of itself in our existing literature.[1]

It is further to be noted that the proportion of feminine caesuras is larger in elegiac verse than in pure hexameters. The above table shows that this is true in literature. In inscriptions the case is thus :

HEXAMETERS.			ELEGIACS.		
	M.	F.		M.	F.
VI-V	28	36	VI-V	27	29
IV-II	114	35	IV-II	204	151
Indeterm.	2	–	Indeterm.	–	1
Cypriote	4	2			
	148	73		231	181
Ratio 100 : 49.			Ratio 100 : 78.		

(Whereby I have thrown out the two inscriptions in hexameters and trimeters, and the indiscernible '*dactylic*' inscriptions.) The reason of this is not far to seek. The feminine caesura gave more variety to elegiac verse : the penthemimeres simply duplicated the cadence of the pentameter.

Elision in the penthemimeral caesura occurs twenty-four times.[2] In the feminine caesura only twice (43, xcvii₂ l. 20). The freedom of short for long in the masculine caesura is hardly certain : see p. 74. Shortening of a vowel before a vowel in the feminine caesura, eight times.[3] For hiatus in this part of the verse see p. 106.

---

[1] I have noted a single instance where the trochaic caesura seems deliberately chosen. Isyllus, xcvii₂ l. 19, has λευκοῖσι δάφνας, where λευκοῖς δάφνας was equally possible.

[2] Nrs. 4, 35, 35a add., 53, 69, 82, 85, 89, 91, 466, 484, 486, 521, 759, 773, 773a RM, 773b RM, 785, 856, 856a prf., 859, xxiii, xcvii₂ (2 examples). A probable example cxxii, where Cauer Μενεκλέα τε ὅς. An uncertain instance, lviii.

[3] Nrs. 63, 78, 87 (where, however, Herwerden conjectures παρεδέξατ'), 255, 768, lxvi, xcvii₃ (l. 68), xcviii.

2.— Bucolic Caesura.

A word-end coincides with the end of the fourth foot in 400 of the 681 hexameters legible at this point; and of these 312 have a dactyl before the caesura in question.

	WITH BUCOLIC CAESURA.			WITHOUT BUCOLIC CAESURA.
	With dactyl.	With spondee.	Total.	
Cent. VI–V	44	16	60	76
Cent. IV–II	265	68	333	201
Cypriote	2	3	5	3
Indeterm.	1	1	2	1
	312	88	400	281

The dactylic cadence is so important a feature of the τομή βουκολική that we may well anticipate a little in discussing it here. I will enumerate the verses which depart from the usual form in having a spondee here. About one-fourth of them form the spondee with καί:

ἀγαθοῦ καὶ σώφρονος ἀνδρός. 4 (Att. vi).
νίκη καὶ τρὶς τὸν ὁπλίτα[ν], 936 (Arg. v).
πόσει καὶ μητρὶ λιποῦσα. 76 (Att. iv).

So 3, 21, 43, 48, 53. 58 a RM, 67, 85, 95, 198, 519, 521, 781, 782, xxiv, xxvi, xxxiv (twice), xcvii₂ l. 24. In all, twenty-two examples. The remainder I quote in full:

κεῖμαι δ' ἐν δήμ[ωι 'Αθηνῶν], 92 (Att. iv–ii).
ποτνίας ἐμ φάρεσι λευκοῖς. 774 (Priene iv–iii).
[φ]οινὴν εἰς γαστέρα θῆται. 1033 (Att. iii).
θεῶν πρὸς δώδεκα βωμόν. 1043 (Att. iv).
[νέ]ατο[ν πρ]ὸς τέρμα κελ[εύ]θο[υ], 29 (Att. iv–iii).
γενεάν. ὃς φείδετο ἄρα Ζεύς. xcvii₃ l. 61 (Epid. iii).
-γεσίας τάς ⟨παῖ⟩ εὖ ποτε ἔρρεξα. lxxvi (Cypriote).
-σύνην ἣν εὔχομεν ἡμεῖς. 78 (Att. iv–ii).
-κράτης τὴγ Γοργίου ἔσχεν. 875 a add. (Olymp. iv).
ὁσίαν τοῖς πᾶσιν ἰδέσθαι. xxxii (Att. iv).
καί με χθὼν ἥδε καλύπτει. xxiv (Att. iv–iii).
καί με χ[θ]ὼν ἥδε καλύπτει. lxxiii (Cypr. Mac.).
ἔχει χθὼν παῖδα τὸν ἡδύν. 90 (Att. iv).

λαμπρὸμ φῶς, Περσεφόνης δέ. 62 (Att. iv).
[τ]ρόπων σῶν ἔσχες ἔπαινον. XXIV (Att. iv-iii).
χιιροπὸς τόνδ' ὤλεσεν Ἄρης. 180 (Corc. vi).
Ἀλεϙότης χόϙ(ν) τά(ν)δ' ἐπέϝασα, LXXVIII (Cypriote), very uncertain. See Appendix.
τὺ δ' εὖ πρᾶσ(σ)', [ὦ] παροδῶτα. CXIII (Haliart. vi).
ταύτην δεῖ πάντας ἀκοῦσαι. 78 (Att. iv-iii).
ἔχει μὲν τοὔνομα κριοῦ. 63 (Att. iv).
ἀεὶ γὰρ πᾶσιν ἀρέσκων. 64 (Att. iv).
νόμον ἀεὶ τόνδε σέβοντας, XCVII₂ l. 25 (Epid. iii).
τόδ' οὔπω πρόσθε ἐπεπόνθεις. CXXVII (Sybaris ii).
Θεογείτων Θυμούχου παῖς. 90 (Att. iv).
[∪ _]μων πατρὸς ἑαυτοῦ. 777 (Salamis iv-ii).
Ἡρακλέων Νι[κ]ιάδο[υ παῖ]. 859 (Tichiussa iv-ii).
ἀτ' οὐδῆς πήποκα τῶν νῖν. CI (Sparta vi-v).
Πειραιεύς, παῖς δὲ Μένωνος. 75 (Att. iv-iii).
Ἀντίστας Φανομαχοσσοῦ. 773 (Panticapaeum Mac.).
Μένανδρο[ς _ ∪ ∪ _ ∪]. 753 (Att. v).
θειάκτης ἐρπέθ' ἄμ' αὐτῶι. 1033 (Att. iii).
Φορύστας παῖς ὁ Τρώκος. 938 (Tanagra iv).
ἰνιπὰ τῶ ἀ(ν)θρώπω. LXXVII (Cypriote).
Θεοσήμου [_ ∪ ∪ _ ∪]. 10 (Att. vi).
Κ[λεοί]του τοῦ Μενεσαίχμου. 1 a add. (Att. vi).
[∪ _]ου παῖς τόδ' ἄγαλμα, X (Att. vi).
Κροβίλου παῖς ἀνέθηκ[εν], LI (Delos iii-ii).
τοῦ Κυπρίου τοῦ Σαλαμι[νί]ου. 188 (Aeg. v).
Διονυσίου· τῶν δ' ἔτι πρόσθεν. 66 (Att. iv-ii).
καὶ [Π]ύρ[ρ]α μεί[ζ]ονα θ[ν]ητ[ῶν]. 844 (Att. iv).
ἐλαίας ἡμεροφύλλου. XCVII₂ l. 20 (Epid. iii).
σῆς ψυχῆς ἐστι παρ' ἀνδρί. 80 (Att. iv-ii).
πόληος τᾶσδ' Ἐπιδαύρου. XCVII₂ l. 14 (Epid. iii).
ὁ Φίλωνος Δήλιος ὧδε. 213 (Delos? iv-ii).
τόδε δ' αὐτῶι δᾶμος ἐποίει. 179 (Corc. vi).
[ἐν] Ἰσθμῶι πανκρατι[αστής], 941 (Att. iii).
ἐν Τρίκκηι πειραθείης. XCVII₃ l. 29 (Epid. iii).
με κοῦρον Μέντορα Χῖον, LXXXIII (Cyme iii-ii).
ἀπαρχὴν τάθηναίαι. II (Att. vi-v).
προφήτην ἠσπάσατ' αὐτός, 858 (Milet. iv-ii).

[προφή]τη[ν ἡσπάσ]α[τ]ο ἱρ[όν]. 859 (Tichiussa iv–ii).
Καλλιστοῖ. γαῖα κ.ιλύπτει. 56 (Att. iv–ii).
κινδύνων εἰκόνα τήνδε. 770 (Att. iv).
[∪ ∪] τέκνων τέκν[α λιπ]όντα[ς]. CXIV (Elatea Mac.).
ἐπαίνων ἄξιός εἰμι. XXXII (Att. iv).
[ἀντ'] ἔργων οὔτι δικαίων. CXXVIII (Sybaris ii).
δισχίλοις ἀνδραπόδοισιν. 26 (Att. iv).
σοφίαισιν καλὸν ἄγαλμα. 1100 (vase v).
τιμωρῶν Δελφίδι χώραι. 490 (Theb. Mac.).
δαιώσας ἑπτὰ μὲν ἄνδρας. 26 (Att. iv).
ἀνέθ[ίη]κ[ε]ν τήρηι ἄγαλμα. LXII (Samos vi–v).
ἔθηκε τὰν ὁμόλεκτρον. 189 (Melos iii); Boeckh ἔθηκε(ν), Kaibel ἔθηκέ (με).
ἀνέθηκεν παῖς Ἀμιάντου. CXLII (Delos, unknown).
περιφείδοιτ' εὐρύοπα Ζεύς. XCVII₂ l. 26 (Epid. iii).
φειδωλός τε ἐνθάδε κεῖται. XXXV (Att. iv).
[∪ —]αι πυρρίχηι ἄθλω. XLVII (Euboea iv–ii).

It is apparent that in some of these there is practically no bucolic caesura at all. This is the case with the twenty-two examples of καί, and the five succeeding examples where a monosyllabic preposition makes the caesura. One might add even the five examples next in order. The monosyllable follows a strong hephthemimeral pause, and leans closely on the next word. In this way thirty-two cases out of eighty-eight would be made to disappear. If, however, we remove these, we should also eliminate the analogous cases from the first — the dactylic — column. There are not nearly so many of these. It is hard to say just how many. But certainly the following two:

προχοὰς καὶ ἐπ' ἔσχατον Ἰνδόν. 197 a add. (Rhodes Mac.);
[ἐπ]ει[ὴ κ]αὶ ὁ κ[λῆ]ρος ὅ[πασσεν]. 859 (Tich. iv–ii);

as well as eight examples with disyllabic prepositions:

ἀρετῆς ἐπὶ τέρμα μολόντα. 49 (Att. iv);

and the like (26, 50, 69, two cases, 211, 1033, CXXVIII). In five others the preposition squints both ways:

ἱερᾶς ἀπὸ νηὸς ἰόντες. 96 (Att. iv–ii);
τάφωι περὶ τῶιδε χυθεῖσα. 184 (Corc. iii);

(also 179, LX, CXIX); but to be quite fair, we will exclude these also.[1] Two verses with ἐς and τό after the trochaic caesura of the fourth foot will be cited below, p. 55. We have therefore seventeen cases on this side. Making these changes in the above table, we should get:

	WITH BUCOLIC CAESURA.			WITHOUT BUCOLIC CAESURA.		
	Dactyl.	Spondee.	Total.	With word-end.	Without word-end.	Total.
Cent. VI–V	42	12	54	6	74	80
Cent. IV–II	250	41	291	42	203	245
Cypriote	2	2	4	1	3	4
Indeterm.	1	1	2	–	1	1
	295	56	351	49	281	330

which is perhaps a fairer statement than the other. Either table shows clearly: (1) the great difference between earlier and later times in the liking for the break after the fourth foot — a difference of at least 1 : 2; and (2) the stronger preference in the later period for the dactylic ending before this break.

As between elegiacs and pure hexameters there is no material difference in the use of the bucolic caesura. Omitting the indistinguishable inscriptions, and using the unsifted statistics as in the first table above, we find:

	HEXAMETERS.				ELEGIACS.			
	Dactyl.	Spondee.	Total.	Without bucolic caesura.	Dactyl.	Spondee.	Total.	Without bucolic caesura.
Cent. VI–V	20	11	33	41	22	4	26	32
Cent. IV–II	70	25	95	71	184	40	224	127
Cypriote	2	3	5	3	–	–	–	–
Indeterm.	1	1	2	–	–	–	–	1

3. — TROCHAIC CAESURA OF THE FOURTH FOOT.

Verses like πολλὰ δ' ἄρ' ἔνθα καὶ ἔνθ' ἴθυσε μάχη πεδίοιο (K 2) are exceedingly rare and commonly regarded as faulty. But our inscriptions of more uncouth composition contain a number of examples of this form. Isyllus of Epidaurus has distinguished himself by several.

---

[1] I do not, of course, count out cases like τίτθην κατὰ γαῖα καλύπτει.

The clearest cases are these:

στοιχέντι κατέφθιτο πότμωι. 77 (Att. iii).
Ἐπιδαυροῖ ἀεὶ ῥέπεν ἀνδρῶν. XCVII₂ l. 23 (Epid. iii).
παρέταξε πόληϊ Λυκοῦργος, XCVII₃ l. 71 (Epid. iii).
βλαστοῦσα γοναῖσι Θόαντος. CXL (Cos iii–ii).
Κάλλωνος ὕπερ. φίλ' Ἄπολλον. CXLI (Delos, unknown).
τόδ' ἐπο(ί)ει Ἱπ(π)ύσ[τρα]το(ς) σῆμα. 8 (Att. vi).[1]

[φίλο]ν τε φίλοισι προσεῖναι. 65 (Att. iv–ii).[2]
οὔ[κ ἄ]ν τις ἀ[ρ]ι[θ]μήσειεν, 926 (Hermione iii).
μή σοί τις ἔχις ἁλίπλανκτος. 1033 (Att. iii).
τοῖόν νυ ἐπάσατο χήειν (?), CXXXIII (vase vi).

τιμὴ δὲ κασιγνήταισιν. 82 (Att. iv).
πᾶσιν δὲ θανοῦσα ποθεινή. 45 (Att. iv–iii).
ἐχθρὰ δὲ φίλοισι γένοιτο. 1136 (Att. iii–ii).
ῥώμην δὲ χερῶν [έ]π[ε]δ[ει]ξ[αν], 941 (Att. iii).

I add further two verses:

μακάρεσσιν ἐς οὐρανὸν εὐρύν, XCVII₂ l. 13 (Epid. iii);
λιπαρὸς δὲ τὸ κ[άδ]ος ὀπίσσω, XLVIII (Chalcis Mac.);

which have in reality the same rhythm, as the break after ἐς and τό is so slight. In the first case the poet might have written μακάρεσσ' εἰς.

Uncertain cases are the following. In XLIX (Ceos vi) Kirchhoff restores φηρῶν [δὲ με]μαότα φῦλα. In LXXIV (Cypriote) we have ἄ(ν)θρωπε θεῶι ἀλ(λ)' ἔτυχ' ἁ κήρ (*a-to-ro-pe-te-o-i-a-le-tu-ka-ke-re*): Deecke assumes 'λλ'; but perhaps θεῶι is shortened. Dittenberger's emendation of the unmetrical verse 778 (see p. 46) gives Ἄπολλον υἱὸς Θρασυμήδεος. but Herwerden's reading is more probable. Finally, the difficult verse 760 may be read Διογένη[ς] ἀνέθηκ' (the stone ἀνέθηκεν) Αἰσσχύλ(ι)ου υἱς Κεφ[α]λῆος. avoiding the hardly credible diaeresis Ἀϊσσχύλου. The name Αἴσχυλλος occurs in 936 (Röhl, IGA, n. 37).

---

[1] Yet see p. 79 (crasis).

[2] Here, as everywhere else, I follow the principle that there is no caesura before an enclitic, nor before μέν and δέ.

I need hardly say that the caesura in question is void of offence when preceded by the stronger hephthemimeral pause : as in δέξαι τόδ' ἀμενφὲς ἄγαλμα (740), Πέλοπος τὸ Πελαζγικὸν Ἄργος (846), and many other cases. Still less is it objectionable when followed by the τομὴ βουκολική, provided that the intervening monosyllable leans backward, not forward. Turns like Ὀπόεντι δὲ πολλάκι τάνδε (855), ἄεθλα γὰρ οἱ παρὰ Δίρκαι (938 a prf.), are quite normal.

4.—CAESURA AFTER THE THIRD FOOT.

A word-end at this point is permissible only on condition that it shall not be perceptible. It is commonly obscured by the foregoing main caesura of the third foot, the poet taking care that the intervening word shall be closer connected with what follows than with what precedes. Verses like [κ]τ[ώμ]ενον εὔκλε(ι)αν [δ]ορὶ καὶ χερὶ τόνδε πρὸς ἀ[νδ]ρός. 24 (Att. iv), are regular, and can be paralleled from any page of Homer.

It becomes, however, a distinct blemish when the sense requires a stronger pause after this intervening word than before it. In this way the verses

σῶμα μὲν ἐνθάδ' ἔχει σόν. Δίφιλε. γαῖα θανόντος. 57 (Att. iv-ii) ;
σοῦ μὲν δὴ πατρὶς δήν. Κέρκινε. Φοξίου υἱέ. 488 (Tanag. v) ;

are slightly cacophonous, unless skilfully read. In Homer, E 580, I 134, γ 34, λ 266, are verses of this sort.

The following are simple atrocities :

μν[ᾶ]μα [τόδ' ἔστ' ἐ]πὶ σ[ώ]ματι κείμενον ἀνδρὸς ἀρίστου. 26 (Att. iv).
μᾶλλόν τοι θεὸν ἔλπομαι ἔμμεναι. ὦ Λυκόερ[γε]. CXIX (Delph. iv-iii).
Ποσειδωνίου ἴσθι με κοῦρον Μέντορα Χῖον, LXXXIII (Cyme iii-ii).

5.—OTHER CAESURAS.

The hephthemimeres occurs 342 times, and is absent in 347 verses, in which this part is legible. I have noted 91 verses which have no caesura in or after the fourth foot.

Caesura of the sixth foot is not frequent: Ζεύς occurs as final word, CVIII and XCVII₃ l. 61 ; Ζεῦ, 941 b RM. ; υἷ[ν]. XXIV ; υοῖς. 850 ; σήν, 776 ; παῖς, 779 (cp. also 859). In 48 is the clumsy ending ἄχρι ἂν ζῶ. The third verse of LIV ended with some monosyllable (μ[ήν] or μ[ε]?). In other cases the final monosyllable is an enclitic (τε, που, με, σε, σοι), or μέν or δέ.

I note a few exceptional rhythms. Two spondiac words at the beginning:

Ἡρ[α]ι Θῆρις τήνδε, CXLII (Delos, unknown);
  1   2   3

ζηλοῖ σ' Ἑλλὰς πᾶσα. 38 (Att. iv);
  1   2   3

θάρσει καιρῶι γάρ σοι. XCVII₃ l. 68 (Epid. iii);
  1   2   3

where ἄπασα and θάρσεε would have sounded better. Two dactylic words:

Λυσέαι ἐνθάδε σῆμα. 5 (Att. vi);
  1   2   3

σῶμα μὲν ἐνθάδε σόν. 35 (Att. iv).
  1   2   3

Trochaic caesura of first and second feet:

χὢ μὲν Ἀχαιός, ὃ δ' ἐξ. XCV (Olymp. Argos v);
 1   2   3

τόνδε νεώ σοι, ἄναξ. XXIII (Att. iv);
  1   2   3

πᾶσι φίληι τε γυναικί. 69 (Att. iv);
  1   2   3

αἱ δὲ θεοῖσι μάλιστα. 88 (Att. iv-ii).
 1   2   3

Trochaic caesura of fourth and fifth feet (α 390, θ 554):

[φίλο]ν τε φίλοισι προσεῖναι. 65 (Att. iv-ii);
   4   5   6

πᾶσιν δὲ θανοῦσα ποθεινή. 45 (Att. iv-iii);
  4   5   6

ἐχθρὰ δὲ φίλοισι γένοιτο. 1136 (Att. iii-ii);
   4   5   6

βλαστοῦσα γοναῖσι Θόαντος. CXL (Cos iii-ii);
    4   5   6

παρέταξε πόληϊ Λυκοῦργος. XCVII₃ l. 71 (Epid. iii).
    4   5   6

The last might have been relieved by writing πόλει Λυκόοργος. Two spondiac words following the penthemimeres (Ξ 199):

βωμοῦ θύσαις Μαλεάτα. XCVII₃ l. 31 (Epid. iii);
   4   5   6

ὦναξ, ὥσπερ τὸ δίκαιον. XCVII₃ l. 79 (Epid. iii).
  4   5   6

Augmented forms are preferred, and elision makes room for the augment. Thus:

μητέρα ἔθηκα, not μητέρα θῆκα, XXXII (Att. iv);

μοῖρ' ἐδάμασσε, not μοῖρα δάμασσε, CXXVIII (Sybar. ii);

εὐδαίμων δὲ ἔθανον, XXV (Att. iv);

οὕσ' ἔθανον, 91 (Att. iv);

μοι τάδε ἔλεξας, XCVII₅ l. 67 (Epid. iii);

ἕνεκ' ἐστεφανώθη, XXV (Att. iv);

γαῖ' ἐκάλυψαν, not γαῖα κάλυψαν, 51 (Att. iv–ii);

Φίλων με ἐποίησεν, XV (Att. vi), if verse;

ταῦτ' ἐνόμιζον, 81 (Att. iv–ii);

πρόσθε ἐπεπόνθεις, CXXVII (Sybar. ii);

'Ολύμπι' ἐνίκων, 940 a RM (Olymp. *Samos* v);

δύ' ἐνίκων, 941 (Att. iii);

[π]οτε ἐν[ίκων], 925 (Att. iv–ii);

ποτε ἔρρεξα, LXXVI (Cypriote).

Preference for the augment outweighs most merely metrical considerations.[1] In particular it is, we see, a more important factor than the choice of a trisyllable or any particular form of word at the end of the verse.[2]

Some other illustrations of the preference for augmented forms will be given below (p. 62). For examples in pentameters, see pp. 64 and 65.

B. — DACTYLS AND SPONDEES.

1. — THE FIFTH FOOT.

Sixteen spondiac verses occur in our inscriptions:

---

[1] Isyllus nevertheless has written ὓς φείδετο, XCVII₅ l. 61, with rather unnecessary squeamishness, as ὓς ἐφείδετο would have been quite defensible.

[2] Accordingly σφ' ἐσάωσας is to be written rather than σφε σάωσας in XCVII₅ l. 75.

ἑκηβόλωι Ἀπόλλωνι, L (Delos vi).
Θεοκρίτου Ἀπόλλωνι, CXLIII (Delos, unknown).
Ἑρμοστράτου Ἀβδηρίτης. 759 (Att. v).
Τᾶνον θεὸν ἱδρύσαντο. 775 (Egypt iv).
Ἀσκλαπιῶι ἰητῆρι. XCVII₂ l. 18 (Epid. iii).
νέην ἔτι Καλλίκλεια[ν]. 857 (Rhod. Mac.).
Μύρτοι. ξένοι, αἰδήσαντες. 205 (Halicarn. ii).
ἀπαρχὴν τἀθηναίαι. II (Att. vi-v).
ἐν Τρίκκηι πειραθείης. XCVII₃ l. 29 (Epid. iii).
Θεογείτων Θυμούχου παῖς. 90 (Att. iv).
ἴνιπα τῶ ἀ(ν)θρώπω. LXXVII (Cypriote).
ἐπιχθονίων ἀνθρώπων. 26 (Att. iv).
οὐ[κ ἄ]ν τις ἀ[ρ]ι[θ]μήσειεν. 926 (Hermione iii).
Ἀθηναίων τρεῖς φυλάς. 26 (Att. iv).
ἐπὶ γούνασι πατρὸς μάρψας. 89 (Att. iv-ii).
ἐκ Βουσπόρου ἦλθεν κάμνω[ν]. XCVII₅ l. 62 (Epid. iii).[1]

It will be seen that seven only of these cases conform to the most frequent norm of spondiac verse — a four-syllable word after a dactyl. Two have the tetrasyllable after a spondee: and the next two have practically the same form, as Θυμούχου παῖς and τῶ ἀνθρώπω are felt as rhythmical equivalents of a tetrasyllable. One verse, a Homeric reminiscence, ends with a trisyllable. All these are well-established forms, and even the ending ἀριθμήσειεν, following the rare trochaic caesura of the fourth foot, can be paralleled from Homer (B 479. etc.). The last three cases are monstrosities. The general character of the inscriptions 26 and 89, both in thought and versification, is such that they can afford but slender support to δήμου φῆμις and the like in Homer. Isyllus is not much better, but we will charitably believe that he meant the graver to cut ἤλυθε κάμνων.[2]

---

[1] The ending ὦρσεν θῆμα which Kabbadias has printed in XCVII₅ l. 72, should obviously be ὦρσε ν᾿ ὁ᾿ ἦμα.

[2] There is plenty of evidence of the avoidance of such cadences. Thus ἐνὶ πόντωι, 179 (Corc. vi); ἐνὶ δήμωι, 26 (Att. iv); ἐνὶ Πυθοῖ, CXVIII (Delphi iv); ἐνὶ ναῶι, LXXX (Cedreae iv-iii); φράζεο σῆμα, XXXVII (Att. Mac.); Βυτρυώδεος οἴνης, 88 (Att. iv-iii); etc.

Ludwich[1] has shown that spondiac verses were more avoided in elegiac poetry than in epic. This explains the comparatively small number of spondiazontes in the inscriptions, the proportion being about half what it is in Homer. Just half our sixteen cases occur in elegiac epigrams, though about two-thirds of the inscriptional hexameters belong in such epigrams.

2. — THE FOURTH FOOT.

The preference of the verse for a dactyl in the fourth foot stands in close connexion with the bucolic caesura. The relative numbers of dactyls and spondees before this caesura have been set forth above (p. 51 flg.). It only remains to point out cases where the form of a word has been influenced by the effort for dactylic endings.

Τηλέκλεες, οὐκ ἀβόητο[ν], 40 (Att. iii-ii).
ἐπικλεές, ὃν πρὶν ἐπ' ἀνδρῶν, 255 (Cypr. iv-iii).

These two verses have a bearing on Π 7 and 754.

περικαλλέα Παλλάδος ἁγνῆς, 850 (Att. iv-iii).
κατ' ἄλσεα Φε[ρ]σε[φ]ονείας, CXXVII (Sybaris ii).
βαρυπενθέος ἀργαλέοιο, CXXVIII (Sybaris ii).
ἔλιπον φάος ἠελίοιο, 521 (Thessalonica Mac.).
προλιπὼν φάος ἀελίοιο, CXXVII (Sybaris ii).
ὧν ἵλαος, οἶκον ἄμ' αὐτοῖ, XXIII (Att. iv).
ἐθαύμασεν ἐμ βίωι ἥδε, 83 (Att. iv-ii) ;

where the sense would suggest rather ἐθαύμαζ'.

La Roche has discussed, in the *Zeitschrift für Oesterreichische Gymnasien*, 1876, p. 413 flg., the Homeric use of ἐνί and ἐν in the fourth foot. His conclusion is that ἔνι is to be written when the preposition leans backwards, ἐν when it leans forward. There is sense in this principle, as the bucolic caesura is felt in the one case and not in the other.[2] The inscriptions follow La Roche's rule three times, and violate it once :

---

[1] *De hexametris poetarum Graecorum spondiacis*, p. 18 flg.
[2] La Roche, however, in applying the second part of the rule, makes an exception in the case of digammated words following the preposition. Before these

ἀκ[μα]ῖς ἔνι σώφρονος ἥβας. CXVII (Elatea Mac.).
ποτνίας ἐμ φάρεσι λεοκοῖς. 774 (Priene iv–iii).
κεῖμαι δ' ἐν δήμ[ωι Ἀθηνῶν]. 92 (Att. iv–ii).

λόγχας ἐνὶ σώματι ἐκείνων. 26 (Att. iv).

No one has attempted to make ποτί (προτί) and πρός conform to any such rule. It would not be very hard. The disyllabic form in this part of the verse is oftenest found before a ϝ-word (ἄστυ, Ἴλιον; Z 113, O 681, etc.). On the other hand, πρὸς τεῖχος ἐρείσας. πρὸς τοῖσί τε ὕπνος (X 112, κ 68), etc. But we have ποτὶ δῶμα γέροντι, ο 442; similarly ζ 297, A 426, etc. Like this is

ἐμὸν ποτὶ πίονα νηόν. CXIX (Delphi iv–iii) = Herod. i, 65.

But for two cases with πρὸς, see above, p. 51.

Where there is no bucolic caesura, no preference for a dactyl is manifest. We find [Ἀ]ριστοκλῆς (not -κλέης), VI (Att. vi), ἐμιμού[μην] (not -εόμην). 85 (Att. iv–ii).

3. — The First and Second Foot.

In verses of which the whole first half can be read with certainty, dactyls and spondees occur as follows:

	With Masc. Caesura of third foot.	With Fem. Caesura of third foot.
Spondee + spondee	50	22
Spondee + dactyl	81	70
Dactyl + spondee	116	69
Dactyl + dactyl	103	80

It will be seen that there is a difference, too large to be accidental, between the verses with the masculine caesura of the third foot, and those with the feminine, in the relative frequency of some forms. In the one class the form with dactyl + spondee distinctly preponderates; in the other, the double dactyl is the favored form.

The theory of a preference for a spondee in the first foot does not find any support in inscriptions. We have, to be sure, τηλοῦ

---

he would write ἐνί. Indeed all the editors of Homer do this. But there is no reason for the distinction. If we write ἐν γούνασι κεῖται, consistency demands also ἐν ϝοίνοπι πόντωι. The manuscripts, of course, have ἐνὶ οἴνοπι, but this may be only a piece of diascevasm to prop up the metre.

πατρίδος, not τηλόθι, 91 (Att. iv) ; Τιμοκλῆς, not Τιμοκλέης, 14 (Att. vi) ; [Παν]τακλῆς, 926 (Hermione iii) ; Ἡρακλεῖ, LIX (Delos Mac.) ; θάρσει καιρῶι, not θάρσεε, XCVII, l. 68 (Epid. iii) ; ζηλοῦτ' ἀλλά, 30 (Att. iii) ; τῶι Δὶ Δαιάλκος, not Διfί, 1098a RM (Melos vi-v) ;[1] — all in accordance with the spoken language. On the other hand, εἰκόνι, not εἰκῶ, eight times, CIX (Olymp. iv), 938 (Tanagra iv), 777 (Salam. iv-ii), 773 (Panticapaeum Mac.), LXIX (Rhod. Mac.), LII (Delos iii-ii), 854 (Delos iii-ii) ; CXL (Cos iii-ii) ; ἄνδρες ἐποίησαν, not ποίησαν, 1100 (vase v) ; ἁμὸς ἐκαρύχθη, not καρύχθη, 941b RM (Olymp. iii), χερσί τε καί, not χερσὶν καί, 776 (Att. iii-ii) ; καί νιν ἅπας, not πᾶς, XCVII₂ l. 12 (Epid. iii) ; ὤλεω, 505 (Tricca iii) ; δέρκεο, 260 (Cyrenaica ii) ; νείκεα, 19 (Att. vi) ; ὀστέα, 90 (Att. iv), 234 (Smyrna iii), 225 (Ephesos Mac.) : — one or two of which are against the every-day language.

Nor is the case different with the second foot. We note, on the one hand, τύχη προὔπεμψε, not προέπεμψε, 39 (Att. iv) ; τοὐμόν, 52 (Att. iv) ; [Π]υθοκλῆς, 71 (Att. iv) ; Ἀριστοκλῆς, 75 (Att. iv-iii) ; Ἑλλὰς πᾶσα, not ἅπασα, 38 (Att. iv) ; ποθεινὸς πᾶσιν, 519 (Thessalon. Mac.). On the other, ποτὶ σῆμ', not πρός, 4 (Att. vi) ; Τιμοκλέην, 492 (Theb. iv) ; ἐν κενεῆι, not κεινῆι, 89 (Att. iv-ii) ; οὐ κενά, 857 (Rhod. iii) ; Ἀλξήνωρ ἐπ[ο]ίησεν, not ποίησεν, 1098 (Orchom. vi-v) ; υἱὸς ἔναιεν, 744 (Olymp. v) ; ἀγχόθι παιδός, not ἀγχοῖ, 491 (Orchom. ii).

One sees that the preference for familiar forms was a much more frequent motive of choice than any liking for dactyls or spondees in these places.

---

[1] The verse is *perhaps* a pentameter.

4. — THE THIRD FOOT.

When the third foot has no caesura, it is oftenest a dactyl. The list of such verses given above (p. 47 flg.) shows only two cases of a spondee.

After the masculine caesura, it makes little difference whether the second half of the verse begins with a long or with two shorts. In xcvii₃ l. 29, Isyllus has chosen to say ἐν Τρίκκηι πειραθείης. where ἱνί would have afforded a slight alleviation of the ponderous rhythm.

IV.

STRUCTURE OF THE PENTAMETER.

The two most essential features — the caesura between the two parts, and the dactylic rhythm of the second part — are always preserved. Elision in the chief caesura occurs 34 times.[1] A short syllable for a long once only, 24; see p. 74. Hiatus at this point only in the wretched doggerel xxvi; see pp. 47 and 107.

1. THE FIRST HALF. — The distribution of dactyls and spondees may be thus shown:

Spondee + spondee . . 50 (14 in Cent. VI-V, 36 in Cent. IV-II).
Spondee + dactyl . . . 71 (23   "   "   48   "   "   ).
Dactyl + spondee . . 143 (25   "   "   118   "   "   ).
Dactyl + dactyl . . 100 (28   "   "   72   "   "   ).

The proportions do not differ greatly from those in hexameters with penthemimeral caesura (see p. 61), but the preponderance of the third form (dactyl + spondee) is more marked.

Among the great variety of rhythmical forms produced by different

---

[1] Nrs. 1 a add., 21, 35, 35 a add. (two examples), 39, 40, 69, 89, 183, 214, 220, 234, 255, 488, 492, 519, 750 a add., 759, 769, 773, 845, 854, 856 a prf., 858, 875 a add., 932, 1043, xxv, LXXXIII (three examples), CXVIII, CXXXIX.

caesuras, some are distinguished by their frequency. Those which occur more than ten times are the following:[1]

— ᴗ | ᴗ — — —	32	— — — | — —	17
— ᴗ ᴗ | — — —	27	— — | — — —	14
— ᴗ ᴗ | — | — —	23	— | — — | — —	11
— ᴗ ᴗ — | — —	16		
— ᴗ | ᴗ — | — —	13	— ᴗ ᴗ | — | ᴗ ᴗ —	15
		— ᴗ ᴗ — | ᴗ ᴗ —	14
— — | — ᴗ ᴗ —	26	— ᴗ ᴗ | — ᴗ ᴗ —	13
		— ᴗ | ᴗ — | ᴗ ᴗ —	12

A single word forms the first half-verse in 184 (ἑπτακαιεικοσετοῦς) and LXXXIII (εἰκοσαπεντaετεῖς).

We note further δέρκεο, not δέρκευ, CXIV (Elatea Mac.) and 855 (Atalante iii); ὀστέα, 183 (Corc. Mac.); χάλκεον ἀντ᾽, 856 a prf. (Hypate Mac.); [Πυθο]κλέης, 926 (Hermione iii); εἰκόνα, 940 a RM (Olymp. *Samos* v), LXXX (Cedreae iv–iii), 260 (Cyren. iii–ii); χαίρειν εἰς, not χαιρέμεν εἰς, 781 (Cnid. iii); βορέου, 214 (Rhenaea iii); εὐκλεiῆ, 851 (Rhodes iii).

Augmented forms preferred: μνῆμ᾽ ἔσ[τησεν], 220 (Amorg. iv); μνῆμα ἔστησεν, LVIII (Amorg. iv);[2] ζῶσα τε ἐκοινώνουν, XLIII (Salam. iv).

2. THE SECOND HALF. — The forms which occur more than ten times are these:

— ᴗ ᴗ — | ᴗ ᴗ —	56	— | ᴗ ᴗ — | ᴗ ᴗ —	29
— ᴗ ᴗ | — ᴗ ᴗ —	52	— ᴗ ᴗ | — | ᴗ ᴗ —	19
— ᴗ | ᴗ — | ᴗ ᴗ —	43	— ᴗ ᴗ | — ᴗ | ᴗ —	19
— ᴗ | ᴗ — ᴗ ᴗ —	42	— | ᴗ ᴗ — ᴗ | ᴗ —	15
— ᴗ | ᴗ — ᴗ | ᴗ —	38	— | ᴗ ᴗ | — ᴗ ᴗ —	15

---

[1] In many cases the less common forms are rhythmically equivalent to these, from the close connexion of words.

[2] The verse may *possibly* be a hexameter.

Comparing these with the two-dactyl forms of the first half, we note that the form _ ∪ ∪ | _ | ∪ ∪ _, which is there first in order of frequency, here takes the seventh place. On the other hand, _ ∪ | ∪ _ ∪ ∪ _, which here is one of the more frequent forms, occurs but four times in the first half. The form _ | ∪ ∪ _ ∪ ∪ _ is found eight times (in the first half only once). A single word, ἐννεακαιδεχέτις, forms the second half-verse in 205. A monosyllable ends the pentameter only once: μ[όρ]σιμ[ό]ν [ἐστ]ι τὸ χρε[ών], 519.

Augment preferred: τοῦτ' ἐτέλεσσε, 740 (Melos vi); γράμμ' ἐτύπωσε, 89 (Att. iv-ii); πάντα [ἐ]κράτεις and [πάντ]α ἐκράτεις, cxviii (Delphi iv); τέρμ' ἔλαβεν, 856 (Atalante Mac.); τοῦδε ἔτυχον, 225 (Ephes. Mac.); τόνδε ἐλάτρευσα, 850 (Att. iv-iii); πατρίδ' ἔ[θηκε], civ (Olymp. vi); ἐλπίδ' ἔθεντο, 21 (Att. v); φίλοις ἔλιπες, not φίλοισι λίπες, 56 (Att. iv-ii); πόλλ' ἔκαμε, 851 (Rhod. iii). In ἔταροι ἐκτέρισαν, 183, it is written against the metre.[1]

The second half exactly repeats the form of the first in three cases:

_ ∪ ∪ _ | ∪ ∪ _ ‖ _ ∪ ∪ _ | ∪ ∪ _, 50.
_ ∪ ∪ | _ ∪ ∪ _ ‖ _ ∪ ∪ | _ ∪ ∪ _, 205 v. 6, 519 v. 4.

V.

STRUCTURE OF OTHER VERSES.

1. IAMBIC TRIMETER. — Out of twenty inscriptions in this metre, thirteen are composed in strict form; that is, without resolutions either of thesis or arsis. Of the remainder, two (93, 1130) have only resolutions which would be permissible in tragic senarii. The other five have the freedom of the comic trimeter: they are numbers LVI, 746, 246, 783, CXXXVII, of which the first two are archaic.

---

[1] In 53, τοῦδ' ἔτυχεν should be read, rather than τοῦδε τύχεν.

The trimeters which form distichs with hexameters in cxvii are strict; those in 211 have one resolution, not transcending tragic limits.

The resolutions of thesis are these:

ἐπὶ νἔο-. 783 (Cnid. iv–ii).   -ται πάρεδρος. 783 (Cnid. iv–ii).
-οι ἀνέθεν. 746 (Olymp. *Arg.* v).   -τα τὸν Ἐρασισθένου, 211 (Syr. iii).
-τω κότυλον. 1130 (vase vi).   Ἀσκληπιοδότου, 246 (Bith. Mac.).
-νὸς γέγονα. 93 (Att. iv–iii).   Λαμψαγορέω. LVI (Amorgos vi).[1]

Disyllabic arses occur as follows:

Ἀφροδίται. 783 (Cnid. iv–ii).   Διΐ τῶν. 746 (Olymp. *Arg.* v).
κατέθηκε. CXXXVII (Cypriote).   πενταέτοις. 246 (Bith. Mac.).

The chief caesura is the ordinary one, after the second trochee, in thirty-seven verses, the whole number of verses being fifty-three. Porson's rule of the fifth foot is nowhere violated.

2. TROCHAIC TETRAMETER.—There are twenty-one verses, sixteen of which have the customary caesura after the fourth foot. Four have the break in the middle of the fourth foot, one in the middle of the fifth.—The inscription 790 and the trochaic part of 79 follow strict rules; 783 and XCVII₁ have the following freedoms:

Resolution of Thesis:

πάλιν ἐπ-. XCVII₁ (Epid. iii).   Κριταγόρας. 783.
ὁ νόμος. XCVII₁.   Ξενόκριτος. 783.
Ἀγαθόδωρος. 783 (Cnid. iv–ii).   ἀριστοκρατίαν. XCVII₁.
ἰσχυρότερος. XCVII₁.   ἀνδραγαθίας. XCVII₁.
ὃν ἀπέδειξα. XCVII₁.

On καὶ ἔλεγον. XCVII₁, see p. 126.

---

[1] But on this see p. 103.

Disyllabic arses:

Τιμοτέλης. 783.   Πōλιάνθης. 783.
Τελέσων. 783.   Σιλεωνίας. 783.
Ἀρισταγάθος. 783. πρ[ο]άγοι. xcvii₁.

The name Σιλεωνίας is, as Kaibel remarks, suspicious. Herwerden guesses Σιμωνίδας. Th dactyl in trochaic tetrameter is defended, even for literature, by Wilamowitz, " Isyllos von Epidauros," p. 7 flg. But these inscriptional examples, nearly all in proper names and in a single inscription of four lines, do not inspire great confidence in its respectability.

3. OTHER IAMBIC VERSES. — The two catalectic trimeters of the vase inscription 1133 have two resolved theses in succession, πλέον [ἀ]π' ἄρα ; and one disyllabic arsis, πάτερ αἴθε. — In 1132, the two iambic tetrameters catalectic both have caesura at the end of the second dipody ; and the second verse has the second arsis disyllabic, ἀποτείσε[ι].

4. ARCHILOCHIAN HEPTAMETER. — The two verses of this form in 187 are of regular construction. The first part is a hexameter cut off at the bucolic caesura : a dactyl precedes this caesura. Both verses have the feminine caesura of the third foot : both have a spondee as the first foot.

5. ISYLLUS'S PAEAN (xcvii₄). — It consists of seventy-eight ionici a minore, written continuously like so much prose. As indications of the ends of periods, we have three catalectic ionics, numbers 18, 45, 65 ; and three hiatus, after numbers 6, 27, 55. If we assume only these certain points of division, we get groups of 6, 12, 9, 18, 10, 10, 13 ionics respectively. But it is very probable that there were more groups. These six dividing-points all coincide with the ends of sentences : Isyllus would seem to have made his rhythmical groups correspond with divisions of the sense. Now there are several other ends of sentences. One of them (at 40) seems to have syllaba

anceps (ἔλυσέ, λεχέων) : but I assign no weight to this, as ἔλυσεν is possible. Following these sense-pauses, the group 12 could be divided into 6, 6 ; the group 18 into 7, 6, 5 ;[1] the group 13 into 2, 9, 2. Strophic responsion is out of the question, and the foregoing figures do not suggest any eurhythmical correlation of the groups among themselves. As to what the distribution of cola inside the groups may have been there is no indication.

The longs of the ionic are freely resolved ; the first long eight times, the second three times, but never both together :

-να θεὸν ἀεί-. foot 2.   -τῶιε κόρε χρυ-. foot 44.
-λυθ' ἐς ἀκοάς. foot 9.   ματρόπολιν αὔξ-. foot 71.
-κοιτιν ὁσίοισ-. foot 17.
πατρίδ' Ἐπίδαυρ-. foot 20.   ὧδε γὰρ φάτις. foot 7.
θυγατέρα Μά-. foot 22.   -λ[ωι] δόμεν παρά-. foot 16.
ἐκ δὲ Φλεγύα. foot 28.   τεμένει τέκετ-, foot 48.

Contraction, producing _ ⊥ _, is not found on the stone, but in foot 68, χαῖρ' Ἀσκλα-, Wilamowitz's conjecture, is demanded by the sense.

Anaclasis of the ordinary form, ᴗ ᴗ ⊥ ᴗ _ ᴗ ⊥ _, occurs five times : τόδ' ἐπώνυμον τὸ κάλλος (foot 31–32) ;[2] κατιδὼν δὲ ὁ χρυσότοξος (35–36) ; γονίμαν δ' ἔλυσεν ὠδῖν- (50–51) ; Λάχεσίς τε μαῖα ἀγανά (54–55) ; -πιὸν ὠνόμαξε Ἀπόλλων (59–60).

More frequent is the freedom of long for short at the beginning of the ionic, _ ᴗ ⊥ _. This may have grown out of the form of anaclasis ᴗ ᴗ ⊥ _ _ ᴗ ⊥ _ (ἀποσείωνται δὲ λύπας. Frogs 346, etc.).[3] But to Isyllus _ ᴗ ⏖ ⏞ is a distinct form of the ionic, to be used at pleasure, without reference to the preceding foot. Twice he begins a rhythmical period with it : ὧδε γὰρ φάτις (7), ἐκ δὲ Φλεγύα (28). Once a resolution of the preceding long is found : παρά | κοιτιν ὁσίοισ- (17). The remaining cases are thirteen on the stone : Φοῖβε Ἀπόλλων (12), -σαν πατὴρ Ζεύς (14), -λ[ωι] δόμεν παρά- (16), -[λ]ου γ[αμ]εῖ τάν (23), Φοῖβος ἐμ Μά- (37), -λου δόμοις παρ- (38), -ραν ἔλυσε (40), -τωιε κόρε χρυ- (44), ματρὸς Ἀσκλα- (58), τὸν νόσων παύσ- (61), ματρόπολιν αὔξ- (71), χαῖρεν Ἀσκλα- (68), -ξων ἐναργῆ (72). The

---

[1] Probably the 7 was originally 8: see foot-note [3] on p. 191.
[2] See, however, p. 191, foot-note [3].   [3] Otherwise Wilamowitz.

last two, however, disappear by the certain emendation of Wilamowitz. In their place come two others: [ἴ]νιν Αἴγλα (49) by Semitelos's conjecture, and το[ῖ]δ' ἐπώνυμος (31) by mine (see p. 192).

The license of short for long at the end of the ionic is admitted by Wilamowitz for two places: δὲ Κορωνὶς ἐπεκλήθη (33), and ὑγίειαν ἐπιπέμποις (73). But this is a needless concession: ὑγιείαν is obviously possible (Aristoph. Birds 604; Homeric ἀληθείη, etc.), and respecting the other place see p. 192.

6. THE DEDICATION OF AGATHON AT DODONA (775 a RM). — The metrical form is obscure. After three anapaestic verses, follow the words πρόξενοι Μολοσσῶν καὶ συμμάχων, ἐν τριάκοντα γενεαῖς; then comes another distinct anapaestic verse, and lastly the single word Ζακύνθιοι. Christ (Rhein. Mus. 1878, p. 610) and Kaibel consider the whole metrical, dividing the words just quoted into an ithyphallic ⏊ ∪ ⏊ ∪ ⏊ —, an iambic dipody — ⏊ ∪ ⏊, and a trochaic dimeter ⏊ ∪ — — ∪ ∪ ∪ —; with another iambic dipody at the end. But I doubt whether any verses except the four anapaestic ones were intended. The diction of the rest is utterly prosaic. Mixed prose and poetry, even joined in one sentence, are not unknown in inscriptions: 762, 936, and 1130 are cases in point.

The first of the four anapaestic verses is a tripody; the other three are dimeters. Only one has the caesura in the middle.

VI.

QUANTITY OF VOWELS.

It has, of course, no significance for us when doubled consonants, in archaic fashion, are written singly: as Ἀπόλ(λ)ωνι, 747; ἀλ(λ)όμενος, 1; τέσ(σ)αρα, 942 a RM; στονόρεσ(σ)αν, 180; χαρίεσ(σ)αν, LXXXIX, XC, XCII; Αἰγίθ(θ)οιο, CXIII; ὀπιδ(δ)ό[μενος], CII. Here belong Κιτ(τ)ύλωι, 484; Καλ(λ)ία, CXXIV. Similar, though due to another cause, is ἠργάατατο for ἠργάσσατο, 778 (Calymn. iv-ii): the graver inadvertently substituted the familiar prose form.

Simple graphic mistakes are εὐσεβείας for εὐσεβίας, 875 a add. (Olymp. iv.); θεῖόν for θεόν. 774 (Priene iv–iii); Σωσειάναξ for Σωσιάναξ, 255 (Cypr. iv–iii); πόλῆας for πόλιας. 759 (Att. *Abdera* v).[1]

Φιλτῶς, as printed at the beginning of a trochaic verse in cxxxvi, is a mistake of the editor. It is the Doric genitive of Φιλτώ, and should read Φιλτός (the letters are ΦΙΛΤΟΣ), like Λατός in CIG. 1688 = CIA. II. 545; compare Ahrens Dor. p. 174.

1. The diphthongs αι, ει, οι before a vowel often lost their ι, producing forms like Μαντινέας. 941 c RM, and Μαντινέαι. 744. As double forms, Πειραιεύς and Πειραεύς, πρυτανεία and πρυτανέα, thus came to stand side by side, it is not surprising that in metrical inscriptions these were sometimes confused. So the following irregularities must be understood:

Αἰνέαι. 14 (Att. vi).[2]   οὐ δικαίαν. 95 (Att. iii).
ἀνδρῶν ἔη (= εἴη) 24 (Att. iv). ἀργιλαίοις. 1136 (Att. iii–ii).
εὐκλέαν. 24 (Att. iv.).   Ἰστιαιεῖς. cxli (Delos, unknown).

Three words require special mention: ποιῶ, υἱός, and αἰεί.

The spelling ποιῶ occurs:

ἐποίει, 179 (Corc. vi).   ἐποίησεν. cxxxviii (Att. vi).
ἐποίει, 1098 a RM, i. t. (Melos vi–v). ἐπ[ο]ίησεν, 1098 (Orchom. vi–v).
ἐποίει, cviii (Olymp. v).   ἐξεποίησ', 759, pent. (Att. v).
ποίησεν. 741 (Att. vi).   ἐποίησεν. xlvi (Euboea v).
ἐποίησαν. 1100 (vase v).   [ἐπ]οίησε. cx (Olymp. iv).
ποίημα. 750 (Paros v).   ἐποίησεν. xiii (Att. vi), if poetry.
ποιεῖν. lxxxi, pent. (Didym. vi), ἐποίησεν. xv (Att. vi), if poetry.
  not quite certain that poetry.
ποίησεν. lxxix (Halic. Mac.).

---

[1] Blass, *Aussprache des Griechischen*, p. 24, and Cauer, *Delectus* (2d ed.), p. 317, think πόληας Ionic spelling for πόλεας.

[2] Bergk, *Litteraturgeschichte* I, p. 385, takes Αἰνέαι τόδε σῆ[μα] as a logaoedic clause.

Furthermore, in κἀποίησε, CXXXV, iamb. trim., where the quantity is indeterminate.

The spelling ποῶ:

ἐπόει, 8 (Att. vi).   ἐπόησεν, VI (Att. vi).

ἐπόει, CXXVI (Metapont. vi).

In κἀπόησε, 1099, iamb. trim., the quantity is not decisive. Neubauer's ἐπέϝυσα = ἐποίησα, LXXVIII, is utterly uncertain. In 773 b RM either ἐπό[ησε] or ἐπο[ίησε] may be supposed.

Wecklein, in his *Curae Epigraphicae*, p. 54, decides that we ought to write ποεῖν in the poets whenever the vowel is short. The inscriptions do not favor this, as against two certain examples of ποεῖν we have five certain ones of ποιεῖν. We are rather led to infer that the pronunciation ποιεῖν with consonantal ι existed alongside of ποιεῖν and ποεῖν.

With υἱός the case is different. Although the word with short first syllable is found in Homer at least ten times (see also Pindar Nem. vi. 37), there is no certain inscriptional instance of this.[1] The one possible instance, Αἰσχῠλ(λ)ου ὑ̆ὺς Κεφ[α]λῆο[ς], 760 (Att. v), is only a possibility. See above, p. 55. On 778, into which Dittenberger has brought υἱός by a more than doubtful conjecture, see p. 48. Everywhere else the syllable, however spelt, is long. The examples are:

With υι: υἱός, 743 a prf. (Att. vi) ; υἱύς, 472 (Sparta vi); υἱοῦ, 179 (Corc. vi) ; υἱός, 752 (Att. v) ; υἱύς, 753 (Att. v) ; υἱέ, 488 (Tanag. v) ; υἱός, 744 (Olymp. v) ; υἱός, CVIII (Olymp. iv, pent) ; υἱός, 942 a RM (Olymp. *Maenal.* iv) ; υἱόν, 492 (Theb. iv) ; υἱέ, CXVIII (Delphi iv) ; υἱός, CXXV (Larisa iv); [υ]ἱός, LXXXII (Ephes. iv, pent.) ; υἱός, 768 (Xanth. iv): υἱός, 774 (Priene iv–iii, pent.) ; υἱεῖ, CXVI (Elat. iv–iii);

---

[1] Meisterhans's statement, *Grammatik der Attischen Inschriften*, p. 29, near bottom, "die poetischen inschriften zeigen je nach bedürfniss des metrums die eine oder die andere form," is misleading.

υἷα, 860 (Chios iv–ii) ; υἷα, 30 (Att. iii) ; [υ]ἱόν, 926 (Hermione iii,
pent.) ; υἰῶι, xcvii₂ l. 18 (Epid. iii) ; υἱός, 851 (Rhod. iii) ; υἷες, 845
(Att. iii–ii, pent.) ; υἷα, 855 (Atalante Mac.) ; υἱός, 856 (Atalante
Mac.) ; υἷα, 856 a prf. (Hypate Mac.) ; υἷες, cxl (Cos iii–ii, pent.) ;
υἱόν, 1135 (vase Mac.).[1]

With ῠ : ὑὺς Ἀθήνηι, xiv (Att. vi) ; ὑὸς Ἀτάρβου, 22 (Att. v) ;
ὑὸς Πρωτάρχου, xxxi (Att. iv) ; φίλος ὑός, 221 (Amorg. iv–iii).[2]

It becomes certain from this that υ in the Attic ὑός, which Herwerden declares to have been the only form known to Attic prose,[3]
was long, not short.[4] The inference for forms like ὀργυά, κατεαγῦα,
παρειληφῦα, etc., is strong ; and Meisterhans, p. 28, note 247, is
wrong in asserting short ῠ for these.

An isolated case of the contrary treatment of υι is perhaps recognizable in the Cypriote inscription lxxvii ; μηδὲ φύῃ. The reading
is not certain. If right, it stands opposed to Homeric δύῃ, but in
agreement with the Homeric measurement of υἱός.

The forms αἰεί, 'ᾱεί, and 'ᾰεί occur as follows :

αἰϝεί, 742 (Crissa vi) ; αἰεί, 6 (Att. vi) ; αἰεί, 197 a add. (Rhod. Mac.).
'ᾱεί, xcvii₂ l. 25 (Epid. iii) ; 'ᾱέναον, same, l. 11.
'ᾱεί, 64 (Att. iv) ; 'ᾱείμνηστον, 35 (Att. iv, pent.) ; 'ᾱειμνήστον, 69
(Att. iv) ; 'ᾱεί, 779 (Chalc. Mac.) ; 'ᾱεί, cxi (iamb. trim., Thesp.
Mac.) ; 'ᾱείμναστον, 855 (Atalante Mac.) ; 'ᾱεινάστους, 932 (Sidon
iii, pent.) ; 'ᾱειμνήστοις, cxv (Elat. iii, pent.).

2. The ω of ἥρως in the oblique cases is sometimes shortened
(cp. ζ 303), sometimes not :

---

[1] Kaibel gives Λαίου [υ]όν, the vase having ΛΛΙΟΥΙΟΝ. But the Υ belongs to
both words: see p. 115, where two similar cases will be given.
[2] In xii (Att. vi) ὑός occurs in what is probably a prose addition.
[3] *Lapidum Testimonia*, p. 12.
[4] So Blass, *Aussprache des Griechischen*, p. 44.

ἥρωϊ. 552 a add. (unknown, Mac.).   ἥρωα. pent., 774 (Priene iv–iii).
ἡρώων. 856 a prf. (Hypate Mac.).   ἥρωος. 781 (Cnid. iii).
ἡρώεισιν. 1037 (Petilia ii).   ἡρωϊ. or ἥρωι?, xxxviii (Att. iv),
   if poetry.

Other shortenings of the long *o*-sound are:

πατρώιης (O), pentam., 13 (Att. vi).

πα[ῖς] Ζωΐλου (Ω), unless Ζωΐλου. 769 (Erythrae iv).[1]

In all these examples (except the archaic one) ω is written, not o. It is hard to believe that there is any reason for this, save preference for the familiar spelling. Ζοίλος and πατροίης would be on a par with Τροία (Rhes. 231, 261, etc.) and ζοίας (Theocr. 29, 5) :[2] ἥροος would be like ζοή.

A similar correption of η. α. in δηίους. xxviii (Att. iv), and δαιώσας, 26 (Att. iv), is in the highest degree improbable, notwithstanding what some Homeric scholars — most recently Christ, *Prolegomena*, p. 112 — have brought themselves to believe. Simple contraction is to be assumed, producing the diphthong ηι (vulgarly written η). This in spite of Hartel, *Homer. Stud.* III, p. 15 flg. There is not the shadow of a reason for supposing Homeric δηιώσαντες to be in any way different from Attic δηοῦτε. ἐδήιωσα.

3. From Homeric imitation come ἱερός. cxv ; ἱερά. pent., 782 and 924 ; ἱερόν. 932 ; ἱερόν. LXXI ; φιλοῖντ'. 79 (Att. iv–ii) ; Ἄϊδος. xcix. καλός occurs not only in dactylic verse (941 b RM, etc.), but even in trochaic tetrameters (καλῶν. 790). Not only Ἀπόλ(λ)ωνι. 747 (Delphi *Lac.* v) ; and Ἄρης. xcix (Tegea Mac.), which are Homeric, but also Ἀπύλλων. 858 (Miletus iv–ii) ; and Ἄρεα. heptam., 187 (Ithaca Mac.) ; Ἄρεα. LIII (Delos ii), which are not.

---

[1] In late inscriptions of Kaibel's collection, Ζωΐλος occurs three times, as ≤ ∪ ∪ ; Ζωΐλου once, with the measurement ≤ _ ≤. Τρωΐλος, pentam., occurs in cviii.

[2] So the editions ; the mss. ζωίας and ζοίας. The trisyllabic Τροία (Τρωία) occurs six times in Pindar: the orthography wavers in the manuscripts.

Noteworthy also are ὑγιείαν in lyric, XCVII₄ (Epid. iii); μηνύει ἀνδρός, LXXXIII (Cyme iii-ii). On Κορωνίς, XCVII₉, see p. 69. χέειν, CXXXIII (vase) is uncertain. If it really means 'to pour with,' it should not be transcribed χήειν, but should be understood as miswritten for χείειν (Hesiod Theog. 83) or *χεύειν.

4. Short final syllables are used, under the ictus, for long in several cases.

In the caesura of the pentameter:

['Αρι]σ[τ]όκ[ριτ]ον ὤλεσε, 24 (Att. iv).

..... Σαωτάνορος ὤλετο. Fick   } CXXII (Pharsalus v);
..... Δωτάνορος ὤλετο. Meister }   both uncertain.

[θάνα]τος ἐξαν[ιόντα], XLI (Att. Mac.), also uncertain.

In the second foot of the hexameter:

γευσάμενον. ἀθιγής, 521 (Thessalon. Mac.).[1]

..... ὃς ἀπὸ μητρός, 95 (Att. iii).

Καλλίστρατος ἀνέθηκε, XCVI (Epid. vi-v).[2]

σῆμα τόδε Κύλων, 9 (Att. vi).

οὐ γάρ τι ἐπισταῖς (*ti-e-pi-si-ta-i-se*), LXXIV (Cypriote);

according to Deecke. If right, 'πισταῖς must be understood.

μνημεῖον ἀρετῆς, according to Köhler, is required by the sense in 73 (Att. v, pent.), the stone having μνημείων, which he thinks is due to a "schreiber noch wenig geübt im gebrauch des ionischen alphabets."

In the third foot:

..... πατρὸς ὑς, XI (Att. vi). But see p. 203.

Κυρστι[ϝά]ναξ κὰ πότι, ϝήπω, LXXIV (Cypriote).

Ἀσταγόρωι πατρὶ [Μ]α[γνη]σικλέας, CXXIII (Pherae iv-iii); but see Appendix, p. 198.

---

[1] Kaibel thinks that a young girl's epitaph was changed to do duty for a boy: so originally γευσαμένην.
[2] It might have been μ' ἀνέθηκε.

In the fifth foot:

ἐχῖς ἀλίπλαγκτο[ς]. 1033 (Att. iii);

or is this the natural quantity? Compare ὄφις.

5. We come now to more palpable irregularities of quantity. Distortions of proper names, for the sake of getting them into dactylic verse, are the most numerous group. The succession _ ∪ _ oftenest made trouble. The short syllable had to be stretched out, or one of the long ones shortened.

Δϝεινία τόδε [σᾶμα]. 463 a add. (Corinth vi).

υἱοῦ Τλασίαϝο. 179 (Corc. vi).

'Αντίου. τόδε σῆ[μα]. XIX (Att. v).

Νικίας με ἀνέθηκεν. 778 (Calymna iv–ii).

Σιμίων μ' ἀνέθηκε. LXXXVI (Corinth vi).

Χαιρίωνος ἐπευχή. XI (Att. vi). But see p. 203.

Θηβάδης [ἐπόησεν]. X (Att. vi).

'Αρτέμης. CXLIII (Delos, unknown).

Εὐμάρους τ[όδ' ἄγαλμα]. IX (Att. vi).[1]

'Αντιστάτης υὸς 'Ατάρβου. 22 (Att. v).

Δημοκύδης τόδ' ἄγαλμα. 750 a add. (Paros v).

'Αθανοδώρου.
'Ασωποδώρου. } XCV (Argos, *Olymp.* v).[2]

Νικόβουλε ἠελίου. 62 (Att. iv);

though in this last, as the stone has O, the name Νικόβολε is perhaps conceivable. I add a few doubtful cases. In CIII (Olymp. v) [Γλαυκία]ι is nearly certain, from the accompanying prose inscription (cp. Paus. v, 27, 8). Καλ(λ)ία Σα[κάδα] or something similar would

---

[1] Εὐμάρεος would have been possible.
[2] Usener suggests that -δότου may have been intended by the poet.

be certain in the pentameter, cxxiv (Pherae Mac.), but for the alternative of Καλ(λ)ίᾳ Σα[οτέλευς], with synizesis. Εὐω[πί]δης τόδε μν|ῆ|μα is a conjecture of Röhl's in lx (Chios v): it is certain that only two letters are gone, the inscription being written στοιχηδόν.

Πυντάρης. cxxxi (Olymp. *Gela* vi), is normal. We have Τιμάρης and Τιμάρεος, Anth. Pal. vii, 652. Ξενϝάρεος in 181 can be read with synizesis. These and most names in -άρης are West-Greek forms of -ήρης. and have nothing to do with Ἄρης. Compare the pairs Ἀμφάρης Ἀμφήρης, Εὐάρης Εὐήρης, Θυμάρης Θυμήρης. Λαχάρης in a very late inscription, Kaibel 470, in which the quantities are generally jumbled, cannot count for much, and may anyhow belong to another group.

The succession ◡ ◡ ◡ was the difficulty in other cases. One of the shorts, oftenest the first, had to be made long:

Θρᾱσυμάχου παῖδες, 1089 a RM (Olymp. *Melos* vi–v).

Πόλῡνόϝαις, 181 a add. (Corc. vi), on pattern of Homeric Πουλυδάμας. etc.

Πν̄υταγόρας. pentam., 846 (Argos iv).[1]

Θεοφίλη οὔποτε λήσει. 60 (Att. iv–ii).[2]

Πολ[ύ]ῑδος. 221 (Amorg. iv–iii);

as in Homer, while Sophocles said Πολυΐδος. Not Πολύειδος. as some ancient Homeric critics wrote, and Christ has lately printed.[3] Still it is possible that the long vowel is here original.

Διογένη[s]. 760 (Att. v), Διογένης. pent., 852 (Att. ii), Διόγενες. 519 (Thessalon. Mac.), also on Homeric model. The actual quantity

---

[1] Cp. Πνῡταγόρην, Anth. Pal. vii, 374.

[2] This belongs with αἰόλον ὄφιν in Homer, φιλόσοφον in Aristophanes (Eccl. 571), etc., in which, it is thought, the aspirate was made to do duty for a double consonant. G. Meyer, *Griech. Gramm.*² p. 212.

[3] Πολυΐδος, CIG. 3053 = Cauer² n. 129.

was Διογένης, like Διώδωρος, etc. See Soph. Ai. 91, Aesch. Sept. 127. But the existence of δῖος made the change easier.

Or the succession ᴗ _ _ ᴗ made the trouble:

Ποσειδωνίου ἴσθι, LXXXIII (Cyme iii–ii).

Here would be put Σαωτάνορος or Δωτάνορος in CXXII (see p. 74) if any dependence could be placed on these readings.

I am uncertain whether the quantity ἐπ' Ἀράθθοιο ῥοϝαῖσι, 180 (Corc. vi), is normal or not. Lycophron and Callimachus[1] have Ἄραιθος with ᾰ. Ἄρατθος, Ἄραχθος, Ἄραιθος, are surely the same river. Ἄραχθος (now removed from Livy and Polybius) is confined to the later sources; and I feel sure that ΑΡΑΙΘΟΣ is nothing but an ancient clerical blunder for ΑΡΑΤΘΟΣ, as Kramer and Ross long since pointed out.

Gratuitous tampering with quantity is much less frequent. In proper names I note:

Χῖος ἀγαλλομένη, pentam., 88 (Att. iv–ii); name of island.[2]
Ἀρτεμῆς Θεοκρίτου, CXLIII (Delos, unknown).
Οἰνόβιος Δίωνος, 220 (Amorg. iv);

against Δίων in Anthol. Pal. vii, 99 (Plat. epigr. 7 Bgk.). It is not likely that Δίων has anything to do with δῖος: more probably it is short for Διόδοτος and like names. For

Κλεινίκη Ἑρμαγόρου, 809 (Pharos ii),

it is better to assume crasis. — Neubauer's construction of LXXVIII (Cypriote) makes Ϝεθόχω Ἀλεϝότης (with crasis, or rather aphaeresis: see p. 48). What he means Ἀλεϝότης to be, I know not. By the omission of χόον, it would be possible to understand Ἀλεϝώτης = Ἀλεάτης as a gentile. See Appendix, p. 187. But the whole is

---

[1] Lycophr. 409; Call. frag. 203 Schn.
[2] Similarly in Anthol. Pal. vii, 510 (Simonid. epigram 119 Bgk.), according to the manuscripts.

very uncertain. — Meister makes [Διω]κλέαι, if I understand him, in the third verse of CXXII, but the verse has been better reconstructed by others. The first verse of the same epitaph measures Διοκλέαι (∪ ∪ ⌣). — Ἱπ(π)οσ[τρά]του σῆμα, 8, I am inclined to read otherwise: see Appendix, p. 162.

6. The residue is now small:

μεμνάμενοι, LXXVI (Cypriote).

ἐν τριάκοντ' ἔτεσιν, 85 (Att. iv–ii) ;

similarly Anth. Pal. ix, 682, τριάκοντα δύο in the latter half of a pentameter.

ἤμυναν καί μοι, 96 (Att. iv–ii).

σᾶμα τοῦ Κυπρίου, 188 (Aegina v).

σ[ῆ]μα μήτηρ, 229 a RM (Erythrae vi) :

where Kaibel thinks μήτηρ has replaced an original πατήρ, but Röhl transposes μήτηρ to the next line : see p. 46.

πημάνας 'ἐπιχθονίων, 26 (Att. iv) ;

in which a tag belonging to the feminine caesura is made to follow the masculine.

Πυρ(ρ)ιάδα ὃς οὐκ, CXLIV (Thess. vi–v).

ἐπόει ὅ τοι, CXXVI (Metapont. vi) :

for which Hiller proposes ὃ (δέ) τοι.

Doubtful is ['Ερχ]σ[εμέ]με[ι 'πα]τήρ restored by Köhler in XXIX (Att. v). Still less probable is κλ[έ]ος, XLVIII ; see Appendix, p. 181. Röhl makes the last two lines of 745 into a hexameter beginning καὶ τοί Συρακύσιοι ; but this seems improbable to me. EMI = 'I am,' has its first syllable short in CXLIV (Thess. vi–v), but this, as Kirchhoff remarks, may well be dialectic.

VII.

QUANTITY BY POSITION.

A.— EXCEPTIONAL CASES.

Neglect of position in final syllables :

τόδε μν[ῆ]μα, LX (Chios v).
κατεστενάχησε Στρατεία, 205 (Halicarn. ii).

The like seems implied in [‿ ‿ Σ]τράτωνος, LXIII (Samos Mac.).

οὐ γὰρ π[ο]νηρός, pentam., LXXIII (Cypr. Mac.).
ἤμυνᾶν καί μοι, 96 (Att. iv–ii) : cp. p. 78.
Uncertain is Ἱπ(π)όσ[τρα]τό(s) σῆμα, 8 (Att. vi) : see p. 78, and Appendix, p. 162. In 744, according to the stone, we have ἔ(μ) Μαντινέαι : but [δ]ὲ Μαντινέαι (Dittenberger) is a certain correction.

The cases in which ν movable is concerned will be registered elsewhere (p. 158).

Neglect of position in the middle of a word :

Καλλίστρατος, XCVI (Epid. vi–v).
Ἱπ(π)όσ[τρα]τό(s), or -σ[τρά]του, 8 (Att. vi) ;

unless crasis with the preceding word is to be preferred : see p. 126. Only one π is written.

ἀνέθηκεν Κάλλωνος, CXLI (Delos, unknown) ;

where Κάλωνος (cp. CIII) was probably meant. The inscription is only a second-hand copy : see Appendix, p. 202.

ἔϝρεξα, LXXVI (Cypriote) ;

(like ἔρεξας, Ψ 570) in spite of the ϝ.

Of Θεοφίλη, 60, we have spoken on p. 76.

We may further remark that in the Cypriote inscriptions, unwritten ν counts for position: πά(ν)τα (*pa-ta*), πα(ν)τακόραστος, ἄ(ν)θρωπε, ἄ(ν)θρωποι, LXXIV; τὰ(ν) δίφατο(ν) δίμαο(ν) Παφίja(ν) γε, LXXV; τά(ν)δ', LXXVIII. So also unwritten σ in Neubauer's Δωλίμελο(ς) Ϝεθόχω, LXXVIII.

B.—MUTE AND LIQUID.

It will here be best to separate the dactylic inscriptions from the rest.

(*A*) IN DACTYLIC INSCRIPTIONS.

KP.

(**κρ** *initial.*)

ποίημᾰ Κριτωνίδεω, 750 (Paros v). ‛ὀ Κριτο[β]ού[λ]ου, LXVI (Thera vi).
χαῖρε Κρίτων, 235 (Smyrna iii).
λῆμμᾰ κρίσιν, pent., 858 (Milet. iv).
δίδωσῐ κρίσι⌈ν⌉, pent., XXII (Att. iv).
τε κράτιστον, 64 (Att. iv).   μέγα κράτος, LIII (Delos ii).
ἅδε Κρατίσταν, 77 (Att. iii).   ὅδε κρατέω[ν], 492 b prf.(Theb.iv).
ἦσθᾰ κρατίστη, 79 (Att. iv–ii).
ἄγαλμᾰ Κροβίλου, LI (Delos ii).   τέκεᾰ κρυεραῖ, pent., 184 a RM
τοὔνομᾰ κριοῦ, 63 (Att. iv).   (Corc. ii).
περὶ κριτ[ί], 786 (Halic. ii).
ἡνίκᾰ Κρήτην, XCIX (Teg. Mac.).
ἀριστερᾰ κρήνην, 1037 (Petil. ii).

(**κρ** *medial in compounds, after augment, etc.*)

[‒ ∪]κράτης, pent., CV (Olymp.   Μενεκράτιος, CXXXI (Olymp.
vi–v).   *Gela* vi).

ON GREEK VERSIFICATION IN INSCRIPTIONS. 81

Δηΐκράτης, 875 a add. (Olymp. iv).

Ἱππŏκράτης, pent., same.

Ἱππŏκράτους, same.

Ἱππŏκράτους, pent., 785 (Cnid. ii).

Ἱππŏκ[ράτης], pent., 799 (unknown, iii–ii).

Ξεινŭκράτης, pent., 768 a prf. (Theb. iv–iii).

Ἀριστŏκρέτης, LXXVI (Cypriote).

Καλλῐκρατε[ς], 203 (Cnid. iii–ii).

Σωσῐκράτης, pent., LIII (Delos ii).

Φανŏ[κ]ρίτη, pent., 229 a RM (Erythrae vi).

[Ἐ]ῠθύκριτον, pent., 49 (Att. iv).

[Ἀρι]σ[τ]ŏκ[ριτ]ον, pent., 24 (Att. iv).

Νικŏκρέων, 846 (Arg. iv).

ἔκράτει, 768 a prf. (Theb. iv–iii).

ἔκράτεις, pent., } cxviii (Delph. iv).
[ἔ]κράτεις, "   }

κέκριυμαι, 96 (Att. iv–ii).

Μενέκρατευς, 179 (Corc. vi).[1]

Ἐχέκρατίδεω. 221 (Amorg. iv–iii).

Φιλόκρατες, 491 (Orchom. ii).

Θεόκρίτου, CXLIII (Delos, unkn'wn).

Πολῠκρίτου, 855 (Atalant. iii).

ἄκριτον, 184 a RM (Corc. ii).

δολιχŏκροτάφου, 937 (Aphid. iv–ii).

(κρ *medial not in compounds.*)

ἄκρον, pent., 88 (Att. iv–ii).

δᾱκρυόεντα, 19 (Att. vi).
δᾱκρυόεν, pent., 219 (Amorg. iv).
δᾱκρυόεν, 214 (Rhenaea iii).
δᾱκρυσιν, pent., 205 (Halicarn. ii).
ἄκρ[οι]. 773 (Panticap. Mac.).

---

[1] ... εκράτεω, 492 b prf., is indecisive. But see p. 103.

ἀκροθί[ναι], cxv (Elat. iii).
        4

Λōκρὸς Ἀστυκλέος, 940 a RM
       3   4
(Olymp. *Samos* v).

ἄκρ[ω]ν, 214 (Rhen. iii).
    1
ἀκροπόλεις, 768 (Xanth. iv).
    2   3
ἀκρόπολιν, pent., 856 (Atalant.
    2   3
Mac.).
Λōκροῖσιν, pent., 849 (Delph.
    2   3
iv–iii).
πικρός, pent., 184 a RM (Corc. ii).
  1
Κέκροπα, 844 (Att. iv).
    2
Κέκροπων, pent., xxii (Att. iv).
    5   6
Κέκροπίας, pent., 88·(Att. iv–ii).
    4   5
Κέκροπιδῶν, pent., 844 (Att. iv).
    2   3
Κέκροπίδαι[ς], pent., 40 (Att. iii–ii).
    5   6
Κέκροπ[ιδῶν], pent., 33 (Att. iii–ii).
    5   6

ΚΛ.

(κλ *initial.*)

τεῖδε κλυτόμ, pent., lxxx (Cedreae iv–iii).
   2   3
σε̄ κλυτά, cxviii (Elat. Mac.).
   4
ἀμειβε̄ κλέος, pent., 941 b RM
   5   6
(Olymp. iii).
λέλοιπε̄ κλέος, pent., 235 (Smyrn.
   5   6
iii).

μέγα κλέος, 197 a add. (Rhod.
   4
Mac.).
ὁ Κλειππίδα, lxxx (Cedreae
        4
iv–iii).

On τὸ κλ|έ|ος, xlviii, see Appendix, p. 181.

(κλ *medial in compounds, etc.*)

[Τ]ουπικλέους, 7 (Att. vi).
       1   2
Ὑψικλέος, 461 a add. (Meg. vi).[1]
   2   3
Ἀστυκλέος, 940 a RM (Ol. *Samos* v).
   3   4
Ἡρᾱκλέους, 492 (Theb. iv).
   4   5

Φρασικλείας, 6 (Att. vi).
    2   3
Προκλείδας, 182 (Anactor. v).
    1   2
Ἡρᾱκλείδου, 71 (Att. iv).
    2   3
Ἡρᾱκλείδης, 213 (Delos iv–ii).
    2   3

---

[1] See note [2] on p. 167.

ON GREEK VERSIFICATION IN INSCRIPTIONS. 83

Ἡρăκλέος, xcvii, l. 61 (Epid. iii). Ἡρᾱκλέων, 859 (Tichiussa iv–ii).

Ἡρᾱκλεώτης, lxxix (Halic. iv–iii). Πατρōκλέ[ος], cx (Olymp. iv).

Πατρŭκλέος, pent., lxxxii (Ephes. iv). Τηλέ̆κλεες, 40 (Att. iii–ii).

[Πυθŏ]κλέης, pent., 926 (Herm. iii). Μεγᾱκλέᾳ, 860 (Chios iv–ii).

Δεινŏκλέους, lxxi (Rhod. Mac.). Σωσίκλειαν(?), 1136 (Att. iii–ii); see p. 45.

... σῐκλίας, cxxiii (Pher. iv–iii). ἐπῑκλεές, 255 (Cypr. iv–iii).

Τιμōκλέην, 492 (Theb. iv). Τιμōκλῆς, 14 (Att. vi).

ἄκλεής, pent., 39 (Att. iv). ['Α]ριστōκλῆς, vi (Att. vi).

ἄκλεᾶ, pent., 850 (Att. iv–iii). Ἀριστōκλῆς, 75 (Att. iv–iii).

Διŏκλέᾳι, cxxii (Phars. v). Ἡράκλει', pent., 488 (Tanag. v).

Ξενῠκλῆς, 942 a RM(Ol. *Maenal.* iv). Ἡρᾱκλεῖ, li (Delos Mac.).

Περῐκλεῖ, pent., 86 (Att. iv). Ἡράκλειτε, 30 (Att. iii).

Πολῠ́κλεις, 854 (Delos ii). [Π]υθōκλῆς, 71 (Att. iv).

περίκλυστος, 846 (Arg. iv). [Παν]τᾱκλῆς, 926 (Hermione iii).

πολῠ́κλαυτε, lxx (Rhod. iii–ii). Καλλίκλεια[ν], 857 (Rhod. Mac.).

ἐκλίθην, pent., 88 (Att. iv–ii). ἔκλινε, 183 (Corc. Mac.).

ἔκλειζεν, 254 (Cypr. iv–iii).

ἔκλινε, pent., 941 b RM (Olymp. iii). κεκλημένη, 505 (Tricca iii).

κέκλησε[τ]αι, 182 (Anactor. v). κεκλήσομαι, 6 (Att. vi).

(κλ medial not in compounds.)

κύκλωι, 73 (Att. v). κύκλος, pent., 184 a RM (Corc. ii).

ἐγ κυκλίοισι, 926 (Herm. iii). κύκλον, cxxviii (Sybar. ii).

ΚΜ.

(κμ medial not in compounds.)

ἀκ[μα]ῖς, cxvii (Elat. Mac.). ἀκμαία, pent., xlviii (Chalc. Mac.).

KN.

(κν initial.)

ἐστὶ Κνίδος, pent., 197 (Rhod. iv–ii).
˰2   ˰3

(κν medial not in compounds.)

τέκνου εὐχ-, pent., 756 (Att. v).
      ˰5

τέκνων τέκν', cxiv (Elat. Mac.).
˰4   ˰5

τέκνον, 205 (Halicarn. ii).
˰1

τέκνων, pent., 43 (Att. iv).
˰6

ἄτεκνον, 184 (Corc. iii).
  ˰3

τέκνων, 81 (Att. iv–ii).
˰4

τέκνων, 776 (Att. iii–ii).
˰3

παντοτέκνου, 44 (Att. iv–iii).
˰2   ˰3

τέκνοις, xcvii₂ l. 22 (Epid. iii).
  ˰4

εὐτέκνωι, pent., 859 (Tich. iv–ii).
˰2 ˰3

ΠΡ.

(πρ initial.)

τόνδε πρός, 24 (Att. iv).
     ˰5

πλεύσαντα πρός, 67 (Att. iv–ii).
         ˰5

ἀλλὰ πρός, 781 (Cnid. iii).
    ˰5

σὲ προσιαντῶν, xcvii₅ l. 65 (Epid. iii).
    ˰6

κἀμὲ προσείπας, 781 (Cnid. iii).
  ˰5   ˰6

φίλοισι προσεῖναι, 65 (Att. iv–ii).
     ˰5   ˰6

τόνδε πρό[σελθε], pent., 85 (Att. iv–ii).
˰4   ˰5

πρόσθε πρίν, pent., 492 (Theb. iv).
˰1

ἁ τὸ πρίν, 260 (Cyren. ii).
˰1

γονάτεσσι Πρίηπον, 782 (Halic. iii–ii).
        ˰5   ˰6

τε π[ρόφρ]ων(?), 55 (Att. iv–iii).
        ˰4

παρὰ προπύλωι, pent., 786
  ˰5   ˰6
(Halic. ii).

με πρόφρων, cxxviii (Sybar. ii).
     ˰2

κατὰ προτόνων, pent., 779
   ˰2   ˰3
(Chalced. Mac.).

σὲ προφήτην, 858 (Milet. iv–ii).
      ˰4

ἔτι πρότερος, 925 (Att. iv).
˰2   ˰3

ἔργᾰ πρέποντα, pent., 492 (Theb. iv). τὸ πρέπον, pent., cxv (Elat. iii).
δῶρᾰ πρέπει, pent., 924 (Att. iii–ii). ἀπὸ πράτας, 491 (Orchom. ii).
ἐπὶ πρᾶγμ', pent., 1 (Att. vi).
ἔτι πρόσθεν, 66 (Att. iv–ii).

In 19, ὃ [πρ]ος, from Lolling's account, must disappear. Usener conjectures δὲ πρώιρ[η] in 96, for δεγπρωιρι.

(**πρ** *medial in compounds.*)

φιλοπρόβατον, pent., xxvii (Att. iv).

ἀπροφασίστως, 65 (Att. iv–ii).

(**πρ** *medial not in compounds.*)

Κύπριος, 774 (Priene iv–iii). Κυπρίου, 188 (Aegin. v).
Κύπρις, 784 (Antipol. v). Κύπρις, pent., 846 (Arg. iv).
 Κύπ[ριν], 89 (Att. iv–ii), not certain.

ΠΛ.

(**πλ** *initial.*)

Ἑλλάδι πλεῖστα, 62 (Att. iv). ἐπὶ πλατε[ῖ], 764 (Att. v).
πένθεᾰ πλεῖστα, pent., 71 (Att. iv).
δὲ π[λ]εῖστα, 768 (Xanth. iv).
σὺ πλοῦτον, 771 (Att. iv).

(**πλ** *medial in compounds, etc.*)

ἁλίπλαγκτος, 1033 (Att. iii). φιλόπλου[ς], 856a prf. (Hypate Mac.).

ἔπλετο, pent., 40 (Att. iii–ii).

ἔπλετο, 855 (Atalante iii).

ἔπλετ', 205 (Halic. ii).

(πλ *medial not in compounds.*)

ὁπλίτα[ν], 936 (Arg. v).

ὁπλίτας, 768 (Xanth. iv).

ὅπλοισιν, XCVII, l. 63 (Epid. iii).

πέπλους, 83 (Att. iv–ii).

ΠΝ.
(πν *medial not in compounds.*)

ἀΰπνοις, 1033 (Att. iii).   ὑπνώδης, 774 (Priene iv–iii).

ὕπνον, 184a RM (Corc. ii).

ΤΡ.
(τρ *initial.*)

Ζηνὶ τρόπαιον, pent., 24 (Att. iv).   ἐνὶ τρισσαῖς, 240 (Smyrn. Mac.).

Ζηνὶ τρόπαια, pent., 768a prf.   ὑπὸ τρίποσιν, pent. (Att. iii–ii).

(Theb. iv–iii).

δουρὶ τρόπαια, same.

πλεῖστα τρόπαια, 62 (Att. iv).

π[λ]εῖστα τρόπαια, 768 (Xanth. iv).

(σ)τῆσα τρόπαια, pent., 25 (Att. iv).

[ν]όημα τρόπους, 84 (Att. iv–ii).

δὲ τρόπους, 78 (Att. iv–ii).

δὲ τρόπων, pent. (Olymp. iv).

ζῶσα [τ]ρύπων, XXIV (Att. iv–iii).

δῶμα Τριάκος, 938a prf. (Theb. iv).

ὁ Τριάκος, 938 (Tanag. iv).

ἐξανύοιτε τρίβου, pent., 89 (Att. iv–ii).

Παλλάδι Τρι[τογενεῖ], XII (Att. vi).

Παλλάδι Τριτογενεῖ, pent., 751 (Att. v).
Παλλάδι Τριτογενεῖ, pent., 770 (Att. iv).
Ποσιδώνιε τρίς, 858 (Milet. iv–ii).

(τρ *medial in compounds.*)

προτρέπει, pent., 940 (Att. iv).
ἄτραπόν, xxxvii (Att. iv–ii).

δυσαπότροπ[ο]ς, 1033 (Att. iii).
ἀτραπιτόν, pent., 781 (Cnid. iii).
ἀτρέστω, pent., 242 (Mytil. Mac.).

(τρ *medial not in compounds.*)

πατρίδα, pent., cxxxix (Att. v).
καὶ πάτ[ρίδ'], pent., 21 (Att. v).
κ[αὶ] πατρίδ', pent., 28 (Att. iv–ii).
λιπὼν πατρίδα, 23 (Att. iv).
πατρίδος, lxxxiii (Cyme iii–ii).
πατρίδι, lxviii (Astypal. iv–iii).
πατρίδες, 35 (Att. iv).

πατρωΐης, pent., 13 (Att. vi).
πατρίδ', pent., civ (Olymp. vi).
πατρίδα, pent., 22 (Att. v).
πατρίδα, pent., 36 (Att. v).
πατρίδα, pent., xxii (Att. iv).
πατρίδος, 179 (Corc. vi).
πατρίδος, xxviii (Att. iv).
πατρίδος, 91 (Att. iv).
πατρίδος, pent., cxxiv (Pher. iv–iii).
πατρίδος, xcvii₂ l. 12 (Epid. iii).
πατρίδος, pent., 856 (Atalant. Mac.).
πατρίδι, pent., 37 (Att. iv).
πατρίδι, 242 (Mytil. Mac.).

πατρὶς ὥς, pent., 25 (Att. iv).
πατρὶς ἅδε, cxvii (Elat. Mac.).
μὲν πά[τρίς], 92 (Att. iv–ii).

[π]ατρίς, pent., 71 (Att. iv).

πατρίς, pent., 197 (Rhod. iv–ii).
πατρίς, 205 (Halic. ii).
πατρίς, pent., 852 (Att. ii).

πατρὸς ἠδ', 52 (Att. iv).
πατρὸς οὖ, 66 (Att. Mac.).
πατρὸς ἡνίκα, XXXIII (Att. iv).
πατρὸς ἄνδρα, XLII (Orop. iv).
πατρὸς ἐξ, 772 (Imbr. iv–ii).
πατρὸς ἐξ, CXL (Cos iii–ii).
... ου πατρός, LII (Delos iii–ii).

πατρὶ τῶι, 76 (Att. iv).
πατρὶ κισσοφοροῦντι, 925 (Att. iv).
πατρὶ μητρί, 213 (Delos? iv–ii).
πατρία, pent., 49 (Att. iv).
πατρίας, pent., 489 (Theb. iv).
πατρί[α], pent., 29 (Att. iv–ii).
πατρικοῦ, 81 (Att. iv–ii).
βοτρυοστεφάνωι, 38 (Att. iv).
βοτρυώδεος, 88 (Att. iv–ii).

Πατροκλέ[ος], CX (Olymp. iv).

θυγατρός, LXIX (Rhod. Mac.).
θυγατρός, same.
πέτρα, 234 (Smyrn. iii).
πέτρωι, pent., 89 (Att. iv–ii).
πατρίς, 489 (Theb. iv).

πατρός, pent., 941 c RM (Olymp. v).
πατρός, 938 a prf. (Theb. iv).
πατρύς, 89 (Att. iv–ii).
πατρός, same.
πατρός, 95 (Att. iii).
πατρός, 189 (Melos iii).
πατρός, 855 (Atal. iii).
πατρός, 777 (Salam. iv–ii).
πατρί, pent., 761 (Aegin. v).
πατρί, 87 (Att. iv).
πατρί, 49 (Att. iv).
πατρί, 85 (Att. iv–ii).
πατρί, 932 (Sidon iii).
πατρί, pent., 505 (Tricca iii).
πατρί, 240 (Smyrn. Mac.).
πατρί, pent., 773 (Pantic. Mac.).
πατρί, 782 (Halic. iii–ii).
πατρί, 260 (Cyr. ii).
πάτρα, 183 (Corc. Mac.).
πάτρας, 854 (Delos ii).
Πατροκλέως, pent., LXXXII (Ephes. iv).
θυγάτρα, 857 (Rhod. Mac.).
θυγάτρα, 205 (Halic. ii).
πέτρος, 240 (Smyrn. Mac.).
Ἀτρειδᾶν, pent., 254 (Cypr. iv–iii).
πατρώιον, LIX (Delos Chios vi).

ON GREEK VERSIFICATION IN INSCRIPTIONS. 89

πατρίς, xcviii (Epid. Mac.).   πατρίς, 488 (Tanag. v).
πατρίς, pent., 88 (Att. iv–ii).   πατρίς, 255 (Cypr. iv–iii).
πατρός, xi (Att. vi).   πατρός, 88 (Att. iv–ii).
πατρό[s], pent.?, 203 (Cnid. iii–ii).   πατρός, 490 (Theb. Mac.).
πάτραν, cxviii (Delph. iv).   πατρί, cxxiii (Pher. iv), but see p. 198.
πάτρας, pent., 938 (Tanag. iv).   πάτραν, 52 (Att. iv).
Ἀντιπάτρου, 779 (Chalced. Mac.).   πάτρῃσιν, xxxvi (Att. Mac.).
Ἀντιπάτροιο, 857 (Rhod. Mac.).   πετρῶν, pent., 773a RM. (Att. iv).

ΤΜ.
(τμ medial not in compounds.)

πότμον ἔκλυε, 183 (Corc. Mac.).   πότμωι, 77 (Att. iii).

ΤΝ.
(τν medial not in compounds.)

πότνιας, 774 (Priene iv–iii).   πότνι', 753 (Att. v).
    πότνια, 34 (Att. iv).
    [π]ότνια, cxv (Elat. iii).
    πότνι', 856a prf. (Hypat. Mac.).

ΧΡ.
(χρ initial.)

μνῆμα χρόνου, 82 (Att. iv).   Ποσειδῶνι Χρόνου, cxvi (Elat. iv–iii).
κείνοισι χρόνοις, xcvii₅ l. 58 (Epid. iii).
σὲ χρόνος, pent., 854 (Delos ii).
δὲ Χρύσω[ν], 197 (Rhod. iv–ii).
τὸ χρέ'ων], pent., 519 (Thessalon. Mac.).

(χρ medial not in compounds.)

ἄχρι ἄν, 48 (Att. iii).

XN.

(**χν** *medial not in compounds.*)

ὅς τέχνηι οὐχί, pent., 38 (Att. iv).
       ἀχνύμενοι, pent., 183 (Corc. Mac.).
       τέχνας, 197 (Rhod. iv–ii).
       τέχνας, 197a add. (Rhod. Mac.).
       τέχνης, 39 (Att. iv).
τέχνης, pent., xxii (Att. iv). τέχνην, 64 (Att. iv).
τέχνην, pent., 875a add. (Olymp. iv). τέχν[ης], pent.?, 780 (Mytil. iv–ii).
καλλιτέχνωι, pent., cxv (Elat. iii). τέχνας, pent., liii (Delos ii).
τεχνιτῶν, 924 (Att. iii–ii).   τέχνην, pent., same.
       ἴχνος?, 1033 (Att. iii): measurement uncertain.

ΦΡ.

(**φρ** *initial.*)

σῆμα Φρασικλείας, 6 (Att. vi). ἀπὸ φρενός, 845 (Att. iii–ii).
ξένε φράζεο, xxxvii (Att. iv–ii).

(**φρ** *medial in compounds.*)

       σαοφροσύνης, pent., 2 (Att. vi).
       μεγαλόφρονος, 34 (Att. iv).
       Εὐθύφρονος, 942a RM (Olymp. *Macnal.* iv).
δίφρων, pent., lxxii (Rhod. Mac.). δίφρων, pent., 932 (Sidon Mac.).

In 741 (Att. vi), it is not clear whether Ἀλκίφρων or Ἀλκίφρον[ος] is to be read.

(**φρ** *medial not in compounds.*)

Ἀφροδίτης, 784 (Antipol. v). ὄφρ', 240 (Smyrn. Mac.).
Ἀφροδ[ίτηι], 809 (Pharos Mac.). ὄ[φ]ρα, lxix (Rhod. Mac.).

ΦΝ.

(**φν** *medial not in compounds.*)

δάφνας, XCVII₂ l. 19 (Epid. iii).   δάφνας, pent., 786 (Halic. ii).

ΘΡ.

(**θρ** *initial.*)

σῆμᾰ Θράσωνος, pent., 2 a RM (Att. vi).
γαῖᾰ θρασυπτολέμων, pent., 183 (Corc. Mac.).

(**θρ** *medial in compounds.*)

πολῡθρήνωι, pent., 184 a RM (Corc. ii).

(**θρ** *medial not in compounds*).

[ἀνδ]ρὸς 'ἄθρῆν, 936 a RM (Lac. v).   πτολίεθρ[ον], 1033 (Att. iii).

ΘΛ.

(**θλ** *medial not in compounds.*)

ἀέθλων, pent., 926 (Hermione iii).   ἀέθλοις, 936 (Arg. v).

ἄεθλα, 938 a prf. (Theb. iv).

[ἄε]θλα, 846 (Arg. iv).

ἀέθλοφόρων, pent., 855 (Atal. iii).

In 492 (Theb. iv), τρὶς ἀέθλοις was probably intended; τρὶς ἐν ἄθλοις being on the stone.

ΘΜ.

(**θμ** *medial not in compounds.*)

ἀρῐθμόν, CXVIII (Delph. iv).

ἀρῐθμόν, 239 (Smyrn. Mac.).

ἀ[ρ]ῐ[θ]μήσειεν, 926 (Hermione iii).

'Ἰθμῶι, CX (Olymp. iv); mistake?

θέθμόν, XCVII₂ l. 12 (Epid. iii).

(σ)τάθ[μ]ηι, 785 (Cnid. ii); not certain.

ΘΝ.

(**θν** *initial.*)

μεί[ζ]ονᾰ θ[ν]ητ[ῶν]. 844 (Att. iv).
εὐδαίμοσῑ θνητοῖς, XLIII (Salam. iv–iii).
σώφρονᾰ θνῄσκω, XXIV (Att. iv–iii).
δαίμ[ο]νᾰ [θ]νητο[ῖς], 519 (Thessalon. Mac.).

(**θν** *medial not in compounds.*)

'ὀθνείαις, 189 (Melos iii).

ΓΡ.

(**γρ** *initial.*)

ἐτέλεσσἔ Γρόφων. pent., 740 (Melos vi).

(**γρ** *medial in compounds, etc.*)

καταγράφεται, pent., 926 (Herm. iii).
ἀνεγραφόμαν, pent., 205 (Halic. ii).

(**γρ** *medial not in compounds.*)

ἀγ[ροῦ], XLV (Aegin. v).
λυγρ[ό]ν, 519 (Thessalon. Mac.). ἀ[γρ]οτέρ[αν], XLVII (Eub. Mac.).
λυγρόμ, 183 (Corc. Mac.). ὑγρός, pent., 41 (Att. iv).

ΓΛ.

(**γλ** *medial not in compounds.*)

ἀγλαόν, CXL (Cos iii–ii).

ΓΜ.

(**γμ** *medial not in compounds.*)

Πυγμαίου, LVII (Amorg. vi).
δόγμασιν, pent., 491 (Orchom. ii).
πεφυλαγμένον, CXXVII (Sybar. ii).

ΓΝ.

(γν *medial in compounds, etc.*)

κα[σ]ίγ[νητ...], LXV (Thera vi), if rightly restored.

[κα]σίγνητοι, LXXVI (Cypriote).

κασιγνήτη. LIV (Delos *Nax*. vi).

κασιγνήτοιο. 179 (Corc. vi).

κασιγνήτηι. pent., 71 (Att. iv).

κασιγνήταις. 35 (Att. iv).

κασιγνήταις. 49 (Att. iv).

κασιγνήτωι, XXIV (Att. iv–iii).

κασιγνήταισιν. 82 (Att. iv).

[αὐτοκασ]ιγνήτων. pent., XXXVII (Att. iv–ii).

αὐτοκασίγνητοι. 772 (Imbr. iv–ii).

γίγνεται. pent., 875 a add. (Olymp. iv).

ἀπογιγνομένοις. pent., XXIV (Att. iv–iii).

ἐπιγιγνομένοι[ς], pent., XXXI (Att. iv).

(γν *medial not in compounds.*)

Ἁγνῄς. 86 (Att. iv).

ἁγνῆς, 850 (Att. iv–iii).

ἁγνῶς, XCVII₂ l. 21 (Epid. iii).

ἁγνόν, 239 (Smyrn. Mac.).

ἁγνοτάτα. pent., 855 (Atal. iii).

ἁγνάς, 774 (Priene iv–iii).

ἁγνήν. CXXVIII (Sybar. ii).

στυγ[νό]ν, 519 (Thessalon. Mac.).

BP.

(βρ *initial.***)**

τήνδε βρότοις, pent., 940a RM (Ol. Samos v).

πᾶσι βροτοῖς. pent., 86 (Att. iv).

τρόπαια β[ρ]οτῶν, 768 (Xanth. iv).

τε βροτοῖς, 65 (Att. iv–ii).

οἱ δὲ βρο[τῶν]. pent., 242 (Mytil. Mac.).

ἔτευξε βροτοῖς, pent., 189 (Melos iii).

στυγέουσι βροτοί τε, 1033 (Att. iii).

ἀντὶ βροτοῖο. cxxviii (Sybar. ii).

(βρ *medial not in compounds.***)**

Σαλυβρίαν. pent., 36 (Att. v). ὄβριμ[οπάτρης]. XLIX (Ceos vi).

ὑβρίσαι. pent., xxviii (Att. iv).

ΔP.

(δρ *initial.***)**

[τ]όνδε δρόμον, 741 (Att. vi).

τε δρόμοις, xxii (Att. iv).

(δρ *medial after augment.***)**

ἔδρασε, pent., 844 (Att. iv). ἐδράμομεν, pent., 768a prf. (Theb. iv–iii).

  ἔδρακεν, pent., 852 (Att. ii).

(δρ *medial not in compounds.***)**

ἱδρυσάμενος, 773b RM (Att. iv–iii).

ἵδρυεται. 781 (Cnid. iii).

πάρεδρον, 924 (Att. iii–ii). ἕδρας, cxxviii (Sybar. ii).

ΔΜ.

(δμ *medial not in compounds.*)

[φ]ρᾱδ[μ]οσύνα[ι]ς. pent., 859
(Tichiussa iv–ii).

[Κ]ᾱδμείωι. pent., 926 (Herm. iii).

Κᾱδμηΐδος. 932 (Sidon iii).

ΔΝ.

(δν *medial not in compounds.*)

Ἀφῐδναίων. 775 (Att. v).

(*B*) IN NON-DACTYLIC INSCRIPTIONS.

ΚΡ.

ἀριστοκρατίαν, troch. tetr., XCVII₁
(Epid. iii).

Ξενόκριτος. troch. tetr., 783 (Cnid. iv–ii).　　δάκρυ, troch. tetr., 790 (Achaia iii).

ἄκρους. iamb. trim., CXI (Helic. Mac.).　　νεκραγωγόν, iamb. tr., 258 (Alexandr. iii–ii).

ΚΛ.

ἠδὲ Κλειτοφῶντα, iamb. tr., 211　　[μ]έγᾱ κλέος. iamb. tr., CXI
(Syros iii).　　(Helic. Mac.).

Ἡρᾰκλεῖ. troch. tetr., 790 (Achaia iii).

Σωσῐκλῆς. troch. tetr., 783 (Cnid. iv–ii).

Τιμοκλείδας. troch. tetr., same.

ἐπεκλήθη. lyric, XCVII₄ l. 45 (Epid. iii).

ἐπίκλησιν, lyric, same, l. 51.

KN.

τέκνου, iamb. tr., 246 (Bith. Mac.).
6

    τέκνου, iamb. tr., cxvii (Elat. Mac.);
        5
    quantity uncertain.

ΠΡ.

    [τ]ὸ πρίν, troch. tetr., 790
     4
    (Achaia iii).

ΠΛ.

αἴθε πλούσιος. iamb., 1133 (vase v);
2 3 4
    quantity uncertain.

ΤΡ.

πέτρος, iamb. tr., 258 (Alex. iii–ii).   πᾱτρός, iamb. tr., 211 (Syros iii).
6   3

πᾱτρίς. iamb. tr., same.
6

πᾱτραι, iamb. tr., cxi (Helic. Mac.).
4

πᾱτρίδ' Ἐπι-, lyric, xcvii₁ l. 42 (Epid. iii).

ΧΡ.

ὃ χρυσότοξος, lyric, xcvii₁ l. 45   μέλιχρον, iamb. tr., cxi (Helic.
    (Epid. iii).   3
                                  Mac.).

κόρε χρυσοκόμα, lyric, same, l. 47.

ΧΜ.

δραχμήν, iamb. tetr., 1132 (vase iv–ii);
   1
    quantity uncertain.

ΧΝ.

Τέχνωνος, iamb. tr., 93 (Att. iv–iii).
2

    τέχναι, iamb. tr., cxi (Helic. Mac.);
        5
    quantity uncertain.

ΦΡ.

Ἑρμᾶς Ἀφροδίται, iamb. tr., 783 (Cnid. iv–ii).
  1   2

ΦΛ.

δὲ Φλεγύα, lyric, xcvii, l. 44 (Epid. iii).

ΘΡ.

νικῶσα θρήνοις, iamb. tr., 246   ἄθρει, iamb. tr., 258 (Alex. iii–ii).
 1   2   2
(Bith. Mac.).

ΘΜ.

ῥυθμῶι, iamb. tr., cxi (Thesp. Mac.).
 6

ΓΡ.

ἔγραψε. iamb. tr., 1099 and cxxxv
   3
(vases v); quantity uncertain.

ΒΡ.

δώρημα βροτοῖς, lyric, xcvii, l. 53 (Epid. iii).

ΔΡ.

πάρεδρος, iamb. tr., 783 (Cnid. iv–ii). ἐπέδραμε, iamb. tr., 258 (Alex. iii–ii).
    3   5 6

———

I have enumerated all the examples, but only the dactylic ones are numerous enough to warrant any inferences. Here it will be useful to note the divergences from the Homeric usage as set forth by La Roche, *Homer. Untersuchungen*, p. 1 flg., and Hartel, *Homerische Studien*, I. p. 80 flg. The count for the dactylic inscriptions may be thus tabulated. The figures in parenthesis indicate the residue after elimination of cases where the form of the word absolutely required the lengthening or shortening. It is obvious that πατρίας, δακρυόεντα, πλεῖστα τρόπαια, and the like, prove nothing as to preferences and tendencies of the verse.

ON GREEK VERSIFICATION IN INSCRIPTIONS.

		short.	long.			short.	long.			short.	long.
κρ	init.	12 (6)	4 (1)	τρ	init.	17 (5)	2 (1)	θν	init.	4	–
	m.c.	18 (2)	8 (1)		m.c.	2	3 (1)		med.	1	–
	med.	3 (2)	16 (5)		med.	40 (35)	51	γρ	init.	1 (0)	–
κλ	init.	4	2	τμ	med.	1	1		m.c.		2 (0)
	m.c.	23 (15)	22 (14)	τν	med.	1 (0)	4		med.	2	3 (2)
	med.	2 (1)	2					γλ	med.	–	1
κμ	med.	1	1	χρ	init.	5 (4)	1	γμ	med.	–	3 (2)
					med.	1	–				
κν	init.	1	–	χν	med.	5 (4)	9 (8)	γν	m.c.	2	12 (8)
	med.	4 (3)	7 (6)						med.	–	8 (7)
πρ	init.	17 (10)	5 (2)	φρ	init.	2	1				
	m.c.	–	2 (0)		m.c.	1	4 (2)	βρ	init.	8 (2)	–
	med.	2	3		med.	2 (0)	2		med.	2 (1)	1 (0)
πλ	init.	4	1	φν	med.	1	1	δρ	init.	2 (1)	–
	m.c.	1	4	θρ	init.	2 (0)	–		m.c.	1	2 (1)
	med.	4	–		m.c.	–	1		med.	3	1
πν	med.	1	2		med.	1	1 (0)	δμ	med.	–	3 (2)
				θλ	med.	1	4 (3)	δν	med.	–	1
				θμ	med.	–	6				

We find illustrated what has often been pointed out before, that γβδ weigh more than κπτχφθ; and the nasals — especially μ — more than ρ and λ (θμ, γμ, δμ, δν make position wherever used): furthermore, that position before an initial group is distinctly weaker than before a medial group. For the rest, the tendency to shortening is stronger than in Homer. The proportion of shortenings is greater, and so is the proportion of *avoidable* shortenings — those not required by the form of the word.

For instance. In Homer πρ makes a short syllable about 273 times, a long syllable about 1150 times;[1] against 19 and 10 of the inscriptions. Before initial πρ Homer has about 272 shorts and about 1000 longs; the inscriptions 17 shorts and 5 longs. Of these 272 shorts, about 60 — less than a fourth — are avoidable, in the sense explained above; in the inscriptions 10 of the 17 are avoidable.

---

[1] An exact count has probably never been made. These figures, partly count and partly estimate, are based on La Roche's statistics.

Shortening before initial mute and liquid is less restricted to particular places of the verse than in Homer. The first short of the third and the first short of the fifth foot — the places to which this shortening in Homer is chiefly confined (Hartel, l. c. p. 81) — show, it is true, a large proportion of our cases (the one 10, the other 14). But the end of the fourth foot (the bucolic caesura) has 3 cases, against 2 in all Homer; and the end of the fifth foot 10 cases, against 3 in Homer! The first short of the first and of the second foot, and the second short of the first foot, have respectively 5, 5, and 3 cases. In the pentameter the favorite place is the first short of the fifth foot (11 cases); next, the first short of the fourth (8 cases).

Lengthening, on the other hand, is restricted. It occurs chiefly in the interior of a word: 193 cases, against 15 before initial mute and liquid. In general it requires the aid of the ictus. Before initial groups there is only one exception to this ('ὁ Κλειππίδα. p. 82), whereas Hartel enumerates 105 Homeric instances of this sort. In the middle of a word 36 out of 193 lengthenings lack the ictus.

A difference between earlier and later inscriptions in the treatment of mute and liquid is not, with the means at our command, demonstrable.

VIII.

CONTRACTION AND SYNIZESIS.

1. Cases of contraction and non-contraction, where either form would fit the verse and the difference is only one of dactyl or spondee, have been enumerated on pp. 62, 64, excepting those in which it is not graphically obvious whether contraction is intended or not.

Such are the patronymics in -ειδης. In dactylic verse there are twelve cases:

Προκλείδας. 182 (Anact. v).   Εὐκλείδης, cxv (Elat. iii).
Κορρείδας. pent., 492 b prf. (Theb. iv).   Ἐρεχθειδᾶν. 852 (Att. ii).

Ὀλ... εἶδα, 486 (Thesp. v).   Ἀτρειδᾶν, pent., 254 (Cypr. iv–iii).
Ἡρακλείδου, 71 (Att. iv).   Λαγείδας, pent., 255 (Cypr. iv–iii).
Ἡρακλείδην, 239 (Smyr. Mac.).   Ἀριστείδου, pent., cxi. (Cos iii–ii).
Ἡρακλείδης, 213 (Delos iv–ii).   Αἰγείδαισι, 852 (Att. ii).

The syllable -ει- is never under the ictus; there is nothing like Ἡρακλείδας ($\smile \_ \smile \_$), Theocr. xvii, 26. On the other hand, it is never in the fifth foot, nor in the latter half of the pentameter. In 486 simple E is written for ει, which is decisive for that case. Indeed it is incredible that -ἐϊ- was intended by the poet in any of these cases. The contracted pronunciation was certainly well established in Pindar's time, if not before.[1] Τιμοκλείδας appears in a trochaic inscription, 783.

In 26 Kaibel has written εὐκλέϊσε Ἀνδοκίδαν, though the same inscription has εὐκλείζων, and 254 ἔκλειζεν. Uncontracted in pentameter εὐκλέϊσαν, cxxxix, and εὐκλ[έϊσαν], 21. I note further εὔκλειαν, pent., 29 (for which εὔκλε(ι)αν with E, 24, is significant); Φρασικλείας, 6; θείης. 1037, and θείοισιν, lii (but θειοτάτην, pent., 846); Ἀργείων, pent., 466; αἰδοίην, pent., 13; ἥρωι or ἥρωϊ. xxxvii (see p. 73); γήραι δή or γήραϊ δή. xlviii (γήραϊ in pentameter 519).

Forms of feminines in -ώ are Καλλιστοῖ. 56; but Καλλιστοῦς, 82; Αἰδοῦς, 34, Πυθοῖ. cxviii.

I need not say that even the oldest inscriptions have no trace of a genitive singular in -οο. Places where it is conspicuous by its absence are these, all of the sixth century: Κ[λεοί]του τοῖ, 1 a add. (Att.); [Ἐχε]τίμου ματρός, 181 a add. (Corc.); υἱοῦ Τλα-, 179 (Corc.); τοῦ Μείξιος. 181 (Corc.); τοῦ Ναξίου, liv (Delos Nax.); τοῦ Μαλί[ου], 1098a RM (Melos). OY is written in the Corcyrean examples, O in the rest.

---

[1] ὠριστοκλείδη in troch. tetr. Anacr. fr. 114 Bgk.⁴ (A.P. xiii, 4). Sappho fr. 118 (A.P. vi, 269) cannot be relied on.

Of δηίους and διμώσας. and of Ζωίλου, we have spoken on p. 73.

The choice, for metrical convenience, of contracted forms of every-day speech on the one hand, or of well-known archaic uncontracted forms on the other — that is, of Ἀιδης. σωφροσύνη. or of Ἀίδαο. σαοφροσύνη — does not here concern us, and no register has been kept of such cases. Still it may be worth while to record a few noteworthy forms. Δέρμιμ. 484 (Tanag. v) is like Homeric ἰξυῖ. etc. Ἀγνῆις. 86, and Ἐρσῆις. pent. 91 (both Att. iv). Τρωίας (with Ω) in anapaests 775 a RM. unless this part is prose. By ποὶ δ' Ἀσκλαπιόν, XCVII₂ l. 20 (Epid. iii), the existence of the preposition ποί = πρός is put beyond doubt, and it is shown to be one syllable, not two. The Homeric ἐϋ- of compounds is avoided. We have εὔκλειαν. pent. 29, εὐκλε(ι)αν 24, εὐκλειῆ. pent. 851, εὐπλοίης. pent. 779, εὔγραπτον. LXI, εἰπόλεμον. pent. 21, εὐπόλεμον. pent. 34, and I dare say others. But ἠϋκόμοιο. 857.

Uncontracted Λυκόεργε (not Λυκόοργε) and Λυκόερ[γε], CXIX (Delphi iv–iii). The common form in Αἰγείδαισι Λυκοῦργος. 852 (Att. ii); and πόληϊ Λυκοῦργος, XCVII₅ l. 71 (Epid. iii); in both cases quite gratuitously, and the older form would, in the second, have improved the rhythm ; see p. 57.

The form ὁράοντι (or ὑράων τις), 756 a RM (Plat. v), is noteworthy as being without the factitious assimilation and "protraction" by which such forms, in our Homeric text, are transmogrified into a semblance of the every-day ὁρῶντι, etc. But these mouthed-over words meet us elsewhere : Δαμοφόων, pent., 761 (Aeg. v) ;[1] Δημοφόων, pent., 86 (Att. iv) ; μνωόμενος. pent., 30 (Att. iii). The occurrence of ἔην in pentameter, LX (Chios v), proves a very respectable antiquity

---

[1] Misprinted Δημοφόων in Kaibel.

for that bogus form. A similar product of rhapsodism is εὐκλειῆ, pent., 851 (Rhod. iii).

The resolution Ἀϊσσχύλον 760, is very doubtful. See p. 55.

2. Of unwritten contraction or 'synizesis' I will enumerate all the examples.

Synizesis of εο:

Οἰανθέος γενεάν, 179 (Corc. vi).

Ξενϝάρεος, 181 (Corc. vi); probable: see p. 76.

Δεινομένεος δέ, LIV (Delos *Nax.* vi).

Δεινομένεος. logaoedic, 745 (Syrac. v).

Παρισάδεος ἄρχοντος, 773 (Panticap. Mac.).

Θρασυμήδεος, 778 (Calymn. iv–ii).[1]

On the other hand, ἔτευς, pent., 184a RM (Corc. ii), like ἔρχευ, 781 (Cnid. iii).

Κλεομάνδρου, 219 (Amorg. iv):

whereas Κλευνίκη, 809 (Pharos ii); Θεύδοτε, 240 (Smyrn. Mac.); Θουτίμο[υ], 766 (Att. v). Cp. Κλεύβουλος, Δεύνυσε in Anacreon (frag. 2 and 3 Bgk.), and Ross, *Arch. Aufsätze*, ii, p. 547.

δώδεκα θεοῖς, pent., 768 (Xanth. iv).

θεοῖς φίλον, pent., 926 (Herm. iii).

θεοῖς φέρε (*te-o-i-se*), LXXIV (Cypriote).

χρυσέοις, XCVII, l. 64 (Epid. iii);

but χρυσῆν, pent., 857 (Rhod. Mac.).

Synizesis of εω:

Δεινοδίκεω, LIV (Delos *Nax.* vi): HO is written.

Κριτωνίδεω, 750 (Paros v): with εω shortened; see p. 119.

Ἐχεκρατίδεω, 221 (Amorg. iv–iii).

---

[1] χρυσαιγίδεος, XLIX, is only a graver's blunder.

The resolution of -εω of the genitive singular is perhaps unknown to the literature of Hellenic times. The epigrammatists of the Anthology have tetrasyllabic Ἀΐδεω and the like; Meleager in Anth. Palat. iv, 1, affording eight examples in fifty verses. But I do not know of any instance which antedates the Roman period. Our inscriptions show two cases:

Λαμψαγόρεω, end of a trimeter, LVI (Amorg. vi).[1]

Λεωνίδεω, pent., XXXVI (Att. iii–ii).

The first ought perhaps not to count, as the other name in the inscription is unmetrical: see p. 47. The second example is certain, but the epitaph is pretty late, and possibly belongs in the Roman epoch. Compare Anth. Pal. vi, 190, 191. The restoration παῖδ[α Μεν]εκράτεω in 492 b prf. (Theb. iv) is not to be trusted; indeed something like παιδ[ὸς Τη]λεκράτεω would conform better to Foucart's copy.

ἀλ(λ)έων, LIV (Delos Nax. vi): HO is written.

νικέων, pent., 768 (Xanth. iv).

αἱμ[α]σιέων, pent., 782 (Halic. iii–ii).

Resolved in:

Βουταδέων, 852 (Att. ii);

as occasionally in literature (H 1, φ 191, etc.).

παρὰ θεῶν, pent., 6 (Att. vi).

θεῶι κυμερῆναι (*te-o-i*), LXXIV (Cypriote).

θεῶι ἀλ(λ)' (*te-o-i*), same; -εωι shortened? See p. 55.

[κοσμ]έων, pent., 489 (Theb. iv).

Ἡρακλέων, 859 (Tichiussa iv–ii).

[ἐστ]ὶ τὸ χρε ῶν], pent., 519 (Thessalon. Mac.).

Κρέων, troch. tetr., 783 (Cnid. iv–ii).

λεωφόρον, pent., LX (Chios v).

---

[1] Not Λαμψάγρεω, as assumed by Usener, *Altgr. Verskunst*, p. 39, note 22.

Synizesis of εα:

  βασιλέως (= βασιλεώς), pent., 768 (Xanth. iv).

  Διοκλέμι, CXXII (Phars. v).

  [Διο]κλέα, Fick,   ⎫
            ⎬ same : neither certain.
  [Μενε]κλέα, Cauer, ⎭

  Μεγακλέα, 860 (Chios iv–ii).

With this last compare βασιλῆ, pent., 846 (Arg. iv), and Ἑρμιονῆ, pent., 926 (Herm. iii).

Synizesis of ιω, ιου: only in epigrams of the clumsier sort.

  Ἀσκ(λ)απιῷ]ι, XCVI (Epid. vi–v).

  Κυπρίου τοῦ, 188 (Aeg. v).

  Σαλαμινίου, same.

  Διονυσίου τῶν, 66 (Att. Mac.).

  Πυθίων, 26 (Att. iv).

On the possibility of Καλλέα, CXXIV, see p. 76.[1]

Other cases: all doubtful.

  χῶρ(ν) τά(ν)δε (*ko-o-ta-te*), LXXVIII (Cypriote) ; see p. 77.

  ὑιής, 760 (Att. v) : but see p. 55. ὓς, contracted, occurs XI.

υἱός as monosyllable, 778, is utterly improbable : see p. 46.

  Significant, as regards the pronunciation of these combinations, are the fifth example of εο, and the second of εω. It is clear that εο was a *long* syllable, consequently that ε was not consonantized.[2] The sound intended was diphthongal, and cannot have differed much from that elsewhere expressed by ευ. That -εω, on the other hand (and perhaps even -εωι : see p. 103 near bottom), can be shortened before a vowel, bears on cases like χρυσέωι ἀνὰ σκήπτρωι (Λ 15), and is easiest understood if we suppose a consonantal ε.

  Synizesis between words will be treated under Crasis.

---

[1] Compare Φειδίας Χαρμίδου υἱὸς Ἀθηναῖος μ' ἐποίησε, Paus. v, 10, 2.

[2] Compare Ἀριστοφάνεος οὐκέτι (∪ — ∪ ∪ — — ∪ —), Pind. Nem. iii. 35.

IX.

HIATUS.

Hiatus is on the whole infrequent, and occurs chiefly in epigrams of unskilful construction in other respects.

I throw out, of course, hiatus in interpolations: καὶ ἐργάτις, 60; πᾶι εὖ, LXXVI; for which see page 46.

The following cases, before former ϝ-words, are due to Homeric reminiscence:

ἐνθάδε οἱ, 86 (Att. iv).
τοῦτο δέ οἱ, 234 (Smyrn. iii).
ἀθάνατο[ί] οἱ, 768 (Xanth. iv).
σ[ύ] οἱ, 786 (Halic. ii); uncertain.
ἔκκριτα ἔργα, LIII (Delos ii).
ὅσσα ἑώργει, LXIII (Samos Mac.).
εὖ εἰδότες, 183 (Corc. Mac.).

ὦ ἄ[να] in 786 is a doubtful conjecture.

The remaining examples I arrange according to their place in the verse. First those in hexameters:

Foot I.
(Shorts). οἳ δὲ ἐκάρυξαν, XCVII₃ l. 76 (Epid. iii).
(ἐγὼ) ἠμὶ Ἀριστοκρέτης, LXXVI (Cypriote).
(End). χαίρετε οἱ παριόντες, 22 (Att. v).
δι[ζ]ῶ εἰ, CXIX (Delph. iv–iii).
ἥρωι εὐξ....., XXXVIII (Att. iv–ii), if verse.

Foot II.
(Middle). σοι ὅτι, 48 (Att. iii).
μεμναμένοι εὐϝεργεσίας, LXXVI (Cypriote).
... ωι ἥρωϊ, 552 a add. (unknown, Mac.).

106   ON GREEK VERSIFICATION IN INSCRIPTIONS.

Foot III.
(Middle). ὁδοῦ ἀγαθοῦ, 3 (Att. vi): the copy has ΗΟΔΟΙ. See p. 151.

ταυτᾶ ἀτ' οὐδῆς, CI (Lac. vi–v).

ἐπόει ὅ τοι, CXXVI (Metapont. vi).

Πυρ(ρ)ιάδα ὃς οἶκ, CXLIV (Thess. vi–v).

[κρύ]πτω οἴας, 95 (Att. iii).

εὐμόχθου ἐπὶ γυμνάδ[ο]ς, 239 (Smyrn. Mac.).

πέμψηι ἕδρας, CXXVIII (Sybar. ii).

(Shorts). ἀνέθηκε Ἀθαναία[ι], CI (Sparta vi–v): see p. 158.

Λυκόεργε ἐμόν, CXIX (Delph. iv–iii).

(End). ὁ Εὐμάρους, IX (Att. vi).

τὰ ὅρκια, 19 (Att. vi).

τὰ ἄ(ν)θρωποι, LXXIV (Cypriote).

Παγαῖς καὶ οὔνο[μα], 469 (Arg. Mac.).

Foot IV.
(Middle). ἐγὼ ἔστα[κ]', 181 a add. (Corc. vi).

Διοκλέαι ἔσστασ', CXXII (Phars. v). See also p. 204.

Foot V.
(Middle). τῶ ἀ(ν)θρώπω, LXXVII (Cypriote).

Ἀσκ(λ)απι[ῶ]ι ὁ μάγιρος, XCVI (Epid. vi–v).

(Shorts). παιδὶ ἀπ(α)ρχήν, XVI (Att. vi).

πάντα ὅμοια, XXVI (Att. iv).

τὰ ἄπ[α]ντα, 768 (Xanth. iv).

πατρὶ ἐπείγηι, 782 (Halic. iii–ii).

(End). ἄχρι ἂν ζῶ, 48 (Att. iii).

ἐ εὔφρων, 936 a RM (Lac. v).

Irreg. τὸν ἄνδρα Ὀνήσιμον, in a 7-foot verse, 79 (Att. iv–ii).

In pentameters :

[δε]ιξαμένωι ἀρετᾶς, 552 a add. (unknown, Mac.).
    1   2   3

ὤλετο ὢν ἀγαθός, CXXII (Phars. v) ; uncertain. See App.
  4   5   5

Furthermore, φροντίδι εὐσεβίας in an unmetrical verse, XXVI. See
p. 47. Even with the transposition there suggested, the hiatus remains.

The instances, as would be expected, are most frequent in the masculine caesura of the third foot of the hexameter.[1] The poet of 492, however, said Τιμοκλέην instead of Τιμοκλέα, in order to avoid hiatus.
                    2   3   2   3

One hiatus is found in an iambic trimeter :

λίθου εἰμὶ ἀνδριάς, 1097 (Delos vi).
  2   3   4

In CXXXIV the blemish is removed by a necessary insertion : see p. 47.

X.

VOWEL SHORTENED BEFORE VOWEL.

1. SHORTENING OF -αι.

καί.

1st short.

Hex. Foot 1. καί Ἀπόλλωνος, 875 a add. (Olymp. iv).
              2   3

καί ἀείμναστον, 855 (Atal. iii).
 2   3

F. 2. καί ἄμωμος, CXVII (Elat. Mac.).
            3

καί ἄτεκνον, 184 (Corc. iii).
       3

F. 3. καί ὑπερφιάλους, 41 (Att. iv).
           4   5

καί ἐμοῦ, 52 (Att. iv).
      4

καί ἐπαίνων, XXXII (Att. iv).
      4

---

[1] Another case of this, Fεθόχω Ἀλεϝώτης, is possibly to be recognized in the Cypriote inscription, LXXVIII. See p. 77.

καὶ Ἐρινύσιν, 1136 (Att. iii-ii).
καὶ ἀνεγκλήτως, 65 (Att. iv-ii).
καὶ ἐν Ἡρακλέους, 492 (Theb. iv).
καὶ ἐπαγγεῖλαι, XCVII₂ l. 15 (Epid. iii).
καὶ ἐπεύχεσθαι, same, l. 21.
καὶ ἀπ' Ἀρκαδίης, 781 (Cnid. iii).
καὶ ἀπόλλυμαι, 1037 (Petil. ii).

F. 4. καὶ ἀδελφός, 86 (Att. iv).
[κ]αὶ ὁ κ[λῆ]ρος, 859 (Tichiuss. iv-ii).
καὶ ἄγαλμ', 785 (Cnid. ii).
καὶ ἐπ' ἔσχατον, 197a add. (Rhod. Mac.).

F. 5. καὶ Ἀθήνῃι, LV (Naxos v).
καὶ ['Ιάνων], XCIV (Olymp. *Corinth* v) : supplement from Pausanias.
καὶ ἐ εὔφρων, 936a RM (Lac. v).
καὶ ἀδελφοί, CIX (Olymp. iv).
καὶ ὁμαίμον, XCIX (Tegea Mac.).

2d short.
Hex. F. 1. καὶ ἰατρός, 45 (Att. iv-iii).
καὶ Εὐκλείδης, CXV (Elat. iii).
καὶ οἱ, 851 (Rhod. iii).
καὶ ἐσσομένοισιν, LIII (Delos ii).

F. 2. καὶ εἰράναν, XCVII₂ l. 24 (Epid. iii).
F. 3. καὶ ἄστεος, 1042 (Att. vi).
καὶ ἡλικίας, 39 (Att. iv).
καὶ αἰνετόν, 30 (Att. iii).
καὶ εὐσεβῆ, 211 (Syr. iii).
καὶ ἐγ κυκλίοισι, 926 (Herm. iii).

ON GREEK VERSIFICATION IN INSCRIPTIONS. 109

καὶ εἰν. 235 (Smyrn. iii).
καὶ εὔγραπτον. LXI (Chios ii).
καὶ οὐρανοῖ. 1037 (Petil. ii).
καὶ ἀθάνατοι. CXXVIII (Syb. ii).
καὶ ἤθεσι. 856 a prf. (Hypate Mac.).
καὶ ἀσφόδολον. 1135 (vase, Mac.).

F. 5. καὶ υἱός. 752 (Att. v).
καὶ αὐτοῦ. 36 (Att. v).
καὶ ἄνδρα. CXIX (Delph. iv–iii).
καὶ αἰδώς. XCVII₂ l. 16 (Epid. iii).
καὶ αὐτοί. 1037 (Petil. ii).
καὶ αὐτῶν. CXVI (Elat. iv–iii).

Pent. F. 1. καὶ οἴκτιρον. 2 a RM (Att. vi).
καὶ ἐν. 89 (Att. iv–ii).
καὶ εὐτέκνωι. 859 (Tichiuss. iv–ii).
καὶ εὐκλειῇ. 851 (Rhod. iii).
ἑπτα-καὶ-εικοσέτους. 184 (Corc. iii).

F. 4. καὶ ὀψιγόνοις. LXXX (Cedr. iv–iii).

-μαι, -ται, -σαι, -σθαι, -ναι *in verbs.*

1st short.
Hex. F. 3. κεῖταί ἔχει. 63 (Att. iv).
παραδείξαί ἀφείλετο. 87 (Att. iv); but see p. 50, note ³.

F. 5. [ἐπι]δείξαί ἀριθμόν. CXVIII (Delph. iv).

Pent. F. 1. ἦσ[θ]αί Ἀθαναίας. LXXI (Rhod. Mac.).

2d short.
Hex. F. 1. τίκτομαί ἐν. 469 (Arg. Mac.).
ἔρχομαί ἐκ. CXXVIII (Sybar. ii).

110   ON GREEK VERSIFICATION IN INSCRIPTIONS.

 F. 3. ἔλπομαῖ ἔμμεναι, CXIX (Delph. iv–iii).
     3 4

 F. 4. μαντεύσομαῖ ἠέ, same.
       4 5

    ἀφίξομαῖ ἀλλά, XCVII₅ l. 68 (Epid. iii).
      4 5

    ἀπόλλυμαῖ ἀλλά, 1037 (Petil. ii).
      4 5

    κεκλῆσε[τ]αῖ ἐγγύς, 182 (Anact. v).
       4 5

    λείπεταῖ ἀλλά, 781 (Cnid. iii).
     4 5

    ἱδρύεταῖ ἠδέ, same.
     4 5

    βοάσεταῖ ὡς, 240 (Smyrn. Mac.).
     4 5

    ἐπιλήσεταῖ ἄνδρα, 858 (Milet. iv–ii).
      4 5

    ἔμμεναῖ ὦ, CXIX (Delph. iv–iii).
     4 5

 F. 5. κεκλήσομαῖ αἰεί, 6 (Att. vi).
      5 6

    εὔχομαῖ εἶναι, CXXVIII (Sybar. ii).
     5 6

Pent. F. 1. δ[ἐρ]κομαῖ ἐν, 858 (Milet. iv–ii).
     1 2

    οἴχεταῖ εἰς, 35 a add. (Att. iv).
    1 2

 F. 4. λείπομα[ῖ]...., 85 (Att. iv–ii) : shortening certain.
     4

    οἴχεταῖ εἰς, 90 (Att. iv).
    4 5

    [μύρ]εταῖ ἠίθ[εον], 33 (Att. iii–ii).
     4 5 6

    γίγνεταῖ Ἱπποκράτης, 875 a add. (Olymp. iv).
     4 5 6

    λείπεταῖ ἡλικίᾳ, XLVIII (Chalcis Mac.).
     4 5 6

2. SHORTENING OF -ει.

      -ει 3d person.
1st short.
 Hex. F. 1. θάλλεῖ ἀγήρατος, 35 a add. (Att. iv).
      1 2 3

 Pent. F. 1. κοσμεῖ ἀειμνήστοις, CXV (Elat. iii).
      1 2 3

  F. 4. ἕξεῖ ἄχος, 488 (Tanagr. v).
     4 5

2d short.
 Hex. F. 4. ἔχεῖ ἐκ, XCIV (Olymp. Cor. v).
      5

  F. 5. μηνύεῖ ἀνδρός, LXXXIII (Cyme iii–ii).
     5 6

-ει *dative.*

2*d short.*
Hex. F. 2. πόλεῖ ὥς, 774 (Prien. iv–iii).
⠀⠀⠀⠀⠀⠀⠀ˆ3
⠀⠀F. 4. Διτρέφεῖ ἐνθάδε, 86 (Att. iv).
⠀⠀⠀⠀⠀⠀⠀4⠀⠀⠀⠀5
⠀⠀⠀⠀⠀⠀ φύσεῖ ἦ, 35 (Att. iv).
⠀⠀⠀⠀⠀⠀⠀⠀⠀⠀⠀7
⠀⠀⠀⠀⠀⠀⠀⠀⠀⠀⠀5
Pent. F. 4. πόσεῖ ἦν, 61 (Att. iv–iii).
⠀⠀⠀⠀⠀⠀⠀⠀⠀⠀5

⠀⠀⠀⠀⠀⠀⠀*Other* -ει's (?).
1*st short.*
Hex. F. 4. ἐπο(ί)ει Ἱπ(π)οσ[τρά]του, 8 (Att. vi), not certain. E is
⠀⠀⠀⠀⠀⠀⠀4⠀⠀⠀⠀⠀5
⠀⠀⠀⠀⠀⠀written: the sound is 'spurious' (monophthongal) ει.
2*d short.*
Hex. F. 3. [ἐπ]εῖ [ἦ], 859 (Tichiussa iv–ii), doubtful.
⠀⠀⠀⠀⠀⠀4

⠀⠀⠀⠀⠀3. SHORTENING OF -οι.

⠀⠀⠀⠀⠀⠀⠀-οι *nomin. plural.*
1*st short.*
Hex. F. 5. ὀνομαστοὶ ἀπ', 254 (Cypr. iv–iii).
⠀⠀⠀⠀⠀⠀⠀⠀⠀⠀⠀5
2*d short.*
Hex. F. 1. Δήλιοῖ ἱδρύσ[αντο], LII (Delos iii–ii).
⠀⠀⠀⠀⠀1⠀⠀⠀⠀2⠀⠀⠀3
⠀⠀F. 4. φίλοῖ οὐκ, 183 (Corc. Mac.).
⠀⠀⠀⠀⠀⠀⠀⠀5
⠀⠀⠀⠀⠀⠀ ξένοῖ αὐδήσαντες, 205 (Halic. ii).
⠀⠀⠀⠀⠀⠀⠀5⠀⠀6
⠀⠀F. 5. [χο]ροὶ or [χο]ρῶι ἀνδρῶ[ν], 923 (Att. v).
⠀⠀⠀⠀⠀⠀⠀⠀⠀⠀⠀⠀⠀⠀⠀6
⠀⠀⠀⠀⠀⠀ θεοὶ ἄλλοι, CXXVIII (Sybar. ii).
⠀⠀⠀⠀⠀⠀⠀⠀6
Pent. F. 1. [ἔ]γ[γ]ονοὶ ἐστήσα[νθ]', 758 (Att. v).
⠀⠀⠀⠀⠀1⠀⠀⠀⠀2⠀⠀3
⠀⠀⠀⠀⠀⠀ ἔκ[γ]ονοὶ Ἀτρειδᾶν, 254 (Cypr. iv–iii).
⠀⠀⠀⠀⠀1⠀⠀⠀2⠀⠀3
⠀⠀F. 4. δεύτεροὶ ἐδράμομεν, 768 a prf. (Theb. iv).
⠀⠀⠀⠀⠀⠀4⠀⠀⠀⠀5⠀6
⠀⠀⠀⠀⠀⠀ φέρτατοῖ οἵ, 242 (Mytil. Mac.).
⠀⠀⠀⠀⠀⠀4⠀⠀⠀5

⠀⠀⠀⠀⠀⠀ μοί, σοί, τοί, οἵ *datives.*
1*st short.*
Hex. F. 2. σοὶ ἄναξ, XXIII (Att. iv).
⠀⠀⠀⠀⠀⠀⠀⠀3
⠀⠀F. 3. σοὶ ἀφίξομαι, XCVII₃ l. 68 (Epid. iii).
⠀⠀⠀⠀⠀⠀⠀4
⠀⠀⠀⠀⠀⠀ οἳ ἀπεμν[ή]σαντο, 768 (Xanth. iv).
⠀⠀⠀⠀⠀⠀4⠀⠀⠀⠀5

2d short.
Hex. F. 1. ταῦτά τοῖ ὦ, XCVII₃ l. 78 (Epid. iii).
           τοῖ ἰφθίμαν, 77 (Att. iii).
   F. 4. μοί ἐστιν, 471 a add. (Sparta iv).
           μοῖ ἵππιον, XCVIII (Epid. Mac.).
           σοῖ εἴ τι, 781 (Cnid. iii).
Pent. F. 1. τοῖ ἱδρύθη, 852 (Att. ii).

           -οι *locative.*
1st short.
Hex. F. 4. Ἐπιδαυροῖ ἀεί, XCVII₂ l. 23 (Epid. iii).

4. Shortening of -ᾱι.

1st short.
Pent. F. 1. Ἥρᾱι ὄν, 846 (Arg. iv).
2d short.
Hex. F. 1. Λυσέᾱι ἐνθάδε, 5 (Att. vi).
   F. 4. κωμωιδίᾱι ἡδυγέλωτι, 38 (Att. iv).
           Ὀλυμπίᾱι ἡνίκα, CVIII (Olymp. iv).
           ἐν ἡμέρᾱι...., 768 (Xanth. iv).

5. Shortening of -ηι.

           -ηι *dative.*
1st short.
Hex. F. 2. Ἑρμῆι ἄγαλμα, 759 (Att. v).
   F. 5. τῆρηι ἄγαλμα, LXII (Samos vi–v).
           Ἑρμῆι ἔρεξεν, 924 (Att. iii–ii).
Pent. F. 1. αὐτῆ ἐπέστησεν, LX (Chios v) : ι omitted!
2d short.
Hex. F. 5. πυρρίχηι ἄθλω, XLVII (Eub. iv–ii).
Pent. F. 4. ὃς τέχνηι οὐχί, 38 (Att. iv).

2d short.
Hex. F. 4. ἔσῆι ἀντί. CXXVIII (Sybar. ii).
　　　　　5

-ηι 2d person.

6. SHORTENING OF -ωι.

1st short.
Hex. F. 1. δήμωι Ἀθηναίων. 741 (Att. vi) ; ΟΙ written.
　　　　　1　　2　　3

σεμνῶι ἐνί, 750 a add. (Paros v).
1　　　2

Φοίβωι ἄνακτι. XCVII₂ l. 18 (Epid. iii).
1　　　2

Φοίβωι Ἀγυιεῖ, 786 (Halic. ii).
1　　　2

F. 3. πέμπτωι ἔτει. 78 (Att. iv–ii).
　　　3　　　4

F. 5. δήμωι Ἀ[θηνῶν]. 844 (Att. iv).
　　　5　　　6

Pent. F. 4. ἔργωι ἔδρασε. same.
　　　　4　　5

χώρωι ἐν. 189 (Melos iii).
4

2d short.
Hex. F. 1. [παρ]θένωι Ἐκφάντου. 752 (Att. v) ; ΟΙ written.
　　　　　1　　　　2　　　3

ποντίωι ἱππομέδοντι. CXVI (Elat. iv–iii).
1　　　2　　　3

F. 3. τῶι Ἀσκ(λ)απιῶ]ι. XCVI (Epid. vi–v) ; ΟΙ written.
　　　4　　　　5

F. 4. ἐκηβόλωι Ἀπόλλωνι, I. (Delos vi) ; ΟΙ written.
　　　4　　　5　　6

ἐκηβόλωι ἰοχεαίρηι, LIV (Delos Nax. vi) ; ΟΙ written.
4　　　5　　6

ἐπὶ Κιτ(τ)ύλοι ἠδ'. 484 (Tanag. v) ; ΟΙ written.[1]
　　4　　　5

Ἀσσκληπιῶι ἠδὲ, 773 b RM (Att. iv–iii).
4　　　5

Ἀσκλαπιῶι ἰατῆρι. XCVII₂ l. 18 (Epid. iii).
4　　　5　6

[ἐ]ν[αγ]ωνίωι Ἑρμῆι. 924 (Att. iii–ii).
　　　4　　　5

δῶρον θεῶι ἐ..., XXXIX (Att. iv), probable.
　　　4　5

δόλωι ἔφθισεν. XCIX (Teg. Mac.).
5

Φιλοξένωι ὅς. 260 (Cyren. iii–ii).
4　　　5

---

[1] It seemed best not to separate this example from the other datives of o-stems. Kaibel writes Κιτύλωι, but the dialect requires rather -οι.

F. 5. ἐμ βίωι ἥδε, 83 (Att. iv–ii).
Pent. F. 1. ἐν δόμωι ὡς, XXIII (Att. iv).
F. 4. παρθένωι Ἀρτέμιδι, 750 a add. (Paros v).
Συμμάχωι ἐστί, 88 (Att. iv–ii).

7. SHORTENING OF -ευ.

1st short.
Hex. F. 3. Ζεῦ Ὀλύνπιε, 743 (Olymp. *Lac.* vi).
2d short.
Hex. F. 4. μεῦ ἔπλετ', 205 (Halic. ii).

8. SHORTENING OF -ου.

I will separate the cases in which simple O is written, from the rest.

-ου *in genitive of o-stems.*

(A.) O is written.

1st short.
Hex. F. 1. Λήμνου ἀπ' ἠγαθέας, XXVII (Att. iv).
F. 3. Κριτο[β]ου̑[λ]ου ἀπὸ Εὐ-, LXVI (Thera vi).
Pent. F. 1. χρυσοῦ Ἀθηναίων, XXV (Att. iv).
2d short.
Hex. F. 2. ...τοῦ Εὐθυμάχου, IV (Att. vi–v); if verse. Unless hiatus.
F. 3. τοῦ ἐν πόντωι, 219 (Amorg. iv).[1]
F. 4. Δαμασιστράτου ἐνθάδε, 7 (Att. vi).
Ναξίου ἔξοχος, LIV (Delos *Nax.* vi).
Δημητρίου ὠ[ι], 753 (Att. v).
Ἑρμοστράτου Ἀβδηρίτης, 759 (Att. *Abdera* v).
Αἰσχύλου υἱός, 760 (Att. v); uncertain; see p. 55.
Διονυσίου ἱππόβοτον δέ, 36 (Att. iv).

---

[1] ΤΩ = ΤΟ is written.

ON GREEK VERSIFICATION IN INSCRIPTIONS. 115

F. 5. Ναυσιστράτου εἰμί. IV (Att. vi–v); if verse.
Φοξίου υἱέ. 488 (Tanag. v).
Pent. F. 1. Σωσίνου ἔστησαν. 54 (Att. iv).
F. 4. Πυθίου ἐν. 743 a prf. (Att. vi).
κἀγαθοῦ ἀνφ[ότερον], 10 (Att. vi).
τοῦ τέκνου εὐχ[σαμένου]. 756 (Att. v).

Kaibel's reading [πρ]ὸς φί[λοῦ] ὤλετ', 19, must now be given up since Lolling's re-examination of the stone.

The following three cases stand by themselves, as showing, not the archaic omission of Y, but rather the neglect to repeat it.

2d short.
Hex. F. 2. Ἁρπάγου υἱός (ΓΟΥΙΟΣ), 768 (Xanth. iv).
F. 5. Χρόνου υἱεῖ (ΟΥΙΕΙ), CXVI (Elat. iv–iii).
Pent. F. 4. Λαΐου υἱόν (ΟΥΙΟΝ), 1135 (vase Mac.); see p. 72.

In 768 πολέμου, and in CXVI τούσδε and ἡμιθέους. are spelt with OY.

(B.) OY is written.
1st short.
Hex. F. 1. Λιν[δο]ῦ ἄν', LXXI (Rhod. Mac.).
. . οῦ ἀποφθιμ[ένη], 84 a RM (Att. iii).
F. 3. Θεοδώρου ὀλυμπικόν. XCVIII (Epid. Mac.).
F. 5. αὐτοῦ ἀδελφόν. 70 (Att. iv–ii).
Pent. F. 1. [κοιν]οῦ ἀνοικτίστη[ς]. 84 a RM (Att. iii).
2d short.
Hex. F. 2. Ἀγεστράτου υἱός. 851 (Rhod. iii).
Ποσειδωνίου ἴσθι. LXXXIII (Cyme iii–ii).
F. 4. Ἀσωπίχου ἠφάνισ'. 492 (Theb. iv).
Ἀσκληπιοῦ εἰ. XCVII₃ l. 30 (Epid. iii).
Βουσπόρου ἦλθεν. XCVII₃ l. 62 (Epid. iii).
Δαμαινέτου ἅδε. 77 (Att. iii).

116   ON GREEK VERSIFICATION IN INSCRIPTIONS.

Δαμα[ι]νέτου ἐκ, 189 (Melos iii).

Διονυσίου Ἡρακλεώτης, LXXIX (Halic. iv–iii).

Νικηράτου ἔκκριτα, LIII (Delos ii).

...ιστράτου ὄλβιος, LXXII (Rhod. Mac.).

Θεοκρίτου Ἀπόλλωνι, CXLIII (Delos, unknown).

Πολυκρίτου υἷα, 855 (Atal. Mac.).

ἀργύρου ἔπλετο, same.

οὐρανοῦ ἀστερόεντος, 1037 (Petil. ii).

θεοῦ εἰς, XCVIII (Epid. Mac.).

ξένο[υ] οὕς, 214 (Rhen. iii).

...οὗ εἷλε, 471 a add. (Sparta iv) ; unless hiatus.

F. 5. [Σω]σιστράτου υἱέ, CXVIII (Delph. iv).

ἡλίου αὐγάς, 78 (Att. iv–ii).

Pent. F. 4. Αἰακοῦ ἐκ, 846 (Arg. iv).

ναυμάχου ἡγεμόνα, LXVIII (Astyp. iv–iii).

-ου *in genitive of ā-stems.*

(A.) O *is written.*

2d short.
Hex. F. 4. Ἀμεινίου ἐστι, XVIII (Att. v).

Κλειδημίδου ἐνθάδε, 34 (Att. iv).

Pent. F. 1. Στησίου ὄν, 15 (Att. vi).

(B.) OY *is written.*

2d short.
Hex. F. 1. Γοργίου ἀσκῆσαι, 875 a add. (Olymp. iv).

F. 5. Γοργίου ἔσχεν, same.

Pent. F. 1. Φαρνάκου αὐθαί[μ]ον, 214 (Rhen. iii).

Ἑρμίου ὀγκωτά, 234 (Smyrn. iii).

-ου *in other words.*

(A.) O is written.

2d short.
Pent. F. 4. δίδου ε[ὐπορίαν]. 773 a RM (Att. iv).

(B.) OY is written.

1st short.
Hex. F. 1. σοῦ ἀποφθιμένου. 183 (Corc. Mac.).
F. 3. μοῦ ὑδοιπόρε. 255 (Cypr. iv–iii).
Pent. F. 1. [τηλ?]οῦ ἄμειψεν. LXIX (Rhod. Mac.).

9. SHORTENING OF -ᾱ.

-ᾱ *in nomin. and vocat. of ᾱ-stems.*

1st short.
Pent. F. 4. κούρᾰ ἀνεγραφόμαν, 205 (Halic. ii).

2d short.
Hex. F. 3. θεᾰ̀ Ἐργάνη. 776 (Att. iii–ii).
F. 4. Διονυσίᾰ ἡλικίας τε. 83 (Att. iv–ii).
Κυδίλᾰ ἐσθλά. 189 (Melos iii).
Pent. F. 1. Εὐθίᾰ οὐκ. 38 (Att. iv), voc. masc.
Πωτάλᾰ ἐγ γαστρός. 505 (Tricca iii).
Χρυσίνᾰ ἐννυχίαν. 785 (Cnid. ii).
ἡμένᾰ ἀγγέλλοι, LXXX (Cedr. iv–iii).
F. 4. Φιλτέρᾰ ἰρ[οπόλ]ος, 852 (Att. ii).

In 183, ἀλκ[ίμᾰ] Ἀμφ- has been made by a doubtful conjecture. See Kaibel.

-ᾱ *in genitive of masculines.*

2d short.
Hex. F. 1. Καλλίᾰ Αἰγίθ(θ)οιο. CXIII (Haliart. vi–v).[1]
[Φ]ειδίᾰ ἐκγεγαώς. XLVIII (Chalcis Mac.).

---

[1] I take Καλλία as genitive, not as vocative (with Röhl) nor as nominative (with G. Meyer, Griech. Gramm., 2d ed., p. 296). The form is not Boeotian, but neither is πρῖσ σ)', in the same inscription.

118 ON GREEK VERSIFICATION IN INSCRIPTIONS.

   Ἀρχίᾳ υἱός, 856 (Atal. Mac.).

F. 4. Κλειππίδᾰ εἴσατο. LXXX (Cedr. iv–iii).

F. 5. ...ίδᾰ υἱύς. 472 (Sparta vi).

10. SHORTENING OF -η.

-η in nomin. and vocat. of ā-stems.

1st short.
Hex. F. 5. [α]ὐτῇ Ἀρίστων. CXII (Theb. ii).

2d short.
Hex. F. 4. Χαιρεστράτῃ ἦν. 44 (Att. iv–iii).
    Πολυξένῃ ἐνθάδε. 76 (Att. iv).
    Φανοστράτῃ ἐνθάδε, 45 (Att. iv–iii).
    χρηστὴ γυνὴ ἐνθάδε. 79 (Att. iv–ii).
    χρηστὴ γυνὴ ἥδ'. 95 (Att. iii).
    Θεοφίλῃ οὔποτε. 60 (Att. iv–ii).
    Ἐργάνῃ ὤν. 776 (Att. iii–ii).
    κεκλημένῃ οὔτε. 505 (Tricca iii).
    Μνησαρχίδῃ ἀπροφασίστως. 65 (Att. iv–ii); vocat. masc.
    Ἀρχεστράτῃ ἔγγονε, XXIV (Att. iv–iii).

F. 5. Ἀρχεστράτῃ ἥδε, same.

Pent. F. 4. Μητρίχῃ αἰνόμορος. 86 (Att. iv).

In Κλευνίκη Ἑρμαγόρου. 809 (compare p. 77), crasis was probably intended.

-η from -εα.

2d short.
Hex. F. 1. εὐσεβῆ ἀσκήσασα. XXIV (Att. iv–iii).

F. 4. εὐσεβῆ ἀμφικαλύπτει. 211 (Syros iii).

Pent. F. 4. συγγενῆ ἐκτέρισαν. 183 (Corc. Mac.).

ON GREEK VERSIFICATION IN INSCRIPTIONS. 119

μή.

1st short.
Hex. F. 5. εἰ μὴ ἐφ' ἁγνοῖ. XCVII₃ l. 30 (Epid. iii).
           5   6

11. SHORTENING OF -ω.

1st short.
Hex. F. 1. δήσω ἐγώ, 1136 (Att. iii–ii), *twice*.
            1   2
Pent. F. 4. μ[ή]πω ὀιόμενος. LXXIII (Cypr. Mac.).
            4   5   6

2d short.
Hex. F. 4. θαυμαζέτω εἰκόνα. 96 (Att. iv–ii).
                4   5
F. 5. ἥδ' ἐγώ εἰμι. 95 (Att. iii).
      5   6
Pent. F. 1. Λ[αμπι]τώ αἰδοίην. 13 (Att. vi).
            1   2   3

12. SHORTENING OF -ῡ (?).

[ἀπ]ώλλῠ ὅς Ἀμ..., CXXI (Anactor. vi–v);
    ?   ?

unless [ἀπ]ώλλυ' is to be understood.

13. SHORTENING OF -εω.

2d short.
Hex. F. 4. Κριτωνίδεω εὔχομαι. 750 (Paros v).
           4   5

Compare Anth. Pal. vii, 77 (= Simonid. fr. 129 Bgk.⁴), where Σιμωνίδεω ἐστὶ σαωτήρ is now restored from Tzetzes and the Scholia to Aristides. — A shortening of -εωι must be assumed in LXXIV, ἄ₁ν)θρωπε θεῶι ἀλ(λ)' ἔτυχ', unless we suppose aphaeresis in ἀλλ': see pp. 55
       5
and 103.

To summarize briefly. We find, neglecting doubtful cases:

-αι 76, -ει 9, -οι 20, -ευ 2 ; total 107.
-ᾱι 5, -ηι 7, -ωι 23 ; total 35.
-ου 54, -ᾱ 14, -η 17, -ω 6 ; total 91.

As in Homer,¹ the diphthongs with short first vowel, taken as a

---

¹ For the statistics of this shortening in Homer, see Hartel, *Homerische Studien* II and III, and the detailed investigation of Grulich, *Quaestiones de quodam hiatus genere in Homeri carminibus*, Halle, 1876.

class, furnish the largest proportion of shortenings. And these are just the cases in which we can best imagine to ourselves the modus of the shortening. For it is easy to suppose that the last part of the diphthong was consonantized, as in ποι̯ῶ.[1] The difficulty is to understand how the other two classes — the diphthongs with long first vowel, and the simple long vowels — were pronounced when shortened. Taking class by class, these last two classes are less numerous than the first. But the disproportion is less than in Homer. For instance, in Homer there is 1 shortening of -ωι to about 13 of -αι; in the inscriptions the ratio is 1 to $3\frac{1}{2}$. So taking -ω as compared with -αι, the ratio in Homer is 1 : 26, in the inscriptions 1 : 13. For -ᾱι and -ηι (taken together), as compared with -αι, the proportions are : Homer 1 : 27,[2] inscriptions 1 : $6\frac{1}{2}$. For -ᾱ and -η (together), Homer 1 : 15, inscriptions 1 : $2\frac{1}{2}$. The greatest difference is with -ου : -ου to -αι in Homer is as 1 : 9, in our inscriptions as 1 : $1\frac{2}{3}$.

Our inscriptions, therefore, show an increase in the shortening of the simple vowels and the diphthongs -ᾱι, -ηι, -ωι — just the reverse, by the way, of what Hartel's statement (*Homerische Studien* III, p. 8)[3] would lead us to expect. It is rather important to know definitely whether these rarer and less explicable shortenings are really an increasing or a diminishing quantity in dactylic verse. To decide positively, a careful examination of the literary remains, from Hesiod to the Alexandrines, would be necessary.[4] If it turns out

---

[1] The entire suppression of the ι, giving, for instance, κἀ ἄλλοι for καὶ ἄλλοι, might naturally be expected to follow. It is noteworthy that we hardly find this in inscriptions. A single case, αὐτῇ ἐπέστησεν (see p. 112), may perhaps be understood as a dialectic dative.

[2] So Grulich: Hartel's figures (based on 8 books only) show a much greater ratio.

[3] "Wenn bereits im epischen und elegischen vers der nachhomerischen dichtung die kürzung abnimmt und immer mehr sich bis auf feste formeln auf die diphthongische ausgänge beschränkt," etc. The context shows that by "diphthongische ausgänge" he means the endings -αι, -οι, -ει, -ου.

[4] I have time at present only for a hasty perlustration of the Works and Days. These do not bear out Hartel's statement. In respect of the matter under consideration, the poem stands between Homer and the inscriptions. The relative frequency of the shortenings of -ηι, -ωι, -ω, and -ου is greater than in Homer; in the case of -η, there is a very small difference on the other side. The numbers are: -αι 113, -ει 9, -οι 30, -ευ 1; -ηι 9, -ωι 13; -η 7, -ω 5, -ου 16; -ε̯ωι 1, -ε̯ηι 1.

that they increase from Homer on, it will look more than ever as if the whole usage had begun with the shortening of -αι, -ει, -οι, -ευ, and had been extended to simple vowels and to -ᾱι, -ηι, -ωι by some supposed analogy. And it is noteworthy that, in connexion with two of these more difficult shortenings — the very two which distinguish themselves by their greater frequency — there are circumstances which point to a possible explanation of the process. The diphthong -ωι is shortened, even in Homer, much oftener than -ηι or -ᾱι. The idea of utilizing the locative termination -οι here occurred to Grulich,[1] though he fails to strengthen his case by pointing out in how many dialects -οι does regular duty as dative.[2] It is perfectly possible to suppose that -οι was a live dative ending at the beginning of the epic period, and that in consequence of its gradual obsolescence, -ωι was, so to speak, forced into its place. This might in turn have prepared the way for a similar use of -ᾱι and -ηι. The other case is that of -ου, which must, of course, be considered as a simple vowel.[3] This is shortened much more frequently than the other simple vowels. The genitive singular furnishes nearly all the examples, and the beginning, I suspect, is to be sought in the elision of the uncontracted form -οο. An ἑκηβόλο' Ἀπόλλωνος, would be felt by and by, when all consciousness of the form -οο was gone, as a simple modification of ἑκηβόλου Ἀπόλλωνος; the more so, as the sound of this -ου was merely that of a prolonged o. What was originally the elision of the uncontracted form would seem to be the shortening of the contracted form. This is just what has happened in εὐσεβῆ ἀσκήσασα and two other cases quoted a little while ago (p. 118). In Homer this would have been understood as εὐσεβέ' ἀσκήσασα; compare Γ 48, λ 125. At what time we should have to imagine this change of consciousness respecting the short -o in our ἑκηβόλο', would be hard to define. The

---

[1] *Quaestiones*, p. 44. The details of his theory, particularly the idea that -ωι developed itself out of -οι by a purely phonetic process (I cannot understand him otherwise), are unsatisfactory.

[2] On this, Gustav Meyer's *Griechische Grammatik*, 2d edit., p. 339 flg., may be conveniently consulted.

[3] Both Hartel and Grulich fall into the serious error of considering -ου as a diphthong, and speaking of the consonantization of its second element. But the sound in question is in all cases the spurious -ο-, and it is entirely certain that this never was a diphthong.

first absolute proof of it would be the writing of OY for it in inscriptions. As long as O was written, it could be taken either way. Hence I have separated, in the above lists, the examples with O from those with OY. But I do not doubt that the change really happened long before, especially as we find, as early as the sixth century, the same shortening applied to the -ου (O) of masculine $\bar{a}$-stems, where there never was an -οο.

It only remains to remark, respecting the unusual proportion of inscriptional shortenings of -$\bar{a}$ and -η, that the greater part of the examples are proper names which could not be otherwise got into the verse (see pp. 117 and 118).

The places of the verse in which the shortenings occur may be thus set forth:

HEXAMETER.

	I		II		III		IV		V	
	— ᴗ	ᴗ	— ᴗ	ᴗ	— ᴗ	ᴗ	— ᴗ	ᴗ	— ᴗ	ᴗ
-αι	2	6	2	1	12	12	4	9	6	8
-ει	1	-	-	1	-	-	-	3	-	1
-οι	-	3	1	-	2	-	1	5	1	2
-ᾱι	-	1	-	-	-	-	-	3	-	-
-ηι	-	-	1	-	-	-	-	1	2	1
-ωι	4	2	-	-	1	1	-	8	1	1
-ευ	-	-	-	-	1	-	-	1	-	-
-ου	4	1	-	3	3	1	-	21	1	6
-ᾱ	-	3	-	-	-	1	-	3	-	1
-η	-	1	-	-	-	-	-	11	2	1
-ω	2	-	-	-	-	-	-	1	-	1
-εω	-	-	-	-	-	-	-	1	-	-
	13	17	4	5	19	15	5	67	13	22

PENTAMETER.

	I		II		IV		V	
	— ⏑	⏑	— ⏑	⏑	— ⏑	⏑	— ⏑	⏑
-αι	1	7	–	–	–	6	–	–
-ει	1	–	–	–	1	1	–	–
-οι	–	3	–	–	–	2	–	–
-ᾱι	1	–	–	–	.–	–	–	–
-ηι	1	–	–	–	–	1	–	–
-ωι	–	1	–	–	2	2	–	–
-ευ	–	–	–	–	–	–	–	–
-ου	3	4	–	–	–	7	–	–
-ᾱ	–	4	–	–	1	1	–	–
-η	–	–	–	–	–	2	–	–
-ω	–	1	–	–	1	–	–	–
	7	20	–	–	5	22	–	–

These proportions, as concerns the hexameter, do not differ much from those given for Homer by Hartel,[1] save that the lead of the second short of the fourth foot is more marked than in Homer. The frequency of the shortening at this point is evidently due to the effort for dactylic word-endings before the bucolic caesura, not to any mysterious affinity. Nor do we find, as Hartel says is the case in Homer, that the heavy endings -η, -ηι, -ω, -ωι are shortened chiefly in the first foot. In the pentameter, the absolute exclusion of the shortening from the second and fifth foot is noteworthy. The same influence would, we should expect, exclude it from the second foot of a pen-

---

[1] *Homerische Studien* II, p. 375.

themimeres standing as the first half of a hexameter. And in fact I find only two instances to the contrary; nearly all the shortenings in the second foot occur in verses which have the trochaic caesura of the third foot.

I append the single case of this shortening outside of dactylic verse.

τἀργ[εῖ]οῖ ἀνέθεν. iamb. trim., 746 (Arg. v).

The extraordinary nature of this correption is matter of comment to Boeckh, CIG. I, p. 885. It is, I think, the only certain example extant in pure iambic or trochaic verse. A possible instance, καῖ ἔλεγον, troch. tetram., xcvii₁, is more probably understood as unwritten crasis; see p. 126.

XI.

CRASIS, WRITTEN AND UNWRITTEN.

1. WRITTEN CRASIS. The following cases occur:

(A.) *In dactylic verse.*

ἁρεσίου (= ὁ Ἀρ-), pent. xxi (Att. v).

αὑτός, xcix (Tegea Mac.).

[τ]οὑπικλέους, 7 (Att. vi); O written.

οὑνπορίωνος (= ὁ Ἐμπ-), xv (Att. vi), if verse.

τοὐμόν, 52 (Att. iv); O written.

τοὔργον, xcvii₃ l. 57 (Epid. iii).

τοὔνεκα, 205 (Italic. ii).

τοὔνομα, 63 (Att. iv); O written.

τοὔνομα, 92 (Att. iv–ii).

ταὔτ', 81 (Att. iv–ii).

τἀμά, pent., 96 (Att. iv–ii).
τἀθηναίαι, 11 (Att. vi–v).
τἀθάναι, pent., cxxix (Posid. vi).
τἤρηι, lxii (Samos vi–v).
κἀθαγοῖ, pent., 10 (Att. vi).
καλοκἀγαθίαν, xcvii₂ l. 23 (Epid. iii).
καὐ[τοί], 1037 (Petil. ii).
κἀμέ, 781 (Cnid. iii).
χὥ, pent., xcv (Olymp. *Arg.* v) : XO written.
χὥ, pent., 852 (Att. ii).
ὦναξ, xcvii₃ l. 79 (Epid. iii).
προὔπεμψε, 39 (Att. iv).

I omit κἀμοί, xxvi, in a conflate and unmetrical verse. ἄνθρωποι, written by Deecke in lxxiv (Cypriote), has no probability.

(B.) *In non-dactylic verse.*

τἄντρον, iamb. trim., 762 (Att. v).
τἀργεῖοι, iamb. trim., 746 (Olymp. *Arg.* v).
τηὐτρητιφάντου, iamb. trim., 1130 (vase vi) ; for ται Ει-.¹
κἀπόησε, iamb. trim., 1099 (vase v).
κἀποιησε, iamb. trim., cxxxv (vase v).
προὐνόησε, iamb. trim., xxxvi (Att. iii–ii).

2. UNWRITTEN CRASIS. 'Synizesis,' that is, between two words :

(A.) *In dactylic verse.*

καὶ Ἀσωποδώρου, xcv (Olymp. *Arg.* v).

The τε before καί should be omitted ; see p. 46.

---

¹ Rather -φαντω, if the vase is really Boeotian.

Κλευνίκη‿Ἑρμαγόρου, 809 (Pharos Mac.),

unless we suppose -νίκη (see p. 77). Ϝεθόχω‿Ἀλεϝότης in the Cypriote inscription LXXVIII is very uncertain: see p. 48 and Appendix. Still less probable is παι‿εῦ in LXXVI: see p. 46. Of a possible ἐπο(ί)ει‿Ἱπ(π)οστρ-, we have spoken on p. 79.

In 189 (Melos iii) the chances are that the stonecutter's copy read καὶ [ἀπο]θανοῦσαν, rather than κά[πο]θανοῦσαν. The stone has
ΚΑΙΘΑΝΟΥΣΑΝ.

(B.) *In non-dactylic verse.*

ἀλλὰ καὶ‿ἐμ μούσαις, iamb. trim., CXI (Helicon Mac.).

καὶ‿ἔλεγον. troch. tetr., XCVII, 1. 6 (Epid. iii).[1]

The old reading [τ]οῦ‿ἀϝυτοῦ λίθου (for τοῦ‿αὐτοῦ) on the well known pedestal in Delos, 1097 (*Naxos* vi), has of late become unfashionable, but in my view is more probable than anything that has yet been suggested.

It appears from these examples that the ancients followed no absolutely fixed rules as to indicating crasis by the spelling. They might so indicate it, or they might leave it to be understood.

XII.

ELISION.

What chiefly interests us here is the inquiry how often and under what circumstances the elided vowel is written. Such cases, in the following enumeration of examples, will be put by themselves in the right-hand column.

The minuscule transcriptions are often misleading in this matter. Some editors (as Boeckh) omit elided vowels in such transcriptions,

---

[1] Similarly καὶ‿ἀδίκων, iamb. trim., in an inscription of Roman time, Kaibel n. 814.

even when they are present on the stone; others write them. Kaibel is inconsistent with himself and untrustworthy. It was therefore essential to verify each case of elision by reference to published copies in capitals, whenever such were accessible to me. In some of the remaining cases an inspection of the stone was possible. There are left, however, a number of examples where a verification was impossible. These I have designated as '*not verified.*' It will be understood that this means simply that, as to the presence or absence of the elided vowel, I have not been able to go behind the minuscule copy. Kumanudes is unusually careful in this respect, and such of the unverified examples as come from his publications I have marked '*Kum.*' These must be considered as well vouched for.

A prefixed ? implies doubt of another kind. For the sake of convenience a number of more or less uncertain cases are printed with the rest, distinguished in this way.

1. ELISION OF -α.

Verbal Forms.

BEFORE

α- ἤγγειλ' αὐθῆμαρ, XCVIII (Epid. Mac.).

ε- ἔστα[κ]' ἐπί, 181 a add. (Corc. vi), nearly certain.[1]   ἐπέδειξα ἔγεντο, troch. tetr., XCVII₁ (Epid. iii).

νίκασα Εὐθύφρονος. 942 a RM (Olymp. *Maen.* iv).

η- [λησό]μεθ' ἤ. pent., 488 (Tanag. v).

ο-   ἔθηκα ὁσίως. XXXII (Att. iv).

Nominative Feminine.

α- πότνι' ἀπαρχήν, 753 (Att. v).   [π]ότνια Ἀθαναία, CXV (Elat. iii).

---

[1] The inscription turns a corner here, and the stone is bevelled off; but there is hardly room for an A.

BEFORE

α- πότνι' ἀγώνων, 856 a prf. (Hyp. ἔχουσα ἀρετήν, pent., 60 (Att. iv-ii).
Mac.), *not verified.*   δόξα ἀρετή. 65 (Att. iv-ii), *not*
γενέτειρ' ἀργαλέοις, pent., LXXXIII   *verified, Kum.*
(Cyme iii-ii), *not verified.*   δεικνῦσα ἀναφαίνει, 84 (Att. iv-ii),
not verified, Kum.
μαῖα ἀγανά (— ∪ — —), lyric,
xcvii₄ l. 50 (Epid. iii).

ε- Ἡράκλει' ἕξει, pent., 488 (Tanag. v).
οὐσ' ἔθανον, 91 (Att. iv).
στέρξῡσ' Ἔρξις. 35 a add. (Att. iv),
not verified.
γυῖ' ἐκάλυψαν. 51 (Att. iv-ii).
θρέπτειρ' ἐνιρηφόρε, 856 a prf.
(Hyp. Mac.), *not verified.*
μοῖρ' ἐδάμασσε. cxxviii (Syb. ii),
not verified.
(?) πρῷρ' [ἐ]γκτετάννυσται. 96 (Att. iv-ii).[1]

η- [λι]ποῦσ' ἥβην. 84 a RM (Att. iii).
ἐνέπουσ' ἤλυθ'. lyric, xcvii₄ l. 38
(Epid. iii).

ο- λαχοῦσ' ὄνομα, pent., 6 (Att. vi).   (?) [χέ]ωσα ὅτ', cxxii (Phars. v)
στέρξῡσ' οἶσι, pent., 35 a add.   acc. to Cauer: similarly Lol-
(Att. iv), *not verified.*   ling. See p. 198.

---

[1] It is certain what the graver cut in this puzzling place, but very uncertain what was meant to be cut. The stone, now in the Central Museum, has ΔΕΓΓΡΩΙΡΙΓΚΤΕ etc., every letter being perfectly distinct. To me it seems clear, first that ΓΚ is a dittography, K being put in to correct the Γ; and secondly that we have a conflation of the two readings περὶ δ' ἐκ πρώιρη τετάνυσται and περὶ δὲ πρῷρ' ἐκτετάνυσται, owing to a boggled and indistinct manuscript copy, which had been put into the graver's hands.

BEFORE

o-   τάλαινα ὀδύρεται, iamb. trim., 246
                           (Bithyn. Mac.).

             στενάζουσα ὀρφανάν, iamb. trim.,
                      cxvii (Elat. Mac.).

ι-   ἰδοῦσα ἱεράν, pent., 785 (Cnid. ii).

υ-   γαῖα ὑπὸ κόλπους, cxii (Theb. ii).

Nouns in -μα.

α- πρᾶγμ' ἀγαθόν, pent., 1 (Att. vi).

σῆμ' ἀγαθοῖ, 4 (Att. vi).

σῆμ' ἀγαθοῖ, 4 a add. (Att. vi).

μνῆμ' ἀρετῆς, pent., cxxxix (Att. v).

μνᾶμ' ἀνέθηκε, pent., 757 a prf. (Thisb. v).

ἀνάθημ' ἀ[π]ό, 747 (Delph. *Lac.* v).

ἄγαλμ' ἀνέθηκε, 761 (Aegina v).

ὄνυμ' αὐτῶι, same.

ἄγαλμ' ἀνέθηκεν, 785 (Cnid. ii).

τέρμ' ἀγαθῆς, pent., 89 (Att. iv–ii),
     not verified, Kum.

δεῖγμ' ἀρετᾶς, pent., 860 (Chios iii–ii).

οὔνομ' ἀγόρευτ', iamb. trim., 258
     (Alex. iii–ii).

(?) χεῖμ' ἀ[π]ό, pent., 214 (Rhen. iii),
     doubtful.

ε- μνῆμ' ἐσορῶν, pent., 1 a add.   ἄγαλμα Ἑρμοστράτου, 759 (Att.
    (Att. vi).   *Abd.* v).

μνᾶμ' ἐμί, cxliv (Thess. vi–v).

μνᾶμ' ἐπ', 486 (Thesp. v).

BEFORE

ε- μνῆμ' ἐπί. pent., LXIX (Rhod. iii).

μνῆμ' ἐσ[τησεν]. pent., 220   μνῆμα ἔστησεν. LVIII (Amorg. iv).
(Amorg. iv).

ὄνομ' ἔσχον. 255 (Cypr. iv–iii).

παράδειγμ' εὐσεβείας. pent.,
875 a add. (Olymp. iv).

γράμμ' ἐτύπωσε. pent., 89 (Att.
iv–ii), *not verified, Kum.*

τέρμ' ἔλαβεν. pent., 856 (Atal.
Mac.), *not verified.*

υ-   ἅμα ὑποδεξάμεναι. pent., 225
                                (Ephes. Mac.).

-α *Accusative Singular.*

α- ἄνδρ' ἀγαθόν. pent., 1 (Att. vi).   ἄνδρα ἀγαθόν. pent., CXXII (Phars. v).

ἔχοντ' ἄνδρα. pent., 69 (Att. iv).   φιλοῦντα ἀντιφιλοῦσα. 79 (Att. iv–

(?) ἐλθόντ' ἀπο[τῆλ]ε, 466   ii), *not verified, Kum.*
(Argos Mac.), not certain.

εἰκόν' ἀναστήσασα. 860 (Chios iii–ii).

παῖδ' ἀγαθόν. pent., 184 (Corc. iii).

ε- πατρίδ' ἔ[θηκε]. pent., CIV   μητέρα ἔθηκα. XXXII (Att. iv).
(Olymp. vi).   πατρίδα ἐνθάδε, 23 (Att. iv), *not*
εἰκόν' ἔχει. pent., 66 (Att. Mac.).   *verified.*
παπταίνοντ' ἐπί. 89 (Att. iv–ii).   πατέρα εὐκλείζων, 26 (Att. iv).
not verified, Kum.   σωτῆρα εὐρυχόρον, XCVII₅ l. 77
πατρίδ' Ἐπίδαυρον. lyric. XCVII₄   (Epid. iii).
l. 42 (Epid. iii).

η- καλλίων' ηὗρε. 875 a add. (Olymp. iv).

ο- χεῖρ' ὀρέγων. XCVII₅ l. 65 (Epid. iii).

BEFORE

υ- παῖδ' ὑπό. 184 (Corc. iii).   δωτῆρα ὑγιείας (— — ∪ ∪ — —), lyric,
                                  XCVII, l. 52 (Epid. iii).

In 28 one has his choice between πατρίδ' α[ἶ]ς (Kaibel) and πατρίδα [ώ]ς (Herwerden).

-α. *Neuter Plural.*

a- ταῦτ' ἀποδυράμενοι. pent., 1   τέσσαρ[α] 'Αθάναι, 43 (Att. iv),
   (Att. vi).   certain from space.
   Τυρ(ρ)άν' ἀπό. lyric. 745   (?) ἐπίδηλα ἀ[π]οφώ.... LVIII
   (Olymp. *Syrac.* v).   (Amorg. iv), not certain.
   ὅσσ' ἀρετῆς. pent. 25 (Att. iv).   βασίλεια 'Αΐδαο. XXXVII (Att. iv-ii).
   μυρί' ἀποφθιμένοιο, 184 (Corc. iii).
   ἑρπέθ' ἄμ'. 1033 (Att. iii), *not
   verified. Kum.*

ε- 'Ολύμπι' ἐνίκων. 940 a RM   [πάντ]α ἐκράτεις. pent., CXVIII
   (Olymp. *Samos* v).   (Delph. iv).
   σώμαθ' ἑλών, pent., 942 a RM   [πάν]τα [ἐ]κράτεις, pent., same.
   (Olymp. *Maen.* iv).
   δώματ' ἐπηγλάϊσεν, pent., 492
   (Theb. iv).
   δώματ' ἔχουσιν, CXIX (Delph. iv-iii).
   ξόαν' εἴκελα. pent., XXIII (Att. iv).
   ταῦτ' ἔσχες, 65 (Att. iv-ii),
   not verified. Kum.
   ταῦτ' ἐνόμιζον. 81 (Att. iv-ii).
   (?) πείρατ' ἐ]φιέ[με]νον. pent.,
   40 (Att. iii-ii).[1]
   τέσσαρ' ἐπεῖδε. pent., 43 (Att. iv).

---

[1] It does not appear quite certain that the gap after T is of one letter only.

BEFORE
ε- ἄριστ' εἰπεῖν, 78 (Att. iv–ii),
   ₄   ₅
    not verified, Kum.

   πόλλ' ἔκαμε, pent., 851 (Rhod. iii).
   ₅   ₆

η- τρίτατ' ἦν, pent., 926 (Herm. iii).
   ₃

ο- πάντ' οὐ, XXIII (Att. iv).
   ₂
   (?) [φ]ῖλ' οὐ[κ], 926 (Herm. iii),
       ₃
    not certain.

ι-   (?) κ[ίβδ]η[λ]α [ῖ]ε[ι]. cxxx (Syrac.
                                    ₃
                         v). So Röhl, very doubtful.

Other Nominal Endings.

a- μέγ' ἄριστε, XCVII₅ l. 78 (Epid. iii).
           ₃
   μέγ' ἀχνύμενοι, pent., 183 (Corc. Mac.).
   ₂   ₃

ε- τεσσαράκοντ' ἐγ, pent., 1043 (Att. iv).
   ₂   ₃   ₄
   τριάκοντ' ἔτεσιν, pent., 85 (Att.
   ₂   ₃
   iv–ii), *not verified, Kum.*

ο- [πε]ν[τ]ήκονθ' ὅς, 32 (Att. iv–ii),
   ₁   ₂
    not verified, Kum.

                        -a *in Adverbs.*
ε- ἀλλ' ἐνί, 179 (Corc. vi).
      ₅
   ἀλλ' ἐσίδεσθε, 1098 (Orch. vi–v).
      ₅   ₆
   ἀλλ' ἔτι, 932 (Sidon iii).
      ₁
   ἀλλ' ἔτυχ' (a-le-tu-), LXXIV (Cypriote).
      ₅

ο- ἀλλ' ὃ μέν, pent., XXXVI (Att. iii–ii).
      ₁
   ἀλλ' ὁπόταν, CXXVII (Sybar. ii),
      ₁   ₂
    not verified.

   ἀλλ' [ο]ὐκ, 519 (Thessalon. Mac.).
      ₁

ι- ἀλλ' ἴτε, pent., 89 (Att. iv–ii),
      ₁
    not verified, Kum.

BEFORE

α-

ε- ἔνεκ' ἐστεφανώθη, XXV (Att.
   iv), *not verified, Kum.*

   ὅς πόκ' ἐν. pent., 187 (Ithac.
   Mac.).

η- τόκ' ἦχον, troch. tetr., XCVII₁.

ο- ὄχ' ὁ παῖς, XCVII₅ l. 62 (Epid. iii).

ι-

α- ἄμ' αὐτοῦ, XXIII (Att. iv).

   ἄμ' αὐτῶι, 1033 (Att. iii), *not
   verified, Kum.*

   ὄφρ' ἄν, 240 (Smyrn. Mac.).

ε- μάλ' ἐξείας XCVII₃ l. 74 (Epid. iii).

   εἶτ' ἐμέ, CXXVIII (Sybar. ii), *not
   verified.*

ο- ἄρ' ὄσσων, troch. tetr., 790 (Achaia iii).

ε- ἦ ῥ' ἐτύμως, 242 (Mytil. Mac.).

α- κ' ἁμῶν, XCVII₂ l. 26 (Epid. iii).

ε- αἴ κ' εἰς, troch. tetr., XCVII₁
   (Epid. iii).

οὕνεκα ἀποφθιμένω, 87 (Att. iv),
   not verified, Kum.

ἕνεκα ἔσχο[ν], 52 (Att. iv), *not
verified, Kum.*

ἕνεκα ἵδρυσεν, pent., 774 (Priene
iv–iii).

-α *in Prepositions.*

ι- ἀν' ἱε[ρό]ν, LXXI (Rhod. Mac.).

ε- δι' εὐξυνέτοιο. 856 a prf. (Hyp.
   Mac.), *not verified.*

   δι' ἔργα. 852 (Att. ii).

   [δ]ι' ἰσχύος. CX (Olymp. iv).

134   ON GREEK VERSIFICATION IN INSCRIPTIONS.

BEFORE

α- κατ' Αἰγυίην. 779 (Chalced. Mac.).[1]

ο- καθ' ὁδόν. 2 a RM (Att. vi).

α- μεθ' ἁγεμόνος, pent., 849 (Delph. iv–iii).
   μετ' ἀστῶν. 240 (Smyrn. Mac.).

η- μεθ' ἡλικίας. 75 (Att. iv–iii).

α- παρ' ἀνδρί. 80 (Att. iv–ii). *not verified, Kum.*

ε- παρ' Ἑλλήσποντον. CXXXIX (Att. v).
   παρ' ἐμοῖ. anap., 775 a RM
   (Dodon. Mac.).

η- [π]α[ρ]' ἥρω. XLII (Orop. iii),
   not certain.

ω- παρ' ὦν. pent., 95 (Att. iii).

2. ELISION OF -ε.

-ε *Third Person Singular.*

α- ⌈θί⌉γ' αὐτός, 936 a RM (Lac. v);
   elision clear, though restoration uncertain.
   ἄειδ' ἀεί. iamb. trim.. CXI
   (Helic. Mac.).
   ἔτυχ' ἁ κήρ (*tu-ka-*), LXXIV
   (Cypriote).

εὐκλέϊσε Ἀνδοκίδαν, 26 (Att. iv).
ἔδρασε ἀγαθά, pent., 844 (Att. iv).
ἱέρωσε Ἀσσκληπιῶι. 773 b RM
   (Att. iv–iii), *not verified, Kum.*
ὠνόμαξε Ἀπόλλων (—∪—∪——),
   lyric, XCVII, l. 51 (Epid. iii).
ἀνέθηκε Ἀφροδ[ίτηι], 809
   (Pharos Mac.).
στῆσε Ἀντίστας. 773 (Pantic. Mac.).

---

[1] κατ' ἄλσεα in CXXVII I omit, as evidently miswritten. The metre requires κατά τ' ἄλσεα.

BEFORE

ε- ἔστησ' ἐγγύς, 3 (Att. vi).
    ἔστασ' ἐπί, 484 (Tanag. v).
    ἔσστασ' Ἐχενάις, CXXII (Phars. v).
    (?)[ἔ]στασ' ἐς, Meister in XLV (Aeg. v), very doubtful.
    εἴασ' ἔστησ[ε]. 85 (Att. iv–ii), *not verified, Kum.*
    ἦλθ' ἐπ[ί], pent., XXVIII (Att. iv).
    ἤλυθ' ἐς. lyric, XCVII₄ l. 39 (Epid. iii).
    ἔλιπ' εὐδαίμων. 44 (Att. iv–iii), *not verified, Kum.*

στῆσε ἐνθάδε. LXVIII (Astyp. iv–iii).
(?) κἀπόησε ἐμέ, iamb. trim., 1099 (vase v); miswritten for -σέ με.

o- (?)[ἀπ]ώλλυ' ὅς. CXXI (Anact. vi–v), unless -ώλλῠ ὅς.
    ἐξεποίησ' οὐκ, pent., 759 (Att. Abder. v).

ἦλθε ὀχ' ὁ. XCVII₃ l. 62 (Epid. iii).
θῆκε ὀνομαστοτέραν, pent., 855 (Atal. iii). *not verified, Kum.*

υ- ἠφάνισ' υἱόν. 492 (Theb. iv).
    παρέδωχ' ὑβρίσαι. pent., XXVIII (Att. iv).

ἀνέθηκε υἱός, CXXV (Laris. iv).

-ε *Imperative Singular.*

α- μέν' αὐτεῖ. XCVII₃ l. 68 (Epid. iii).
    αὔξ' ἐν. pent., 750 a add. (Paros v).
    χαῖρ' εἰπών. pent., 184 (Corc. iii).
ω- οἴκτιρ' ὡς. pent., 1 a add. (Att. vi).
    πρᾶσ(σ)'[ὦ]. CXIII (Haliart. vi–v), probable from space.

-τε, -σθε *Imperative Plural.*

α- ζηλοῖτ' ἀλλά. 30 (Att. iii).
    δότ' αἶψα. 1037 (Petil. ii).

BEFORE

ε-   νεῖσθε ἐπί. pent., 1 (Att. vi).
                                             4

o- [κρά]ναθ' ὀδίτηι, XLVI (Eub. v) :
      1   2
   supplement uncertain.

                              -ε *Vocative.*

a- φίλτατ' ἀνδρῶν. troch. tetr., 79   Φοῖβε 'Απόλλων(_ ⌣ _ _), lyric.
        3   4
   (Att. iv–ii), *not verified, Kum.*   XCVII₄ l. 39 (Epid. iii).

   ἑκατηβόλ' "Απολλον. 799 (unknown,
        5   6
   iii–ii).

   φίλ' "Απολλον. CXLI (Delos, unknown).
        6

ε- φίλ' ἐν, iamb. trim., 258 (Alex.
       4
   iii–ii).

   [ξ]έν' Εὐ[θ]υδάμ[ω]. Arch. hept.,
        6   7
   187 (Ithaca Mac.).

η-   Νικόβουλε ἡελίου. 62 (Att. iv),
                                            1   2   3
                                         not verified, Kum.

                                         [π]ερίσαμε 'Ηρακλέων. 859 (Tich.
                                                3   4
                                         iv–ii).

o-   ἄνθρωπε ὅς, 2 a RM (Att. vi).
                                            1   2

ω- Διόνυσ' ὤν. XXIII (Att. iv).
      3

                              -ε *Dual and Numeral.*

   (?)[πέν]τ' ἐπί. 33 (Att. iii–ii),   λιπόντε ἀμφοῖμ. 87 (Att. iv), *not*
       4?   4   5
   uncertain.   *verified, Kum.*

                              με, σε, *etc.*

a- μ' ἀνέθ[ηκεν], 739 (Att. vi).   (?) με [ἀνέθεν]. pent., 1098 a RM
         6?   6
   μ' ἀ[νέθηκε], VIII (Att. vi).   (Melos vi–v), not certain.
        3
   μ' ἀνέθη[κεν]. XII (Att. vi).   με ἀνέθηκεν. 778 (Calymn. iv–ii).
         7   3
   μ' ἀνέθη[κεν]. XIII (Att. vi).   (?)με ἀνέθηκε. 809 (Pharos Mac.),
         7   3
   μ' ἀνέθηκεν, LIV (Delos *Nax.* vi). not certain : Boeckh omits με.
          3

ON GREEK VERSIFICATION IN INSCRIPTIONS. 137

BEFORE

a- μ' ἀνέθηκεν. l. (Delos vi).   με ἀγοραίωι. 772 (Imbr. iv–ii).
　μ' ἀνέθ[η]κ[ε]ν. LXII (Sam. vi–v).　τιμήσω σε ἄχρι ἄν ζῶ. 48 (Att. iii).
　μ' ἀνέθηκε. LXXXVI (Corinth. vi).
　μ' ἀνέ[θη]κε. LXXXVIII (Corinth. vi).
　μ' ἀνέθηκε. CXXVI (Metap. vi).
　μ' ἀνέθηκε. CXXXI (Olymp. *Gela* vi).
　μ' ἀ[νέθηκε]. CII (Sellas. vi–v).
　μ' ἀν[έθηκ]εν. 755 (Att. v).
　μ' ἀνέθηκεν. 756 (Att. v).
　μ' ἀνέθηκεν. 926 (Herm. iii).
　μ' ἀνέθηκεν, CXLI (Delos, unknown).
　σ' ἀρετᾶς. 69 (Att. iv).

ε- μ' ἐπόει. CXXVI (Metap. vi).[1]　(?) Φίλων με ἐποίησεν, XV (Att.
　μ' ἐποίησεν. XLVI (Eub. v).　　vi), if verse.
　μ' ἐκάμοντο. 782 (Halic. iii–ii).　ζηλοῖ σε Ἑλλάς. 38 (Att. iv).
　σ' ἐφίλουν. 48 (Att. iii).　　σέβομαί σε ἐν (∪ ∪ — —), lyric,
　　　　　　　　　　　　　　　　XCVII, l. 48 (Epid. iii).
　σφ' ἐσάωσας, XCVII, l. 75 (Epid. iii).
　μ' ἐποίκτειρον. same, l. 67.
　σ' ἔτι [τι]μῶ. 48 (Att. iii).
　καὶ σ' ἐν, pent., 860 (Chios iii–ii).
　μ' ἔχει. pent., 197 (Rhod. iv–ii).
　μ' ἔχει. LXIX (Rhod. Mac.).

η- σ' ἢ μέν. 35 (Att. iv).　　θανοῦσάν σε ἦσθα, troch. tetr., 79
　　　　　　　　　　　　　　　(Att. iv–ii).

---

[1] This and the following four examples might in theory be taken as με πόει, με ποίησεν, etc. Nevertheless after what we have observed on pp. 58, 62, 64, 65, we are justified in assuming the contrary.

ON GREEK VERSIFICATION IN INSCRIPTIONS.

BEFORE

o- μ' ὁ πατήρ, 486 (Thesp. v).
⏑- δὺς δέ ϝ' ἰν. pent., CXXVI (Metap. vi).

σ' ἱερωͱε. 773 b RM (Att. iv–iii),
 not verified, Kum.

(?) μ' ἰ[δοῖ]. CVI (Olymp. v),
 according to Roehl.

ὅδε, ἐνθάδε, *etc.*

a- τόδ' ἀντ', pent., 2 (Att. vi).   τόδε 'Αρνιάδα, 180 (Corc. vi).
τόδ' ἀμενφές. 740 (Melos vi).
τόδ' ἄγ[αλμα], v (Att. vi).   τόδε ἄγαλμα. 750 (Paros v).
τόδ' ἄγαλμα. x (Att. vi).   [τ]οίδε ἀπό. LXXXV (Meg. vi–v).
τόδ' ἄγ[α]λμα. XI (Att. vi).   ἥδε ἀγορεύ[ει]. 52 (Att. iv), *not*
τόδ' ἄγαλμ'. 761 (Aeg. v).   *verified, Kum.*
τόδ' ἄγαλμα. 756 a RM (Plat. v).   ὅδε αὐτόχθων, pent.?, 771 (Att. iv).
τόδ' ἄγαλμα. 744 (Olymp. v).   ὅδε 'Αρπάγου. 768 (Xanth. iv).
τοδ' ἄγαλμα. 750 a add. (Paros v).   τόδε ἀθάν[α]τον, pent., same.
τόδ' ἀπαρχήν. 754 (Att. v).
[τ]όδ' ἀ, CXXII (Phars. v).
[τ]οῦδ' Αἰσσχρος, LV (Nax. v).
[τόν]δ' ἀνέθηκεν. 941 c RM (Olymp. v).
ἐνθάδ' ἀνήρ. 19 (Att. vi).
ἐνθάδ' 'Αθηναίηι. pent., 752 (Att. v).
ἐνθάδ' 'Αθηναῖοι. pent., 36 (Att. v).
τόδ' ἄγαλμα. XXXI (Att. iv), *not*
 verified.
τόδ' ἄγαλμα. LI (Delos ii).
τόδ' ἀώρον, 220 (Amorg. iv).

ON GREEK VERSIFICATION IN INSCRIPTIONS.

BEFORE

a. τήνδ' ἀνέθηκεν, 875 a add.
   5
   (Olymp. iv).

τήνδ' ἀνέθηκε, 70 (Att. iv–ii).
2   3

τούσδ' ἀνέθηκε, pent., CXVI (Elat.
   4   5
iv–iii).

τοῦδ' ἀνδρός, XXVI (Att. iv).
   3

τοιῶιδ' ἀνδρί, pent., 845 (Att. iii–ii).
  3   4

τοιούσδ' ἄνδρας. pent., 856 a prf.
   3   4
(Hyp. Mac.), not verified.

ἐνθάδ' ἀγῶνα. XCVIII (Epid. Mac.).
5   6

e. τόδ' ἐστ'. pent., 744 (Olymp. v).
     5

τόδ' ἔσται. 23 (Att. iv), not verified.
     6

τόδ' ἐστίν. iamb. trim., 210 (Ceos
     2
iv–iii), not verified.

ὅδ' ἔστ', 856 (Atal. Mac.), not
   3
verified.

ὅδ' ἔχει. 72 (Att. iv), not verified,
    4
Kum.

ἥδ' ἐγώ. 95 (Att. iii).
   5

ὅδ' εὐθάν[ατον]. pent.?, 68 (Att.
   2   3
iv–ii), not verified, Kum.

τόδ' ἐν. 89 (Att. iv–ii), not verified.
    2

τόνδ' ἔτι. same, not verified.
   1

[τ]αῖδ' ἕταροι. pent., 183 (Corc. Mac).
   4   5

τᾶσδ' Ἐπιδαύρου, XCVII₂ l. 14 (Epid. iii).
  5   6

τᾶσδ' Ἐπιδαύρου, lyric, XCVII₄ l. 38
(Epid. iii).

τόδ' ἐπώνυμον, lyric, same, l. 44.

τήνδε ἀνέθηκε. 938 (Tanag. iv).
   2   3

τήνδε ἀνέθεντο. pent., LII (Delos
   4   5
iii–ii).

τήνδε ἀνέθηκεν, CXLII (Delos,
   3   4
unknown).

τοιῶνδε ἀνδρῶν. 24 (Att. iv).
   2   3

το[ι]άνδε ἀνέθηκ[ε]ν, 768 (Xanth.
   5   6
iv).

ἅδε Ἐλάτεια. CXVII (Elat. Mac.).
 5   6

ἥδε ἐλθόντα. 466 (Arg. Mac.).
  3   4

BEFORE

ε- τόνδ' ἐ[σό]ρα, CXIV (Elat. Mac.),
    if space rightly measured.
τοιόσδ' ἐών. iamb. trim., CXI
    (Helic. Mac.).
ἐνθάδ' ἔχει. 57 (Att. iv–ii).
[ἐνθ]άδ' ἐγώ. LXXIII (Cypr. Mac.).
ἥδ' ἔθανε(ὦν. 58 a RM (Att. iv),   τόνδε ἐλάτρευσα, pent., 850 (Att.
    not verified.[1]   iv–iii).
τοῦδ' ἔτυχεγ. pent., 53 (Att. iv),   μοι τάδε ἔλεξας. XCVII₅ l. 67
    not verified, Kum.   (Epid. iii).
τοῦδ' ἔτυχον. pent., XXV (Att. iv),   τοῖδε ἔτυχον. pent., 225 (Eph.
    not verified, Kum.   Mac.).
τόνδ' ἐπό[ησε]. 773 b RM (Att.
    iv–iii), *not verified*.
τάνδ' ἔ[στασε]. CIX (Olymp. iv),
    certain from traces of letters.
τήνδ' ἔκτισε. 844 (Att. iv).
ἐνθάδ' ἔθηκεν. 86 (Att. iv).
τήνδ' ἐ[θ]ἐ[μην], pent., LXXIII (Cypr.
    Mac.), if space rightly indicated.
(?) τάι(ν)δ' ἐπέρυσα (*ta-te-pe-*), LXXVIII
    (Cypriote), uncertain.
τόνδ' ἐβώσε. pent., 932 (Sidon iii).
τόδ' ἔτευξεν. 260 (Cyren. ii).
τόδ' ἔγραψ[εν]. 1037 (Petil. ii).

η- ἅδ' Ἡρακλείδην. 239 (Smyr. Mac.).   μνῆμα τόδε ἧς. 743 a prf. (Att. vi).

---

[1] Here and in the next eleven examples the augmented form is to be understood; ἥδ' ἔθανεν, not ἥδε θάνεν. See note [1], on p. 137.

BEFORE

o- τόδ' Οἰναίου, 66 (Att. Mac.).
       2 3

τοδ' οὔπω, CXXVII (Syb. ii).
     4

ι- τόνδ' ἱαρόν, XCVII₂ l. 10 (Epid. iii). [ἧς] ο[ἷ]δε ἱέ[μ]ενοι, pent., 28
   1   2   1   2   3
                                                    (Att. iv–iii), not quite certain.

τῆιδ' ἱερῆα, 211 (Syros iii).
    2   3

υ-   τόδε Ὑψικλέος, 461 a add.
                                     2   3
                                     (Meg. vi).¹

Particle δέ.

a- δ' ἄλοχος, pent., LIV (Del. *Nax*. vi).
     6

τόδε δ' αὐτῶι, 179 (Corc. vi).
       4

δ' αὐτῶι, same.
   3

ἡ δ' αὐ[τοῖς], pent., v (Att. vi).
2   3

δ' ἀθάνατον, pent., CXXXIX (Att. v).
   2   3

ἡ δ' αὐτοῖς, XX (Att. v).
2?   3?

δ' ἀντίρρο[πα], 21 (Att. v).   ἐγὼ δὲ Ἀντιστάτης, 22 (Att. v).
   5   4   5

δ' ἀμφι, same.   ἔστι δὲ ἀ[ρ' αὐτῶι], XVIII (Att. v).
   4   5   6

ὀργῆς δ' ἀ[ντ'], LX (Chios v).   ηὕρηται δὲ ἄφθονος, pent., 35
1   2   2   3   4

δ' ἀνέθηκεν, 757 (Thisb. v).   (Att. iv).
   5

δ' ἀρετῆι, pent., 39 (Att. iv).   ψυχὴν δὲ ἀθάνατον, pent., same.
   3   1   2   3

δισσαὶ δ' αἴ, 35 (Att. iv).   ἑπτὰ δὲ ἀπορρήξυς, 26 (Att. iv).
1   2   1   2   3

δ' ἀνθρώποισι, XXVI (Att. iv).   μητρὸς δὲ Ἀριστίδος, 71 (Att. iv).
   2   3   4   5

δ' Ἀργεῖοι, 846 (Arg. iv).   [πο]λλὰς δὲ ἀκροπόλεις, 768
   2   3   1   2   3

[τ]οὺς δ' ἄλλους, CXVIII (Delph. iv).   (Xanth. iv).
 1   2

δ' ἀντι[πάλους], pent., same.   εἰμὶ δὲ Ἀριστοκλῆς, 75 (Att.
   2   3   1   2   3
                                        iv–iii).
δ' αὐτῶι, pent., 875 a add.
   3
   (Olymp. iv).

---

¹ See note 2, p. 167.

ON GREEK VERSIFICATION IN INSCRIPTIONS.

BEFORE

a. δ' αὐτῆς, XXIV (Att. iv–iii).

δ' Ἀσκλαπιόν, XCVII₂ l. 20 (Epid. iii).

δ' Ἀσκληπιό[ς], XCVII₃ l. 60 (Epid. iii).

δ' αὐδήσαντος, XCVII₅ l. 74 (Epid. iii).

[σ]ῆς δ' ἀρετῆς, 59 (Att. iv–ii).

δ' ἀμφί, CXVII (Elat. Mac.).

δ' ἀριθμόν, 239 (Smyrn. Mac.).

δ' ἀπόνοσφιν, LXXXIII (Cyme iii–ii), *not verified.*

δ' ἄλγεα, pent., same, *not verified.*

δ' ἀγχόθι, 491 (Orch. ii).

δ' Ἀριστάνδροιο, 184 a RM (Corc. iii), *not verified.*

δ' ἄνθησαν, 852 (Att. ii).

δ' ἀρτιγάλακτον, 205 (Halic. ii).

δ' Ἀΐδαο, 1037 (Petil. ii).

δ' αὐτῆι, same.

δ' ἀνταπέτισ[α], CXXVIII (Syb. ii), *not verified.*

e. δ' ἐπάτει, CIV (Olymp. vi).[3]

δ' ἔστησεν, pent., 940 a RM (Olymp. *Samos* v).

σωθεὶς δὲ Ἀσκληπιέ, 773 a RM (Att. iv), *not verified, Kum.*

τιμῶν δὲ ἀρ[ετάν], CXXIV (Pher. iv–iii).

σω[φροσύνη]ς δὲ ἀρετῆς, 55 (Att. iv–iii).

σῆς δὲ ἀρετῆς, LVIII (Amorg. iv).

σῆς δὲ (ἀ)ρετῆς, 56 (Att. iv–ii), *not verified, Kum.*[1]

ἐν δὲ ἀρχαῖς, 855 (Atal. iii), *not verified, Kum.*

ὀγκωτὰ δὲ [ἀ]μφιβέβακε, pent., 234 (Smyrna iii).[2]

κόσμον δὲ αὐτοῖσι, 772 (Imbr. iv–ii).

βαρὺν δὲ ἀπὸ δεσμόν, 849 (Delph. iv–iii).

ψυχὴ δὲ αἰθέριον, 225 (Ephes. Mac.).

Ἱπποκράτους δὲ ἄλοχος, pent., 785 (Cnid. ii).

Ἀθηναίων δὲ ἐστεφάνωσε, pent., XXV (Att. iv), *not verified, Kum.*

---

[1] The stone has δερετης: the cutter left out α by mistake.

[2] The copy ΔΕΜΜΦ.

[3] In this and the next seven examples, the augment is to be assumed; see note [1], p. 137.

BEFORE

ε- δ' εὐκλεῖσαν. pent., CXXXIX
  4   5
  (Att. v).

δ' ἔστησεν. 211 (Syros iii).
  2   3

φῶς δ' ἔλιπ'. 44 (Att. iv-iii), *not*
  1
verified, *Kum*.

δ' ἔλιπεν. XXXIV (Att. iv-iii), *not*
  3
verified, *Kum*.

(?) δ' ἔλιπον. 96 (Att. iv-ii),
  3
others δὲ λιπ[ώ]ν.

δ' ἔλιπον, 521 (Thessalon. Mac.).
  4

δ' ἔλυσεν, lyric, XCVII, 1. 49 (Epid.
iii).

τὺ δ' εὖ. CXIII (Haliart. vi-v).
  4

ὃ δ' ἐξ, pent., XCV (Olymp. *Arg.* v).
  3

τάφου δ' ἐπί. 69 (Att. iv).
  4

δ' ἐστι. pent., 71 (Att. iv).
  2

δ' ἐν, same.
  2

δ' ἔπαινος. XXVIII (Att. iv).
  6

δ' ἔτη. 43 (Att. iv).
  4

δ' εὐσεβέων. pent., 90 (Att. iv),
  2   3
not verified, *Kum*.

δ' εἰκών, pent., XXII (Att. iv).
  3

(?) δ' ἔτ' ἔχειν. pent., XXXIII (Att.
  6
iv), uncertain.

δὶς δ' ἐνί, CXVIII (Delph. iv).
  5

δώδεκα δ' ἐξ. pent., same.
  1   2

δ' Εὔμολπος, 875 a add. (Olymp. iv).
  3

δ' ἔργοις. 768 (Xanth. iv).
  3

εὐδαίμων δὲ ἔθανον. same, *not*
  1   2   3
verified, *Kum*.

(?) δὲ εἶπεν, LXXXI (Didym. vi),
       5
unless hiatus.

πιστῶν δὲ ἔργων. 52 (Att. iv),
  4   3
not verified, *Kum*.

τοῦδε δὲ ἔτι, 925 (Att. iv).
  1   2

BEFORE

δ' ἔ[ργο]ν. pent., 769 (Eryth. iv).

ὄψεσι δ' ἐν. pent., 774 (Priene iv–iii).

τῶν δ' ἔτι. 66 (Att. Mac.).   λύπαις δὲ ἐλαχίσταις, 88 (Att.
κεῖμαι δ' ἐν, 92 (Att. iv–ii).   iv–ii), *not verified, Kum.*

δ' ἐκτελέσαι. pent., 85 (Att. iv–ii),
not verified, Kum.

δ' ἐπιδοῦσ[α], 81 (Att. iv–ii).[1]

περὶ δ' ἐγ, 96 (Att. iv–ii).[2]

δ' ἐσθλά[ν]. 860 (Chios iii–ii).

δ' ἐστί. pent., 197 (Rhod. iv–ii).

τὰ δ' εἰς, 552 a add. (unkn. Mac.).

δ' ἐξ. pent., 519 (Thessalon. Mac.).   μήτηρ δὲ ἐν οἴκοις. iamb. trim.,

δ' ἐξέρυσαν, pent., 183 (Corc. Mac.).   246 (Bith. Mac.).

ὄστεα δ' ἐν, pent., same.

θνήσκω δ' ἐν. 490 (Theb. Mac.).

δ' εἰμί, same.

δ' ἔοικεν. iamb. trim., CXI (Helic.
Mac.).

ἐγ δ' ἑνός. XLII (Orop. iii).

δ' ἐσιδών. XCVII₅ l. 64 (Epid. iii).

δ' ἐσορᾶν. XCIX (Tegea Mac.).

δ' εἷλε. same.

εὖ δ' ἐν. 33 (Att. iii–ii).

δ' ἐσ[θλ]ός. pent., 40 (Att. iii–ii).

---

[1] Kaibel tacitly omits this δ'; I cannot find out on what authority. Ross, the Ephem. Arch. n. 311, and Kumanudes, all give it.

[2] See note 1, p. 128.

BEFORE
ε- δ' εἰς, 260 (Cyren. ii).
  δ' ἐκείν[ου], 926 (Herm. iii).[1]
  δ' Εὐβούλου, pent., 205 (Halic. ii).
  δ' ἑτέραν, 1037 (Petil. ii).
  δ' ἐπίπροσθεν, same.
  δ' εἰμί, same.
  δ' ἐξέπταν, cxxviii (Syb. ii), *not verified*.
  δ' ἐπέβαν, same, *not verified*.
  θεὸς δ' ἔσηι, same, *not verified*.

η- δ' ἡλικίην, pent., 220 (Amorg. iv).   παῖς δὲ Ἡρακλείδου, 71 (Att. iv).
  δ' ἦν, pent., cviii (Olymp. iv).
  δ' ἦ[ε]ν, pent., 255 (Cypr. iv–iii).
  δ' ἦλθε, xcvii₅ l. 62 (Epid. iii).
  δ' ἦλθες, pent., 932 (Sidon iii).
  δ' ἡγεμόσιν, 242 (Mytil. Mac.).

ο- δ' οἶ, 21 (Att. v).   αὐτῶ δὲ οὔ, 87 (Att. iv), *not verified, Kum.*
  δ' οἶ, 23 (Att. iv), *not verified*.
  δ' ὄνομα, 90 (Att. iv), *not verified*.
  δ' ὄνομα, pent., xxvii (Att. iv).   ἑπτὰ δὲ ὁπλίτας, 768 (Xanth. iv).
  Πραξαγόρας δ' ὄνομ', 255 (Cypr. iv–iii).
  δ' ὀνομαστοί, 254 (Cypr. iv–iii).
  δ' οὔνομα, 189 (Melos iii), *not verified*.   κατιδὼν δὲ ὁ (∪ ∪ _ ∪), lyric, xcvii₄ l. 45 (Epid. iii).
  δ' οὔνομ', iamb. trim., 258 (Alex. iii–ii).

---

[1] Not δὲ κείνου, as the familar form has the preference. Cp. pp. 58 and 62.

BEFORE

o- δ' οὔνομα, 89 (Att. iv-ii), *not
       ₂
   verified, Kum.*

   δ' ὁσίαν, same, *not verified, Kum.*
      ₂

   οἵτινες δ' οἱ, troch. tetr., 783
   ₁   ₂
   (Cnid. iv-ii).

   δ' ὀνομάσθη. lyric, xcvii₄ l. 43
   (Epid.,iii).

   δ' ὀνομάσθη. lyric, same, l. 44.

   δ' οὐκ. troch. tetr., xcvii₁ (Epid. iii).
      ₆

   δ' οὐ. pent., 854 (Delos ii).
      ₄

   δ' οἴακι, 491 (Orch. ii).
      ₃

   δ' Οἰδιπόδαν, pent., 1135 (vase Mac.).
      ₂   ₃

ω- δ' ὦρσε, xcvii₃ l. 72 (Epid. iii).
      ₅

ι- δ' ἱμεροέντων. lyric, xcvii₄ l. 47   νικήσας δὲ ἵππων, XXII (Att. iv).
   (Epid. iii).   ₁   ₂   ₃

   δ' ἴστε. 1037 (Petil. ii).   πεζοὶ δὲ ἱππῆες. 849 (Delph.
      ₅   ₁   ₂   ₃
                                            iv-iii).

   δ' ἱκέτης. cxxviii (Syb. ii), *not
      ₂
   verified.*

υ- δ' ὑγιείαν. lyric, xcvii₄ l. 55 (Epid. iii.)

   δ' ὕστατον. 184a RM (Corc. ii),
      ₄
   not verified.

   δ' ὑπὸ κολπόν. cxxviii (Syb. ii),
              ₃
   not verified.

α- οὐδ' αἰών. 858 (Milet. iv-ii).
      ₂   ₃

ε- ἠδ' ἐπί. 484 (Tanag. v).
       ₅

   οὐδ' Ἐπαμινώνδαν, pent., 768a prf.
   ₁   ₂   ₃
   (Theb. iv-iii), *not verified.*

ON GREEK VERSIFICATION IN INSCRIPTIONS.

BEFORE

o.-

ἠδὲ ὁμοβώμοις, 773 b RM (Att.
iv–iii), *not verified, Kum.*

Particle τέ.

a.- πόλεμόν θ' ἅμα. 19 (Att. vi).

[συμ]μαχία τ' ἀν[έθεν]. pent.,
XCIV (Olymp. *Corinth* v).

Τελεστοδίκη τ' ἀπό. 750 a add.
(Paros v).

βίοτόν τ' αὐξ', pent., same.

χῶρόν τ' ἀπέδειξαν, 774 (Prien.
iv–iii).

τῶν τ' ἄλλων. pent., 66 (Att.
Mac.).

ὄφρα τ' Ἀπόλλων, LXIX (Rhod.
Mac.).

αὐθαί[μ]ου τ' αἰπύ. pent., 214
(Rhen. iii).

τ' ἀστεροπῆι. CXXVIII (Syb. ii),
not verified.

e- Ἀγνήις τ' ἐνθάδε. 86 (Att. iv).

τοῖς τ' ἐπιγιγνομένοι[ς]. pent.,
XXXI (Att. iv).

παιδί τ' ἐμῶι, XXIV (Att. iv–iii).

οὔ τ' Εὐρώπην. 768 (Xanth. iv).

ἀγαθῆς τ' ἐξανύοιτε. pent., 89 (Att.
iv–ii), *not verified, Kum.*

εὐπόλεμόν τε ἀρετήν. pent., 34
(Att. iv).

φύσιν τε ἀρετῆς. pent., 64
(Att. iv).

ἔν τε ἀνδρῶν, pent., 62 (Att. iv).

ἄλλους τε ἀθλοφόρους. 938
(Tanag. iv).

θεσμοφόρους τε ἁγνάς, 774 (Prien.
iv–iii).

λέξασθαί τε ἄνδρας, XCVII₂ l. 15
(Epid. iii).

υἱῶι τε Ἀσκλαπιῶι. same, l. 18.

θνητοῖσι τε Ἀθνῆναι. 88 (Att.
iv–ii), *not verified, Kum.*

πόσιν τε αὐτῆς, pent., 83 (Att.
iv–ii), *not verified.*

παίδων τε ἀκμαίαι. pent., XLVIII
(Chalcis Mac.).

πᾶσ[ί] τε ἑταίροισιν. pent., 49
(Att. iv).

ἔργων τε ἐν ἁμίλλα[ις]. XXII
(Att. iv).

φειδωλός τε ἐνθάδε, XXXV (Att. iv).

[ζ]ῶσά τε ἐκοινώνουν. pent., XLIII
(Salam. iv–iii).

BEFORE

ε- χρηστῶν τ' ἔργων, 65 (Att. iv–ii),
   not verified, Kum.

μοῖραι τ' ἐλεεινό[ν], XL. (Att. Mac.).

μητρός τ' εὐσεβίην. pent., 858 (Milet. iv–ii).

Κασταλίων τ' ἐλ[α]βον. pent., 926 (Herm. iii).[1]

τέκνοις τ' ἐρατάν. XCVII₂ l. 22 (Epid. iii).

(?) τ' ἐστι [γ]έρας. pent., 249 (Byz. Mac.), changed by Kaibel.

σύν θ' Ἑκάτηι, 1136 (Att. iii–ii).

η- καλλίστοις τ' ἠγλάϊσας, pent., CXVIII (Delph. iv).

ναοῦ θ' ἥδε, 780 (Mytil. iv–ii).

θ' ἥλιον, pent., LXXXIII (Cyme iii–ii), not verified.

ο- ἐμόν θ' ὅδε, 89 (Att. iv–ii), not verified, Kum.

ω-

ι- ποθεῖ θ' ἱεροῖς, 38 (Att. iv).

ἀμφοτέροισί θ' ἶσον, LXXXIII (Cyme iii–ii), not verified.

Καυκάσιός τε ἐντός, pent., 773 (Panticap. Mac.).

πενταέτους τε εἰκώ, iamb. trim., 246 (Bith. Mac.).

πλείστην τε εὐφροσύνηι, pent., LXXXIV (Heracl. Pont. iii–ii).

(?)-κλέα τε ὅς ἀδελφεός, CXXII (Phars. v), so Cauer; probable.

Φιλῆς τε οἷν ἡ, 82 (Att. iv).

ἀρετῆι τε οὐκ, pent., 39 (Att. iv).

Ἧραι τε ὥς, 742 (Crissa vi).

οἷσί τε ἴ[σον], pent., 35 a add. (Att. iv). not verified.

λειμῶνάς τε ἱερούς, CXXVII (Syb. ii), not verified.

---

[1] See note 1, p. 137.

BEFORE
υ- τόν θ' ὑπό, same, *not verified*.
      3
α-   οὔτε ἀπὸ δαιμονίου, pent., 95
                                 4   5   6
                                (Att. iii).

ε- εἶτ' ἐπί, 779 (Chalced. Mac.).
     1
   ὦττ' ἐχθρούς, CXXXIX (Att. v).
   1   2
ο- ἀτ' οὐδής, CI (Lac. vi–v).
     4
                    Particle γέ.
α- τάσδε γ' Ἀθαναίαι, 742 (Crissa vi).
    1   2   3
   (?) τύ γ' ἀποστείχοντι, XCVII₅ l. 63
        1   2   3
      (Epid. iii) ; see p. 192.
ε- ἆ γ' ἐνί, LXXX (Cedr. iv–iii).
     5
   (?) ἐνθάδε γ' [εἰ]σοράοντι, 756 a RM
       1   2   3
      (Plat. v), restoration not certain.
η- ἐλπίδι γ' ἦσθα, pent., 39 (Att. iv).
    1
   (?) φίλοι γ' ἤμυναν, 96 (Att.
         2   3
      iv–ii), not certain.[1]
ο-   τῶνγε ὀνόσαιτ', pent., LIII (Del. ii).
                                  4   5
ω-   καὶ σοί γε ὡραία, CXII (Theb. ii).
                                 1   2   3

           Adverbs πότε, πρόσθε, *etc.*
α- ποτ' ἀρισστεύων, pent., 487
      2   3
   (Thisb. v).
   (?) ὄτ' ἀνώρως, Lolling CXXII
          3
      (Phars. v), similarly Röhl and
      Cauer : Meister and Fick
      otherwise.
   [τ]ότ' αἰχμήν, 749 (Att. v).
        6
   οὔποτ' ἄν, 24 (Att. iv).
      5

---
[1] It is hard to tell whether ΓH or TH was originally cut.

BEFORE

ε- [οὔ]ποτ' ἐπαίνου, 488 (Tanag. v).   εὖ ποτε ἔρρεξα (*po-te-e-ve-re-xa*)
   LXXVI (Cypriote).

(?) ποτ' ἐ[ϝ]ώ[λπει, 489 (Theb.
iv), if rightly restored.¹

τῶν τότ' ἐν. pent., 768 (Xanth. iv).   σ[ύ]μ [π]οτε ἐν[ίκων], 925 (Att.
   iv).

(?) ποτ' ἐϝείσης (*po-te-*), LXXIV
(Cypriote), if rightly read.

τότ' ἔπειτα, 1037 (Petil. ii).

ο-   τότε 'Ολυμπίαι, CVIII (Olymp. iv).

υ- ἃ ποθ' ὑπ', 77 (Att. iii).

α- (?) πρόσθ' ἀρ', pent., 744 (Olymp.   καθύπερθε ἀγορεύει, 234 (Smyrn.
v), according to the stone, but   iii).
πρόσθα [δ]έ is sure ; cp. p. 79.

ε-   πρόσθε ἐπεπόνθεις, CXXVII (Syb.
                                          ii), *not verified*.

3. ELISION OF -O.

-το *Verbal Ending.*

α- ἡ[λλ]άξαντ' ἀρετήν, pent., 21 (Att. v).

ἵκετ' ἄχος, pent., 36 (Att. v).

ὤλετ' ἄωρος, pent., 221 (Amorg.
iv–iii).

ἠσπάσατ' αὐτός, 858 (Milet.   γένετο Αἴγλα (∪ ∪ — —), lyric,
iv–ii).   XCVII₄ l. 44 (Epid. iii).

γένετ' ἀνδρῶν, LXIII (Samos Mac.). φείδετο ἄρα Ζεύς, XCVII₅ l. 61
                                    (Epid. iii).

---

¹ ποτε [ἐ]ώ[λπει] seems possible.

BEFORE

ε- ἀγορεύετ' ἐκ, iamb. trim., 258
   3   4   5
   (Alex. iii–ii).

περιφείδοιτ' εὐρύοπα, XCVII₂ l. 26
    4   5   6
   (Epid. iii).

ὀνόσαιτ' ἐσιδών, pent., LIII (Del. ii).
    5   6

ω-

ι- ἔ[γ]ε[ν]τ' Ἰθάκαι, pent., 187
      5   6
   (Ithac. Mac.).

ἔπλετ' Ἰάσων, 205 (Halic. ii).
  5   6

υ- εἴσαθ' ὑπό, pent., 924 (Att. iii–ii).
    4   5

ᾤχετο ἐπί, XCVII₃ l. 72 (Epid. iii).
  2   3

(?) ὡς ὄλετο ὤν, pent., CXXII
       4   5
(Phars. v), acc. to Köhl.

The cases [ὤ]ναθ' ὅ and ὤλετ' ἐ[κείνου] in 19, disappear in consequence of Lolling's re-examination of the stone.

-o *Nominal Endings*.

a- τοῦτ' ἀπένειμε, unmetrical verse,
   XXVI (Att. iv).

ε- τοῦτ' ἐτέλεσσε, pent., 740
     4   5
   (Melos vi).

[δ]ύ' ἔτη, 74 (Att. iv–ii).
      3

δύ' ἐνίκων, 941 (Att. iii).
       6

a- (?) ἐγγὺς ὁδοῖ' ἀγαθοῦ, 3 (Att. vi),
        2   3   4
   according to copy.¹

-o *in Prepositions*.

[ἀ]π' ἄρα, iamb., 1133 (vase v).
      4

ἀπ' ἀν[δρ]ῶν, 768 (Xanth. iv).
       6

---

¹ HOΔOI. The stone seems no longer to exist. ὁδῶι is out of the question. Kaibel, after Kiessling, makes ὁδοῦ, by taking I as ; ; see p. 106. Respecting the possibility of elided -o in -οιο, Bergk on Archil. fr. 77 (Poet. Lyr.⁴ II, p. 404), Lugebil in Fleckeisen's Jahrb. suppl. vol. XII. p. 212, and Christ's Proleg. ad Iliad. p. 135, may be consulted.

BEFORE

α- ἀπ' Ἀρκαδίης. 781 (Cnid. iii).

ε- ἀπ' Εὐδόξοιο, 941 c RM   ἀπὸ Ε[ὑμ]νάστας. LXVI (Thera
(Olymp. v).   vi), not certain.
ἀπ' Εὐρώτα. 768 a prf. (Theb.
iv–iii), *not verified*.
ἀφ' Ἑλλάδος, 932 (Sidon iii).

η- ἀπ' ἠγαθέας, XXVII (Att. iv).
ἀπ' ἠϊθέων, pent., 938 a prf.
(Theb. iv).
ἀφ' ἡμετέρης. 781 (Cnid. iii).

α- ὑπ' ἄγκει, same.
ὑπ' ἀργύρου, 855 (Atal. iii), *not
verified*, *Kum*.
ὑπ' αἰχμῆς. troch., tetr., 790
(Dyme iii).

ο- ὑπ' ὄχθαις. 234 (Smyrn. iii).

ω- ὑπ' ὠδίνων, 77 (Att. iii).

ι- ὑφ' ἱππομάχοισι, 183 (Corc. Mac.).

4. ELISION OF -ι.

εἰμί, ἐστί.

α-   εἰμὶ ἀνδριάς. iamb. trim., 1097
                             (Del. vi).
                         εἰμὶ αὔη. 1037 (Petil. ii).

ε- εἰμ' ἐπί, 181 (Corc. vi).   εἰμὶ Εὐανορίδα, 490 (Theb. Mac.).

α- ἔστ' ἀρετᾶς, pent., 744 (Olymp. v).
ἔστ' Ἀλκαίνετος, 856 (Atal.
Mac.), *not verified*.

ON GREEK VERSIFICATION IN INSCRIPTIONS. 153

BEFORE

ε-   ἐστι Ἔφεσος, pent., 71 (Att. iv).
          2   3

ο- ἐστ' ὄνυμ', 761 (Aeg. v).
  5

 ἔστ' οὐδέν, 492 (Theb. iv).
  2

Meister's reading ἐσστ' Ἀγέλ[αος] in CXXII is not very probable.
        5   6

     -ι *Dative Singular*.

α-   Παλ(λ)άδι Ἀθαναίαι, X (Att. vi).
         1   2   3
       κήρυκι ἀθανάτων, 772 (Imbr.
        1   2   3
         iv–ii).
       γυναικὶ ἐσθλήν, 53 (Att. iv),[1]
        3   4
        not verified.
      (?) σώματι ἐκείνων, 26 (Att. iv),
        5   6
       probably mistake for σώματι
       κείνων.

ο-   Δάματρι οἶκον, 785 (Cnid. ii).
        3   4

υ-   ἄνακτι υἱῶι, XCVII₂ l. 18 (Epid. iii).
        2   3

I count out Ἀπόλλωνι υἱός, 778, on which see pp. 46 and 104.
     4   5

       Dative Plural.

ε-   ἔρνεσι ἐλαίας, XCVII₂ l. 20
        3   4
        (Epid. iii).

      εἴκοσι, ἔτι.

ε- εἴκοσ' ἐτῶν, pent., 519 (Thessalon.
  1   2
 Mac.).

 (?) δ' ἔτ' ἔχαιν, pent., XXXIII
      6

  (Att. iv), very uncertain ; δέ τ' ?

     -ι *in Prepositions*.

α- ἀντ' ἀρετῆς, pent., 2 (Att. vi).
 2   3

---

[1] On this see p. 38.

BEFORE

a. ἀντ' ἀγαθῶν, pent., 757 a prf.
   (Thisb. v).

   ἀ[ντ]' ἀγαθῆς, LX (Chios v).[1]

   ἀντ' ἀρετᾶς, pent., 856 a prf. (Hyp. Mac.), *not verified*.

ω- ἀνθ' ὦν, pent., XXXII (Att. iv).

   [ἀ]νθ' ὦν, XXIII (Att. iv).

   ἀνθ ὦν, 780 (Mytil. iv–ii).

a. ἐπ' Ἀράθθοιο, 180 (Corc. vi).

   ἐπ' ἀνδράσι, 35 (Att. iv).

   ἐπ' ἀνδρῶν, 255 (Cypr. iv–iii).

   ἐφ' ἁγνοῦ, XCVII₃ l. 30 (Epid. iii).

   ἐπ' Ἀλφειῶι, 941 b RM (Olymp. iii).

   ἐπ' ἀϊόσιν, pent., 234 (Smyrn. iii).

   ἐπ' ἀριστερά, 1037 (Petil. ii).

ε- ἐπ' ἔσχατον, 197 a add. (Rhod. Mac.).

   ἐπ' εὐσεβίαι, pent., 786 (Halic. ii).

o- ἐπ' Ὀλ..ειδαι, 486 (Thesp. v).

ω- ἐπ' ὠκυμο[ί]ρ[ου], iamb. trim.,
   246 (Bith. Mac.).

a. ποτ' Ἀπόλλω, XCVII₂ l. 19 (Epid. iii), unless we assume πότ.

---

[1] Omission of ι is certain from the number of letters, as the inscription is cut στοιχηδόν.

5. ELISION OF DIPHTHONGS.

BEFORE

α- χάριτας μοι ἀπέδωκα|ν ϳ. 95 (Att. iii), unless μοι ἔδωκαν was intended.

ε- ἐνδείξασθ' ἔργα (for -σθαι), pent., 492 (Theb. iv).

η- κεῖθ' Ἡρακλείδης (for κεῖται), 213 (Del. iv–ii).

From these lists several interesting facts appear. First the difference between prepositions and other words. The elided vowel of a preposition is not written. There is only one instance, and that is not entirely certain. In other words than prepositions the elided vowel is written between one-third and one-fourth of the time. The numbers are, seriously doubtful cases eliminated :

Words not Prepositions.				Prepositions.		
-α omitted	91,	written	29	-α omitted	14	
-ε "	275	"	104	-ο "	15	(written 1?)
-ο "	15	"	3	-ι "	19	
-ι "	6	"	10			
	387		146		48	

The natural deduction from this is, that elision of prepositions was total, but that elision of other words was — or might be — partial.

Was it always partial or only sometimes? Two things are conceivable. Either the elided vowel was always sounded a little, but so slightly that the Greeks did not know whether to write it or not. Or it was sometimes slightly sounded and sometimes entirely suppressed, according to the caprice of the speaker. On the first supposition the diversity between τόδε ἄγαλμα and τόδ' ἄγαλμα is merely graphic, on the second it represents a difference of pronunciation. Decisive in favor of the second alternative is the fact that we find on the one hand σώμαθ' ἑλών, ἑρπέθ' ἅμ'. πεντήκονθ' ὅς. οὐχ ὁ. παρέδωχ' ὑβρίσαι. ... ναθ' ὁδίτηι. θ' ἅμα. θ' Ἑκάτηι. θ' ἥδε. θ' ἥλιον. θ' ὅδε. θ' ἱεροῖς. θ' ἴσον.[1]

---

[1] See G. Meyer, Griech. Gramm.² p. 244.

θ' ὑπό, ποθ' ὑπ', εἴσαθ' ὑπό, and on the other ἔθηκα ὁσίως, ἕνεκα ἵδρυσεν, ἀνέθηκε υἱός, ἄνθρωπε ὅς, τε ἁγνάς, τε αὐτῆς, τε ἑταίροισιν, τε οἶν, τε ὡς, τε ἱεροῖς, ἄνακτι υἱῶι, the distinction in the employment of the aspirate being consistently observed. It is certain that in σώμαθ' ἑλών the aspirate was written simply because the *h* of ἑλών was unconsciously brought into connection with the *τ* of σώματ'; what was pronounced was *sōmat helōn*. Now if there had been even the slightest vowel-sound between the *t* and the *h*, no one could possibly have imagined that he heard a θ.

As among the three vowels α, ε, ο, there does not appear to be any significant difference in the relative frequency with which they are written or omitted. But different words do differ in this respect. It can hardly be accident that τε is written nearly as often as τ' or θ', while δέ and δ' are as 1 to 3⅔. I subjoin the figures for the most numerous classes :

-α	nom. fem.,	omitted	13,	written	9.	-ε 3d pers.,	omitted 13,	written 10.
-μα	"	"	21	"	3.	-ε imp. sg. pl.,	" 8	" 1.
-α	acc. sg.,	"	11	"	7.	-ε vocat.,	" 6	" 4.
-α	neut. pl.,	"	17	"	4.	με, etc. . . .	" 31	" 6.
-α	adverbs,	"	21	"	3.	ὅδε, etc. . .	" 59	" 20.
-το	3d pers.,	"	11	"	3.	δέ, ...	" 118	" 32.
						τε, ...	" 30	" 23.

The succeeding vowel seems also to make a difference in the tendency to write the elided vowel. It is oftenest written before α-. This is strikingly illustrated in the cases of -α of the nominative singular, -ε of the 3d person, ὅδε, and δέ, as will be seen on reference to the foregoing lists. Altogether (omitting still the prepositions) :

		-α		-ε		-ο		-ι	
		Omitted.	Written.	Omitted.	Written.	Omitted.	Written.	Omitted.	Written.
Before	α-	31	10	99	54	6	2	2	4
"	ε-	42	11	120	25	6	1	2	4
"	η-	6	–	12	5	–	–	–	–
"	ο-	10	3	24	11	–	–	2	1
"	ω-	–	–	4	2	–	–	–	–
"	ι-	1	2	9	5	2	–	–	–
"	υ-	1	3	7	2	1	–	–	1

The elisibility of -ι in the dative singular is attested by five certain examples. But the -ι is written in all five examples, and it is clear that here at least we have to deal with *consonantization* of the vowel, not suppression. The statement of Eustathius on K 277 (p. 805, 18) is fully borne out. The "παλαιοί," he says, wrote ὄρνιθι Ὀδυσεύς in full, and not ὄρνιθ' Ὀδυσεύς, "κατ' ἔκθλιψιν." As to further traces of this usage in our Homeric tradition — traces uniformly neglected by the editors — see La Roche, *Homerische Untersuchungen*, p. 127 flg.[1] Altogether it is evident that this treatment of dative -ι does not stand on the same footing as ordinary elision. It was evidently not considered an ornament to the verse. The augment was omitted to avoid it: παιδὶ θέσαν, pent., LXIX (Rhod. Mac.), παιδὶ λίπες, pent., 505 (Tricca iii).

Diphthongs are elided three times; in two cases the diphthong is not written, and its entire suppression is shown, in one of these, by the form κεῖθ'.

There is no discernible difference between earlier and later inscriptions in the usages of elision.

XIII.

APHAERESIS.

There is only one clear case of 'aphaeresis,' and in that the suppressed vowel is written:

τῶι ἐπιγόνου, pent., 781 (Cnid. iii).

The Cypriote inscriptions furnish three more — all problematical. Of Φεθόχω Ἀλεϝότης, LXXVIII, we have spoken on pp. 48 and 77. Of θεῶι ἀλ(λ)' ἔτυχ' ἁ κήρ (or θεῶι ἀλ(λ)' ἔτυχ' ἁ κήρ), LXXIV, on pp. 55, 103, and 119. Of οὐ γάρ τι ἐπιστᾶις, in the same inscription,

---

[1] A few additional *testimonia* may be found in La Roche's critical editions. The passages in which the reading with -ι has come down to us, either in manuscripts or through Eustathius, are: Γ 349 (= P 45), Δ 259, E 5, K 277, Λ 544, 588, P 324 (all the manuscripts), Ω 26, ε 62.

on p. 74. Kaibel's reading πρώιρ[η] 'κτετάνυσται in 96 has no adequate foundation : see p. 128, note.

Of course we do not count instances of omitted augment, nor those like ἐγὼ κείνην (1136); not even when the ἐ- is written by mistake, as in ἕταροι ἐκτέρισαν. pent., 183. σώματι ἐκείνων. 26.

XIV.

N MOVABLE.

1. Of ν movable as employed or omitted according to ordinary poetic custom, to avoid hiatus or to make or avoid position (ὤλεσεν Ἄρης, 180 ; πᾶσιν μακάριστος. 26 ; θῆκε τόδ' ἀντ', 2 ; ἐτέλεσσε Γρόφων, 740), no record has been kept. Violations of these usages occur as follows :

Wrongly written.

[ἀνέθη]κεν Διώς. 738 (Att. vi).

ἀνέθηκεν Κάλλωνος. CXLI (Delos, unknown).

ἐπέθηκεν θανόι ν)τοι(ν). 9 (Att. vi).

εἶπεν δί[κ]αιον. LXXXI (Didym. vi).

ἔστησεν τόδε (unless ἔστησεν τοῦδε), LVIII (Amorg. iv).

φροντίσιν θαητόν. pent., 189 (Melos iii).

Wrongly omitted.

ἥρωσι φίλτρων, pent., 189 (Melos iii).

ἔθηκε τὰν ὁμόλεκτρον. same.[1]

ἀνέθηκε Ἀθαναία[ι]. CI (Lac. vi–v).

In the last example the omission of the ν is doubtless due to dialectic influence.[2]

---

[1] Boeckh guessed ἔθηκε[ν ἐ]ὰν, Kaibel ἔθηκέ [με] τάν.
[2] See G. Meyer, *Griech. Gramm.*,[2] p. 298.

ON GREEK VERSIFICATION IN INSCRIPTIONS.

2. At the end of a verse ν movable is nearly always written. The examples are subjoined. Except where the contrary is stated, each case has been verified by reference to the publications in capitals, or to the stone itself. '*Not verified*' means simply that only minuscule copies were accessible to me (compare p. 127).

ἐπέθηκεν. 5 (Att. vi).
κατέθηκεν. 15 (Att. vi).
ἐπόησεν. vi (Att. vi).
ἐποίησεν. xv (Att. vi), if verse.
[ἴ]σασιν. 25 (Att. iv)..
ἀνδραπόδοισιν, 26 (Att. iv).
ἀγαθοῖσιν. 35 (Att. iv).[1]
νόμοισιν. same.
ἀγῶσιν, 38 (Att. iv).
ἐπέβησεν, 39 (Att. iv).
ἐστίν. 61 (Att. iv–iii), *not verified, Kum.*
κασιγνήτοισιν. 82 (Att. iv).
διέμεινεν, same.
ἔθηκεν. 86 (Att. iv).
ἔχουσιν. same.
ἔτυχεν. xxxiii (Att. iv).
ἅπασιν. 59 (Att. iv–ii).
ἐκάλυψεν. 51 (Att. iv–ii).
ἐστίν, 48 (Att. iii).
ἅπασιν, 95 (Att. iii).
ἐπόνησεν. 776 (Att. iii–ii).
ἔρεξεν, 924 (Att. iii–ii).
τρίποσιν. same.
ἔτευξεν. 260 (Cyren. ii).
πράπισιν. 491 (Orch. ii).
μελέεσσιν, same.
ἔασιν. 1037 (Petil. ii).

ἐποίησεν. xlvi (Eub. v).
... σύνησιν. lv (Nax. v).
ἀνέθηκ[ε]ν. 768 (Xanth. iv).
ἐστεφάνωσεν. same.[2]
ἐπηγλάϊσεν. 492 (Theb. iv).
εἷλεν. 768 a prf. (Theb. iv–iii), *not verified*.
αὖσεν. cxvii (Elat. Mac.).
ἔπεσιν. cxv (Elat. iii).
ἔσχεν, 875 a add. (Olymp. iv).
ἀνέθηκεν. same.
ἔχουσιν, cxix (Delph. iv–iii).
προέηκεν, 849 (Delph. iv–iii).
ἐπέθεικεν. cxxiii (Pher. iv–iii).
Στροφάσιν. 184 (Corc. iii).
ἴαχεν, troch., 790 (Dyme iii).
ἀ[ρ]ι[θ]μήσειεν, 926 (Herm. iii).
χοροῖσιν, same.
ἐστεφάν[ω]σεν, same.
θεοῖσιν, xcvii₂ l. 11 (Epid. iii).
ὅπλοισιν. xcvii₅ l. 63 (Epid. iii).
χάρισιν, 189 (Melos iii), *not verified*.
ἦλθεν, lxiii (Sam. Mac.).
ἀϊόσιν. 234 (Smyrn. iii).
δεκάδεσσιν. 240 (Smyrn. Mac.).
εἶ δ᾽εν. 858 (Milet. iv–ii).
ἀγαθοῖσιν. 249 (Byz. Mac.).
νέμουσιν. 781 (Cnid. iii).
ἀνέθηκεν. 785 (Cnid. ii).
ἔκλειζεν. 254 (Cypr. iv–iii).

---
[1] Kaibel wrong.
[2] The N is incomplete on the stone, but certain.

The next verse begins with a consonant in 23 cases, with a vowel in 18. In 4 instances the beginning of the next verse is uncertain, and in 11 the word stands at the end of the epigram.

Ν movable is omitted at the end of a verse in these instances:

ἔθανε, 1 a add. (Att. vi).
ἔθηκε, 742 (Crissa vi).
ἀνέθηκε, cxxvi (Metap. vi).
ῥοραῖσι, 180 (Corc. vi).
ἐποίει, 179 (Corc. vi).
βέβακε, iamb., 1133 (vase v); omission perhaps due to lack of room.

ἐστί, 71 (Att. iv).
ἐστί, 235 (Smyrn. iii).
ἔκαμε, 851 (Rhod. iii).
ἐπέδραμε, iamb., 258 (Alex. iii–ii).
καρπαλίμοισι, cxxviii (Syb. ii), *not verified*.

A comparatively large number of these omissions, it will be observed, occur in early inscriptions. The second, third, and fourth cases may be due to dialectic influence, although 180 has -ν in ὤλεσεν. In 6 cases a consonant begins the next verse, in 2 a vowel; in 3 cases the word ends the epigram.

In 17, Kaibel's [κατέ]θηκεν should be [κατέ]θηκε[ν]: the stone is broken off, and it is impossible to tell whether Ν was there or not. Similarly in φίλοισ[ι], 71.

3. Respecting the writing of -ν movable before two consonants, the testimony of the inscriptions is altogether affirmative.

ἀνέστασεν πρεσβυτάτα, pent., 857 (Rhod. Mac.).
  2 3 4 5

ἔθανε⟨ι⟩ν προλιποῦσα. 58 a RM (Att. iv); mistake for
  2   3
ἔθανεν.

γέγονεν χρηστή. 95 (Att. iii).
  3 4

εὐσεβέσιν κλήροις. 858 (Milet. iv–ii).
 1 2 3

ἔτυχεγ Γλυκέρα, pent., 53 (Att. iv).
  5 6

ἀμφέβαλεν πτέρυγας. pent., 89 (Att. iv–ii).
  4 5 6

ἐστιν μνῆμα, iamb. trim., 210 (Ceos iv–iii).
  2 3

ἀστοῖσιγ Ξενόφαντος. 851 (Rhod. iii).
  4 5 6

So [ἔ]στασες σκοπόν, xlv (Aeg. v) is probably to be understood (like ἐς στήληι for ἐν στήληι), with Roehl.

APPENDIX.

LIST OF INSCRIPTIONS USED.

Abbreviations are employed as follows:

  add. . . . Addenda to Kaibel's Epigrammata.
  prf. . . . Preface to the same.
  RM . . . Rhein. Museum, vol. xxxiv (1879), pp. 181 flg.
  CIA . . . Corpus Inscriptionum Atticarum.
  CIG . . . Corpus Inscriptionum Graecarum.
  IGA . . . Roehl's Inscriptiones Graecae Antiquissimae.
  IBM . . . Inscriptions of the British Museum.
  Kum. . . . Kumanudes' Ἀττικῆς ἐπιγραφαὶ ἐπιτύμβιοι.
  Eph. . . . Ἐφημερὶς ἀρχαιολογική.
  Löwy . . . Löwy's Inschriften Griechischer Bildhauer.

Other abbreviations will hardly need explanation.

In designating the metres, *hex.* = hexameter; *el.* = elegiac; *dact.* indicates that from the fragmentary condition of the epigram it cannot be discerned whether it was in elegiacs or hexameters; *i.t.* = iambic trimeters; *t.t.* = trochaic tetrameters; *el. irr.* means that the "pentameters" do not alternate with the hexameters in the usual way.

In giving the number of verses, the sign + indicates that the epigram originally had a greater, but no longer ascertainable, number of verses. Two numbers (2. 1) indicate separate epigrams on the same stone.

Small Roman numerals (vi) mean centuries B.C.

A. — KAIBEL'S INSCRIPTIONS.

Kaibel.	Elsewhere Published.	Place.	Age.	Metre.	Nr. Verses.
1	CIA. I. 463.	Att.	vi	el.	4
1 a add.	CIA. IV. 477 c.	"	"	el.	2
2	Better CIA. IV. 477 b. Löwy 395.	"	"	el.	2
2 a RM[1]	Roehl, Imagines Insc. Ant. xxxi, 21.	"	"	el.	2
3	CIA. I. 465.	"	"	hex.	2
4	" " 466. Löwy 11.	"	"	dact.	1+
4 a add.	CIA. IV. 477 a. Löwy 18.	"	"	hex.	1
5	CIA. I. 468.	"	"	hex.	1
6	" " 469. Better Löwy 12.	"	"	el.	2
7	" " 470.	"	"	hex.	2
8[2]	" " 471. Löwy 13.	"	"	el. + hex.	2.1
9	" " 472.	"	"	dact.	2
10	" " 473.	"	"	el.	2
11	" " 475.	"	"	.. i.t.	1
12	" " 476.	"	"	dact.	2?
13	" " 477. Better Löwy 8.	"	"	el.	2
14	" " 478.	"	"	dact.[3]	2?
15	" " 479.	"	"	el.	2
16	" " 481.	"	"	el.	2
17	" " 482. Löwy 396.	"	"	el.	2
18	" " 487.	"	"	el.	1+
19	" " 492. Better Lolling, Mittheilungen, v, 1880, p. 244 flg.	"	"	hex.	2
20	CIA. I. 441.	"	v	dact.	?
21	" " 442. IBM. I. 111.	"	"	el.	4.4.4.
22	IGA. 368.	Att. Aeg.	"	el.	2
23		Att.	iv	el. irr.	3
24	CIG. 173.	"	"	el.	2.2+

---

[1] ἄνθρωπε ὃς (σ)τείχεις καθ' ὁδὸν φρασὶν ἄλ(λ)α μενοινῶν,
στῆθι καὶ οἴκτιρον σῆμα Θράσωνος ἰδών.

[2] It appears to be taken for granted that [Ep]istemon is the artist's name. But [οὐκ ἀνεπ]ιστήμων τόδ' ἐπόει Ἰπ(π)όσ(τρα]τος (σ)ῆμα seems possible. Compare 759. οὐκ ἀδαὴς Πάριος.

[3] According to Bergk, Litteraturgesch. I. p. 385, two logaoedic cola.

ON GREEK VERSIFICATION IN INSCRIPTIONS. 163

Kaibel.	Elsewhere Published.	Place.	Age.	Metre.		Nr. Verses.
25	Rhein. Museum, viii, p. 625.	Att.	iv	el.	..	4
26	CIG. 175. Kum. 16.	"	"	hex.	..	9
27	Eph. 545.	"	"	el.	..	2+
28	Rang. 2204. Kum. 3480. Cp. Herwerden, Mnem. x, p. 386.	"	iv–iii	el.	..	4
29	CIG. 1042.	"	iv–ii	dact.	..	4
30	Eph. 2565.	"	iii	el.	..	6
31	Kum. 3483.	"	iv–ii	dact.	..	2
32	" 3492.	"	"	dact.	..	2
33	" 3493.	"	iii–ii	el.	..	10
34	Bull. Arch. 1870, p. 146. Kum. 858.	"	iv	el.	..	4[1]
35	Kum. 2784.	"	"	el.	..	4.6
35 a add.		"	"	el.	..	4.4
36	Arch. Zt. 1871, p. 29. Köhler, Mittheilungen x (1885), p. 366.	"	v	el.	..	4
37	Arch. Zt. 1871, p. 28.	"	iv	el.	..	4
38	" " " p. 27.	"	"	el.	..	4
39	Bull. Arch. 1864, p. 40. Kum. 735.	"	"	el.	..	4
40	Bull. Arch. 1873, p. 248.	"	iii–ii	el.	..	5+
41	Arch. Zt. 1856, p. 139.	"	iv	el.	..	2
43[2]	Better Löwy 64.	"	"	el.	..	4
44	Kum. 585.	"	iv–iii	hex.	..	4
45	" 3406.	"	"	hex.	..	2
46	CIG. 930.	"	iv–ii	hex.	..	1
47	Bull. Arch. 1841, p. 59.	"	iv	el.	..	2
48	CIG. 808.	"	iii	hex.	+iamb.	6
49	" 805.	"	iv	el.	..	4
50	" 800 b.	"	"	el.	..	2
51	Kekulé, Theseion, n. 269.	"	iv–ii	el.	..	2
52	Kum. 1412.	"	iv	el. irr.	..	3
53	" 2716. Cp. Herwerden Mnem. x, p. 386.	"	"	el.	..	2
54	CIG. 837.	"	"	el.		2

[1] In spite of Kaibel's assurance, there are distinct traces of a fourth verse.
[2] N. 42 falls out: see CIA. III. 1308, Löwy 550.

Kaibel.	Elsewhere Published.	Place.	Age.	Metre.		Nr. Verses.
55[1]	Kum. 3499.	Att.	iv–iii	el.	..	4
56	" 3037.	"	iv–ii	el.	..	2
57	Kekulé, Theseion, n. 224.	"	"	el.	..	2
58	Rang. 1518.	"	"	el.	..	2
58 a RM[2]		"	iv	el.	..	2
59	Bull. Arch. 1874, p. 170.	"	iv–ii	hex.	..	2+
60	CIG. 954.	"	"	el.	..	2
61	Kum. 699.	"	iv–iii	el.	..	4
62	" 426.	"	iv	el.	..	4
63	" 3076.	"	"	el.	..	2
64	" 1052.	"	"	el.	..	4
65	" 170 and p. 444.	"	iv–ii	hex.	..	4
66	Ross, Demen v. Attika, p. 87.	"	Mac.	el. irr.	..	3
67	Rhein. Mus. xx, p. 558.	"	iv–ii	el. irr.	..	4
68	Kum. 3500 β (p. 451). Gomperz, Arch. Mitt. Oest. x (1886), p. 42.	"	"	dact.	..	2
69	Ross, Demen v. Attika, p. 101.	"	iv	el.	..	4
70	CIG. 747. IBM. I. 56.	"	iv–ii	el.	..	2
71	Bull. Arch. 1840, p. 104.	"	iv	el.	..	6
72	Kum. 3391 β.	"	"	hex.	..	1
73	" 2961. Köhler, Mittheilungen x (1885), p. 363.	"	v	el.	..	2
74	Kum. 305.	"	iv–ii	el. irr.	..	5
75	CIG. 749. IBM. I. 92.	"	iv–iii	el. irr.	..	3
76	Kum. 3264.	"	iv	hex.	..	2
77	" 3074. Ross, Arch. Aufs. II. p. 673.	"	iii	el.	..	4
78	Kum. 24.	"	iv–ii	hex.	..	4
79	" 3125.	"	"	hex.	+ t. t.	4
80	" 3498.	"	"	dact.	..	1+
81	" 254. Eph. 311.	"	"	hex. + el.	..	2.2
82	" 3484. Fleck. Jahrb. 1873, p. 810.	"	iv	el. ?	..	4

[1] In l. 2 [ἐν βιότωι γενεῆ]ν ἢ λιπα[ρῶι] προλιπών? Cp. nr. XXXVII.

[2] ἥδ' ἔθανε⟨ι⟩ν προλιποῦσα πόσιν καὶ μητ[έρα σεμνήν]
[κ]αὶ κλέος ἀθάνατον σωφροσύνης [ἔλαβεν].

ON GREEK VERSIFICATION IN INSCRIPTIONS.

Kaibel.	Elsewhere Published.	Place.	Age.	Metre.		Nr. Verses.
83[1]	Kum. 2777. Completer Brückner, *Ornament u. Form d. Att. Grabstelen*, p. 47.	Att.	iv–ii	el.	..	4
84	Kum. 3491.	"	"	el.	..	4
84 a RM[2]	Bull. Corr. II. p. 417.	"	iii	el. irr.	..	3
85	Kum. 3500.	"	iv–ii	el.	..	6
86	CIG. 3648. Kum. 2767.	"	iv	el.	..	4
87	Kum. 3153. Cp. Herwerden, Mnem. x, p. 387.	"	"	hex.	..	4
88	Kum. 2486.	"	iv–ii	el.	..	4.4
89	" 1651.	"	"	el.	..	8
90	" 1825.	"	iv	el. irr.	..	4
91	" 2856. Bull. Arch. 1841, p. 55.	"	"	el.	..	2
92	Arch. Zt. 1856, p. 141.	"	iv–ii	hex.	..	2
93	CIG. 2322 b. 42.	"	iv–iii.	..	i. t.	2
95[3]	Kekulé, Theseion, n. 358. Kum. 3151.	"	iii	el. irr.	..	7
96[4]	Kekulé, Theseion, n. 57. Kum. 1607.	"	iv–ii	el. irr.	..	6
179	IGA. 342.	Corcyra	vi	hex.	..	6
180	" 343.	"	"	hex.	..	3
181	" 344.	"	"	hex.	..	1
181a add.	CIG. 20. Better IGA. 340.	"	"	hex.	..	2
182	IGA. 329.	Anactorium	v	el.	..	2
183	CIG. 1914.	Corcyra	Mac.	el.	..	8

[1] οὐχὶ πέπλους οὐ χρυσὸν ἐθαύμασεν ἐμ βίωι ἥδε,
ἀλλὰ πόσιν τε αὐτῆς σωφροσύν[ην τ' ἐφίλει].
ἀντὶ δὲ σῆς ἥβης, Διονυσία, ἡλικίας τε
τόνδε τάφον κοσμεῖ σὸς πόσις 'Αντίφ[ιλος].

[2] 'Ηράκλ ει' ἐρατὴν προλι[ποῦσ' ἥβην ͵πόσιός τε]
[Φαίδρ]ου ἀποφθιμ[έ]νη μέγαρα π[ρ]ολιποῦσα με τέσχεν]
[κοιν]οῦ ἀνοικτίστη[s Περσεφό[νης θαλάμου.

[3] Nr. 94 is of Roman period, according to the copy in the BM, and falls out.

[4] On the reading of the second verse see p. 128, note. That the Phoenician merchant, who set up the monument, himself composed this epigram, is a very improbable supposition, nor are its peculiarities of language *barbarisms*, least of all οὔτηι, on which see G. Meyer, *Griech. Gramm.*[2] p. 396.

Kaibel.	Elsewhere Published.	Place.	Age.	Metre.		Nr. Verses.
184	CIG. 1886.	Corcyra	iii	el.	..	8
184 a RM[1]	Mittheilungen II. (1877), p. 290.	"	ii	el.	..	8
187	CIG. 1925.	Ithaca	Mac.	Arch. hept. + pentam.		4
188	IGA. 362.	Aegina	v	hex.	..	1
189	CIG. 2439.	Melos	iii	el.	..	10
197	Arch. Zt. 1844, p. 133.	Rhodes	iv–ii	el.	..	2
197 a add.	CIG. 2545.	"	Mac.	hex.	..	2
198	Ross, Inscr. ined. 281.	"	iv–ii	el.	..	2
203[2]	Newton, Disc. I. pl. 95, 58. Löwy 159.	Cnidos	iii–ii	dact.	..	4
205	Rev. Arch. 1864, II. p. 134. Cp. Herwerden, Mnem. x, p. 389.	Halicarnassus	ii	el.		8
210	Eph. 3248.	Ceos	iv–iii	..	i. t.	1
211	Lebas IV. 1896.	Syros	iii	hex.	+ i. t.	4
213	CIG. 2316.	Delos ?	iv–ii	hex.	..	2
214	Arch. Zt. 1851, p. 295.	Rhenea	iii	el.	..	8
219	CIG. Add. II. 2264 v.	Amorgos	iv	el.	..	2
220	Ann. Inst. 1864, p. 103.	Amorgos	"	el.	..	2
221	CIG. Add. II. 2264 w. Kaib. add. p. 519.	"	iv–iii	el.	..	2
225	CIG. 3026.	Ephesus	Mac.	el.	..	4
229 a RM[3]	Better IGA. 495.	Erythrae	vi	el.	..	2
234	Monatsber. Berl. Akad. 1874, p. 727.	Smyrna	iii	el.		6

[1] δοιαὶ μὲν δεκάδες σε τελειοτόκων ἐνιαυτῶν
ἤδη καὶ τριτάτου κύκλος ἐπεῖχεν ἔτευς
μισγομέναν φθιμένοισι, Φιλίστιον, ἄνικα πένθος
ματρὶ πολυθρήνωι κάλλιπες Ἁρπαλίδι,
δῶμα δ' Ἀριστάνδροιο λελονχότος ἄκριτον αἶ[σαν]
καὶ τέκεα κρυεραῖ θῆκας ἐν ὀρφανίαι,
Ἀγῆνος κλυτὸν αἷμα, σὲ δ' ὕστατον ὕπνον ἑλο[ῦσαν]
πικρὸς ὅδε ζοφεραῖ τύμβος ἔδεκ[το κόνει].

[2] Nr. 199 is omitted, on ground of the better copy in Bull. Corr. 1879, p. 44.

[3] . . . . τόδε σ[ῆ]μα μήτηρ ἐπέθηκε θανόντι
Φανο[κ]ρίτη παιδὶ χαριζομένη.

Kaibel.	Elsewhere Published.	Place.	Age.	Metre.		Nr. Verses.
235	Monatsber. Berl. Akad. 1874, p. 727.	Smyrna	iii	el.	..	4
239	CIG. 3326.	"	Mac.	el.	..	6
240	" 3328.	"	"	el.	..	8
242 [1]	" 2168. Bechtel, Collitz, Dial. n. 217.	Mytilene	"	el.	..	5+
246	Lebas V. 1145.	Bithyn.	"	..	i. t.	8
249	Wien. Akad. 1864 (XIII), p. 49.	Byzant.	"	el.	..	4
254	Lebas VII. 2802.	Cyprus	iv–iii	el.	..	4
255	CIG. 2613. IBM. II. 389.	"	"	el.	..	4
258	Ἀθήναιον, III. p. 22.	Alexandria	iii–ii	..	i. t.	9
260	CIG. 5362 b. Better Rev. Arch. 1886 (VII), p. 273.	Cyrenaica	ii	el.	..	6
461 a add.[2]	Lenormant, Rhein. Mus. xxi, p. 390, n. 230. IGA. 14.	Megara	vi	hex.	..	1
463 a add.	IGA. 15.	Corinth	"	hex.	..	1
466 [3]	CIG. 1141. New copy, Mittheil. IV. (1879), p. 158.	Argos	Mac.	el.		2
469	CIG. 1155.	"	"	el.	..	2
471 a add.	Mittheilungen I. (1876), p. 233.	Sparta	iv	el.	..	4
472	IGA. 54. Löwy 22.	"	vi	hex.	..	1 ?
484	" 765.	Tanagra	v	hex.	..	1
486	" 146.	Thespiae	"	el.	..	2
487	" 167.	Thisbe	"	el.	..	2
488	Hermes viii. p. 422.	Tanagra?	"	el.	..	4
489	Lebas III. 553.	Thebes	iv	el. + hex.		6.1
490	CIG. 1652.	"	Mac.	el. irr.		4
491	Missions Scientif. 1867, p. 498.	Orchom.	ii	el.		8

[1] The absence of ι in the dative ἀτρέστω is dialectic.
[2] The authenticity of this inscription is doubted by Kaibel and Roehl.
[3] From a comparison of Milchhoefer's new copy with the older ones of Fourmont and Lebas, it seems probable that the first line should read ... σόθεν ἥδε ἐλθόντ' ἀπυ[τῆλ]ε κέκευθ[εν].

Kaibel.	Elsewhere Published.	Place.	Age.	Metre.		Nr. Verses.
492	Rev. Arch. 1875, I. p. 110. Löwy 93 a.	Thebes	iv	el.	..	6
492 b prf.	Rev. Arch. 1875, I. p. 110. Better Löwy 93 b.	"	"	el.		4
505 [1]	Rev. Arch. 1844, I. p. 315.	Tricca	iii	el.	..	4
519	Better Lolling, Mittheil. VII (1882), p. 225.	Thessalonica	Mac.	el.	..	6
521	CIG. 1966.	"	"	hex.	..	3
552 a add.	" 6314.	unknown (Rome?)	"	el.	..	6
738	CIA. I. 355.	Att.	vi	hex.	..	1
739	" " 343.	"	"	hex.	..	1
740	CIG. 3. IGA. 412. Löwy 5.	Melos	"	el.	..	2
741	CIA. I. 332.	Att.	"	hex.?	..	2
742	CIG. I. IGA. 314.	Crissa	"	hex.	..	2
743	IGA. 75, with add. p. 174.	Olympia (Lacon.)	"	el.	..	2
743 a prf.	CIA. IV. 373 e.	Att.	"	el.	..	2
744	IGA. 95. Löwy 30 b, c.	Olympia	v	el.	..	4
745	CIG. 16. IGA. 510.	Olympia (Syrac.)	"	..	log.[2]	3
746	CIG. 29. IGA. 32.	Olympia (Argos)	"		i. t.	1
747	IGA. 70.	Delphi (Lacon.)	"	hex.	..	1
748	CIA. I. 334.	Att.	"	el.	..	4
749	" " 333.	"	"	el.	..	5 +
750	CIG. 24. IGA. 402. Completer Arch. Zt. 1882, p. 391. Löwy 6.	Paros	"	el. + hex.	..	2.1
750 a add.	IGA. 401.	"	"	el.	..	4
751	CIA. I. 403. Löwy 47.	Att.	"	el.	+ i. t.	2.1
752	" " 374. Löwy 40.	"	"	el.	..	4
753	" " 397.	"	"	el.	..	4
754	" " 382.	"	"	el.	..	2

[1] 504 I omit: it seems not to be verse. See Fick in Bezz. Beitr. v. p. 10, and in Collitz, Dial. n. 335.

[2] According to Roehl, prose and a hexameter.

ON GREEK VERSIFICATION IN INSCRIPTIONS.

Kaibel.	Elsewhere Published.	Place.	Age.	Metre.		Nr. Verses.
755	CIA. I. 350.	Att.	v	dact.	..	2?
756	" " 349.	"	"	el.	..	2
756 a	Bull. Corr. III. 134. IGA.	Plataeae	"	hex.	..	2
RM¹	143. Löwy 44.					
757	CIG. 1592. IGA. 148.	Thisbe	"	hex.	..	1
757 a prf.	IGA. 284.	"	"	el.	..	2
758	CIA. I. 381.	Att.	"	el.	..	2
759	IGA. 349. Löwy 48.	Att. (Abdera)	"	el.+pent.	..	2.1
760	CIA. I. 398.	Att.	"	hex.	..	1
761	CIG. 2138 d. IGA. 354.	Aegina	"	el.	..	2
762	CIA. I. 431.	Att.	"	..	i. t.	1
763	" " 418. Löwy 42.	"	"	el.	..	2?
764	" " 414.	"	"	dact.	..	2?
765	" " 353 and add. Löwy 36.	"	"	el.	..	2
766	CIA. I. 347.	"	"	dact.	..	2?
767	" " 354.	"	"	dact.	..	?
768	CIG. 4269 and add. vol. III. p. 1122.	Xanthus	iv	el. irr.	..	12
768 a prf.	Bull. Corr. I. 351.	Thebes	iv–iii	el.	..	6
769	Better Löwy 59.	Erythrae	iv	el.	..	2
770	Eph. 22.	Att.	"	el.	..	2
771	Arch. Zt, 1872, p. 20. Löwy 62.	"	"	dact.	..	4
772	CIG. 2156. IBM. I. 58.	Imbros	iv–ii	hex.	..	3
773	" 2104.	Panticapaeum	Mac.	el.	..	4
773 a RM²	Ἀθήναιον, VI. p. 371.	Att.	iv	el.	..	4

¹ [Δ]αματρο[ς] τόδ᾽ ἄγαλμα . . . .
ἐνθάδε γ᾽ [εἰ]σοράοντι σέ[βας θέσαν ἀνέρες οἵδε].

So Kaibel; γ[ά]ς ὁράοντι σε[βάσμιον] Löwy; γ᾽ [εἰ]σοράων τίς ἔ[τευξεν] ἐρεῖς Foucart.

² This epigram must have run somewhat thus:

[. . . . . . Με]νανδ[ρος . . . . . . ὤλισθεν]
[ἠλιβάτ]ων πετρῶν ἡγεμόνο˙ς χατέων].
[πημοσυνῶ]ν σωθεὶς δέ, Ἀσκληπιέ, τό[νδε λέβητα]
[θῆκε σὸ]ν εἰς τέμενος · τῶι δίδου ε[ὐπορίαν].

Kaibel.	Elsewhere Published.	Place.	Age.	Metre.		Nr. Verses.
773 b RM¹	'Αθήναιον, VI. p. 137. Mittheilungen II (1877), p. 241.	Att.	iv–iii	hex.	..	4
774	Ross, Arch. Aufs. II. p. 582.	Priene	"	el.	..	6
775	CIG. 4702.	Egypt	iv	hex.	..	1 +
775 a RM²	Carapanos, *Dodone*, plate 22.	Dodona	Mac.	..	lyr.	8?
776	Ross, Arch. Aufs. I. p. 83.	Att.	iii–ii	hex.	..	4
777	CIG. 408.	Salamis	iv–ii	hex.	..	2
778	Ross, Inscr. ined., 298. Löwy 467. See Dittenberger, Hermes XIII. p. 393; Herwerden, Mnem. x, p. 393.	Calymna	"	hex.	..	2
779	CIG. 3797.	Chalcedon	Mac.	el.		8
780	Conze, *Lesbos*, pl. v. 2.	Mytilene	iv–ii	dact.	..	4
781	Newton, *Disc.* I. pl. 90, 29.	Cnidos	iii	el.	..	12
782	" " " 96, 65.	Halicarn.	iii–ii	el.	..	6
783	" " " 90, 31.	Cnidos	iv–ii	..	i. t. + t. t.	2.4
784	Comp. Kaibel's pref. IGA. 551.	Antipolis	v	hex.	..	2
785	Newton, *Disc.* I. pl. 89, 15.	Cnidos	ii	el. irr.		4
786	CIG. 2661.	Halicarn.	"	el.		6
789 ³	" 2037.	Constantinople.	iv–ii	hex.		1

¹ .... ος σ' ίέρωσε Ἀσσκληπιῶι ἠδὲ ὁμοβώμοις
πρῶτος ἰδρυσάμενος θυσίαις θείαις ὑποθήκαις.
σαῖς ὑποθημοσ[ύναις . . . .]
Βωμὸν τόνδ' ἐπό[ησε . . . .]

² Ζεῦ Δωδώνης μεδέων
τόδε σοι δῶρ ιν πέμπω παρ' ἐμοῦ,
Ἀγάθων Ἐχεφύλου καὶ γενεά,
πρόξενοι Μυλοσσῶν
καὶ συμμάχων
ἐν τριάκοντα γενεαῖς
ἐκ Τρώιας Κασσάνδρας γενεά,
Ζακύνθιοι.

³ Nrs. 787 and 788, together with others of the same group since published, seem too late for our purpose: see especially Kumanudes in 'Αθήν. VII. p. 282.

ON GREEK VERSIFICATION IN INSCRIPTIONS.

Kaibel.	Elsewhere Published.	Place.	Age.	Metre.	Nr. Verses.
790	Rang. 2218.	Dyme	iii	t. t.	8+
799	CIG. 1946. Better Wolters, Rhein. Mus. xli, p. 346.	unknown	iii–ii	el.	2
809	CIG. Add. II. 1837 d.	Pharos	ii	hex.	1
844	See Kaibel's Add. CIA. II. 555.	Att.	iv	el. irr.	4
845	See Kaibel's Add. CIG. 411, and Add.	"	iii–ii	el.	4
846	Ross, Arch. Aufs. II. p. 662.	Argos	iv	el.	6
849 [1]	Lebas II. 890.	Delphi	iv–iii	el.	4+
850	Ross, Arch. Aufs. I. p. 174. Löwy 75.	Att.	"	el. irr.	4
851	Better Löwy 170.	Rhodes	iii	el.	6
852	CIG. 666 and add. Better Löwy 224.	Att.	ii	el.	8
854 [2]	CIG. 2308.	Delos	"	el.	4
855	Ἀθήναιον, I. p. 484.	Atalante	iii	el.	10
856	Rhein. Mus. xxvii, p. 614.	"	Mac.	el.	2
856 a prf.[3]	Bull. Corr. I. p. 120.	Hypate	"	el.	8
857	Ross, Arch. Aufs. II. p. 609.	Rhodes	"	el.	4
858	CIG. 2884.	Miletus	iv–ii	el.	6
859 [4]	Lebas V. 243.	Tichiussa	"	el.	8
860	CIG. 2221.	Chios	iii–ii	el.	6
875 a add.	Better Fränkel, Arch. Zt. 35 (1877), p. 43.	Olympia	iv	el.	44
923	CIA. I. 493.	Att.	v	el.	4
924	Better Löwy 533.	"	iii–ii	el.	4
925	Lebas I. 85. Correcter Köhler, Mitth. VII (1882), p. 348.	"	iv	hex.	4
926	CIG. 1212.	Hermione	iii	el.	16
932	Lebas VI. 1866 a. Löwy 167.	Sidon	"	el.	12
936	CIG. 17. Lebas II. 108. IGA. 37.	Argos	v	hex.	2

---

[1] 847 and 848 omitted: see Dittenberger CIA. III. n. 947 and 948.
[2] 853 (CIA. III. 779) omitted.
[3] The third verse should apparently end Λάτυια φιλόπλου s].
[4] At end of verse 7: Νικιάδο[υ παῖς]?

Kaibel.	Elsewhere Published.	Place.	Age.	Metre.	Nr. Verses.
936 a RM[1]	Mittheil. II (1877), p. 434. IGA. 62.	Lacon.	v	hex.	5+
937[2]	Rang. 992.	Aphidna	iv–ii	dact.	5+
938	See Kaibel's Pref. Better Löwy 119.	Tanagra	iv	el.	4
938 a prf.	Löwy 120.	Thebes	"	el.	6
940	Eph. 179.	Att.	"	el.	2
940 a RM[3]	IGA. 388. Löwy 23.	Olympia (Samos)	v	el.	2
941	Bull. Acad. St. Petersb. 1859, XVI. p. 98.	Att.	iii	hex.	3
941 b RM[4]	Arch. Zt. 36 (1878), p. 84. Löwy 126.	Olympia	"	el.	6

[1] Röhl thus:

['Αλκιμάχω τάνδ' εἰκόν' ἔνεστ' ἀγαθῶ καὶ ἀγαυῶ]
[ἀνδ]ρὸς ἀθρῆν · δ[ιαμιλλαθὴς δ' ἤδη τε θί]γ' αὐτός
νίκας [καὶ θορύβως κατὰ τρα]χυτάτως ἐδ[αμάσθη.]
[οἰχομένωι δ]ὲ χαριζόμεν[ος στᾶσεν τόδε σᾶμα]
ἐνθάδε παῖς Π[ολυκλῆς · ἀλλ' ἴλαθι τ]ῶι καί ἑ εὔφρων
[δέξο, ϝάναξ ἐνέρων,] Διὸς αἰγιόχ[ω κάσι σεμνέ].

[2] Probably in elegiacs and so distributed:

. . . .
. . . . ν [τ'] ἀναδεξάμενοι
. . . . [Οἰ]νῆος ἐν ἄστει
πάντη ἐπ . . . .
καὶ δολιχοκροτάφου ν . . . .
ΦΥΙΟΥ τε στάδιον ΕΩΣ . . . . ˙ . . .
. . . . πουν . . . νεσ . . λ . .

[3] Εὔθυμος Λοκρὸς Ἀστυκλέος τρὶς Ὀλύμπι' ἐνίκων,
εἰκόνα δ' ἔστησεν τήνδε βροτοῖς ἐσορᾶν.

[4] ὧδε στὰς ὁ Πελασγὸς ἐπ' Ἀλφειῶι ποκα πύκτας
τὸμ Πολυδεύκειογ χερσὶν ἔφανε νόμον.
ἆμος ἐκαρύχθη νικαφόρος · ἀλλὰ πάτερ Ζεῦ,
καὶ πάλιν Ἀρκαδίαι καλὸν ἄμειβε κλέος,
τίμασον δὲ Φίλιππον, ὃς ἐνθάδε τοὺς ἀπὸ νάσων
τέσσαρας εὐθείαι παῖδας ἔκλινε μάχαι.

Kaibel.	Elsewhere Published.	Place.	Age.	Metre.		Nr. Verses.
941 c RM[1]	IGA. 99, add. p. 175. Löwy 50.	Olympia	v	el.	..	2
942 a RM[2]	Arch. Zt. 36 (1878), p. 83. Löwy 90.	Olympia (*Maenalos*)	iv	el.	..	2
1033	Kum. 3482.	Att.	iii	hex.	..	23+
1037	Better Journal Hell. Studies III. p. 111.	Petilia	ii	hex.	..	11+
1042	CIA. I. 522.	Att.	vi	hex.	..	1
1043	CIG. 525.	"	iv	el.	..	4
1097	CIG. 10. Better IGA. 409.	Delos	vi	..	i. t.	1
1098	Better IGA. 410. Löwy 7.	Orchom.	vi-v	hex.	..	1
1098 a RM[3]	Completer IGA. 12, add. p. 169. Löwy 25.	Olympia (*Melos*)	"	dact.	+ i. t.	2.1
1099	CIG. 8154.	vase	v	..	i. t.	1
1100	Benndorf, *Vasenbilder* XXVIII. n. 24.	"	"	hex.	..	1
1130		"	vi	..	i. t.	2
1131	IGA. 588.	lamp	iv?	pent.	..	1
1132	CIG. 545.	vase	iv-ii	.	iamb. tetr.	2
1133	Monum. ined. II. pl. 44 b.	"	v?	..	i. t. catal.	2
1134	Ann. inst. 1864, p. 183, 197.	"	v-iv	hex.	..	1
1135	CIG. 8429. Heydemann, *Vasensammlung*, n. 2868.	"	Mac.	el.	..	2
1136	Eph. 1869. Kum. 2583.	Att.	iii-ii	el.?	..	5

[1] πύ[κ]τα[ς τόν]δ' ἀνέθηκεν ἀπ' εὐδόξοιο Κυνίσκος
Μαντινέας νικῶν, πατρὸς ἔχων ὄνομα.

[2] Μαινάλιος Ξενοκλῆς νίκασα Εὐθύφρονος υἱός,
ἁπτὴς μουνοπαλᾶν τέσ(σ)αρα σώμαθ' ἑλών.

[3] With Röhl's supplements :
Θρασυμάχου παῖδες τοῦ Μαλί[ου ἐν Μεγαρεῦσι]
τῶι Δὶ Δαίαλκος καὶ [Στρατυκλῆς] με [ἀνέθεν].
γρόφων ἐποίει Μάλιος Κα[βειροκλ]ῆς.
But I incline to think that Γρόφων, both here and in n. 740, is the artist's name.

B.—INSCRIPTIONS NOT IN KAIBEL'S COLLECTIONS.

I.

Att. (Eleusis) vi, bustrophedon. Philios in Eph. 1883, p. 190. On an ἀλτήρ.

ἀλ(λ)όμενος νίκησεν Ἐπαίνετος οὕνεκα τοῦδε
HA . . . .

II.

Att. vi-v. Mylonas Eph. 1883, p. 35.

. . . . ἀνέθηκε Τύχανδρος
. . . . ἀπαρχὴν τἀθηναίαι.

III.

Att. vi-v. Kum. in Ἀθήναιον, VII, p. 386. Löwy 419. Not certain that verse.

. . . καλλίμαχος . . .
. . . . σοφίαι.

IV.

Att. vi-v. Mylonas in Bull. Corr. 1879, p. 179. If verse, to be restored somewhat thus:

[ἀνδρὸς φιλτά]του Εὐθυμάχου Ναυσιστράτου εἰμί.

V.

Att. vi. Köhler in Mittheilungen VII (1882), p. 222. (A part, inaccurately, in CIA. IV, 373 x.)

. . . νης καὶ παῖδες Ἀ[θηνα]ίαι τοδ' ἄγ[αλμα]
[στήσανθ']· ἣ δ' αὐ[τοῖς εὔφρ]ονα θ[υμ]ὸ[ν ἔχοι].

VI.

Att. vi, bustrophedon. CIA. I, 344 (cp. IV, p. 40). Löwy 9. Recognized as verse by Benndorf.

[. . . . μ'] ἀνέθηκ[εν · Ἀ]ριστοκλῆς ἐπόησεν.

VII.

Att. vi-v. CIA. I, 352. Löwy 420.

. . . . ὁ Χολαργ[εύς]
· [. . . . . εἰργασ]μένος ἔργον
[. . . . . ἀνέθηκ]εν ἀπαρχήν.

VIII.

Att. vi. Kabbadias in Eph. 1886, p. 79, n. 1. My supplements.

'Αλκίμαχος μ' ἀ‚νέθηκε Διὸς γλαυκώπιδι κούρηι]
εὐχωλὴν ἐσθλοῦ δ[αίμονος ἐκτελέων].

IX.

Att. vi. Kabbadias in Eph. 1886, p. 81, n. 4.

Νέαρχος ἀν[έθηκε . . . . . . υἱ]ὺς ἔργων ἀπαρχήν.
'Αντήνωρ ἐπ[όησεν] ὁ Εὐμάρους τ[όδ' ἄγαλμα].

The second inscription is verse. Kabbadias Εὐμάρου στ . . . . But the name Εὔμαρος is improbable, and the text of Pliny (xxxv, 34) is an insufficient guarantee for it.

X.

Att. vi; leftward. Unpublished. Acropolis 1886. Dedication in one elegiac distich; artist's inscription in one hexameter.

XI.

Att. vi. Unpublished. Acropolis 1886. Dedication in two hexameters and the beginning of another verse.

XII.

Att. vi. Unpublished. Acropolis 1886. Dedication in one hexameter (or two?) and prose addition.

XIII.

Att. vi. Unpublished. Acropolis 1886. Dedication. Parts of two hexameters, with artist's inscription in prose.

XIV.

Att. vi. Unpublished. Acropolis 1886. Dedication in elegiac distich; ends of lines.

XV.

Att. vi. Unpublished. Acropolis 1886. Ends of two hexameters; the second the artist's inscription. Not quite certain that verse.

XVI.

Att. vi. Unpublished. Acropolis 1886. Dedication. Parts of a hexameter.

XVII.

Att. vi. Yard of Central Museum. Bottoms of letters. Less correct Kum.
3476.

σὲ μένει θάνατος or σὲ μὲν εὐθάνατος.

XVIII.

Att. v. CIG. 913. CIA. IV, 477 e.

[ἤδ' εἰκ]ὼν ἔστ[ηκ]εν 'Αμεινίου· ἔστι δὲ ἀ[ρ' αὐτῶι]
[μνῆμα δικαιοσύν]ης εἵνεκα καὶ γενεᾶς.

XIX.

Att. v. CIA. IV, 486.

'Αντίου (or [Μ]αντίου, [Φ]αντίου) τόδε σῆ[μα].

XX.

Att. v. CIA. IV, 373 x.

....νης καὶ παῖδες ἄμεμ[πτοι]
... ἢ δ' αὐτοῖς ....

XXI.

Att. vi–v. Mylonas in Eph. 1883, p. 35.

τόνδε Φίλων ἀν[έθηκεν] 'Αθηναίαι τριποδίσκον
θαύμασι νικήσας [ἐ]ς πόλιν 'Αρεσίου.

XXII.

Att. iv. Kumanudes in Eph. 1883, p. 22.

δόξα μὲν Ἑλλήνων ἱεροῖς ἀναθήμασιν αὔξει
τόνδε, τέχνης δ' εἰκὼν ἥδε δίδωσι κρίσι[ν].
νικήσας δὲ ἵππων τε δρόμοις ἔργων τε ἐν ἁμίλλα[ις]
τὴν ἱερὰν στεφανοῖ πατρίδα Κεκροπίαν.

'Ιλίεια   Κλάρια   Ἐφέσεια
συνωρίδ[ι].   ἵππωι.   ἵππωι.

XXIII.

Att. iv. Dragatzes in Eph. 1884, p. 48. Köhler, Mittheilungen IX (1884), p. 284.

τόνδε νεώ σοι, ἄναξ, Διονύσιος εἴσατο τῆιδε
καὶ τέμενος θυόεν καὶ ξόαν' εἰκελά σοι,
καὶ πάντ', οὐ πλοῦτον κρίνας πολυάργυρον αὔξειν
ἐν δόμωι, ὡς τὸ σέβειν, Βάκχε, τὰ σοὶ νόμιμα.
[ἀ]νθ' ὧν, ὦ Διόνυσ'. ὢν ἴλαος. οἶκον ἅμ' αὐτοῦ
[καὶ] γενεὴν σώιζοις πάντα τε σὸν θίασον.

XXIV.

Att. iv-iii. Meletopulos in Eph. 1884, p. 65.

(a) πλεῖστομ μὲν καὶ ζῶσα [τ]ρόπων σῶν ἔσχες ἔπαινον,
Λυσάνδρου Πιθέως Ἀρχεστράτη ἔγγονε, καὶ νῦ[ν]
[λ]είπεις σοῖσι φίλοισι μέγαν πόθον, ἔξοχα δ' αὐτῆς
ἀνδρί, λιποῦσα φάος μοιριδίωι θανάτωι.

(b) εὐσεβῆ ἀσκήσασα βίον καὶ σώφρονα θνήισκω
ἡνίκα μοι βιοτοῦ μόρσιμον ἦλθε τέλος.

(c) πένθος μητρὶ λιποῦσα κασιγνήτωι τε πόσει τε
παιδί τ' ἐμῶι θνήισκω καί με χθὼν ἥδε καλύπτει,
ἣ πᾶσιν κοινὴ τοῖς ἀπογιγνομένοις.
εἰμὶ δὲ Λυσάνδρου Πιθέως Ἀρχεστράτη ἥδε.

XXV.

Att. iv. Kumanudes Ἀθήναιον III, p. 595. (O = ου.)

Ἄρχιππος Σκαμβωνίδης

εἴ τις ἐν ἀνθρώποις ἀρετῆς ἕνεκ' ἐστεφανώθη
πλεῖστον ἐγὼ μετέχων τοῦδ' ἔτυχον στεφάν[ου]
χρυσοῦ· Ἀθηναίων δὲ ἐστεφάνωσε πόλις.
εὐδαίμων δὲ ἔθυνον, παίδων παῖδας καταλείπω[ν].

XXVI.

Att. iv. Köhler, Mittheilungen x (1885), p. 404. Bull. Corr. 1886, p. 162.

Γῆρυς ἰσοτελής. Νικὼ Γήρυος γυνή. Θεόφιλος ἰσοτελής.

εἰ τὸ καλῶς ἐστὶ θανεῖν κἀμοὶ τοῦτ' ἀπένειμε τύχη
οὐδὲ φάος λεύσ(σ)ων ὅγε δαίμοσιν ἦν ἀγέραστος,
πᾶσιν δ' ἀνθρώποισι παρέσχον ἀνέγκλητον ἐμαυτό[ν].
ἔντιμον χθονίοισι θεοῖς ὑπεδέξατο γαῖα.

See pp. 38 and 47.

καὶ ἐγὼ τοῦδ᾽ ἀνδρὸς ἔφυν καὶ πάντα ὅμοια
γήραι καὶ φροντίδι εὐσεβίας ἕνεκα.

XXVII.

Att. iv. Bull. Corr. 1880, p. 131. (O = ου, E = ει.)

Λήμνου ἀπ᾽ ἠγαθέας κεύθει τάφος ἐνθάδε γαίας
ἄνδρα φιλοπρόβατον· Νικόμαχος δ᾽ ὄνομα.

XXVIII.

Att. iv. Mylonas in Bull. Corr. 1879, p. 359. (O = ου.)

τοὺς ἀγαθοὺς ἔστερξεν Ἄρης, ἐφίλησε δ᾽ ἔπαινος
καὶ γήραι νεότης οὐ παρέδωχ᾽ ὑβρίσαι·
ὧν καὶ Γ[λ]αυκιάδης δήμους ἀπὸ πατρίδος εἴργω[ν]
ἦλθ᾽ ἐπ[ὶ] πάνδεκτον Φερσεφόνης θάλαμον.

XXIX.

Att. v. Köhler in Mittheilungen x (1885), p. 402.

|σῆμα τόδ᾽ Ἐρχ]σ[εμέ]νε[ι πα]τὴρ Κάλλαισχρος ἔ[θηκεν].

XXX.

Att. iv. Köhler in Mittheilungen x (1885), p. 405.

γηραιὰν ἄνοσον, παῖδας παίδων ἐπιδοῦσαν,
Λύσιλλαν κατέχει κοινοταφὴς θάλαμος.

XXXI.

Att. iv. Köhler in Mittheilungen VII (1882), p. 222.

[Φιλ]ιδιμίδης ἀνέθηκεν Ἀθηναίαι τόδ᾽ ἄγαλμα
υὸς Πρωτάρχου Προβαλίσιος, ὧι σὺ δὸς ὄλβον
αὐτῶι καὶ παισὶν τοῖς τ᾽ ἐπιγιγνομένοι[ς].

XXXII.

Att. iv. Παρνασσός 1882, p. 250. (O = ου.)

Βελτίστη Νουμηνίου Ἡρακλειῶτις.

μητέρα ἔθηκα ὁπίως ὁσίαν τοῖς πᾶσιν ἰδέσθαι,
ἀνθ᾽ ὧν εὐλογίας καὶ ἐπαίνων ἄξιός εἰμι.

XXXIII.

Att. iv (?). CIG. 1041. Kum. 3486. IBM. 1, 132. Στοιχηδόν. χ in v. 2 is noted as certain by Hicks.

. . . . οτιων . . . .
. . . . . . [σο]φία[ν] δ' ἔτ' ἔχειν (?)
. . . . πατρὸς ἡνίκα τένξη
. . . . ὧν ἔτυχεν.

XXXIV.

Att. iv–iii. Kumanudes in 'Αθήναιον III, p. 596.

εἴ τινα γῆ κατέχει χρηστήν, καὶ τήνδε γυναῖκα,
οὐδεμιᾶς θνητῆς λειπομένην ἀρετῆι·
εὐδαίμων δ' ἔλιπεν βίοτον καὶ πᾶσι ποθεινή.
. . . φίλη . . . [β]ούλου. Ξανθιππίδης Σκαμβωνίδης.

XXXV.

Att. iv. Unpublished. Yard Central Museum. (O = ου.)

ἐργ[ά]τις οὖσα γυνὴ φειδωλός τε ἐνθάδε κεῖμαι.
Νικαρέτη.

XXXVI.

Att. iii–ii. Bull. Corr. 1884, p. 470.

. . . . . ἥ]ρως οὗτος ἀρήϊον ἔργον ἀνύσσας
. . . . . . μέζων τοῦτο Λεωνίδεω·
ἄμφω γὰρ πάτρησιν ἀμύνετον [α]ἴμ[α]τ[ι . . .
ἀλλ' ὃ μὲν ἐν βαιοῖς ο[ἴκ]ε[ε . . .]σίο[ις]
. . . .
. . . .
ὁ συντραφείς μοι προυνόησέ μου [καλῶς].

In the fourth line the editor gives ο ἴχ ε ται] ἥ'λυ]σίο[ις], but questions it himself. Obviously the poet is contrasting the humble home of this hero with the Sparta of Leonidas. The sense requires something like ᾤκεε Θριασίοις (or Τειθρασίοις, Φυλασίοις). The iambic verse I venture to fill out with καλῶς, although the copy indicates no break.

XXXVII.

Att. (Rhamnus) iv–ii. Lolling, Mittheilungen IV (1879), p. 282. The use of a completer copy, made by Löwy, was kindly granted me by Professor Köhler. Supplements mine.

[τρισσῶν δὴ στε]ίχων ἀτραπόν. ξένε, φράζεο σῆμα
[αὐτοκασ]ιγνήτων οἳ γενεὴν ἔλιπον·
[ὧν ἄρ' ἐγ]ὼν [ἔμ]ολ[ο]ν πύματος βασίλεια Ἀΐδαο.
[ἐν βίωι] ἃ λιπαρῶι θυμὸν ἀποπρολιπών.

XXXVIII.

Att. iv-ii. Köhler, Mittheilungen II (1877), p. 246. Ἀθήναιον v, p. 161.
Not certain that verse.

. . . . της
ἥρωι εὐξ[άμενος . . . ἀνέθηκε]ν ἀπαρχήν.

XXXIX.

Att. iv. Philios, Ἀθήναιον v, p. 321. Löwy 73.

Ἀσκληπιῶ[ι] Κιχήσιππος Διον[υσίου] Ἀνακαιεὺς ἀνέ[θηκεν]. Στρατ-
ωνίδης ἐπόη[σεν].
. . . . . . τοῦ χαλεποῦ δο . . . .
. . . . . . ος δῶρον θεῶι . . . . .

XL.

Att. Mac. Yard of Central Museum. Unpublished?

. . . . μοῖραι τ' ἐλεεινό[ν]
. . . . ων γῇ κατέχει φθίμε[νον].

XLI.

Att. Mac. Central Museum. Kum. 3481, not quite correctly. I use my own copy. Supplements uncertain.

μνῆμα τό[δ' εὔτυκ]τον θνητ[ῶν ἡγή]τορος ἀν[δρῶν],
Εὐκτίτο[υ, ὃν θάνα]τος ἐξαν[ιόντα πλα]νῶν
βλαψίφ[ρων ἔκιχ', ἤ]σχαλ[λεν . . . .

XLII.

Oropus iii. Unpublished. Mentioned by Löwy, p. xxii ("zu 135 a"). I am indebted to Mr. Leonardos for the use of his copy and squeeze. A connected passage of three verses could be read with an approach to assurance. In all there were at least four distichs. The speedy publication of this inscription in the Ἐφημερίς may be hoped for.

XLIII.

Salamis, iv-iii. Bull. Corr. 1882, p. 534.

[π]άντων ὧν θέμις ἐστὶ τυχεῖν εὐδαίμοσι θνητοῖς.
[ζ]ῶσά τε ἐκοινώνουν, καὶ φθιμένη μ[ετ]έχω.
ἡλικίας δὲ πόθον νεαρᾶς μνήμην τε λιποῦσα
σωφροσύνης ἔθ[υ]νον, Λογχὶς ἐπωνυμίαν.

XLIV.

Aegina, vi. IGA. 356. Complete.

Ἐγδήλου τόδε σᾶμα.

XLV.

Aegina, v. IGA. 360. Compare Cauer, *Delectus* (2d ed.), n. 69; Meister, *Jahrb. für Philol.*, 1882, p 525. One line of prose precedes.

[τόνδ'] Ἄβων λίθον [ἔ]στασες σκοπὸν ἀγ[ροῦ, ὀδῖτα].

So Roehl. See p. 160 Meister [ἔ]στασ' ἐς σκοπόν; Cauer [ἔ]στασε σκοπόν. — The absence of medial caesura (see p. 48) does not seem necessary. We may suppose, for instance, [τόνδ'] Ἄβων λίθον [ὧδε κατέ]στασες σκοπὸν ἀγ[ροῦ], or [ἐνθάδε τόνδ'] Ἄβων λίθον [ἔ]στασες σκοπὸν ἀγ[ροῦ].

XLVI.

Euboea, v. IGA. 7. Roehl so:

[κρά]νιθ' Ὁδίτηι [ἀρωγοὶ ἐέλδωρ, ὅ]ς μ' ἐποίησεν,
τόνδε β[όλον, ξυν]θαὶ Σιράδες, εὐξάμ[ενος].

XLVII.

Artemision, Euboea, iv-ii. Lolling, Mittheilungen, VIII (1883), p. 202.

. . . . αι πυρρίχηι ἄθλω
. . . . πα]ρ[θ]ένον Ἀ[γρ]οτέρ[αν].

XLVIII.

Chalcis, Mac. Lolling, Mittheilungen x (1885). p. 283.

γήραϊ δή, Κλεόνικε, λιπὼν βίον αἰνετὸς ἀστοῖς
κεῖσαι τόνδε μέγαν τύμβον ἐφεσσάμενος.
[Φ]ειδία ἐκγεγαώς, λιπαρὸς δὲ τὸ κ[ᾶδ]ος ὀπίσσω,
παίδων τε ἀκμαία λείπεται ἁλικία.
Κλεόνικος Φειδίου.

v. 3 ΚΛΙΟΣ, Lolling κλ'έ]ος.

XLIX.

Ceos, vi. IGA. 393. Roehl thus:

[εἰκόν' 'Αθη]ναίης χρυσαιγίδεος ὀβριμ[οπάτρης]
[τήνδ' ἐθέτην τόσ]σην Στω[μύ]λος 'Α[λκι]δάμας.
[ὧδε θεῶν προῦσ]τη, φηρῶν [δὲ με]μαότα φῦλα
|ἔγχεϊ γηγενέων δάμ]νατ' [ἀλεξομένη].

Kirchhoff's supplements, who however reads in v. 2 [ἄνθετο τὴν χρυ]σῆν Στώ[λι]ος 'Α[ντιδ]άμας.

L.

Delos. vi. Arch. Zt. 37 (1879), p. 84. IGA. 408.

Δειναγόρας μ' ἀνέθηκεν ἐκηβόλωι 'Απόλλωνι.
[δε]κά[τη].

LI.

Delos, ii. Bull. Corr. 1883, p. 331.

Ἡρακλεῖ τόδ' ἄγαλμα Κροβίλου παῖς ἀνέθηκ[εν]
Ἄσπασις Ἰνωποῦ γείτονι καλλιρόου.

LII.

Delos, iii–ii. Homolle, Rev. Arch. 1884 (3me série, vol. IV), p. 215. Löwy 122, Nachtrag (p. 385). A part of these readings Homolle does not himself vouch for.

Δήλιοι ἱδρύσ[αντο] . . . . ΟΛΙΟ
ἔργα ΤΛΙΞΕΙ . . . . ι Πολυκρ . . .
εἰκόνι σ . . . . χαριου πατρὸς ον . . .
ἔργων ἀθανάτων τήνδε ἀνέθεντο θεοῖς.
Θοινίας Τειπικράτου.

LIII.

Delos, ii. Homolle in Monuments grecs, 1879, p. 44. Löwy 147.

ὦ μάκαρ, ὦ Φιλέταιρε, σὺ καὶ θείοισιν ἀοιδοῖς
καὶ πλάστηισιν, ἄναξ, εὐπαλάμοισι μέλεις.
οἳ τὸ σὸν ἐξενέπουσι μέγα κράτος, οἳ μὲν ἐν ὕμνοις,
οἳ δὲ χερῶν τέχναις δεικνύμενοι σφετέρων.
ὥς ποτε δυσπολέμοις Γαλάταις θοὸν Ἄρεα μείξας
ἤλασας οἰκείων πολλὸν ὕπερθεν ὅρων·
ὧν ἕνεκεν τάδε σοι Νικηράτου ἔκκριτα ἔργα
Σωσικράτης Δήλωι θῆκεν ἐν ἀμφιρύτηι.

LIV.

Delos, *Naxos*, vi. Bull. Corr. 1879, p. 3. Arch. Zt. 37 (1879), p. 85. IGA. 407. Löwy 430. Bustrophedon.

Νικάνδρη μ' ἀνέθηκεν ἐκηβόλωι ἰοχεαίρηι
ϟούρη Δεινοδίκεω τοῦ Ναξίου, ἔξοχος ἀλ(λ)έων.
Δεινομένεος δὲ κασιγνήτη, 'Φράξου δ' ἄλοχος μ[ήν].

At the end, Homolle assumes μ̞ε and another line; Gomperz μ[ε] as 'anadiplosis.'

LV.

Naxos, vi. Bull. Corr. 1885, p. 494. Section of a column, the inscription running up and down in 17 lines. No connected reading is possible from this copy. The end seems to be τοῦδ' Αἴσχρος καὶ 'Αθήνηι. The editor suggests also ἐπὶ σῆμ[α˙ l. 1, [ἀμ]ύνεεν l. 14. One might add σὺν ἧσιν or κ[αλλο]σύνησιν, end of l. 15; ... τι ἐῆς φυ[λῆς] l. 10.

LVI.

Amorgos, vi. Kumanudes in Eph. 1884, p. 86. Bustrophedon.

Δημαινέτης εἰμὶ μνῆμα τῆς Λαμψαγόρεω.

LVII.

Amorgos, vi. Mittheilungen XI (1886), p. 97. Leftward.

Δηϊδάμας
Πυγμαίου πατέρος ....

LVIII.

Amorgos, iv. Mittheilungen XI (1886), p. 106.

Νύμφη ....
σῆς δὲ ἀρετῆς ἐπίδηλα ἀ[˙π]οφω ....
μνῆμα ἔστησεν τόδε ....

LIX.

Delos, *Chios*, vi. Bull. Corr. 1883, p. 254. Löwy 1. (Incomplete, IGA. 380a add. p. 182.) Restoration uncertain: I give Röhl's.

Μικκιάδης τε ἅ]μα καλὸ[ν ἄγαλμ' ἐπόησε καὶ υἱός]
["Α]ρχερμος β. ουλ]ῆισιν ἐκηβό[λου ἰοχεαίρης]
οἱ Χῖοι. Μέ[λαν]ος πατρώϊον ἄσ[τυ νέμοντες].

LX.

Chios, v. Bull. Corr. 1879, p. 316. IGA. 382. Στοιχηδόν.

ἐσλῆ[ς] τοῦ[τ]ο [γ]υναικὸς ὁδὸν παρὰ τ[ή]νδε τὸ σ[ῆ]μα
λεωφόρον Ἀσπασίης ἐσ[τ]ὶ καταπθιμ[έν]ης·
ὀργῆς δ' ἀ[ντ]' ἀγαθῆς Εὔω.. δης τόδε μν[ῆμ]α
αὐτῇ ἐπέστησεν, τοῦ παράκοιτις ἔην.

The dative without ι, αὐτῆ, is not unparalleled in Ionic inscriptions of the fifth and fourth centuries. See Röhl's note.

LXI.

Chios, ii. Bull. Corr. 1879, p. 326.

Ἀσπασίας ναόν τε καὶ εὔγραπτον θέτο μορφὰν
Διογενὶς (σ)τοργᾶς ἀντιτίνουσα χάριν.

LXII.

Samos, vi-y. Bull. Corr. 1880, p. 485. IGA. 384.

[ἐνθάδε] Χηραμύης μ' ἀνέθ[η]κ[ε]ν τῆρηι ἄγαλμα.

LXIII.

Samos, Mac. Bull. Corr. 1881, p. 486.

. . . . Σ]τράτωνος
. . . . ος ἦλθεν
. . . . ιν ὅσσαι ἐώργει
. . . . ἀρίδηλα
. . . . ς γένετ' ἀνδρῶν
. . . . οις
. . . . Β]άκχον
. . . . α]ν.

LXIV.

Olympia, *Melos*, vi-v. IGA. 12a add. (p. 169). Löwy 25 Anhang (p. 21). Fragment of a duplicate of 1098a RM.

[Θρασυ]μάχου παῖδες τ[οῦ . . . .

LXV.

Thera, vi. IGA. 465.

[Ε]ὐμεν[ίδ]ας κα[σ]ιγ[νητ . . . .

LXVI.

Thera, vi. IGA. 466.

Κώ[θι]ος ὁ Κριτο[β]ού[λ]ου ἀπὸ Ε[ὐμ]νάστας νεα(ρ)ηβῶν.

So Köhl. The ρ of the last word is omitted on the stone.

LXVII.

Thera iv-ii. Weil, Mittheilungen II (1877), p. 65. "Vierzeilige metrische Inschrift." The only words legible are τέταρται (end of v. 1) and τοῖσδε (end of v. 3).

LXVIII.

Astypalaea, iv-iii. Bull. Corr. 1879, p. 483.

κόσμον Ἄρης πατρίδι στῆσε ἐνθάδε παῖδα Πίδωνος
Τιμαγόραν, νίκης ναυμάχου ἡγεμόνα.

LXIX.

Rhodes, Mac. Bull. Corr. 1885, p. 117.

(a) [εἰκόνα Παρμενίδο]ς θυγατρὸς σφετέρας με Δαήμων
    [καὶ Κλεινὼ μ]άτηρ μνᾶμ' ἐπὶ παιδὶ θέσαν.
    . . . . ου δέ μ' ἔχει τέμενος Διός, ὄ[φ]ρα τ' Ἀπόλλων
    [τηλ]οῦ ἄμειψεν ἑλὼν ἐκ πυρὸς ἀθάνατον.

(b) [ε]ἰκόνα Παρμενίδος (σ)τᾶσεν θυγατρός μ[ε Δαήμων]
    [κ]αὶ Κλεινὼ μάτηρ . . . .
    φογ . . . .

LXX.

Rhodes, iii-ii. Bull. Corr. 1878, p. 617.

χαῖρε Συρακοσία Μελίτη πολύκλαυτε Μενίσκωι
ἀνδρὶ θανοῦσα, τεᾶς οὕνεκα σωφροσύνας.

LXXI.

Rhodes, Mac. Löwy 186. Supplements of Benndorf and Gomperz.

. . . . Δει]νοκλ[ῆ] Φιλί[ππου . . . . .
. . . . καὶ Ἀθαναία[ς Λινδίας . . . .
[Ἀθαναί]αι Λινδίαι καὶ Διὶ . . . . . .

Δεινοκλέους θαεῖσθε [γ]ε[γ]ηθότο[ς ἐνθάδε μορφάν],
στ[λεν]γίδι καὶ δοιοῖς [βρ]ιθομέν[ου στεφάνοις],
Λίν[δο]ν ἀν' ἰε[ρὸ]ν ἄστυ [παρ]αστ[αδὸν ἡρώεσσι]
ἦσ[θ]αι Ἀθαναίας ἄνθεμα π . . . . . .
ἅ τε φιλόζωος ψυχὰ [προφυγοῦσα Φιλίππου]
παῖδα [λ]ι[θ]ο[ξ]έστωι [πρόσδετές ἐστι τύπωι].

Θέων Ἀντιοχ[εύς].

LXXII.

Rhodes, Mac. Löwy 201. A prose inscription accompanies.

. . . . . Καλ]λίστ[ρ]ατε χεῖρα Ποσειδάν
. . . . . . ς καθύπερθε δίφρων
. . . . οσ . . το νίκα
. . . . φέρουσα γέρας.
. . . . Καλλ]ιστράτου ὄλβιος οἶκος
. . . κυδιά]νειρ' ἀ[π]όδος (?).

LXXIII.

Cyprus, Mac. Bull. Corr. 1879, p. 168. Deecke (Collitz *Dial.*) n. 30. An accompanying inscription in Cypriote characters reads Ὄνασος [Ὀνά]σα(ν)τος (*o-na-so-se-o-na-sa-to-se*).

[ἐνθ]άδ' ἐγὼ κεῖμαι καί με χ[θ]ὼν ἥδε καλύπτει
[Ὄ]νασο[ς Ὀν]άσ[αν]τος μ[ή]πω οἰόμενος.
οὐ γὰρ π[ο]νηρὸς ἐών, [ἀ]λλὰ δικαιότατος,
τήνδ' ἐ[θ]έ[μη]ν ἀ[ρ]ετὴν τοῖς παριοῦσιν ὁρᾶν.

LXXIV.

Cyprus; Cypriote characters. Deecke (Collitz *Dial.*) n. 68.

χαίρετε.
Καρστι[ϝά]ναξ κὰ πότι, ϝήπω μέγα· μή ποτ' ἐϝείσης
θεοῖς φέρε [κὰ θ]νυτοῖς ἐρεραμένα πα(ν)τακόραστος·
οὐ γάρ τι ἐπισταῖς, ἄ(ν)θρωπε, θεῶι ἀλ(λ)' ἔτυχ' ἀ κὴρ
θεοῖς. κυμερῆναι πά(ν)τα τὰ ἄνθρωποι φρονέωί.
χαίρετε.

LXXV.

Cyprus; Cypriote characters. Deecke (Collitz *Dial.*) n. 69.

τιμῶ τὰ(ν) δίφατο(ν) δίμαο(ν) Παφίϳα(ν) γε διμώοις.

LXXVI.

Cyprus; Cypriote characters. Deecke (Collitz *Dial.*) n. 71.

ἐγώ ἠ[μι] 'Αριστοκρέτης κά μεν ἔστασαν [κα]σίγνητοι
μεμναμένοι εὐϝεργεσίας τάς παι εὖ ποτε ἔϝρεξα.

LXXVII.

Cyprus; Cypriote characters. Deecke (Collitz *Dial.*) n. 126.

Θεάνωρ Θεοκλέος ἔκιστα μ' ὡρίσετυ·
σί(ς) τε τόδε ἄγος συλήσῃ τὸ(ν) δόμε(ν) Ἄδῃ
μισαάτω.
μηδὲ φύϳη φιδωλὸς ἰνιπὰ τῶ ἀ(ν)θρώπω.

The first line is prose: the remainder (an imprecation against the violator of a grave) is meant as verse. After σί(ς) τε two syllables seem to have fallen out.

LXXVIII.

Cypriote characters on vase. Neubauer in *Commentationes in honorem Theodori Mommseni*, p. 689. Deecke n. 88. The beginning, according to Neubauer, is:

Δωλίμελο(ς) Ϝεθόχω 'Αλεϝότης χόρ(ν) τά(ν)δ' ἐπέϝασα

(the last word being equivalent to ἐποίησα). The rest is yet more uncertain. Several metrical difficulties would be removed by omitting χόον. Compare CXLII.

LXXIX.

Halicarnassus, iv-iii. CIG. 2260. Löwy 60. A prose inscription precedes.

ποίησεν Μακεδὼν Διονυσίου Ἡρακλεώτης.

LXXX.

Cedreae, iv-iii. Bull. Corr. 1886, p. 424.

ἦ μάλα καὶ ταύταν ὁ Κλειππίδα εἴσατο Νίκων
εἰκόνα τεῖδε κλυτὸμ μνᾶμα καὶ ὀψιγόνοις.
δαρὸν ὅπως θυόεντι θεοῦ γέρας ἅ γ' ἐνὶ ναῶι
ἡμένα ἀγγέλλοι δῶρα θυαπολίας.

LXXXI.

Didymi, vi. IGA. 489. Bustrophedon.

... ημιστοιφ .... δὲ εἶπεν δί[κ]αιον
ποιεῖν .... ὡς πατέρες.

LXXXII.

Ephesus, iv. CIG. 2984. Löwy 88.

Εὔθηνος Εὐπείθεος.
[υ]ἰὸς Πατροκλέος Δαίδαλος εἰργάσατο.

LXXXIII.

Cyme, iii-ii. Revue Arch., 1884 (3me série, vol. IV), p. 93.

(a) Ποσειδωνίου ἴσθι με κοῦρον Μέντορα Χῖον.

(b) Μέντορα τὸν Χῖον λεύσσεις, ξένε, τόν θ' ὑπὸ μητρὸς
Χίας, εἰς Ἄϊδος δῶμα καθελκόμενον.
ὃν λίπεν ὀκταέτη, πατριδὸς δ' ἀπόνοσφιν ἰδοῦσα
ξείνισεν ἡ γενέτειρ' ἀγγυλέοις ξενίοις.
ἀμφοτέροισι θ' ἴσον ζωῆς χρόνον ἤνυσε Μοῖρα.
εἰκοσαπεντάετεις θ' ἥλιον ἐξέλιπον.
δήμου δὲ στέφανος πινυτὴν φρένα μηνύει ἀνδρὸς
ἀρτιφυοῦς· λείπει δ' ἄλγεα πατρὶ φίλωι.

LXXXIV.

Heraclea Ponti, iii-ii. Mittheilungen IV (1879), p. 48; corrected V (1880), p. 83.

Ἡρώνδης Ἀλκιάδα Ἡρακλεώτ[ης].

ἄρμενος ἦν ξείνοισιν ἀνὴρ ὅδε καὶ φίλ[ος ἀστοῖς],
πλείστην τε εὐφροσύνηι δόξα[ν ἀειράμενος].

LXXXV.

Megara, vi-v. Mittheilungen VIII (1883), p. 181.

[τ]οίδε ἀπὸ λ[αία]ς τὰν δεκάτα[ν] ἀνέθηκαν Ἀθ[ά]ναι.

LXXXVI.

Corinth, vi. IGA. 20 (7).

Σιμίων μ' ἀνέθηκε Ποτειδάϝων[ι ϝάνακτι].

LXXXVII.
Corinth, vi. IGA. 20 (12).
[. . . . . Ποτ]ειδάϝωνι ϝάνικτι.

LXXXVIII.
Corinth, vi. IGA. 20 (8).
. . . ων μ' ἀνέ[θη]κε Ποτειδᾶνι ϝάν[ακτι].

LXXXIX.
Corinth, vi. IGA. 20 (62). Bustrophedon.
. . . . δὸς χαρίεσ(σ)αν ἀφορμάν.

Röhl -δοι or -δωι; but δός is surely meant, in spite of the different form of the s.

XC.
Corinth, vi. IGA. 20 (63).
[. . . ἐπαγγείλα]ς. τὺ δὲ δὸς χαρίεσ(σ)αν [ἀφορμάν].

XCI.
Corinth, vi. IGA. 20 (64).
. . . . . . ἀνέ]θηκε [Ποτει]δᾶνι ϝ[άνακτι].
. . . . τὺ δὲ δ[ὸς χαρίεσσαν ἀφορμάν].

XCII.
Corinth, vi. IGA. 20 (108 a) add., p. 171.
[. . . ἐπ]αγγείλας. τὺ δὲ δὺ[ς χα]ρίεσ(σ)αν ἀμοιϝάν.

XCIII.
Corinth, vi. IGA. 18.
[Μαν]δροπύλου τόδε σᾶμα.

XCIV.
Olympia, *Corinth*, v. IGA. 26 a add., p. 171. Cp. Paus. 5, 10, 4.
[ναϝὸς μὲν φιαλὰν χρυσέα]ν ἔχει, ἐκ δὲ [Τανάγρας]
[τοὶ Λακεδαιμόνιοι συμ μαχία τ' ἀν[έθεν].
[δῶρον ἀπ' Ἀργείων καὶ Ἀθι]ναίων καὶ ['Ιάνων],
[τὰν δεκάταν νίκας εἵν]εκα τοῦ πο[λέμου].
. . . . Κο⌜ρινθ⌝ί⌜ο . . . . . .
. . . . . . ρ . . . .

XCV.

Olympia, *Argos*, v. IGA. 41. Löwy 30.

ξυνὸν Ἀθανοδώρου τε καὶ Ἀσωποδώρου τόδε ϝέργον.
χὠ μὲν Ἀχαιός, ὃ δ' ἐξ Ἄργεος εὐρυχόρου.

Usener (*Altgriechischer Versbau*, p. 38) guesses that the poet may have intended to say Ἀθανοδότου and Ἀσωποδότου.

XCVI.

Epidaurus, vi–v. Kabbadias, Eph. 1885, p. 198.

Καλλίστρατος ἀνέθηκε τῶι Ἀσκ(λ)απι[ῶ]ι ὁ μάγιρος.

Probably meant as a verse. The λ of the god's name is omitted.

XCVII.

Epidaurus, iii. Inscription in five parts. Kabbadias, Eph. 1885, p. 65 flg. Wilamowitz-Moellendorf, *Isyllos von Epidauros*, Berlin 1886. Compare Baunack, '*Studien*,' I. 1, Leipsic 1886; Blass, *der Paean des Isyllos*, Jahrb. für Philol., 1885, p. 822.

(1)

Ἴσυλλος Σωκράτευς Ἐπιδαύριος ἀνέθηκε
Ἀπόλλωνι Μαλεάται καὶ Ἀσκλαπιῶι.

δᾶμος εἰς ἀριστοκρατίαν ἄνδρας α[ἰ] πρ[ο]άγοι καλῶς.
αὐτὸς ἰσχυρότερος. ὀρθοῦται γὰρ ἐξ ἀνδραγαθίας·
5 αἰ δέ τις καλῶς προαχθεὶς θιγγάνοι πονηρῶς,
πάλιν ἐπαγκρούων. κολάζων δᾶμος ἀσφαλέστερος.
τάνδε τὰν γνώμαν τόκ' ἦχον καὶ ἔλεγον καὶ νῦν λέγω.
εὐξάμιν ἀνγράψεν, αἴ κ' εἰς τάνδε τὰν γνώμαν πέτη
ὁ νόμος ἁμίν, ὃν ἐπέδειξα. ἔγεντο δ' οὐκ ἄνευ θε[ῶ]ν.[1]

(2)

10 τόνδ' ἱαρὸν θείαι μοίραι νόμον ηὗρεν Ἴσυλλος
ἄφθιτον ἀένιον γέρας ἀθανάτοισι θεοῖσιν.
καί νιν ἅπας δᾶμος θεθμὸν θέτο πατρίδος ἁμᾶς.
χεῖρας ἀνισχόντες μακάρεσσιν ἐς οὐρανὸν εὐρύ[ν].
οἵ κεν ἀριστεύωσι πόληος τᾶσδ' Ἐπιδαύρου.
15 λέξασθαί τε ἄνδρας καὶ ἐπαγγεῖλαι κατὰ φυλάς,
οἷς πολιοῦχος ὑπὸ στέρνοις ἀρετά τε καὶ αἰδώς.

---

[1] The stone has ΘΕΟΝ.

τοῖσιν ἐπαγγέλλεν καὶ πομπεύεν σφε κομῶντας
Φοίβωι ἄνακτι υἱῶι τε Ἀσκλαπιῶι ἰατῆρι
εἵμασιν ἐν λευκοῖσι, δάφνας στεφάνοις ποτ' Ἀπόλλω,
20 ποὶ δ' Ἀσκλαπιὸν ἔρνεσι ἐλαίας ἡμεροφύλλου,
ἁγνῶς πομπεύειν καὶ ἐπεύχεσθαι πολιάταις
πᾶσιν ἀεὶ διδόμεν τέκνοις τ' ἐρατὰν ὑγίειαν,
τὰν καλοκαγαθίαν τ' Ἐπιδαυροῖ ἀεὶ ῥέπεν[1] ἀνδρῶν
εὐνομίαν τε καὶ εἰράναν καὶ πλοῦτον ἀμεμφῆ,
25 ὥραις ἐξ ὡρᾶν νόμον ἀεὶ τόνδε σέβοντας.
οὕτω τοι κ' ἀμῶν περιφείδοιτ' εὐρύοπα Ζεύς.

(3)

πρῶτος Μᾶλος ἔτευξεν Ἀπόλλωνος Μαλεάτα
βωμὸν καὶ θυσίαις ἠγλάϊσεν τέμενος.
οὐδέ κε Θεσσαλίας ἐν Τρίκκῃ πειραθείης
30 εἰς ἄδυτον καταβὰς Ἀσκληπιοῦ, εἰ μὴ ἐφ' ἁγνοῦ
πρῶτον Ἀπόλλωνος βωμοῦ θύσαις Μαλεάτα.

(4)

Ἴσυλλος Ἀστυλαΐδαι ἐπέθηκε μαντεύσασθαί οἱ
περὶ τοῦ παιᾶνος ἐν Δελφοῖς, ὃν ἐπόησε εἰς τὸν Ἀπόλ-
λωνα καὶ τὸν Ἀσκλαπιόν, ἦ λώϊόν οἵ κα εἴη ἀγγρά-
35 φοντι τὸν παιᾶνα. ἐμάντευσε λώϊόν οἵ κα εἶμεν ἀγ-
γράφοντι καὶ αὐτίκα καὶ ἐς τὸν ὕστερον χρόνον.

	FEET.
ἴε παιᾶνα θεὸν ἀείσατε λαοὶ ζαθέας ἐνναέτα|ν|[2]	1–5
τᾶσδ' Ἐπιδαύρου. ὧδε γὰρ φάτις ἐνέπουσ' ἠλι-	6–9
θ' ἐς ἀκοὰς προγόνων ἀμετέρων, ὦ Φοῖβε Ἀπόλ-	10–12
40 λων. Ἐρατὼ μοῖσαν πατὴρ Ζεὺς λέγεται Μάλ\[ωι\]	13–16
δόμεν παράκοιτιν ὁσίοισι γάμοις. Φλεγύας δ'. \[ὃς\]	17–19
πατρίδ' Ἐπίδαυρον ἔναιεν, θυγατέρα Μά\λ\ ον γ\αμ\]-	20–23
εῖ, τὰν Ἐρατὼ γείνατο μάτηρ. Κλεοφήμαι δ' ὀνομάσθη, ἐκ	24–28
δὲ Φλεγύα γένετο. Αἴγλα δ' ὀνομάσθη · τόδ' ἐπώνυμον.	29–32
45 τὸ κάλλος δὲ Κορωνὶς ἐπεκλήθη.[3] κατιδὼν δὲ ὁ χρυ-	33–36

---

[1] Wilamowitz conjectures ἰσορρέπεν, with much probability.
[2] So Kabbadias. Wilamowitz ἐνναέτα ιʹ.
[3] Wilamowitz has persuaded himself that the words ἐκ δὲ ... ἐπεκλήθη stand as Isyllus intended. But the author, however little merit he may have as a poet, has not elsewhere put words without meaning or construction. The sense demands

		FEET.
	σότοξος Φοῖβος ἐμ Μάλου δόμοις παρθενίαν ὥραν	37-40
	ἔλυσε. λεχέων δ' ἱμεροέντων ἐπέβας. Λατῶιε κόρε	41-44
	χρυσοκόμα. σέβομαί σε· ἐν δὲ θυώδει τεμένει τέ-	45-48
	κετό[1] νιν Αἴγλα. γονίμαν δ' ἔλυσεν ὠδῖνα Διὸς	49-52
50	[π]αῖς μετὰ Μ[ο]ιρᾶν, Λάχεσίς τε μαῖα ἀγανά. ἐπίκλη-	53-56
	σιν δέ νιν Αἴγλας ματρὸς Ἀσκλαπιὸν ὠνόμαξε	57-60
	Ἀπόλλων. τὸν νόσων παύστορα, δωτῆρι ὑγιείας,	61-63
	μέγα δώρημα βροτοῖς. ἰὲ παιάν. ἰὲ παιάν. χαῖρεν[2]	64-68
	Ἀσκλαπιέ. τὰν σὰν Ἐπίδαυρον μιτρόπολιν αὔ-	69-71
55	ξων. ἐναργῆ δ' ὑγιείαν ἐπιπέμποις φρεσὶ καὶ σώ-	72-75
	μασιν ἁμοῖς. ἰὲ παιάν, ἰὲ παιάν.	76-78

(5)

καὶ τόδε σῆς ἀρετῆς, Ἀσκληπιέ, τοὔργον ἔδειξας
ἐγ κείνοισι χρόνοις ὅκα δὴ στρατὸν ἦγε Φίλιππος
εἰς Σπάρτην. ἐθέλων ἀνελεῖν βασιληίδα τιμήν.
60 τοῖς δ' Ἀσκληπιὸ[ς ἦ]λθε βοαθόο[ς] ἐξ Ἐπιδαύρου
τιμῶν Ἡρακλέος γενεάν, ἃς φείδετο ἄρα Ζεύς.
τουτάκι δ' ἦλθε ὄχ' ὁ παῖς ἐκ Βουσπόρου ἦλθεν κάμνω[ν],[3]
τῶ τύ γα ποστείχοντι[4] συνάντησας σὺν ὅπλοισιν
λαμπόμενος χρυσέοις, Ἀσκλαπιέ. παῖς δ' ἐσιδών σε
65 λίσσετο χεῖρ' ὀρέγων ἱκέτηι μύθωι σε προσαντῶν.
"ἄμπορός εἰμι τεῶν δώρων. Ἀσκληπιὲ Παιάν.
ἀλλά μ' ἐποίκτειρον." τύ δέ μοι τάδε ἔλεξας ἐναργῆ,
"θάρσει. καιρῶι γάρ σοι ἀφίξομαι. ἀλλὰ μέν' αὐτεῖ,
τοῖς Λακεδαιμονίοις χαλεπὰς ἀπὸ κῆρας ἐρύξας,

---

something like ἐκ δὲ Φλεγύα θυγάτηρ οἱ γένετο, Αἴγλα δ' ὀνομάσθη το(ῦ)δ' ἐπώνυμος, ἀπὸ κάλλευς δὲ Κορωνὶς ἐπεκλήθη (still better would be ἀπὸ κάλλεος Κορωνὶς δ' ἐπεκλήθη). That is, she was named Αἴγλα after her father Φλεγύας, which is intelligible enough. Compare v. 51. G. Schultz in the Berliner Philol. Wochenschritt, 1887, n. 4, p. 101, proposes to omit δ' ὀνομάσθη after Αἴγλα, but this is not a satisfactory remedy.

[1] τέκετο (ῐ)νιν Semitelos, — a certain correction.
[2] χαῖρε Ἀσκλαπιέ and (just below) αὖξον were certainly intended, as Wilamowitz has pointed out.
[3] See p. 59. Wilamowitz ἦλθεν (ὁ) κάμνων.
[4] τύ γα ποστείχοντι (Wilamowitz) is more probable than τύ γ' ἀποστείχοντι. The moment meant seems to be that of the arrival of the boy (ἦλθεν v. 62) at the temple.

70 οὕνεκα τοὺς Φοίβου χρησμοῖς σώζοντι δικαίως.
    οὕς μαντευσάμενος παρέταξε πόληϊ Λυκοῦργος."
    ὡς ὁ μὲν ὤχετο ἐπὶ Σπάρτην. ἐμὲ δ' ὠ̣[ρ]ῃσε ν[όη]μα
    ἀγγεῖλαι Λακεδαιμονίοις ἐλθόντα τὸ θεῖον.
    πάντα μάλ' ἐξείας. οἱ δ' αἰδήσαντος ἄκουσαν
75 σώτειραν φήμαν, Ἀσκληπιέ. καί σφ' ἐσάωσας.
    οἳ δὲ ἐκάρυξαν πάντας ξενύαις σε δέκεσθαι
    σωτῆρα εὐρυχόρου Λακεδαίμονος ἀγκαλέοντες.
    ταῦτά τοι. ὦ μέγ' ἄριστε θεῶν, ἀνέθηκεν Ἴσυλλος
    τιμῶν σὴν ἀρετήν, ὦναξ, ὥσπερ τὸ δίκαιον.

XCVIII.

Epidaurus, Mac. Kabbadias in Eph. 1885, p. 194.

Δρυμὸς παῖς Θεοδώρου ὀλυμπικὸν ἐνθάδ' ἀγῶνα
ἤνγειλ' αὐθῆμιρ δρομέων θεοῦ εἰς κλυτὸν ἄλσος.
ἀνδρείας παράδειγμα. πατρὶς δέ μοι ἵππιον Ἄργος.

XCIX.

Tegea, Mac. Bull. Corr. 1885, p. 512.

Ἄϊδος εἰς εὐνὰς ὁ Λάκων δόλωι ἔφθισεν Ἄρης
Λα . . . .
αὐτὸς δ' εἷλε μόρος καὶ σύγγονον. ἡνίκα Κρήτην
. . . .
ἄ[ψ]υχον δ' ἐσορᾶν Ἀνδροσθένεος καὶ ὁμαίμου
. . . .

C.

Sparta, vi. IGA. 56. Bustrophedon. A very difficult inscription. As a possible contribution to its solution, I will suggest that the C in the middle of the second line is probably the Laconian mark of interpunction (see IGA. 29 and 54), and that in two of the older inscriptions found at Delos (see above n. LIV and LIX) HK does duty as ἐκ-. We have, unless I am mistaken, two iambic trimeters. In the first line τῶννε ἰών (= ἐών), and in the second, [πα]χνεῖον αἴ τις δισκίοι may be worth considering, but I cannot propose a probable restoration of the whole.

CI.

Sparta, vi–v. IGA. 78.

Δαμώνων ἀνέθηκε Ἀθαναία[ι] Πολιάχωι,
νικάας ταυτᾶ ἅτ' οὐδὴς πήποκα τῶν νῦν.

A prose inscription follows.

CII.

Sellasia, vi-v. IGA. 62 a add., p. 174.

Πλειστιάδας μ' ἀ[νέθηκε] Διοσκώροισιν ἄ[γαλμα]
Τινδαριδᾶν δ[ιδύμων] μᾶνιν ὀπιδ(δ)ό[μενος].

CIII.

Olympia, v. Kirchhoff, Arch. Zt. 39 (1881), p. 83. IGA. 536. Löwy 33.

[Γλαυκία]ι? με Κάλων γενε[ᾶι Ϝ]αλεῖ[ο]ς ἐποίει.

[Γλ]αυκίης ὁ Λυκκίδεω [τῶ]ι Ἑρμῆι Ῥ[η]γῖνος.

Inscription mentioned by Pausanias, 5, 27, 8. The hexameter of the artist is in Elean, the prose dedication in the Ionic of Rhegium.

CIV.

Olympia, vi. Kirchhoff, Arch. Zt. 39 (1881), p. 84. IGA. 552 a.

[. . . . . . . προ]τέρω δ' ἐπάτει Δ[αμάσ]ιππος
κλεινοτέραν δὲ πόλιν πατρίδ' ἔ[θηκε . . .]

CV.

Olympia, vi-v. Kirchhoff, Arch. Zt. 39 (1881), p. 169. IGA. 563.

. . . . ἀνέθηκέ με παῖς ὁ [Π]ίθωνος
[παῖδας νικήσας . . .]κράτης στάδιον.

CVI.

Olympia, v. Kirchhoff, Arch. Zt. 37 (1879), p. 161. IGA. 355. Löwy 416.
Two fragments. Röhl's restoration, based on Pausanias 6, 10, 9, but not certain, is as follows:

[εἰκόνα Ϝαλεῖος τάνδ' Ἀγι]άδας ἀνέθ[ηκε],
[πὺξ παῖς νικάσα]ς καλὸν ἀ[γῶνα Διός].

[Σηράμβου τοῦ ἐν Αἰγ]ίναι μ' ἰ[δοῦ ἐνθάδε Ϝέργον].

CVII.

Olympia, Orestheum, v. IGA. 98. A fragment; but the inscription was repeated on the same stone, in much later times; the restoration is therefore easy. See also Pausanias 6, 10, 9.

(Τέλλων τόνδ' ἀνέθηκε Δαήμ)[ονος ἀγλαὸς υἱός]
(Ἄρκας Ὀ[ρ]ε)σθάσιος. π[ὺξ ἐνὶ παισὶ κρατῶν].

Here [ ] means lost entirely, ( ) preserved only in the later copy.

CVIII.

Olympia, iv. Arch. Zt. 37 (1879), p. 145. Löwy 94. Compare Paus. 6, 1, 4.

Ἑλλήνων ἦρχον τότε Ὀλυμπίαι ἡνίκα μοι Ζεὺς
δῶκεν νικῆσαι πρῶτον Ὀλυμπιάδα
ἵπποις ἀθλοφόροις· τὸ δὲ δεύτερον αὖτις ἐφεξῆς
ἵπποις. υἱὸς δ᾽ ἦν Τρώϊλος Ἀλκινόου.

CIX.

Olympia, Sparta, iv. Arch. Zt. 37 (1879), p. 151. Löwy 99. Anthol. Pal. xiii, 16.

Σπάρτας μὲν [βασιλῆες ἐμοὶ] πατέρες καὶ ἀδελφοί.
[ἅρμισι δ᾽ ὠκυπόδων ἵππων] νικῶσα Κυνίσκα
εἰκόνα τάνδ᾽ ἔ[στασε·] μόν[αν] δέ με φαμὶ γυναικῶν
Ἑλλάδος ἐκ πάσας τό[ν]δε λαβεῖν στέφανον.

Ἀπελλέας Καλλικλέος ἐπόησε.

CX.

Olympia, iv. Arch. Zt. 37 (1879), p. 144. Löwy 103, with new facsimile.

. . . . δ]ι᾽ ἰσχύος ἔσχον
. . . . άρισα
. . . . τρὶς ἐν Ἰθμῶι
. . . . λεύς
[. . . . . ἐπ]οίησε Πατροκλέ[ος . . . υ]ἱός.

Despite the objections of Purgold (see Löwy) to the reading υἱός, the artist's inscription seems to me a verse, on account of the position of the genitive Πατροκλέος.

CXI.

Helicon, Mac. Bull. Corr. 1879, p. 447. Another copy, Mittheilungen, v (1880), p. 124. I have made some tentative supplements.

. . . . ΤΙΔΕΜΕ . . . .
. . . ἄ[εθ]λον; ἀλλὰ τᾶι τέχναι σοφός
. . . ος αὐλῶι φθόγγον εὖ προσαρμόσας.
[κροτεῖθ᾽], ὅπως μελιχρὸν ἀπύσαι μέλος
[πάλι]ν τι[θεὶ]ς πρὸς τέρμα καίριον ῥυθμῶι.
[ἅ]λις δέ [π]α παρ[η]μένοις ἄειδ᾽ ἀεί,
οὕτως ἐνῆς ἐν τῶι μέλει πολλὰ φάτις.
τοιόσδ᾽ ἐὼν ἀείρατ᾽ ἐγ Μουσᾶν ἐμέ.

[κ]ρατῶν ἀγῶνος, σφᾶι πάτρηι [μ]έγα κλέος.
ά Θεσπιὰ δ' ἔοικεν οὐ μόνομ φέρειν
ἄνδρας μαχητὰς ἀλλὰ καὶ ἐμ μούσαις ἄκρους.

CXII.

Thebes, Mac. Bull. Corr. 1879, p. 387.

Ἀρίστων.
ἦ μάλα δή σε φίλως ὑπεδέξατο γαῖα ὑπὸ κόλπους
ὄλβιον αἰῶνος μᾶκος ἀμειψάμενο[ν]·
καὶ σοί γε ὡραία χάρις ἥλυ[θεν α]ὖτη, Ἀρίστων,
δεινοῦ [ἐλευθ]ερίαν τοῦ δέσμο[ῦ . . . .]

The editor questions his own restoration of the last line.

CXIII.

Haliartus, vi–v. Mittheilungen v (1880), p. 133. IGA. 149.

Καλλία Λιγίθ(θ)οιο. τὺ δ' εὖ πρᾶσ(σ)', [ὦ] παροδῶτα

See note [1], p. 117.

CXIV.

Elatea, Mac. Bull. Corr. 1881, p. 451.

ἐπὶ Φιλαι.   ἐπὶ Διονυσίωι.

ὦ ξένε, τόνδ' ἐ[σό]ρα Διονύσιον. ἠδὲ γυναῖκα
δέρκεο τοῖδε [Φ]ίλαν. πνεῦμα λιποῦ[σαν ὁμοῦ].
ἄμφω γηραλέω . . . . . . τέκνων τέκν[υ λιπ]όντα[ς],
ὀλβίστους θά[να]τος [π]λ[ηθοδόκ]ος κιτέχ[ει].

In verse 4 ΕΩ . . ΕΕΔΕΤΕΚ: τε ἰδὲ seems unlikely. In verse 5, after θάνατος, ΓΛ . . . . . . ΟΣ: I have little confidence in what I have written, but γλισχρότατος does not commend itself.

CXV.

Elatea, iii. Löwy 135 c, Nachtrag, p. 388. Bull. Corr. 1887, p. 345.

[π]ότνια Ἀθαναία τόδε . . . .
τὸ πρέπον ἐν χαλκῶι σ . . . .
ἐξ ὁσίων ἔργων ἀκροθί[νια] . . . . . καὶ . . .
πολλάκι καλλιτέχνωι φωτὶ . . σ . . ημ . .
τῶι σφε καὶ Εὐκλείδης μοῖσα . . . ἱερὸς . . .
κοσμεῖ ἀειμνήστοις εὐλογ[ί]ας ἔπεσιν.

Ξενοκράτης Ἐργοφίλου ἐπόησε.

CXVI.

Elatea, iv-iii. Bull. Corr. 1886, p. 367

ποντίωι ἱππομέδοντι Ποσειδῶνι Χρόνου υἱεῖ
ἡ πόλις εὐξαμένη τοῦσδ' ἀνέθηκε θεῶι
ἡμιθέους σωτῆρας ὑπὲρ προγόνων τε καὶ αὐτῶν
καὶ γῆς καὶ τεκέων καὶ σφετέρων ἀλόχων.

CXVII.

Elatea, Mac. Bull. Corr. 1886, p. 383.

ἦ μάλα δὴ φθίμενόν σε κλυτὰ πατρίς, ἅδε Ἐλάτεια,
καλοῖσι, Δαμότιμε, κυδαίνει λόγοις.
ἐσθλὸς γὰρ καὶ ἄμωμος, ἀκ[μα]ῖς ἐνὶ σώφρονος ἥβας,
θνῄσκεις δαμασθεὶς θυμὸν ὠκείαι νόσωι.
πολλά[κι] δ' ἀμφὶ τεὸν μάτηρ τάφον οἰκτρὸν ἄϋσεν
Δεξὼ στενάζουσα ὀρφανὰν τέκνου χάριν.

CXVIII.

Delphi, iv. Bull. Corr. 1882, p. 447. Compare Paus. 6, 4, 1.

. . . .
. . . . στεφ]άνους . . . . . .
. . . . πάντ]α ἐκράτεις ἀμ[αχεί].
[πλ]είστοις δὴ Σικυῶνα πάτραν. | Σω]σιστράτου υἱέ.
Σώστρατε, καλλίστοις τ' ἠγλάϊσας στεφάνοις.
[ν]ικῶ[ν] παγκράτιον τρὶς Ὀλύμπια, δὶς δ' ἐνὶ Πυθοῖ,
δώδεκα δ' ἐξ Ἰσθμο[ῦ καὶ Νεμ]έας στεφάνους.
[τ]οὺς δ' ἄλλους ἀπο[ρον στεφάν]ους [ἐπι]δεῖξαι ἀριθμόν·
[πα]ύσας δ' ἀντι[πάλους πάν]τα [ἐ]κράτεις ἀμαχεί.

CXIX.

Delphi, iv-iii. Bull. Corr. 1881, p. 434. A version of the oracle of Herod. 1. 65, in letters of the fourth century or later. From a manuscript in the Barberini library at Rome, containing copies, by another hand, of inscriptions collected by Cyriacus of Ancona. This inscription must share, to some extent, in the grave doubts which have been cast on the other oracle, CIG. 1724. Other instances of humbuggery on Cyriacus's part in the matter of inscriptions have been lately pointed out by Mommsen, *Jahrbücher der kön. preuss. Kunstsamml.* IV (1883), p. 78, and Kubitschek, *Arch. Epigr. Mittheil. aus Oesterreich*, VIII (1884), p. 102.

The nature of the mistakes in the present document are in favor of its genuineness; particularly Τ for Ι in διζῶ.

[ἦλ]υθες, ὦ Λυκόεργε, ἐμὸν ποτὶ πίονα νηόν,
[Ζ]ηνὶ φίλος καὶ πᾶσιν Ὀλύμπια δώματ' ἔχουσιν.
δι[ζ]ῶ εἴ σε θεὸν μιντεύσομαι ἠὲ καὶ ἄνδρα·
μᾶλλόν τοι θεὸν ἔλπομαι ἔμμεναι, ὦ Λυκόερ[γε].

CXX.

Delphi. Mac. J. Schmidt, Mittheilungen v (1880), p. 198. He fancies a restoration like the following:

[. . . . . τόδε σῆμα] πατὴρ ἀνέθηκε Κ . . . . .
[εἰς Ἀίδαν τὸν ἔπεμψε θοῶι νέ]ον ἄμπυκι Μοῖρα,

understanding ἄμπυξ as 'wheel.'

CXXI.

Anactorium, vi–v. CIG. 1794g, restored by Röhl, IGA. 330, thus:

[πόντος . . . ἀπ]ώλλυ' ὃς Ἀμ[πρακίαν ποτ' ἔναιεν].

CXXII.

Pharsalus, v. IGA. 325. Better Lolling, Mittheilungen VII (1882), p. 226. Fick (Collitz *Dial.*) n. 324. Meister, *Griech. Dialekte* I. p. 291. Cauer, *Delectus* (2d edit.) n. 393. I give Cauer's version:

[σᾶμι τ]οδ' ἁ μάτηρ Διοκλέαι ἔσστασ' Ἐχεναίς,
[δάκρυ χέ]ωσα ὅτ' ἀνώρ ὣς ὄλετο ὢν ἀγαθός·
[τᾶς δῶρον? Μενε]κλέα τε, ὃς ἀδελφεὸς ἔσσταγε λο[ιβάν].
[πᾶς δὲ κα]τοικτίρας ἄνδρα ἀγαθὸν παρίτω.

Verse 2: Röhl [ἐσγόνωι, ὅς ποτ' ἀνώρ ὣς ὄλετο; Meister [υἱ]ὸς Δωτάνορος ὤλετο; Fick [παῖς; ὁ Σαωτάνορος ὤλετο; Lolling [. . . γο]ῶτα ὗτ' ἀνώρως ὤλετο. Verse 3: Röhl . . . . . ἔλτειος ἀδελφεὸς ἔσσταγε λο[ιβάν]; Meister [πὰρ δὲ Διο]κλέα[ι ϝ]ὸς ἀδελφεὸς ἐσστ' Ἀγέλ[αος]; Fick [σοὶ δέ, Διο]κλέα, τεῖυς ἀδελφεὸς ἔσσταγε λο[ιβάν].

CXXIII.

Pherae, iv–iii. Lolling, Mittheilungen VII (1882), p. 234.

Ἀσταγόραι πατρὶ [Μ]α[γνη]σικλάας ἐπέθεικεν.
ἀπ . . . [ἔ]θεικαν μναμμεῖον.

The last words, according to Lolling, are a '*nachträglicher zusatz*.' He restores Π[α]γα[σικλ]έ as, which does not seem a very probable name. Could we suppose the beginning gone, [σᾶμα τόδ'] Ἀσταγόραι πατρὶ | Π[ασικλίας ἐπέθεικεν would be possible.

CXXIV.

Pherae, iv–iii. Bull. Corr. 1883, p. 61.

σώιζων μὲν πίστιν, τιμῶν δὲ ἀρ[ετὰν] θάνες ὧδε,
Καλλία Σα . . . . . . πατρίδος ἐκ Τεγέας.

CXXV.

Larisa, iv. Lolling, Mittheilungen VIII (1883), p. 23.

μούσαις Εὐρυδάμας ἀνέθηκε υἱὸς Κρατεραίου,
τόμ ποτε μὴ λε[ί]ποι τερψίχορος σοφία.

CXXVI.

Metapontum, vi. Bustrophedon. Röhl, *Imagines* XV, 5 (p. 37). Cauer, *Delectus* (2d ed.) n. 277.

χαῖρε ϝάναξ Ἡράκλεις.
Νικόμαχός μ' ἐπόει. ὅ τοι κεραμεὺς μ' ἀνέθηκε.
δὸς δέ ϝ' ἐν ἀνθρώποις δόξαν ἔχειν ἀγαθ(ά)ν.

Hiller, *Jahrb. für Philol.* 127, p. 144, proposes ὁ (δέ) τοι.

CXXVII.

Sybaris, ii. Comparetti, *Journal of Hellenic Studies* III, p. 114. Orphic gold tablet from a tomb, like Kaibel 1037.

ἀλλ' ὁπόταν ψυχὴ προλιπὼν φάος ἀελίοιο
δεξιὸν ἐ[ὶνν]οίας δεῖ τινα πεφυλαγμένον εὖ μάλα πάντα.
χαῖρε, παθὼν τὸ πάθημα. τόδ' οὔπω πρόσθε ἐπεπόνθεις·
θεὸς εἰ ἐ(λεει)νοῦ ἐξ ἀνθρώπου. ἔριφος ἐς γάλα ἔπετες.
χαῖρ(ε), χαῖρε. δεξιὰν ὁδοιπόρ(ῶν).
λειμῶνάς τε ἱεροὺς κατ' ἄλσεα Φε[ρ]σε[φ]ονείας.

CXXVIII.

Sybaris, ii. Comparetti, *Journal Hell. Studies* III, p. 115. Three more gold tablets of the same sort. Their contents partly coincide. Comparetti gives conflate readings thus (*a, b, c* distinguishing the parts that are peculiar to one or two):

ἔρχομαι ἐκ καθαρῶν, καθαρὰ χθονίων βασίλεια,
Εὐκλῆς Εὐβουλεύς τε [θεοί τ' εὐδαίμονες ἄλλοι].
καὶ γὰρ ἐγὼν ὑμῶν γένος ὄλβιον εὔχομαι εἶναι,
ποινὰν δ' ἀνταπέτισ' [ἀντ'] ἔργων οὔτι δικαίων·
εἴτ' ἐμὲ Μοῖρ' ἐδάμασσε καὶ ἀθάνατοι θεοὶ ἄλλοι
(βροντῆι) τ' ἀστεροπῆι τε καὶ (αἰθαλόεντι) κεραυνῶι

a { κύκλου δ' ἐξέπταν βαρυπενθέος ἀργαλέοιο,
   ἱμερτὸν δ' ἐπέβαν στέφανον ποσὶ καρπαλίμοισι
   δεσποίνας δ' ὑπὸ κολπὸν ἔδυν χθονίας βασιλείας.

b, c { νῦν δ' ἱκέτης ἁγνὴν ἥκω παρὰ Περσεφόνειαν
     ὥς με πρόφρων πέμψῃ ἕδρας ἐς (τὰς μακαριστὰς)
     εὐαγέων . . . .

a { ὄλβιε καὶ μακαριστέ. θεὸς δ' ἔσῃ ἀντὶ βροτοῖο
   ἔριφος ἐς γάλ' ἔπετον.

CXXIX.

Posidonia, vi. Leftward. Curtius, Arch. Zt. 38 (1880), p. 27. IGA. 542.

Τάθάναι Φιλλὼ Χαρμυλίδα δεκάτα[ν].

CXXX.

Syracuse, v. IGA. 509. Köhl restores:

Κλεομέ[ν]ης ἐποίησε [τ]ὠπέλ(λ)ωνι.
οὗ κ[ίβδ]η[λ]α [ἴ]ε[ι χρ]ῆσι[ν λ]η[τ]ὰ κα[τὰ] ϝέργ[α],

as prose followed by a hexameter.

CXXXI.

Olympia, Gela, vi. Arch. Zt. 40 (1882), p. 87. IGA. 512 a.

Πανταρης μ' ἀνέθηκε Μενεκράτιος. Διὸ[ς ἄθλον]
[ἅρματι νικάσας, πέδου ἐκ κλει]τοῦ Γελοαίου.

CXXXII.

Vase, Athens, vi. Leftward. Kumanudes in 'Αθήναιον, IX (1881), p. 3.
Kirchhoff, Mittheilungen VI (1881), p. 106.

ὃς νῦν ὀρχηστῶν πάντων ἀταλώτατα παίζει
τοῦ τόδε . . . .

CXXXIII.

Vase, Magna Graecia, vi. Köhl, IGA. 550, reads doubtingly:

δίς πει πὺ[ξ] Ἶρος τοιόν νυ ἐπάσατο χήειν.

"bis alicubi pugilatu Irus tale vas adeptus est quo funderet." The last word is
ΧΕΕΝ. See p. 74.

CXXXIV.

Vase, Boeotia, v. IGA. 219.

See p. 47.

Χάρης ἔδωκε Εὐπλοίωνί με.

CXXXV.

Vase, v. CIG. 8157. Counterpart of Kaibel 1099 (CIG. 8154), but with two orthographical differences.

Ἐξηκίας ἔγραψε κἀποίησέ με.

CXXXVI.

Vase, iv. C. Smith in *Journal of Hellenic Studies*, VI (1885), p. 372. Smith guesses from Rhodes.

Φιλτός ἠμι τᾶς καλᾶς ἁ κύλιξ ἁ ποικίλα.

The editor Φιλτῶς; but see p. 70.

CXXXVII.

Silver spoon with Cypriote characters. Deecke (Collitz *Dial.*) n. 61.

Ἀμ(μ)ῦς κατέθηκε τᾶι θιῶι τᾶι Γολγίαι.

CXXXVIII.

Attic, vi. Kabbadias in Eph. 1886, p. 133. Acropolis 1886.

["Α]ρχερμος ἐποίησεν ὁ Χῖ[ος].
[. . . . . . ἀνέ]θηκεν Ἀθηναίαι πολιούχω[ι].

I have not taken the first line as verse. If it is, Ἄρχερμος ποίησεν was intended.

CXXXIX.

Att. v. Kumanudes, Ἀθήναιον, x, p. 523. Kirchhoff, Hermes XVII (1882), p. 623.

οἴδε παρ' Ἑλλήσποντον ἀπώλεσαν ἀγλαὸν ἥβην
βαρνάμενοι. σφετέραν δ' εὐκλέϊσαμ πατρίδα,
ὥστ' ἐχθροὺς στενάχειμ πολέμου θέρος ἐκκομίσαντας·
αὑτοῖς δ' ἀθάνατον μνῆμ' ἀρετῆς ἔθεσαν.

CXL.

Cos, iii–ii. *Journal of Hellenic Studies*, VI, p. 259.

εἰκόνα μητρὸς τήνδε Θόας . . ΓΙΟ . . . . . .
υἷες Ἀριστείδου στῆσαν Ἀθηναΐδος.

ἢ πατρὸς ἐξ ἀγαθοῦ βλαστοῦσα γονᾶισι Θόαντος
γνήσιον εὐλογίας ἀμφέθετο στέφανον.

Δυμάν. Θόας. Ἀναξαγόρας. Διοκλῆς. Λεωνίδας. Ἀνδροτέλης.

CXLI.

Delos, unknown time. Vase-inscription, quoted in a temple-inventory of the second century, Bull. Corr. 1882, p. 29 flg. (= Dittenberger, Syll. Inscr., n. 367), l. 41.

Ἱστιαιεύς μ' ἀνέθηκεν Κάλλωνος ὕπερ. φίλ' Ἄπολλον,
τήνδε συναμφοτέροις εὐτυχίην ὄπασον.

Usener conjectures τὺν δὲ for τήνδε.

CXLII.

Delos, unknown time. Similar vase-inscription, quoted in same inventory, l. 46.

Ἡρ[α]ι Θῆρις τήνδε ἀνέθηκεν παῖς Ἀμιάντου.

Before Dittenberger, Ηρχίθηρις was read.

CXLIII.

Delos, unknown time. Another quoted vase-inscription in same inventory, l. 49.

Μύνδιος Ἀρτεμῆς Θεοκρίτου Ἀπόλλωνι
Δηλίωι.

Meant as verse, according to Dittenberger.

CXLIV.

Thessaly, vi–v. Kirchhoff, Hermes xx (1885), p. 158.

μνᾶμ' ἐμὶ Πυρ(ρ)ιάδα. ὃς οὐκ ἠπ[ί]στατο φεύγειν,
ἀλλ' αὖθε πὲρ γᾶς τᾶσδε
πολ(λ)ὸν ἀριστεύων ἔθανε.

POSTSCRIPT.

Just as the last pages of this article are casting comes the second fascicle of the CIA. vol. IV. This contains a good many of the newer inscriptions of our collection, and among these are the hitherto unpublished ones numbered above X–XVI. Although possessing copies of these inscriptions, I did not feel myself at liberty to print them. Now, however, I may be permitted to add the text of these documents.

x (= CIA. IV., I, n. 373^{105}).

Παλ(λ)άδι 'Αθαναίαι Λύσων ἀνέθηκεν ἀπαρχὴν
ὧν αὐτοῦ κτ[εά͵]νων, τῆι δὲ θεῶι χαρίεν.
Θηβάδης ἐ[πόησεν . .]νου παῖς τόδ' ἄγαλμα.

xi (= CIA. IV., I, n. 373^{94}).

. . . ης θῆκε Διὸς κούρηι τόδ' ἄγαλμα.
. . . . . . πατρὸς ῦς Χαιρίωνος ἐπευχή
ταῖν . . . . . .

So I had written, without pretending to understand the sense. Kirchhoff, I see, has made the second verse [ὅσπερ δὴ] πατρὸς ῦς Χαιρίωνος ἐπεύχεται (εἶ)ν[αι]͵, supposing the letter Ε to have been omitted by the cutter in the last word. Assuming this to be right (and it is very probable), Χαιρίωνος on p. 75 should give
                                                                                              4 5
place to Χαιρίωνος; πατρός on p. 74 should disappear; and ἐπεύχεταῖ (εἶ)ν[αι]
       4   3   5   6
should be added on p. 110.

xii (= CIA. IV., I, n. 373^{100}).

Παλλάδι Τρι[τογενεῖ . . . Γόρ]γυλ(λ)ος μ' ἀνέθη[κεν]
καὶ Χρέμης ὑύς.

xiii (= CIA. IV., I, n. 373^{57}).

. . . λιτύς μ' ἀνέθη͵κε . . . .
[πότνι'] 'Αθηναία, χεχ[αρίσθω σοι τόδε δῶρον].
Εὐήνωρ ἐποίησεν.

The name looks to me like 'Ανγέλιτος. Α, Ν and ϒ are marked in my copy as certain, though not entirely intact; the third letter must be Λ, Α or Δ; the fourth Ε or +.

xiv (= CIA. IV., I, n. 373^{107}).

. . . . ὑὺς 'Αθήνηι
. . . . χ]άριν ἀντιδίδου.

xv (= CIA. IV., 1, n. 373¹⁰³)

. . . . οὐνποριωνος
. . . . Φίλων με ἐποίησεν.

xvi (= CIA. IV., 1, n. 373¹⁰⁴; cp. p. 131).

. . . . . ἀνέθηκεν . . . . ι παιδὶ ἀπ(α)ρχήν.

The new fascicle of the CIA. contains a number of new archaic epigrams hitherto unknown to me. I wish they had appeared in time to be used in my work; but these, and two or three others which have recently been printed in other publications, must be reserved for a supplementary article, for which the next few years will doubtless bring ample material. Meanwhile I note one or two things. Another trochaic caesura of the fourth foot is seen in CIA. IV. n. 373²³¹, p. 131: Τελεσῖνος ἄγαλμ' ἀνέθηκεν. Another maltreated proper name in Αἰσχίνης ἀνέθηκεν, n. 373²³². Omitted ν movable in the chief caesura (compare pp. 106 and 158) in an old Thessalian dedication, Mittheilungen XI, p. 450; 'Αργεία μ' ἀνέθηκε ὑπὲρ παιδὸς τόδ' ἄγαλμα.

I observe at the last moment a case of hiatus, τοῖόν νυ ἐπάσατο, CXXXII', which was inadvertently omitted in its proper place on page 106.

THE ATHENIAN PNYX.

BY

JOHN M. CROW.

WITH A SURVEY AND NOTES,

BY

JOSEPH THACHER CLARKE.

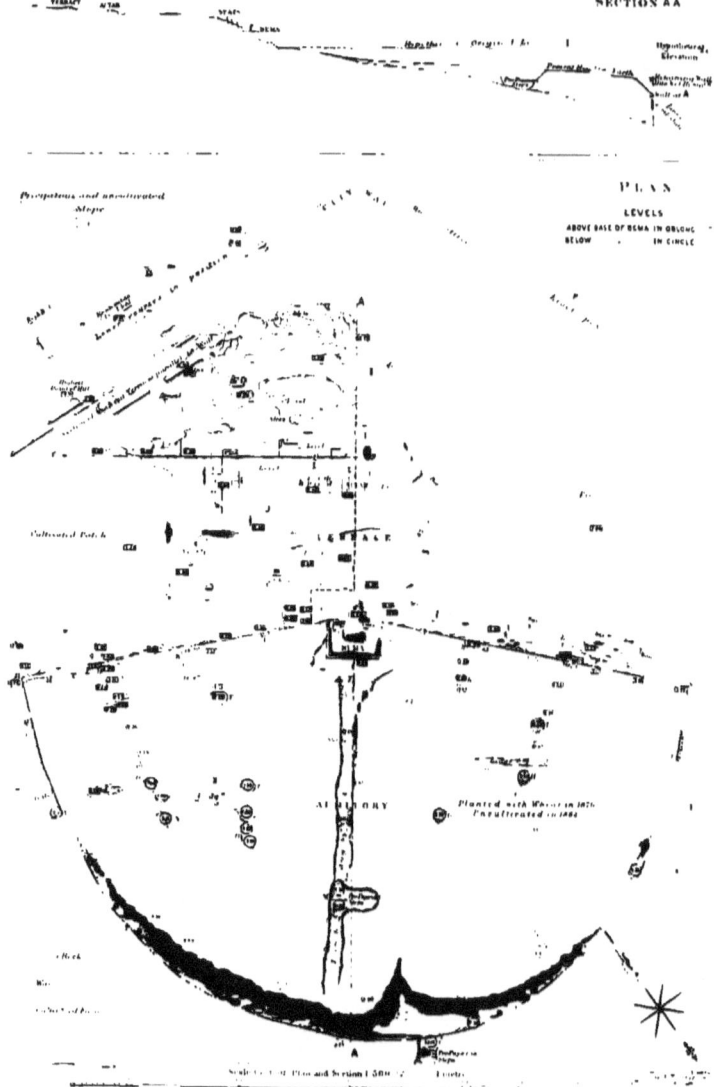

THE ATHENIAN PNYX.

THE ATHENIAN PNYX.

No greater effort has been made to settle any point in the topography of Athens than has been devoted to the site of the Pnyx. Scholars of different nationalities have become interested in the discussion, and valuable contributions to it have been made in French, German, Norwegian, and English. These investigations have led to conclusions differing widely from each other. Our attention was especially called to this fact by Professor Kirchhoff's lectures on Greek antiquities. We afterwards availed ourselves of the opportunities for study and personal observation furnished by a residence of six months in the city of Athens in 1882–83, when we made some excavations for the purpose of determining more definitely the nature of the floor of the Pnyx. Though not extensive, they led to the conclusion that some of the hypotheses entertained by writers on the topography of Athens in regard to the Pnyx question are incorrect.

It happened also at this time that Mr. Joseph Thacher Clarke,[1] who had been engaged in excavations in Asia Minor for the Archæological Institute of America, was spending his vacation in Athens, and he was induced to make a survey of the entire Pnyx Hill.[A] As no very thorough discussion of the question has yet appeared in America, we hope that our own work, illustrated and explained by Mr. Clarke's drawings and survey, will justify us in asking archæological students to accompany us in a reconsideration of the whole subject.

What we have to say arranges itself naturally under three heads: first, a study of the most important passages in classical authors in

---

[1] The notes designated by letters and signed J. T. C. are Mr. Clarke's.

[A] The transit and level used in the survey were lent for the purpose by Dr. Henry Schliemann, to whom we desire to express our thanks. — J. T. C.

which the Pnyx is mentioned or referred to ; second, an examination of the Pnyx itself in the light of the information thus gathered ; third, a survey of what has been recently written by others on the subject.

I.

In the earliest history of Athens the public life of the city gathered around the Acropolis. Later, as the city continued to grow, even before Solon's time, the assemblies of the people, a portion of their legal proceedings, and certain festal meetings were transferred from the citadel to the Cerameicus. About this place many of the public buildings were erected. Later still, the participation of the people in public life, which naturally resulted from the political institutions of Solon and Cleisthenes, together with the party conflicts of the sixth century B.C., led to the selection of a more convenient and comfortable place for holding the popular assemblies.

That a place of such importance cannot be definitely located is greatly to be regretted. There is no passage in the Greek literature that will enable us to identify the Pnyx with absolute certainty. But, however vague the references to it may be, it is to them that every student must come. Tradition that might have survived the long night of gloom through which Greece has passed could not possibly have any scientific value ; nor can fancy be allowed to play any rôle here.[1] Notwithstanding this lack of absolute certainty, there is no question about our ability to determine certain limits within which the Pnyx must have been situated.[2] This is admitted by all writers on the topography of Athens.

I. The first passage to which we call attention is in the Onomas-

---

[1] "Bei keiner Art historischer Untersuchungen darf vorgefassten Meinungen oder der ergänzenden Phantasie weniger Spielraum gegönnt werden als bei der Erörterung von Fragen der Topographie. Sorgsame Abwägung der litterarischen Zeugnisse, ... unbefangene Prüfung der erhaltenen Reste, genaue Kenntniss und Beachtung der Natur und Eigenthümlichkeiten des betreffenden Terrains, ... sind hier ein unerlässliches Erforderniss."— Ludwig Ross, *Die Pnyx und das Pelasgikon in Athen*, pp. v. and vi.

[2] "Ueber die Lage der Pnyx finden sich einige Bestimmungen vor die nicht täuschen können."— Welcker, *Der Felsaltar des Höchsten Zeus*, u. s. w., p. 325 (61).

ticon of Pollux, VIII, 132, where we find these words: Ἐνεκλησίαζον δὲ πάλαι μὲν ἐν τῇ Πυκνί. Πνὺξ δὲ ἦν χωρίον πρὸς τῇ Ἀκροπόλει κατεσκευασμένον κατὰ τὴν παλαιὰν ἁπλότητα οὐκ εἰς θέατρον πολυπραγμοσύνην. αὖθις δὲ τὰ μὲν ἄλλα ἐν τῷ Διονυσιακῷ θεάτρῳ, μόναις δὲ τὰς ἀρχαιρεσίας ἐν τῇ Πυκνί.[1]

This passage is important, as in it a direct attempt is made to describe the Pnyx. By it we are informed on the following points:

The word Πνύξ was used to designate the place in which the assemblies of the people were held; this was a *place* and not a *building*;[2] it was at no great distance from the Acropolis; it was arranged with simplicity and not with the elaborateness of a theatre; it was abandoned at some time after the construction of the Dionysiac theatre, and was then used for special meetings only.

II. In the imaginary city which Plato pictures in Critias, 112 A, he thus describes the conformation of the site of Athens: τὸ δὲ πρὶν ἐν ἑτέρῳ χρόνῳ μέγεθος μὲν ἦν πρὸς τὸν Ἠριδανὸν καὶ τὸν Ἰλισὸν ἀποβεβηκυῖα καὶ περιειληφυῖα ἐντὸς τὴν Πύκνα καὶ τὸν Λυκαβηττὸν ὅρον ἐκ τοῦ καταντικρὺ τῆς Πυκνὸς ἔχουσα.[3]

In this passage Plato gives a description of the oldest citadel of Athens, as he imagined it, before inundations, earthquakes, and the like had torn it into several pieces. He imagines the space between the heights (Acropolis, Lycabettus, and Pnyx) closed up so that the three hills form one great citadel rock; and he mentions on one side of the Acropolis the Pnyx, on the other Lycabettus over against the Pnyx, ἐκ τοῦ καταντικρὺ τῆς Πυκνός. Now Lycabettus is one of the points in the topography of Athens about which there is no longer any doubt.[4] It is the conical hill north-east of the city, the top

---

[1] "The assemblies were formerly held in the Pnyx. The Pnyx was a place near the Acropolis, arranged with ancient simplicity, and not with the elaborateness (?) of a theatre. Later the other assemblies were held in the Dionysiac theatre, and only those for the election of officers in the Pnyx."

[2] As was common in designating εὐρυχωρίαι in Athens, it was called a τόπος or χωρίον. Aeschines, *in Tim.* § 82, also has the words ὁ τόπος ὁ ἐν τῇ Πυκνί; and Hesychius, *s.v.* Πνύξ, says the Pnyx was a *place*, τόπος.

[3] "But in primitive times the hill of the Acropolis extended to the Eridanus and Ilissus, and included the Pnyx on one side, and the Lycabettus as a boundary on the opposite side to the Pnyx." — Jowett.

[4] Christensen, *Athens Pnyx*. p. 78.

of which is dedicated to St. George. The Pnyx must, therefore, be sought in the south-western portion of the city, over against Lycabettus. It is also spoken of as a separate hill, and consequently could not have been situated on the slope of the Acropolis. This fact will aid us in interpreting the words of Pollux πρὸς τῇ Ἀκροπόλει. They must be allowed to refer to a point at some distance from the Acropolis as well as to one situated on it. The Pnyx was πρὸς τῇ Ἀκροπόλει, and also constituted a part of the boundary of Plato's imaginary citadel on one side, as Lycabettus did on the other.

In the south-western part of the ancient city we find three hills, now known in Athens as the Museum Hill, the Pnyx Hill, and the Hill of the Nymphs. On the last is the astronomical observatory. For convenience, and in accordance with common usage at Athens, we shall call them all the Pnyx Hills when we have occasion to refer to them collectively; and, in like manner, we shall use the word Pnyx in referring to the ruin on the middle one of these hills. These three hills lie in a line from the south-east to the north-west along the western foot of the Acropolis, and are separated from it by a depression which is less deep toward the Pnyx Hill than toward the other two. On the side toward the Acropolis, the Museum Hill and the Hill of the Nymphs are rather precipitous, but the Pnyx Hill descends gradually into the depression. This part of the city is now generally understood to be that which the ancients called Melite. It has been thoroughly studied and described by Curtius, Christensen, and others.

III. In Lucian (*bis accus.* 9). Dike is represented as going to Athens to assist in the administration of Justice. Hermes, who accompanies her, says to her: αὐτὴ μὲν ἐνταῦθά που ἐπὶ τοῦ πάγου κάθησο ἐς τὴν Πνύκα ὁρῶσα καὶ περιμένουσα ἔστ' ἂν κηρύξω τὰ παρὰ τοῦ Διός, ἐγὼ δὲ ἐς τὴν Ἀκρόπολιν ἀναβὰς ῥᾷον οὕτως ἅπαντας ἐκ τοῦ ἐπηκόου προσκαλέσομαι.[1]

The word πάγου in this passage is generally understood to refer to the Areopagus. Dike, therefore, seated herself on the spot where the ancient court formerly held its sessions. From here she looked into the Pnyx. From the passage already cited from Plato we learn that the Pnyx was west of the Acropolis, and therefore west of the

[1] "Seat yourself somewhere on the Areopagus looking towards the Pnyx, and remain until I have announced the message from Zeus; and I will ascend into the Acropolis and there summon more easily all who are within hearing."

place where Dike was now sitting. As she was there to await the coming of the people, it is highly probable that she looked in the direction from which they were expected to come. This supposition is rendered almost necessary by the nature of the place. The Areopagus is precipitous on all sides except the west, where it slopes gradually to the open space south of the temple known as the Theseum. Such a crowd as Dike seems to have expected could scarcely have come from any other direction. The topography of the place is thus seen to correspond with the testimony of the ancients. Nor does it weigh against this supposition that Dike sat looking towards the west, that she saw Pan and asked Hermes who he was before he went to summon the people. Pan's grotto was east of where Dike was sitting, under the north-west corner of the Acropolis; but there is no intimation of the direction from which he was coming. Lucian says simply that he was approaching, προσιών. From this passage we conclude that the Pnyx was visible from the Areopagus and was probably in a south-western direction from it.

IV. In the *Life of Theseus* (§ 27), Plutarch gives an account of the battle between the Amazons and the Athenians. The encampment of the Amazons was within the city, ἐν ἄστει, and the battle was fought in the vicinity of the Pnyx and the Museum Hill, περὶ τὴν Πνύκα καὶ τὸ Μουσεῖον. In regard to the encampment, he adds further that it was ἐν τῇ πόλει σχεδόν, which is tautological unless we understand the word πόλει in this clause to refer to the Acropolis. Otherwise it is difficult to understand why Plutarch should say that the encampment was ἐν ἄστει, and then add immediately afterwards that it was *almost ἐν τῇ πόλει*. That he means that the encampment was almost on the Acropolis is also favored by a not uncommon usage by which the word πόλις takes the place of 'Ακρόπολις. Plutarch then quotes Cleidemus, who, he says, gives us accurate details, as saying: τὸ μὲν εὐώνυμον τῶν 'Αμαζόνων κέρας ἐπιστρέφειν πρὸς τὸ νῦν καλούμενον 'Αμαζόνειον. τῷ δὲ δεξιῷ πρὸς τὴν Πνύκα κατὰ τὴν Χρύσαν ἥκειν. μάχεσθαι δὲ πρὸς τοῦτο τοὺς 'Αθηναίους ἀπὸ τοῦ Μουσείου ταῖς 'Αμαζόσι συμπεσόντας, καὶ τάφους τῶν πεσόντων περὶ τὴν πλατεῖαν εἶναι τὴν φέρουσαν ἐπὶ τὰς πύλας παρὰ τὸ Χαλκώδοντος ἡρῷον, ἃς νῦν Πειραϊκὰς ὀνομάζουσι.[1]

---

[1] "The left wing of the Amazons turned towards the place now called the Amazoneum, while the right wing extended to the Pnyx at a place called

This passage leaves no doubt as to the site of the battle. It was the depression already spoken of, bounded on one side by the Acropolis and Areopagus, and on the other by the Pnyx Hills, and opening toward the north in the level space south of the Theseum. Though it may not be possible to determine all the places mentioned by Plutarch in this description, those of greatest importance are generally agreed upon. The Museum and Areopagus we know certainly. The Amazoneum is believed to have been north or north-west of the Areopagus;[1] and the Peiraic gate was north-west of the Hill of the Nymphs, as it is represented on Curtius's map of Athens. The Athenians were on the Museum Hill, and the Amazons faced them, having their left wing on or near the Areopagus. Aeschylus (*Eumen.* 685) says the camp of the Amazons was on the Areopagus, πάγον δ' Ἄρειον τόνδ', Ἀμαζόνων ἕδραν. As their line would naturally be near or in front of their encampment, their right wing would of necessity extend to some point in the vicinity of the Hill of the Nymphs or of the Pnyx Hill. The fact that Aeschylus represents the encampment as on the Areopagus makes the latter the more probable. A careful study of this passage and of the site of the battle leaves little doubt as to the details; and these words support very strongly the conclusion reached from the passages from Lucian and Plato, that the Pnyx was south-west of the Areopagus.

V. In Aeschines (*de falsa legat.* § 74) we find the following words: ἀνιστάμενοι οἱ ῥήτορες ἀποβλέπειν εἰς τὰ προπύλαια τῆς Ἀκροπόλεως ἐκέλευον ἡμᾶς καὶ τῆς ἐν Σαλαμῖνι πρὸς τὸν Πέρσην ναυμαχίας μεμνῆσθαι.[2] Harpocration (*s.v.* Προπύλαια ταῦτα, quoted from Demosthenes) says: δύναται μὲν δεικτικῶς λέγεσθαι ἅτε ὁρωμένων τῶν προπυλαίων ἀπὸ τῆς Πυκνός.[3]

From these words it is plain that the Propylaea were visible from the Pnyx, and that the Pnyx lay west of the Propylaea.

Χρύσα (?). The Athenians attacked the Amazons on this side (πρὸς τοῦτο = against the right wing), issuing from the Museum Hill; and tombs of the fallen are to be seen along the street which leads to the gate near the shrine of Chalkodon, now called the Peiraic gate."

[1] Literarisches Centralblatt, 1863, No. 30, 712.

[2] "The orators, rising, used to call on us to look at the Propylaea of the Acropolis, and remind us of the naval battle against the Persian at Salamis."

[3] "This can be said δεικτικῶς (German *hindeutend*), pointing towards the object, for the Propylaea are visible from the Pnyx."

VI. In the Knights of Aristophanes (v. 313) the chorus says that Cleon looked down from the rocks, ἀπὸ τῶν πετρῶν ἄνωθεν, as a tunny-fisher from the rocks on the seashore. The word πετρῶν in this passage is understood to refer to the Pnyx. In the passage quoted above, Plato also refers to the Pnyx as a hill or height opposite Lycabettus. Demosthenes (de cor. § 169) uses the words πᾶς ὁ δῆμος ἄνω καθῆτο; and Plutarch (Nicias 7) has the words ἐκκλησίας ποτὲ οὔσης τὸν δῆμον καθήμενον ἄνω. In the Scholia to Aeschines in Tim. § 81, the Pnyx is called a height or hill, πάγος ὑψηλὸς, λόφος καλούμενος Πνύξ. When the people met it was common to speak of going up into the place of assembly, ἀναβαίνειν εἰς τὴν ἐκκλησίαν.[1] In the Acharnians of Aristophanes (v. 20) Dicaeopolis is represented as looking into the Agora.

The Pnyx must, therefore, have been situated on one of the prominent hills of the city, and from it it must have been possible to look into the Agora.

VII. In the Knights of Aristophanes, v. 754, Demos is spoken of as sitting on a rock or stone seat, ὅταν δ' ἐπὶ ταυτησὶ καθῆται τῆς πέτρας. In v. 783 of the same play he is told that Cleon does not care for his sitting uncomfortably on the rocks, ἐπὶ ταῖσι πέτραις. In the Ecclesiazusae, v. 21, Praxagora speaks of the women as about to take *seats* in the Pnyx; and in v. 92 ff., of the danger that they might expose themselves by stepping over the *seats* unless they should be seated before the assembly became full. In the Wasps, v. 33, the Athenians are derided for their sheepishness, and Sosias is made to say that he saw in a dream the sheep *sitting* together, πρόβατα συγκαθήμενα, in the Pnyx. The words καθέζομαι and κάθημαι are often used in speaking of the people in the Pnyx. The scholiast on v. 784 of the Knights uses the word βάθρα in speaking of the stone seats in the Pnyx, and explains the word τουτί, which is used by the Sausage-seller to designate something which he had brought to Demos, to mean a cushion. The connection leaves no doubt about this. In the Wasps, v. 42, Sosias says he thought he saw Theorus *sitting* on the ground, χαμαί, but this is the only passage in which this word is used, and Sosias here speaks of a single per-

---

[1] Welcker, *Felsaltar des Höchsten Zeus*, p. 329 (65); Ross, *Die Pnyx und das Pelasgikon in Athen*, p. 1.

son. In the Acharnians, v. 20, Dicaeopolis is represented as sitting in the Pnyx early in the morning while it is still empty, and complaining of the tardiness of the people in coming to the assembly. He says further, that when they do come, the Prytanes will jostle each other for the front seat, περὶ πρώτου ξύλου. That πρώτου ξύλου here means the front seat is plainly shown by v. 42 of the same play, where προεδρίαν is synonymous with it. The Scholiast on v. 24 also explains ξύλον to mean προεδρία, and then cites vs. 754 and 783 of the Knights to show that all the seats were made of stone. But in these verses the seats are spoken of in a general way, and, consequently, they do not materially stand in the way of the supposition that part of the seats may have been made of wood. Nevertheless the Scholiast's remark has its value, as it shows that at his time the Pnyx was thought of as supplied with seats. The expression ὁ ἐπὶ τῶν ξύλων was used in early times at Athens in speaking of the slave who had charge of the seats in the theatre; and this usage survived after the construction of the Dionysiac theatre on the south slope of the Acropolis, in which all the seats were made of stone.

VIII. That the Pnyx was also in a certain sense a sacred place may be inferred from the existence in it of a statue of Zeus Agoraeus, Ἀγοραῖος Ζεὺς ἵδρυται ἐν τῇ ἀγορᾷ καὶ ἐν τῇ ἐκκλησίᾳ, Schol. Aristoph. Eq. 410. This inference is favored also by the words λίθος, τὸ ἐν τῇ θεία ἐκκλησία βῆμα, in Hesychius. s.v. λιθωμότα. This point will come up again in the discussion of the tablets found by Lord Aberdeen.[1]

IX. From the Scholia on the Birds of Aristophanes, v. 997, we learn that the Pnyx was probably a place from which astronomical observations were made. In this place we are informed that Meton, whose name has come down to us in the Metonic Cycle, set up a sundial on the wall in the Pnyx: ἡλιοτρόπιον ἐν τῇ νῦν οὔσῃ ἐκκλησίᾳ, πρὸς τῷ τείχει τῷ ἐν τῇ Πνυκί. About the word τεῖχος in this passage the most widely different opinions are entertained.[2] Wherever this wall may have been, it is certain that the top of this hill is very well adapted for astronomical observations; and it would be very natural

---

[1] See Schoemann, de Comit. pp. 91–95; Ross, Die Pnyx und das Pelasgikon, p. 12; Welcker, Der Felsaltar des Höchsten Zeus, p. 69.
[2] See Welcker, ibid. p. 331 (67); Ross, ibid. p. 4.

that a sundial should be placed on such a site, whether on the city wall or on a wall erected especially for it.

X. In Plato's Republic, vi. 492 C, in speaking of the applause in an assembly, court, theatre, camp, or other place of resort, it is said: ὅταν αἴ τε πέτραι καὶ ὁ τόπος ἐν ᾧ ἂν ὦσιν ἐπηχοῦντες διπλάσιον θόρυβον παρέχωσι τοῦ ψόγου καὶ ἐπαίνου.[1] But as the Pnyx is not mentioned in this passage, and so many other places are mentioned, no conclusion can be drawn from it as to the situation of the Pnyx. The only reason for introducing it here is that it has been used to favor the opinion that the Pnyx was situated in a low place.

XI. In Plutarch's Themistocles, § 19, it is said that Themistocles did not so much make Peiraeus dependent on the city as make the city dependent on Peiraeus, and the land dependent on the sea. By this means he transferred the power from the nobles to the people, because the sailors and the pilots became the real strength of the state. Then Plutarch adds: διὸ καὶ τὸ βῆμα τὸ ἐν Πνυκὶ πεποιημένον ὥστ' ἀποβλέπειν πρὸς τὴν θάλασσαν ὕστερον οἱ τριάκοντα πρὸς τὴν χώραν ἀπέστρεψαν, οἰόμενοι τὴν μὲν κατὰ θάλατταν ἀρχὴν γένεσιν εἶναι δημοκρατίας, ὀλιγαρχίᾳ δ' ἧττον δυσχεραίνειν τοὺς γεωργοῦντας.[2]

About this passage we shall have something to say elsewhere. For the present we only call attention to the fact that the Thirty Tyrants left the bema in the same position in which the stage in the Pnyx now stands, looking toward the land, πρὸς τὴν χώραν.

From what has been gathered, we may describe the Pnyx as follows. The Pnyx, the place of public assembly in ancient Athens, was elevated, and of simple arrangement; it was an open *place* and not a *building:* it was situated on a height south-west of the Areopagus, from which it could be seen, and in the same direction from the Acropolis, from which it was not distant; it was furnished with stone seats for the people in general, wooden seats for the dignitaries, and a stage for a speaker; the Propylaea were visible from it, and from it one could look into the Agora; it was to a certain extent sacred in

---

[1] "And when the rocks and the place in which they are assembled re-echo and so redouble the sound of blame or praise."

[2] "For this reason the Thirty Tyrants afterwards turned the bema in the Pnyx, which was made to look toward the sea, toward the land, because they thought that naval supremacy had been the origin of democracy, but that tillers of the soil were less ill-disposed toward oligarchy."

character, and may have served as a site for astronomical observations; after the construction of the Dionysiac theatre it was abandoned as the regular place of popular assemblies, and was used only for special meetings.

Possessed of this information, and being acquainted with the position of the Acropolis, Areopagus, and other points mentioned, the student will find no difficulty in selecting, almost with certainty, a place answering to the given conditions. On arriving at the place he will be surprised to find himself in presence of a ruin, the first view of which will convince him that it is one of the most venerable within the limits of the ancient city.

II.

A study of the survey which accompanies this paper will aid in forming a correct conception of both the ruin and the hill on which it is situated.

It lies on the middle one of the three hills mentioned above, which bound Athens on the west. It faces north-east, and is so near the top of the hill that the upper boundary is but a short distance from the summit. It is bounded on this side by what we will designate as a back wall; *i.e.*, the rock of the hill is cut down, so that when you stand within the enclosure, with your face turned to the hill, a perpendicular wall of native rock rises before you. This wall is not straight, but consists of two parts, $R\theta$ and θS, which form an angle of 158° at the middle point θ. The top of the wall is very irregular. The height varies, and is greatest toward the south-east, where it is 7.40 metres. This altitude decreases gradually toward the north-west. The half marked θS varies in altitude from two to three metres. In cutting away the rock to make this back wall a large block was left, which stands in the angle made by its two parts. This is marked "bema" on the survey, and has for a long time been supposed to be the tribune of the Attic orators. The rock has been removed to a sufficient depth to produce a floor which is nearly on a level with the base of the bema. This floor is bounded on the right and left by walls of native rock, of the same nature as the back wall. These side walls meet the back wall at the points R and S. Their altitude, which is greatest near these points, gradually decreases to the points where the slope of the hill reaches the level of the floor. On the right this point is marked U on the survey; on the left it is between Q and V.

At some distance below the last-named points, between Z and W on the right and V and Y on the left, are the ends of a massive wall, which, for want of a better term, we will call semicircular, though in reality it is not more than the third of a circle. This wall forms the boundary of the ruin on the north-east. It is built of immense blocks of stone, which seem to have been quarried from the hill above. By reference to the survey it is seen that an arc of a circle whose centre is at the point T almost coincides with the course of this wall." As it lies on the side of the hill, its greatest perpendicular height is, of course, at the point A.^{c} The top of the wall, however, is not in the same level throughout its course; at A it is 3.39 metres lower than at W, and 3.11 metres lower than at Y. The space above the wall is filled in with broken stones, covered by a stratum of fine earth. Above the point A the earth is 2.37 metres higher than the top of the wall. This stratum of earth extends over the entire enclosure and constitutes the present surface. It is only by removing it that the nature of the rock-floor below can be determined. Its depth varies from a few inches in the upper part to five or six feet in the lower. See Section AA'.

As was said above, the back wall whose ends are designated on the survey by the letters R and S and which forms the south-western boundary, is not straight, but its two halves make an angle of 158° at

---

B. A dotted semicircle, $RYZS$, having its centre at T, is drawn upon the map in order to show the deviation of the retaining wall, in plan, from a true arc. The close agreement in length between the radii TR and TS with TY and TZ makes it evident that the Greek constructor endeavored to lay out an exact semicircle as the plan of the auditory. The deviation observable, reaching a maximum of 5½ metres, is to be ascribed to the difficulty experienced by the primitive surveyor in laying out such a figure upon an irregular slope. The arc was evidently determined by holding one end of a cord about 60 metres in length at the point T, in front of the middle of the bema, and moving the other end around the periphery to be occupied by the wall. At first, near the corners, no correction was made for the diminution of the horizontal distance through the dip, — with the result that the cuttings and wall from R to Y and from S to Z were disposed somewhat within the ideal arc. Below these points the error of method became apparent and a correction was allowed, — the addition proving to be excessive. — J. T. C.

C. Namely, 5.13 metres. — J. T. C.

the point marked θ. If a straight line be drawn from R to S, it will intersect the line AA' at the point T in front of the bema. Taking this point as a centre, the part of the enclosure below the line RS is found to be nearly a semicircle, the radius RT being but 0.4 of a metre longer than TS." The greater part of the semicircular wall, YAW, is seen to lie outside of the arc of the circle. From these dimensions the area can be easily computed.[e]

After this general survey of the whole ruin, we will now describe its different parts in detail, beginning with the back wall RS. In this wall between the corner R and the bema are more than fifty rectangular niches, cut as if to receive tablets. All except one are from five to eight inches in width and height, and an inch or so deep. The "Cut" (marked on the survey) between S and the bema is so irregular that it seems to have had no such object as the others. The largest of all, which is marked "Niche," is forty feet to the left of the bema. Of the smaller ones, forty are between this large one and the bema; the remainder are beyond the large one toward R on the survey. Several have been enlarged, the last cutting being less deep than the first. One of the small niches has been cut through in making the large one. This fact is of some importance, as it indicates that the small niches were not cut with any reference to the large niche. One of them at least was there before the large niche was made. In some of the small ones holes are still to be seen, in which the nails were inserted which held in position the tablets for which the niches seem to have been made. A number of the tablets that were in the niches were found buried in the earth at the foot of the wall when Lord Aberdeen made excavations here in 1803, and they are now in the British Museum. The inscriptions which they bear have been copied into the *C.I.G.*, Nos. 497 ff.[1] Most of them consist of the names of the donor, the words εὐχήν or χαριστήριον and ὑψίστῳ. Two add the word Διί to ὑψίστῳ. They have also a picture

---

D. RT 59.9 metres. TS = 59.5 metres. — J. T. C.

E. The area of the entire auditory, excluding the bema, is 6240.5 square metres. Deducting about 160 square metres for the masses of rock at the south-eastern corner which were not removed, this provides standing-room for twenty-five or thirty thousand auditors. About eighteen thousand seats might have been placed within the same space. — J. T. C.

[1] Ross, *Die Pnyx und das Pelasgikon*, p. 15.

THE ATHENIAN PNYX.

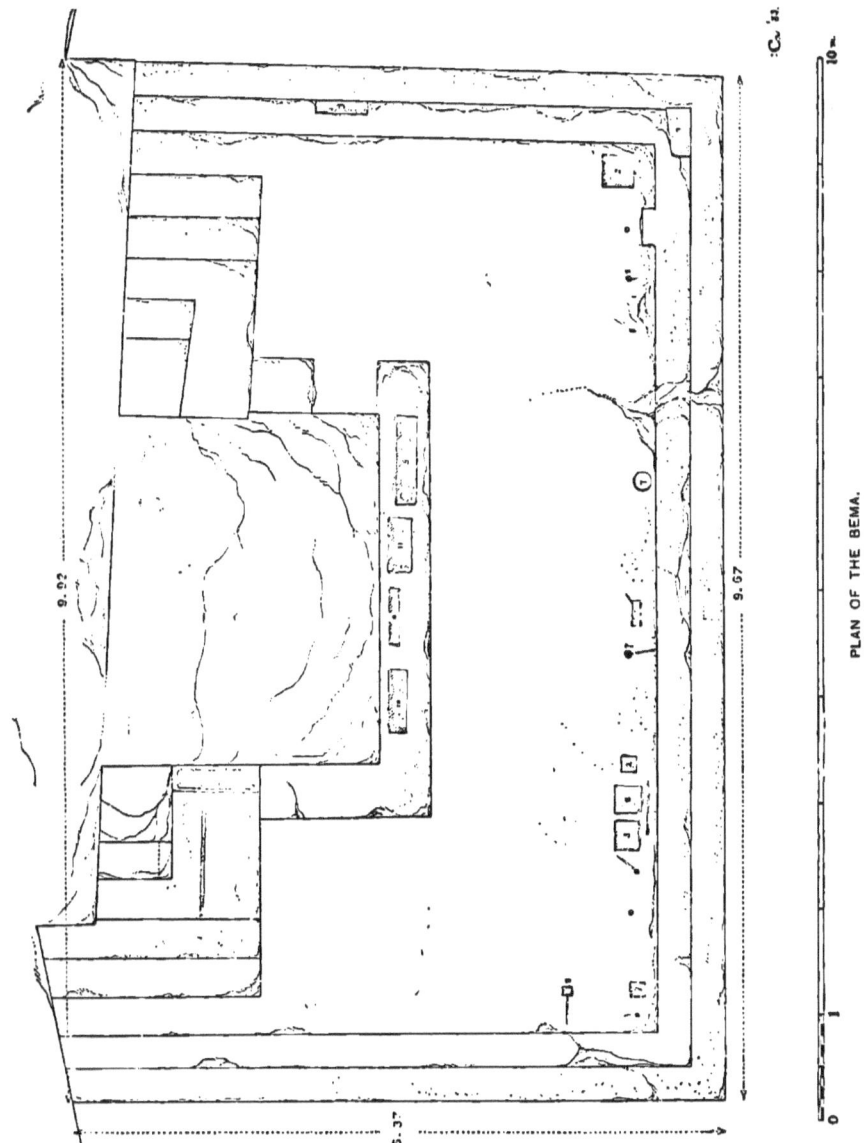

PLAN OF THE BEMA.

220 THE ATHENIAN PNYX.

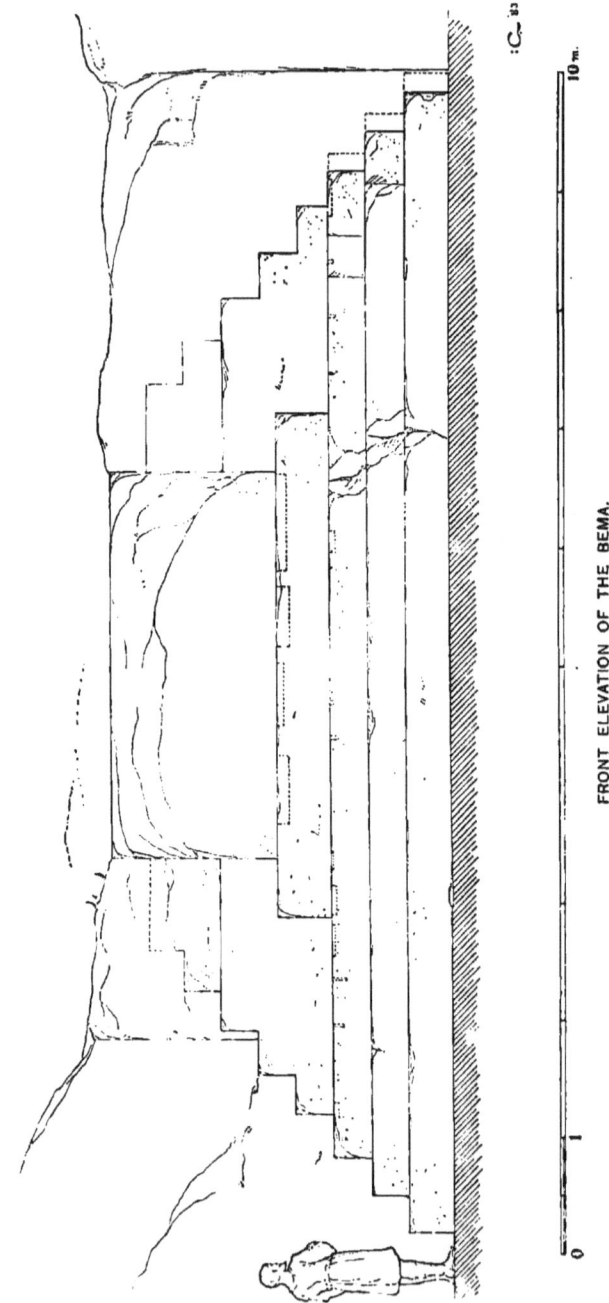

FRONT ELEVATION OF THE BEMA.

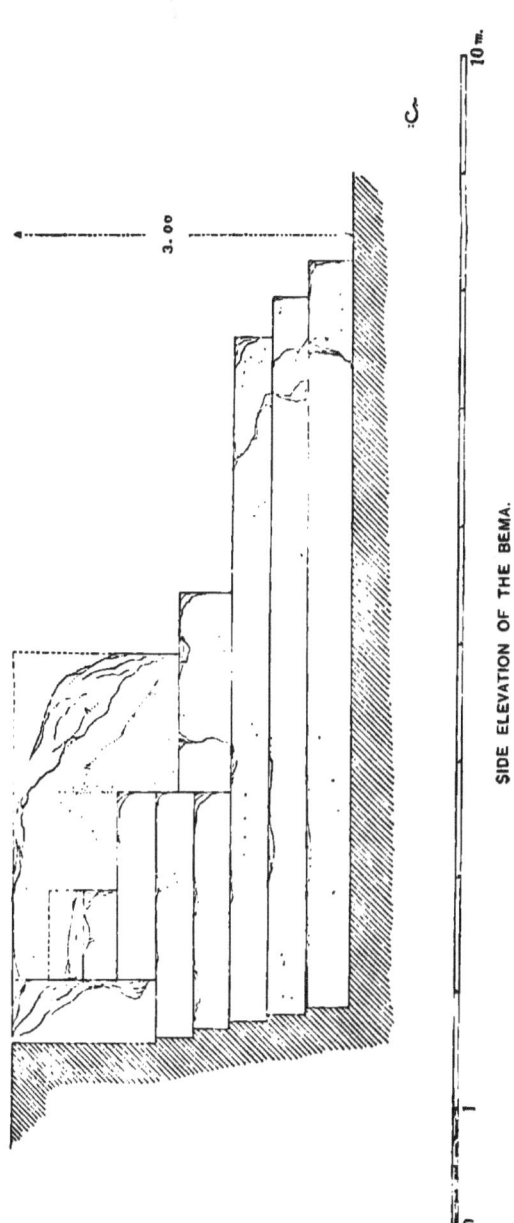

SIDE ELEVATION OF THE BEMA.

of some part of the human body, doubtless that which was thought to have been healed by Zeus the Highest, to whom the tablets are dedicated. Ross has noticed that the names are mostly of the lower class.

In the angle of the back wall stands the bema, which is 9.67 metres wide in front, and projects 6.37 metres from the back wall. It is a mass of rock which was left when the rock about it was removed in producing the back wall. Its position and its relation to other parts of the Pnyx are clearly indicated on the survey. The drawing on page 219 is an enlargement of the same view which is presented there, and represents the bema as seen from above. It consists of two distinct parts: a platform approached by three steps, and a block of rock rising from the platform against the back wall. These two parts are separated by a step-like portion of rock which is left around the block; this may be thought of as a second smaller platform resting on the first and supporting the block. On the upper step of the large platform in front of the bema are a number of cuttings, which are represented on the drawing and marked with Arabic numerals, indicating their depth in centimetres. The larger ones seem to have been designed to receive stelae, the smaller for the insertion of iron pins which held in position statues or similar objects placed here. Small grooves cut in the stone lead into the holes, forming channels by which melted lead was poured in to hold the pins in place. Larger slots of the same character appear in the second platform immediately under the bema, and no doubt had the same object as those in the lower platform, but are not so neatly made. Against the back wall on each side of the bema is a flight of steps reaching from the floor of the Pnyx to the top of the bema. The steps of the platform constitute the first three steps of each flight. At the top they are irregular and broken, as is also the top of the block or bema proper. The relation of the parts to each other is shown by the front and side elevations on pages 220 and 221.

The height of the whole structure is three metres. Back of the bema are several seats or steps cut in the rock, as represented in the section AA' on the survey. In the direction of the letter R they are parallel with the back wall. On the other side of the bema this is not the case; and their line of direction, if continued, would meet that of the back wall toward the point S. They are wider and lower than the steps of the bema. These facts would lead to the supposition that they are older than the bema and rock wall.

Continuing our survey from the extremities of the back wall, R and S, we come first upon the other two low rock walls mentioned above. For a distance below these there is no boundary line whatever. Curtius supposes that there were entrances to the enclosure at these places; they are marked "Gate?" on the survey. Still further down we come upon the two ends of the great semicircular wall, a structure no less interesting than is the back wall above.[F] The ends consist of immense blocks of rock which lie at some distance from each other, but in the line of the wall. The continuous wall begins at the points W and Y. Its greatest height is at the point A, opposite the bema. It consists of enormous blocks of stone, almost rectangular on the face, and skilfully fitted together without mortar. The stones are of the same kind of rock as the back wall, and seem to have been cut from the hill. Seventy-five blocks are still in position. The largest block measures six by twelve feet, and many others are but little smaller. There is what seems to be a rude attempt at ornamentation by furrows, which are near the edges of the stones and run parallel with the joints.[G] The blocks of the upper course are dressed smooth on top, as if to receive another course. At the point marked Z on the survey there is a single block, which rests on the native rock and rises to a height of three feet above the wall as it now stands. This block is in the line of the wall and is also dressed smooth on top. If, as Curtius suggests, the smooth upper surface of the blocks of the upper course of the continuous wall furnishes sufficient evidence for assuming that the wall was originally one course higher than it now is, this block furnishes similar evidence that it was two courses higher. The portion still standing is 5.13 metres high at the point A, and has three courses

---

F. Dodwell, in the volume of plates cited page 233, note *J*, remarks on the similarity of this masonry to that of the south-western side of the Gate of Lions at Mycenae, a resemblance, however, which cannot be admitted as an argument in favor of the view that the construction of the Pnyx is to be ascribed to an age equally remote. The character of the walls, at both places, is largely determined by the nature of the building material at hand. — J. T. C.

G. For an explanation of the origin of these furrows parallel to the joints, see note *I*, page 228.

with the thicker blocks in the portion opposite the bema. If these two courses that have disappeared were in place, the height of the wall would become 8.55 metres; *i.e.* on the supposition that the courses which have disappeared consisted of blocks of the same thickness as those now to be seen, it would be but 4.55 metres lower than the base of the bema. The difference of level between this middle point and a point (near *IV*) due north of the bema, which is near one end of the wall, is shown on Section *AA'*, which accompanies the survey. The attempt of the builders seems to have been to bring the top of the wall along its entire length to a level by placing the thicker blocks of the course at the lowest point.[11]

Below this wall, a little to the west of the middle point *A*, are a few shallow steps cut in the rock. They are older than the wall itself, as is shown by their disappearance under it. A few paces east of the steps is a square hole in the wall, probably caused by the falling out of a small block of stone. Through it the rubble which fills the space above the wall can be seen.

The next question in order, and the one of greatest importance, is that in regard to the nature of the floor of the enclosure. If this place was arranged for people to assemble in, and all are agreed that it was, did they assemble on the earth that now covers the rock, or on the rock itself, or on neither of these? When the topography of Athens began to be studied carefully, the enclosure was covered with earth and rubble as it now is. Since that time the condition of the Pnyx has changed but little. At the points marked *B* and *C* on the survey, ledges come to the surface. Below these the covering of the rock at once becomes deeper.

---

11. The angle of earth-slide, indicated upon the Section *AA'*, is uniform along the crescent. It is of particular importance as indicating the existence of a much greater height of earth within the retaining wall at a period anterior to the removal of its stones by Christian or Turkish builders. Much of the earth which originally raised the auditory to the requisite level has been washed down upon the low-lying tract between the eastern front of the Theseum and the houses of the present town. This is proved by the excavations recently (February, 1887) made in this region by Dr. Dörpfeld, for the purpose of determining the site of the ancient Agora. All the remains of Roman, and even of early Christian date, were found to be deeply buried by gravel and earth, which can have been carried down upon them only from the enormous terrace of the Pnyx auditory. — J. T. C.

The first removal of earth in the upper part was made by Lord Aberdeen in 1803. He laid bare the rock about the bema to a distance of several feet from it. Nothing further was done till 1863, when Curtius made extensive investigations. He removed the earth from the foot of the semicircular wall, from the foot of the back wall, and dug a trench running about three-fourths of the distance from the back wall to the semicircular wall below, down to a point just below M.[1] In the line of this trench he found the rock dressed with tools. It is rather smooth near the bema, but gets rougher further down the hill. At the lower end of the trench, M on the survey, he found three steps cut in the rock. In the course of the trench are also several incisions that resemble mortises, from six to eight inches long, four or five inches wide, and of considerable depth. Possibly they were used for the insertion of bars to which was attached the machinery by which the blocks of the lower wall were brought to their present position. Ropes were used in various ways by the ancients in lifting the blocks of their temple walls to their place, and it is probable that some such devices were used here. Extensive as were Curtius's excavations, they left the nature of the floor below the ledges B and C practically undetermined. A knowledge of its character seemed necessary to a satisfactory conclusion. To this matter, therefore, we applied ourselves. Through the kindness of Professor Goodwin and others, permission was obtained from the minister of education, Mr. Eustratiades, to make some excavations. We exposed the rock at the points N, D, G, and H on the survey. We also laid bare the steps which Curtius found, which by the action of the rains had been buried again to the depth of six or eight feet. The dressing of the rock to produce a smooth floor seems not to have extended below the ledges B and C. There are no hammer marks on it at any of the points N, D, G, or H. At N and D it declines at an angle of 30 degrees. At H the declivity is not so great; at G it descends at nearly the same angle with the slope of the hill. At the point G we removed a piece of the rubble, which was so large that three men with difficulty lifted it from the hole. The opening up of the steps

---

[1] Clarke's survey appears to represent this trench as extending below the point M; but Curtius made no excavations below this point.

showed that the rock descends uniformly from the bema to the uppermost of the three steps. No great depth of the rock has been removed in the dressing which appears in the track of the trench, as is shown by the fact that the rock at the bottom of the trench is not so low as it is at D and G, where it has not been wrought at all. The three steps found by Curtius are of little more than half the height of the steps of the bema. Their edges are so irregular and so much rounded that they seem to belong to a different period from the steps of the bema itself.

The accompanying figure will aid in making clear which parts of the floor bear hammer marks and which do not.

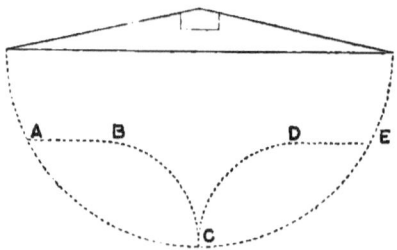

The region above and between the lines ABC and CDE bears marks of tools. That below these lines, so far as it was explored, bears no such indications of work. There is no propriety in applying the term "rock-floor" to this lower region; and this should be reserved for the nearly horizontal upper part. The levellings show that it was the design of the workmen to make the upper part of the enclosure approximate a level with the base of the bema. The points L, F, P, J, and K are seen to be in the same plane with this base, while the point I and the ledges at O, B, and C are but slightly below it. But below the ledges B and C the rock begins at once to sink rapidly. From the bema along the track of the trench which Curtius dug the descent is more gradual. That the rock below the ledges cannot have been used as a floor is plainly shown by the levellings on the lines $\alpha\beta$ and $\gamma\delta$. Where they pass over the ledges there is a difference of level of from one to two metres between points within two or three metres of each other. Between the points E and D, which are comparatively near together, there is a difference of two metres. Thus it will be seen that the rapid descent of the rock is below the ledges and in the region of the trench dug by Curtius. The lowest point at which the rock has been exposed is just below the steps found by Curtius, where it is 6.90 metres below the base of the bema.[1]

In the south-east corner of the enclosure is a large mass of rock which appears to have been left when that at each side of the bema was removed. It is twenty-five metres long, and not of uniform width. The widest portion is in the corner near *R*. From here toward the bema it grows narrower, the part next to the bema being very irregular and broken. It is separated from the rock of the hill by a deep, narrow trench. This trench is so cut as to have a neat, smooth wall on both sides, and is of an average width of one foot and a half,— a width barely sufficient to allow a man to work in the trench. The bottom is evenly finished, and is on a level with the base of the bema. The width of the mass where it is the greatest is 7.50 metres ; at the end toward the bema it is not more than two or three metres. The rock below it has been cut away, and the narrower portion of it, *n* on the survey, has been entirely surrounded by a trench which is left unfinished. The smaller portion is by no means regular. At the point *b*, where the section line $\alpha\beta$ crosses this mass, it is 5.20 metres lower than the top of the back wall ; while at other points, as *c* and *d*, the difference in altitude is not so great. At *Q* the original surface of the rock is seen on both sides of the trench. The conclusion seems evident that it was the designer's intention to remove this mass of rock and make this corner of the Pnyx like the other. That the sides of the trench are wrought smooth, that the bottom of the trench along its whole length is found to be exactly on a level with the base of the bema, and that the end of the mass nearest the bema presents almost unmistakable evidences of interrupted or unfinished work, can be reasonably accounted for on no other supposition.[1]

· [1] The figures on the survey which seem to be 6190 are meant for 6.90.

I. The manner in which the removal of the native rock was effected is evident from these unfinished portions. Trenches of sufficient width to allow a workman the free use of his arms were sunk to the depth determined upon for the floor of the auditory, namely, to the level of the base of the bema, which is taken as zero in the levellings of the plan. These trenches were hewn out with pick-

Above the Pnyx, near the corner S, are two immense blocks of stone, not unlike those of the semicircular wall below. They are marked "Wall" on the survey. This designates them well, as the supposition that they are a part of an old wall seems more probable than any other. This supposition is favored by the facts that they bear hammer marks and have been fitted together in a neat joint. These blocks, the steps which disappear under the wall below, and the steps which Curtius found, all seem to be much older than the bema and than much of the other work about the Pnyx. This is

---

hammers and chisels of tempered iron, the marks of which are plainly visible upon the rock. Specimens of such tools, used by the ancient quarrymen of Attica, have been found among the débris of the neighboring quarries of Pentelicus, and are described by Welcker, *Tagebuch einer Griechischen Reise*, Berlin, 1865, Vol. II. The islands of native rock remaining, from six to seven metres in length and from three to four metres in width, when they were of suitable material, homogeneous, and free from cracks, were split into blocks to be employed in the construction of the retaining wall. This was done by means of wedges of dried wood, driven tightly into holes drilled for the purpose, and then wetted. Traces of such holes can be detected upon the edges of some of the huge stones which form the wall. From the character of the grooving upon the sides of these perfectly circular sinkings it is evident that they were bored with a cylindrical drill, probably of bronze, the cutting circle of which was set with diamonds or other jewels. Tubular drills of this kind, generally reputed a modern invention, were in common use among the ancients. Holes drilled by them are visible, for instance, among the prehistoric remains of Tiryns and Mycenae, as the writer can testify from recent examination. W. M. F. Petrie, *The Pyramids and Temples of Gizeh*, London, 1883, Chap. xix., has found the cylindrical cores which resulted from this method of boring among the débris of ancient Memphis. It appears that upon the Pnyx, as in the quarries of Egypt, from five to eight of these holes were drilled to the metre (compare De la Rosière, *Description de l'Égypte*, Paris, 1809-28; and Wilkinson, *Manners and Customs of the Ancient Egyptians*, fourth edition, London, 1878). Along the lines thus marked out slight grooves were cut, to conduct and hold the water by which the wedges were moistened and swollen. There thus resulted upon the blocks those bosses and edges tooled with parallel furrows, referred to in the text, page 223, as a rude attempt at ornamentation.

When, however, the islands of rock which remained between the chiselled trenches were too shallow to provide such building blocks, or were of too poor and cracked a material, they were removed in small fragments, after being disintegrated through the action of fire, aided by water or some other liquid dashed upon the red-hot stone. This is certainly the simplest method of removing large masses of rock when it is not desired to preserve the blocks for building

especially plain in the two sets of steps. One of them actually
disappears under the wall; and the other, the one found by Curtius,
though buried for ages, is much more irregular, and more antique and
worn in appearance, than the steps of the bema, though these have
apparently been exposed to the action of the elements ever since
they were cut from the rock.

On the right of the bema, between it and the corner *S*, is a flight
of steps, which seem to lead from the Pnyx to the top of the hill.
But if they were ever used as part of a stairway, they must have been

purposes. Diodorus (iii. 12, 4) gives a clear account of the manner in which
gold-bearing rock was so rent asunder by large fires that it could readily be
worked with pickaxes. This was among the Egyptians, the earliest teachers of
the Greeks in all that appertains to the quarrying and tooling of stone. Tedious
as it is, this primitive method is occasionally adopted even at this day, in order to
economize blasting powder. The writer has seen traces of it in the mines of the
Hartz. H. H. Gorringe (*Egyptian Obelisks*, New York, 1882), though apparently
unaware of the above-mentioned passage of Diodorus, so directly bearing upon
the subject, refers to the employment of fire in the quarries of Egypt, quoting as
an authority attesting the splitting of rock by this means one Agatharcides (?), —
possibly meaning Agatharchides, who is mentioned by the Sicilian historian as an
authority upon Egyptian matters, though among the fragments of his writings no
such reference is to be found. In the construction of the stupendous rock-cut structures of India fire was constantly employed to aid in the removal of material. Thus
we are informed (J. F. W. Herschel, *A Manual of Scientific Enquiry*, London,
1871) that in a quarry of Seringapatam a block not less than 26 metres long by
3 metres square was procured by maintaining a narrow line of fire along a shallow
groove, chiselled upon the surface of the rock, until the stone was sufficiently
heated, when the ashes were suddenly swept off by a long row of men, each of
whom dashed a bucket of cold water upon the rock, which was thereby severed
with a clear fracture.

The Greeks and Romans were possessed of the idea that vinegar was peculiarly
effective in splitting the heated rock. Galen, Περὶ Κράσεως καὶ Δυνάμεως τῶν
Ἁπλῶν Φαρμάκων, XXII. p. 16; and Pliny, *Nat. Hist.*, XXIII. 27: "Saxa
rumpit infusum (acetum), quae non ruperet ignis antecedens." It is difficult to
account for this belief except on the assumption that it arose through an observation of the effects of vinegar — the most important acid known to the ancients —
as a solvent. But Pliny elsewhere (XXXIII. 21) ascribes to it even the power of
splitting silicious stone, which, when heated, would yield as readily to water as to
any acid. An almost miraculous potency was attributed to this agent. Dion
Cassius (XXXVI. 1, 2) relates that a breach was made in the walls of a tower of
the Cretan Eleuthera by the use of fire and vinegar; and Apollodorus, the architect (in Wescher, *Poliorcétique des Grecs*, Paris, 1867, p. 153), describes a

supplemented by some steps placed on the rock beneath them, as the lowest of them is two or three feet from the floor.

This concludes the description of the Pnyx proper. We pass from it to notice some remains of the city wall on the top of the hill, and also a small plateau which has been produced by cutting down the rock in a way in some respects similar to that which has been pursued in making the Pnyx itself. Many of the details of this place can be seen at once by referring to the survey. It is approached on the east and west from the level field, and is limited on the north by the back wall, *R.S.* of the Pnyx, and on the south by a back wall, *fg*, resembling

---

furnace, the flames of which could be directed against the walls of a besieged town. After having been heated by this gigantic blow-pipe the stones were to be sprinkled with vinegar " or some other mordant." A curious attempt to employ this ancient means of effecting a breach in fortification walls was made by the Duc de Guise in his expedition against Naples (*Les Mémoires de Feu Monsieur le Duc de Guise*, Paris, 1668).

The most memorable occasion on which we hear of the use of fire in this way is, of course, the passage of the Alps by Hannibal. The construction of a road, rendered necessary by the presence of elephants in the invading army, required the removal of large masses of native rock. This was effected by the disintegrating action of fire (Silius Italicus, *Punica*, III.; and Orosius, *Hist.*, IV. 14). Other authors (Livy, XXI. 37; Appian, IV.; Juvenal, *Sat.*, X. 152; Ammianus Marcellinus, XV. 10; Servius, *Ad Aeneid*, X. 13) state that vinegar was also employed by Hannibal,—a story which has given rise to many wild comments. A discussion of the recent literature of this subject may be found in E. Hennebert, *Histoire d'Annibal*, Paris, 1870, Vol. II., who himself comes to the startling conclusion that the ὄξος or *acetum* of the passages quoted was an actual explosive, now unknown, with a force comparable to that of gunpowder or dynamite. Scarcely less amusing is an explanation given by R. Ellis, *A Treatise on Hannibal's Passage of the Alps*, Cambridge, 1853, who, regardless of the explicit testimony of the ancient authors, asserts the fire and vinegar to have been used, not in splitting rocks, but in thawing out great masses of "snow, solidified by frost." In point of fact, the peasants of the high Alps still employ fire in breaking up the enormous boulders which at times block the roads; compare C. Chappuis, *Rapport au Ministre de l'Instruction Publique*, Paris, 1860.

That a very considerable portion of the rock removed from the Pnyx hill in the excavation of the auditory was disintegrated by fire, is proved by the presence of many fragments of partially calcined rock in this vicinity. This method, as regards both fire and vinegar, would have been far more efficacious upon the limestone of this formation than upon the granite and gneiss of the Alpine passes. — J. T. C.

somewhat that of the Pnyx, but of much less extent, and running in
a straight line. Another important difference is that there is nothing
on this plateau bearing any resemblance to the bema.

The floor has been wrought with tools so as to approach a level
surface, which is broken by rectangular spaces slightly above or
below the general level. See h, i, j, k on the survey.

Toward the south-west, at l, a rectangular portion of rock has been
cut around and left standing. It is about a foot high, and is probably
an altar that was finished by being built up with stones. The top has
the same appearance as the native rock in the vicinity which has been
neither cut nor broken. The depth of rock removed in order to
produce the level plateau was not great in this place, as is shown by
the native rock near by. If we suppose that much has been broken
from the top of the altar, we are forced also to suppose that the altar
was higher than the native rock which originally surrounded it. In
several places on this plateau, as in the Pnyx and bema below, are
slots cut in the rock as if to receive staves.

Toward the top of the back wall of the Pnyx, at m, are several
ruts in the rock, which are supposed to be chariot tracks. In the
rock-wall fg at the back of this plateau is a niche, and west of it are
steps leading from the plateau to the top of the hill. This niche differs from the largest of those in the back wall of the Pnyx in being
semi-cylindrical in form and arched over at the top, while the one
below is in the form of a rectangular prism and extends to the top of
the rock.

Beyond this level place, on top of the hill, at n, o, p, are some remains of the city wall, an angle of which was in the straight line that
passes over the bema and through the central part of the Pnyx.

The information thus gathered approaches so near to a demonstration, that we are forced to the conclusion that the so-called Pnyx is the
real Pnyx. There seems to be no good reason for abandoning this view.
We hope to be able to show that the views of those who are of a different opinion are based on inaccuracies in the description of the
Pnyx. As far as its ruined condition justifies us in expecting it, we
find that the place corresponds to the description. It would be inconsistent to apply the language of Pollux to anything but this ruin or to
some other nearly like it. To apply all these passages and references
to a place of assembly in some other part of the city would be a

difficult task. When Pollux spoke of the Pnyx as κατεσκευασμένον κατὰ τὴν παλαιὰν ἁπλότητα, οὐκ εἰς θεάτρου πολυπραγμοσύνην, he evidently had in mind a place resembling a theatre, and πολυπραγμοσύνη was that in which the theatre and the Pnyx differed. If we accept for a moment that the question is settled and that this ruin is the Pnyx, we easily understand how it happened that Pollux mentioned the πολυπραγμοσύνη of a theatre and not that of some one of the other splendid buildings near. A comparison of the Pnyx with the Dionysiac theatre brings out several very important points of resemblance. The bema is in the same position as the stage, the back wall in that of the scene-building, and the outline is almost exactly that of a theatre. The one striking difference, that the hill slopes down from the bema instead of rising, is not nearly so formidable as it has been thought. The first popular assemblies were doubtless held on level ground. As the Pnyx is much older than any theatre, its floor was probably nearly on a level with the base of the bema. A *gradual* change from an auditorium which consisted of a flat, open space to one which elevated the people above the speaker, as does the cavea of a theatre, would seem to be in accordance with the natural order of things. This leads to the inquiry as to the probability of the existence at any time of such a floor or flat auditorium in the Pnyx. The fall of the ground towards *A* is 1 in 10.7; due north of the bema, 1 in 13.5; in the direction of *Z*, 1 in 29.7. The levellings above the ledges *B* and *C* show that the floor in this part of the enclosure was practically on a level with the base of the bema. The smoothness of the rock shows also that in this part it served for the people to stand on. The unevenness of the rock below the ledges shows with equal certainty that here it never served for this purpose. The natural inference is that the floor, which in the upper part approaches a level with the lowest step of the bema, was continued artificially in nearly the same plane over the entire enclosure. If this was not the case, there is no reasonable explanation of the fact that the space above the circular wall was filled in as it is. A floor produced in this way, by supplementing the rock-floor above the ledge *B* and *C* by an artificial floor in the lower part, becomes, therefore, almost a necessity. On this supposition the structure is also in good keeping with the apparent idea of Pollux that the place was in the main like a theatre.

III.

The literature on this subject, though not extensive, is widely scattered. The ruin on the Pnyx Hill naturally attracted the attention of travellers, and every one who described his travels had something to say of it. Many of these descriptions, however, contain mere repetitions of what others had already said, and possess no scientific value. The following list is a sufficiently complete enumeration :

SPON AND WHELER. *Voyage d'Italie, de Dalmatie, de Grèce, et du Levant.* Lyon, 1678; La Haye, 1724.

RICHARD CHANDLER. *Travels in Asia Minor and Greece.* 3d edition. London, 1817.[1]

STUART AND REVETT. *Antiquities of Athens*, I.-III., London, 1787: with Supplement, Vol. IV., London, 1830.

J. L. BARTHOLDY AND C. AUG. BÖTTIGER. In Wieland's *Deutscher Mercur* for 1806.

J. C. HOBHOUSE. *A Journey through Albania*, etc., Vol. I. London, 1813.

EDWARD DANIEL CLARKE. *Travels*, Part II., Sect. II. London, 1814.

W. WILKINS.[2] *Atheniensia or Remarks on the Topography and Buildings of Athens.* London, 1816.

HAWKINS.[3] *On the Topography of Athens in Robert Walpole's Memoirs Relative to European and Asiatic Turkey.* 2 vols. London, 1817. 1820.

G. F. SCHOEMANN. *De Comitiis Atheniensium.* Greifswald, 1819.

EDWARD DODWELL. *Tour through Greece during the Years* 1801, 1805, *and* 1806. London, 1819.ʲ

W. GELL. *The Itinerary of Greece.* London, 1810.

W. KINARD. In the *Supplement to* Stuart and Revett's *Antiquities of Athens.* London, 1830.

W. M. LEAKE. *Topography of Athens.* London, 1821. 2d edition, 1841.

P. W. FORCHHAMMER. *Zur Topographie Athens.* Kiel, 1841.

W. MURE OF CALDWELL. *Journal of a Tour in Greece*, Vol. II. Edinburgh and London, 1842.

---

[1] Travelled in 1765.   [2] Travelled in 1802.   [3] Travelled in 1797.

ʲ A drawing of the Pnyx, showing a portion of the semicircular retaining wall, is given by E. Dodwell, *Views and Descriptions of Cyclopian and Pelasgic Remains in Greece and Italy*, London, 1834, Pl. LV. — J. T. C.

LUDWIG ROSS. *Tablettes votives d'Athènes et de Mélos.* In the *Ann. dell' Inst. Archeol.*, XV. p. 322. 1843.

H. N. ULRICHS. *Topographie der Häfen von Athen*, in *Reisen und Forschungen in Griechenland.* 2 vols. Bremen, 1840, 1863. See Vol. II. p. 168.

C. W. GOETTLING. *Das Pelasgikon in Athen*, in *Gesammelte Abhandlungen aus dem classischen Alterthume.* Vol. I. p. 68. Halle, 1851.

F. G. WELCKER. *Der Felsaltar des Höchsten Zeus oder das Pelasgikon zu Athen, bisher genannt die Pnyx.* Berlin, 1852.[K]

LUDWIG ROSS. *Das Theseion und der Tempel des Ares in Athen.* Halle, 1852.

CARL W. GOETTLING. *Das Pelasgikon und die Pnyx in Athen.* Jena, 1853.

LUDWIG ROSS. *Die Pnyx und das Pelasgikon in Athen.* Braunschweig, 1853.

F. G. WELCKER. *Pnyx oder Pelasgikon.* In the *Rhein. Museum, N. F.*, X. 30 ff., 1854.

CONRAD BURSIAN. *Die athenische Pnyx.* In *Philologus.* IX. 631 ff., 1854.

LUDWIG ROSS. In the *Neue Jahrbücher für Philol. und Pädag.* LXXI. 181 ff., 1855.

F. G. WELCKER. *Ueber C. Bursian's "Athenische Pnyx."* In the *Rhein. Museum, N. F.*, X. 591 ff., 1856.

F. G. WELCKER. In the *Rhein. Museum, N. F.*, X. 56.

ERNST CURTIUS. In the *Göttingsche Gelehrte Anzeigen.* 1859. p. 2016.

ERNST CURTIUS. *Attische Studien.* No. 1. In the *Abhandl. d. k. Ges. d. Wissenschaften zu Göttingen*, Vol. XI 1862.

[K]. The best map hitherto published is that given by Welcker, in this work, in the form of an engraving based upon a tracing of a fine watercolor drawing made by Sebastian Ittar for Lord Elgin. This drawing, now in the British Museum (P. R. Elgin, Vol. III. 8), bears the title "Piano (*sic*) del trigonio e tutto ciò che esiste su il (*sic*) Pnix." It is on a large scale, 1 to 420, and measures .56 by .89 metres. At the time when this drawing was made many more blocks of the city wall must have been in position than at present, and many more traces of the cutting upon the native rock must have been visible. Notwithstanding this, nothing was found upon Ittar's plan which had not been indicated upon the map here given, — while many features of the greatest importance are omitted altogether from the Italian drawing. No real survey can have been made by Ittar. After taking a few measurements he seems to have drawn in the outlines by eye. Thus the position of the great retaining wall, which is represented as the arc of a true circle, is wrong by several metres. In Welcker's reduction from a tracing the errors of the original were, as was unavoidable, considerably exaggerated. — J. T. C.

CONRAD BURSIAN. *Geographie von Griechenland*, Vol. I. p. 276. Leipzig, 1862.

CONRAD BURSIAN. In the article *Athenae* in *Pauly's Real-encyclopädie*, Vol. I. p. 1970 (2 ed.).

CONRAD BURSIAN. In the *Neue Jahrbücher für Philol. und Pädag.*, Vol. 71, 182.

CONRAD BURSIAN. In the *Literarisches Centralblatt*, No. 30, for July, 1863.

ERNST CURTIUS. In the *Erläut. Text der Sieben Karten zur Topographie von Athen*, p. 16. Gotha, 1868.

P. PERVANOGLU. In the *Neue Jahrbücher für Philol. und Pädag.*, Vol. 101, 55 ff., 1870.

W. GURLITT. In the *Neue Jahrbücher für Philol. und Pädag.*, Vol. 99, 153. 1869.

CURT WACHSMUTH. In the *Rhein. Museum, N. F.*, XXIV. 1869.

P. W. FORCHHAMMER. In *Philologus*, XXXIII. pp. 101, 109, 119, 125 f., 1873.

THOMAS HENRY DYER. *Ancient Athens*. London. 1873.

H. G. LOLLING. In the *Göttinger Nachrichten*, p. 463 ff., 1873.

CURT WACHSMUTH. *Die Stadt Athen im Alterthum*, Vol. I. Leipzig, 1874.

RICHARD CHRISTENSEN. *Athens Pnyx*. In the *Nordisk Tidskrift for Filologi og Paedagogik*, p. 77. Copenhagen, 1875.

E. GUHL AND W. KONER. *The Life of the Greeks and Romans Described from Antique Monuments*. Translated by F. Hueffer. p. 49. New York. 1876.

CHRISTOPHER WORDSWORTH. *Greece, Pictorial, Descriptive, and Historical*. Revised by H. F. Tozer. p. 214. London, 1882.

K. B. STARK. *Nach dem Griechischen Orient*, p. 319 ff. Heidelberg, 1882.

A. BAUMEISTER. *Denkmäler des Klass. Altertums*, article *Athen*. Munich, 1885.

During the Dark Ages the names of almost all the places and points in the topography of Athens were lost.[*L*] As a consequence, when scholars first began to study the topography of the city, they were compelled to re-identify, as well as possible, the places men-

---

[*L*] The mediæval name of the Pnyx, or rather of the bema, Σκάλα τοῦ Δημοσθένου, continued in popular use until the beginning of the present century, and may with good reason be regarded as a tradition derived from classic ages, and urged in favor of the identification of the place. — J. T. C.

tioned in classical writers. As investigations advanced, it became necessary to change many of the names which had been given to places and buildings in the city. Thus the Pnyx at different times bore names corresponding with the conjectures of successive travellers. *Areopagus, Odeum, Theatre of Bacchus, Theatre of Regilla,* and *Theatre of Herodes Atticus* are all names which have served at different times to designate it. Chandler was the first to suggest that this place was the Pnyx. His opinion was at once adopted; and until about the middle of our own century it has been the one entertained by nearly all writers on the topography of Athens. How thoroughly satisfied they were with this opinion is seen from the following notes from some of the different writers mentioned above.[1] Clarke and Mure believed the Pnyx to be the place in which Demosthenes and other Greek orators delivered their orations. Clarke says the site of the Pnyx may perhaps be regarded as more certainly settled than that of any other structure not determined by an inscription.

In the last edition of Stuart's works the editors still adhere to the opinion that it would be in vain to undertake to prove that this ruin is anything else than the ancient Pnyx. Leake, after stating briefly the evidence presented in the first part of this paper for believing this ruin to be the Pnyx, says, " All these data accord so exactly with the remains of a monument still existing on a height to the north of the Museum and to the west of the Areopagus, that it is singular there should ever have been a difference of opinion in regard to those remains."[2] Leake has for almost half a century been one of the highest authorities on all questions of Attic topography. Wilkins says, " A public assembly is comfortably accommodated in a structure similar in form to the theatre, which was afterwards appropriated to this use. Such is the form of the building about whose remains we are speaking. It is so constructed that the orator on the bema had a position similar to that of an actor on the stage."[3] Bartholdy says, "The appearance of the place forbids us to take the Pnyx for the remains of a temple, or the bema for an altar."[4] Goettling says, "The

---

[1] Welcker, *Der Felsaltar,* u.s.w., p. (30) 294 ff.
[2] *Topography of Athens,* p. 41 (1821).
[3] Welcker, *Der Felsaltar,* u.s.w., p 32, note.
[4] Welcker, *Der Felsaltar,* u.s.w., **p. 295 (31).**

Pnyx is without any doubt to be sought in the place where it has hitherto been thought to be."[1] Forchhammer says, "In regard to the Ilissos, the Acropolis, and the Pnyx, no difference of opinion can prevail." Raoul Rochette says, "Cette détermination [of the site of the Pnyx] ne saurait plus, à notre avis, comporter la moindre objection."

Many others have expressed themselves with equal decision. The division of opinion arose among the Germans, some of whom still hold Chandler's view, while others follow Welcker and Curtius in accepting the altar theory. We regret very much that we are not at liberty to present here the opinions of some German scholars whose conclusions in regard to the Pnyx have not yet been published.

The Pnyx question has been narrowed down by the identification with other places of all the names mentioned above as having been given at different times to the Pnyx, so that at present but two views prevail: one, that the so-called Pnyx is the real Pnyx; and another, that it is a place of ancient worship sacred to Zeus, and that the bema is the altar. The latter idea originated with Ulrichs, who travelled with Welcker in Greece in 1842. He did not express himself decidedly about it when this thought first occurred to him, because he knew of no other suitable place for the Pnyx; but later he refers to it in his article "Ueber das attische Emporium in Piraeus" in such a way as to show that this was his conclusion. Ulrichs's suggestion received no particular attention for ten years. During this time (in 1851) C. W. Goettling published a paper on "Das Pelasgikon in Athen." In this he introduced into the discussion the novel idea that the Pelasgicum, which Leake located under the north-west corner of the Acropolis, is not to be sought near the Acropolis or on its slope, but in the ruin usually known as the Pnyx. According to his view, the semicircular wall and the blocks on the top of the hill (marked "wall" on the survey) are the remains of a fortification which was constructed here by the Pelasgians.[M] In this old fort, he thinks, the Athenians afterwards

---

[1] *Das Pelasgikon und die Pnyx*, p. 19.

[M]. The error of this assumption is evident from the fact that the semicircular masonry is not a bulwark, but simply and only the retaining wall of a terrace of earth. It has no counterscarp whatever, not having been intended to be seen from the inner side. It is even probable, from constructive reasons, that the space within it was filled in with rubble and earth as rapidly as the blocks

arranged a place for public assemblies by cutting away the rock on each side of the bema and filling up the space above the circular wall so as to produce a level floor. An elaborate attempt is made to show wherein this supposition elucidates many passages in which the Pelasgicum is spoken of or referred to. This newly discovered Pelasgicum, Goettling claims, was afterward taken possession of by the Pisistratidae, and used as a fortification. The block of rock at the point *l* on the plateau above the Pnyx he supposes to have been the altar of Zeus Agoraeus. This altar was later taken for the bema, and as the sea is visible from it and not from the bema in the Pnyx, the story of the turning of the bema by the Thirty Tyrants may have arisen from this confusion. This may be true; but it is unreasonable to suppose, as Goettling does, that Lucian, when he speaks of Parrhesiades as sitting on the Acropolis and fishing the stones up out of the Pelasgicum (Piscator 47), could have thought of the rocks of the semicircular wall of this ruin. It lies on another hill a half a mile or so distant from the Acropolis, and in a part of the city that was thinly populated and given over to the lower class. Nor does Parrhesiades throw his line in the direction of this ruin, but into the city where the philosophers were to be expected. This is seen from the connection in which this passage stands.

Goettling, in defending this idea, feels the necessity of disposing of a passage in which Lucian describes Pan's grotto as $\mu\iota\kappa\rho\grave{o}\nu$ $\dot{\upsilon}\pi\grave{\epsilon}\rho$ $\tau o\hat{\upsilon}$ $\Pi\epsilon\lambda\alpha\sigma\gamma\iota\kappa o\hat{\upsilon}$, and so changes $\dot{\upsilon}\pi\acute{\epsilon}\rho$ to $\dot{\alpha}\pi\acute{o}$. But even if this change be made, it would be difficult to understand why Pan's grotto should be spoken of as $\dot{\alpha}\pi\grave{o}$ $\tau o\hat{\upsilon}$ $\Pi\epsilon\lambda\alpha\sigma\gamma\iota\kappa o\hat{\upsilon}$, for the grotto was under the north-west corner of the Acropolis, a long distance from Goettling's newly found Pelasgicum.

The inscriptions in the rock on the Pnyx hill to which Goettling refers we were not able to find, though we sought them diligently. There are many little furrows in the rock that one might fancy to be letters, though they are only marks of time and weather. While

---

were placed in position. The laying of the upper courses would thus have been greatly facilitated.

It would, indeed, have been well-nigh impossible to construct a fort at this point, — on the side of a hill which is commanded by an unprotected summit. Goettling's explanation is thus in disaccord with the character of the site and remains, and with the most fundamental practices of military engineering. — J. T. C.

it is impossible to regard the argument of Goettling for the identity of the Pelasgicum and the Pnyx as convincing. he should have credit for suggesting one thing of which the place itself is the all-sufficient proof: that there is pre-Pnyxian work to be found in many places on and about the Pnyx.

In 1852 Welcker read his paper, " Der Felsaltar des Höchsten Zeus oder das Pelasgikon zu Athen, bisher genannt die Pnyx," to the Academy of Sciences in Berlin. He had come into possession of a leaf from Ulrichs's note-book. On this Ulrichs had collected the material for an article which he doubtless intended afterward to publish. The substance of this note is as follows: —

According to Plato the Pnyx must have been surrounded by echoing rocks (πέτραι) ; the real βῆμα was a λίθος and not a πέτρα ; according to Plutarch the βῆμα is movable ; according to Demosthenes the Pnyx was capable of seating 6000 people. It was, therefore, probably situated between the Areopagus, the so-called Pnyx, the Museum, and the Acropolis. Aristophanes's words about sitting ἐπὶ ταῖς πέτραις σκληρῶς (Eq. 783) cannot be taken as a description of the place usually called the Pnyx. The Pnyx doubtless had rude seats, like the κριτήριον in Argos, which is situated near the theatre. On account of this primitive character of the Pnyx the Dionysiac theatre was afterwards used for the popular assemblies ; and, as soon as similar theatres were constructed in other cities, it became the common custom throughout Greece to hold the assemblies in the theatres. Pollux (8, 132) seems to note the difference between the Pnyx and the theatre when he contrasts the παλαιὰ ἁπλότης and the later πολυπραγμοσύνη. Aristophanes (Eq. 750, Ach. 29, and Eccles. 428) testifies that the people sat in the Pnyx. The Prytanes, as it seems, sat on wooden seats, the others on stones. Euripides (Orestes, 871) pictures a popular assembly in Argos, which is to be understood as referring to Athens. What has become of the Pnyx Ulrichs says he does not know. He says Plutarch seems to know of it ; Pausanias does not mention it at all. Probably the place was used for buildings. Harpocration's citation from Apollodorus is important because it says the old ἐκκλησία was held near the Pandemos. Thither the people could be driven, but not to the place now called the Pnyx. This is a sanctuary of Zeus Hypsistos ; the rock with the steps is the altar ; and of the ten inscriptions, *C.I.G.* 497–506, eight belong to votive offerings which were set up in the niches of the back wall by women. The Pnyx must, according to Plutarch, have been so situated that, in spite of the city wall, the sea could be seen, perhaps in the direction of Aegina. This is impossible from the so-called Pnyx. The Pnyx appears to have been situated to the south of the Areopagus. From the bema in the so-called Pnyx the sea is not now visible; much less was it so when the city wall was still standing. But from the western declivity of the citadel, below the entrance, the sea is plainly seen; here the Pnyx may have been situated. Pausanias (v. 15, 4) mentions two altars of Zeus in Olympia. According to Aeschines, *in Timarch*, § 81, περὶ τῶν οἰκήσεων τῶν ἐν τῇ Πυκνί, the word Pnyx must have had a wider signification and have embraced a valley. Probably the site of the Pnyx lay toward the Ilissus, for the Pandemos, from which the sea could be seen, was in this vicinity. Perhaps the Pnyx was in the place where Forchhammer supposes the new agora to have been. The north wind blows over the so-called Pnyx so strongly that it would have been impossible for an orator to make himself heard from the bema.

At the end of Ulrichs's own remarks he quotes Welcker, who was with him at the time of the visit, as suggesting that, since at the time of the democracy every good-for-nothing could harangue the people, a smaller stage would have been more democratic; and that as the rostra in the Roman Forum consisted of a narrow stone with a step by which it was ascended, so the βῆμα in the Pnyx may have been something less stately than the block in the so-called Pnyx. Welcker is also quoted as suggesting that the Pnyx probably lay in the southern part of the city, on the Museum Hill.

Starting from these notes which Ulrichs had jotted down while in Athens, Welcker elaborated the paper mentioned above. It is by far the most exhaustive discussion of the subject published up to that time, and is the foundation of the work done by Curtius. After discussing the antiquity of the worship of Zeus in the city of Athens, he takes as a starting-point the tablets found by Lord Aberdeen in 1803. He seeks to show that the terrace is an altar-terrace from the Pelasgic age, consecrated to Zeus Hypsistos, and that the bema is his altar. In his opinion the place was abandoned as a place of worship in early times, and the worship was transferred to the Acropolis, where the name was changed, and Zeus *Hypsistos* was worshipped as Zeus *Hypatos*. A tradition of the original use of the place maintained itself through the ages, and, in later times, the worship was taken up on the altar-terrace. He agrees with Goettling in supposing that this ruin was the Pelasgicum, and thinks it was spoken of as τὸ Πελασγικόν, while τὸ Πελασγικὸν τεῖχος refers to the oldest fortification of the Acropolis. He thinks the oracle found in Thucydides, II. 17, refers to this ruin, and that the land within the enclosure lay uncultivated, as sacred soil, in compensation for the giving up of the Zeus-cultus here. Finally he attempts to determine the site of the Pnyx, — of which more hereafter.

Welcker was opposed by Ludwig Ross, who on account of his long residence in Athens regarded himself as almost infallible in all questions about the topography of the city. His paper, " Die Pnyx und das Pelasgikon in Athen " was published in 1853. He collected all the important passages from Greek authors that bear on the question, and set forth in a very conclusive way that the ruin under consideration must have been the Pnyx. He emphasizes the fact, which is also recognized by Welcker, that the tablets found in the Pnyx and the statue supposed to have been in the large niche in the back wall undoubtedly belonged to the times of the Roman emperors, and introduces the very probable supposition that some pious soul for reasons unknown to us — perhaps in consequence of a revelation from a god by a dream or otherwise — had founded here a worship of Zeus Hypsistos as the giver of health, and that this worship, from the respectability of the founder or from the wonder-working power of the statue, had met with special sympathy among women of the lower classes. He also shows, by two inscriptions found by himself in a house north of the Acropolis, that Zeus Hypsistos was worshipped elsewhere in Athens as the giver of health. That such a cult was afterward established in the Pnyx, he thinks very natural, since it was desolate, and Zeus had undoubtedly been worshipped there earlier as Agoraeus. He therefore regards Welcker's position as untenable when he infers from this later cult that Zeus Hypsistos was worshipped here in earliest times. He also argues that the support which Welcker sought for his theory in the distinction which he made between τὸ Πελασγικόν and τὸ Πελασγικὸν τεῖχος is of no force, since these expressions were both used in speaking of the oldest fortification of the Acropolis. He regards it as absurd to suppose that the bema was an altar and the terrace a temenos, since so large a place of worship around so small an altar would be without analogy in antiquity; and he concludes by condemning Welcker's location of the Pnyx as in conflict with the testimony of the ancients and on the whole unsatisfactory.

Welcker answered in a paper entitled " Pnyx oder Pelasgikon," in the Rhein. Mus. (N. F.) X. 30 (1854). In this he maintains that it is impossible to understand how the people happened to worship Zeus as the giver of health on this terrace under the name of Hypsistos, and not as Παιάν or Σωτήρ, unless such a worship had already existed there at an earlier time and been preserved by tradition. As to the two inscriptions found on the north of the Acropolis, he assumes that they were carried there from the Pnyx. About the site of the Pnyx he again expresses himself vaguely; but he rightly urges against Ross that it is absurd to maintain that the name Pnyx cannot be given up as a name for this ruin until the situation of the real Pnyx is fixed with certainty.

Ross answered in the Neue Jahrb. f. Philol. und Paedag., LXXI. 181 (1855), but contributed nothing new. In the meanwhile Welcker's theory had also been attacked by Bursian in Philologus, IX. 631 (1854). Bursian sees no reason for calling either the semicircular wall or the back wall Pelasgic; he does not even consider the former very old.[N] Like Ross, he finds the place fairly well adapted for a place of popular assembly. The bema could not, in his opinion, possibly be an altar, since an altar must stand free and without contact with anything profane, while here one could easily step down from the upper terrace

---

[N]. There are certainly no technical grounds for asserting that the construction of the retaining wall, and the excavation of the native rock so as to form a level auditory, necessarily took place in a prehistoric age. Nay, it is not altogether impossible that the tradition preserved by Plutarch (loc. cit.) is actually correct, and that it was not before the age of the Thirty Tyrants that this bema was constructed, from which it was impossible for the orator to look upon the sea. The character of the masonry must have been determined almost entirely by the manner in which the blocks were obtained, and by the nature of the limestone of the Pnyx hill, which is readily split into these enormous parallelopipedons. On the other hand it should be borne in mind that the troublous times immediately succeeding the Peloponnesian War were certainly not favorable for the execution of so gigantic a design. The supposition of Bursian, that the Pnyx, as we at present see it, is a work of the age of Cleisthenes, is much more probable. — J. T. C.

upon the top of the altar. He supposes that the hill had been dwelt upon in most ancient times, abandoned later, and in Cleisthenes's time arranged as a place of assembly by widening the terrace and supporting it by the semicircular wall. He also thinks that Welcker fails to establish his distinction between τὸ Πελασγικόν and τὸ Πελασγικὸν τεῖχος. Welcker's answer, in an article entitled "*Ueber C. Bursians Athenische Pnyx*," in the Rhein. Museum (N. F.) X. 591 (1856), was not convincing to Bursian, as is seen by reference to his Geographie von Griechenland, I. 276 f.; however, he slightly modified his views later in the article "Athenae" in Pauly's Realencyclopädie, I. p. 1970 (2 ed.), but is still of the same opinion on the main question, the situation of the Pnyx.

When Curtius visited Athens in 1862, he made extensive excavations, and subjected the whole question to a new and comprehensive investigation. The result he published in his "Attische Studien, No. 1." As he, rather than Ulrichs or Welcker, is held responsible for the altar theory in regard to the Pnyx, his arguments deserve special attention. He begins with a most minute and fascinating description of the plain of Attica, and then discusses at length the divisions of the city and the region about it in the most ancient times.

The remainder of his article may be epitomized as follows : —

These small districts, even in the earliest period of their existence, were united in some way, though these relations may have been but vaguely defined. The first basis of union was doubtless their religion. The cults of the nymphs and heroes, and especially that of Zeus, united the people. Of these cults the worship of Zeus is the oldest. It is the one to which all the others were related. It was the primeval religion, common to all classes of citizens. In this all the inhabitants of the different districts formed at first a whole, and from this cult arose that in which Zeus was worshipped as a god of the herds, as a patron of the household and family. The people must have prepared suitable places in which this common service could take place, and these must be sought in the parts of the city then most thickly populated. These thickly settled parts were doubtless the heights. These were preferred because they were a more healthy place for abodes than the damper valleys, and because of the fresh air and the outlook towards the sea. These conditions were fulfilled especially on the south-west slope of the ridge which culminates toward the north-west in the Hill of the Nymphs and toward the south-east in the Museum Hill. Here the Attic Pelasgians settled, and from this fact they bear, by the most ancient tradition, the name Κραναοί, the rock-dwelling Pelasgians. Of this settlement, the very beginning of the city of Athens, extensive remains have come down to us. They consist of terraces, spaces before the houses (Vorplätze), steps leading from one terrace to another, drains to carry off water, cisterns, altars, and graves. If the union of these different districts was brought about in Athens, as in all other Greek cities, by a common worship of some deity, we must expect to find suitable places and altars for this service. We know of two such places in Athens, — one near the fountain *Callirrhoe*, and the other the *so-called Pnyx*. No one can doubt that the work on this last-named place belongs to the same period as the rock-dwellings of the Κραναοί. The only difference is that this is a more extensive piece of work and that this place was designed for public gatherings. In preparing a place for popular assemblies, the first task was the levelling of the floor, so as to make it suitable for the assembling of an audience. Here we find two terraces, one on the top and one on the slope of the hill, which are alike, except that one is larger than the other. On the upper terrace is a block of rock, now about a foot and a half high, which seems to have been violently destroyed. The lower terrace has often been described, says Curtius, but it seemed worth the trouble to investigate it further. The excavations undertaken with this intention were directed to three points: the boundary of the enclosure and the entrances to it, the altitude of the back wall, and the nature of the floor in its original condition. To find the foot of the back wall, a ditch was dug along it, and at the points on the right and left of the bema (marked by a and β on Curtius's plan) the foot of the wall was found to be respectively 4.302 metres and 3.50 metres below the base of the bema.

In the south-east corner of the enclosure is left a mass of rock, which (Curtius thinks) probably served for people to stand on during the ceremonies at the bema.[o] Next Curtius dug a trench from the

---

O. It is hardly necessary here to enter into a serious consideration of this. The masses of rock remaining unexcavated in the south-eastern corner of the enclosure were plainly intended to be removed by the means described in note *l*, p. 227. The Pnyx, like many other public works of the Greeks, was never entirely completed. Far from providing a standpoint for favored spectators, the presence of these islands of rock decreased the available area of the auditory. — J. T. C.

bema down the hill to the semicircular wall, in order to determine the nature of the floor. It was found that the rock bore hammer marks and had been wrought smooth. This led him to the conclusion that the old floor was much below the surface of the earth that now covers the rock. At a distance of thirty-six metres from the bema and under six metres of earth three steps were found, which are probably the steps of a block of rock similar to the bema. Below the steps the floor is covered with earth and pieces of broken rock so large as to render its investigation impossible. The investigations were, however, sufficiently extensive to lead to important conclusions in regard to the so-called Pnyx. They show that, although it was arranged for public assemblies, these assemblies must have been of a different character from those usually supposed to have been held in this place. The most important question is as to the kind of assemblies held here. They were not assemblies where an orator was to deliver an oration, for he could not be heard. The north wind, which blows very strong over this hill, would make this impossible. The audience would have been seated on ground which was lower than the stand of the speaker. Thus the orator would not have been able to see the effect of his speech on the faces of his auditors. More than this, the enclosure is much too small for the general political assemblies of Athens, its area being but 2586 square metres.[P] From this 70 square metres must be deducted for the bema. The remaining space down to the semicircular wall would accommodate at most 5000 men standing, not to mention sitting. Nor was the entire surface of the enclosure used for an assembly : it was partly occupied by an altar at the point where the steps were found below the bema. The whole structure has the appearance of greater age than is consistent with Chandler's theory ; and the story told by Plutarch, that the Thirty Tyrants turned the bema so as to make it look away from the sea, renders it impossible that this block cut from the living rock should ever have been the bema. If we inquire for what kind of assemblies this place was arranged, we learn from the inscriptions found by Lord Aberdeen that it was

---

[P]. Even when calculated from the measurements given by Curtius himself, these figures are inexplicably wrong, giving less than one-half of the actual area of the enclosure, which is 6240.5 square metres. The extent of the bema, on the other hand, is only about 62 square metres. — J. T. C.

dedicated to Zeus the Highest. The religious character is to be seen in the structure itself. Its unchangeable and monumental nature favors the idea that the supposed bema is an altar. It is a surprising fact that we find here three altars almost in a line, one on top of the hill, one at the upper side of the enclosure (the so-called bema), and one in the middle of it. It is probable that we have before us here a θεῶν ἀγορά, such as are mentioned in Greek writers. If we take into consideration the great antiquity of this double terrace, its suitable situation for uniting the different districts of city and country, its unmistakable connection with the old rock city of the Κρανιοί, the adaptability of the place for a common religious service, the inscriptions which testify to the antiquity of the service of Zeus in this place, the traces of different altars, the tradition of an ἀγορὰ θεῶν in Cyzicus, Eleusis, and Athens, we shall probably be justified in assuming, Curtius concludes, that this is the ἀγορὰ θεῶν of Athens, in whose midst Zeus was worshipped as the Highest.

As to the site of the real Pnyx, Curtius supposes that it was on the north side of the Museum Hill. Here he made excavations, but without material result.

Of the articles published since 1862 that of Christensen is by far the most important. He concludes that the Pnyx could not have been situated in any other place than on the ridge of hills on which the quarter of the city called Melite lay, *i.e.* the Pnyx Hills; and further that it must have been on the eastern slope of one of these hills. Then he presents the usual arguments against Chandler's theory. The age, the size, the slope of the hill, the north wind, the unfitness of the bema for a speaker's stage, the impossibility of turning it around, and the inscriptions, are all considered, and a conclusion is reached, that "neither the upper nor the lower terrace can have been, in historical times, the well-known place of popular assembly on the Pnyx." This leads naturally to an inquiry about the use of the place. As to this Christensen agrees, except in one point, with Curtius and Welcker. The name of the hill, he thinks, could well be changed to Altar Hill. He then criticises the advocates of the altar theory for claiming that the place was sacred to Zeus. He questions the consistency of assuming the worship of Zeus here in the most ancient times on the uncertain evidence of inscriptions which, as all admit, were set up in Roman times. He cannot understand why a god of healing should be worshipped as the *Highest* and not as Παιάν, Σωτήρ, or the like. Further, the worship of Zeus as a god of healing was not confined to this place, as is shown by inscriptions found by Ross north of the Acropolis. He thinks that these tablets were more probably set in some of the niches of the rock of the Acropolis than carried there from the Pnyx, as Welcker supposes; for there are niches in the north side of the citadel rock very similar to those in the Pnyx. So the inscription ὅρος Διός below the little church Hagia Marina is rather against Welcker and Curtius than for them, for this slope is distinctly separated from the Pnyx Hill. The τέμενος of Zeus can scarcely have extended over the ravine between these two hills. If, with Welcker, we admit that Zeus, who was worshipped on the Acropolis as Zeus Hypatos, was formerly worshipped here as Hypsistos, he thinks it an unsafe supposition that the tradition of this worship was preserved and the worship renewed here in Roman times in consequence of this tradition. Or if, as Curtius supposes, the service of Zeus was never given up in this place, why do we not find more distinct references to it in literature than the very vague ones which Curtius cites? If it had been the "Götter Markt" of Athens, it is not likely that it would not have been mentioned. We have no right, he says, to identify Zeus Hypatos and Zeus Hypsistos, nor do we even know that Curtius's old Κραναοί ever worshipped Zeus. We dare not, he thinks, go further than to say that the hill was sacred to one or more of the deities worshipped in this part of the city.

When we inquire where the Pnyx was, he proceeds to say, other locations than those suggested by Curtius and Lolling can be left out of consideration, as he has already shown that its site must be sought on one of the three Pnyx hills. Christensen then reviews Dr. Lolling's paper, which was published in the *Göttinger Nachrichten* in 1873, and is decidedly inclined, with him, to place the Pnyx on the north-eastern slope of the Hill of the Nymphs. This we cannot but regard as an unfortunate conclusion. Dr. Lolling has lived in Athens most of the time, we believe, since he wrote this paper, and he gave us permission to say that he had entirely abandoned this idea. In minor details Christensen has followed Curtius very closely. His paper is marred by a few inaccuracies in the descriptive part, which, however, do not affect the main question.

From this review of the discussion the following objections to Chandler's view may be easily gathered: —

1. *The slope of the terrace away from the bema unfits it for popular assemblies.*

This was frequently noticed as a difficulty by writers on Attic topography before Curtius; but when he gave the world his picture of the floor of the enclosure, it seemed fatal to the Pnyx theory. It would certainly continue to be so regarded, if his description of the floor were accepted as correct. He says that at the points on the right and left of the bema, which he marks a and β on his plan, and which are marked λ and π on Clarke's survey, the rock floor is respectively 4.302 metres and 3.50 metres below the base of the bema.[1] This gives the impression that the floor sinks very rapidly on both sides of the bema. Thus the bema would stand on an elevation above the people who assembled around and below it and gazed up at the offering on the supposed altar. This statement we fail to find in accordance with the facts. The points which he marks a and β are not below, but on a level with the base of the bema. The levellings show this also to be approximately true of that entire portion of the floor which lies above the ledges marked B and C. We here call attention to the levellings at the points H, I, J, K, F, and L, and to those on the ledges B and C. Only in the middle, where Curtius dug his trench, and below the ledges B and C does the rock sink rapidly. The inaccuracy of this description is manifest on first entering the Pnyx, and it was this observation that finally led to our study of the question.

On the section of the hill which Curtius has published with his paper, the steps found thirty-six metres from the bema are represented as nearly a metre and a half below the top of the semicircular wall at A. This is not exactly correct; but let us suppose for the time being that Curtius's section is correct, and see to what it will lead. He says the wall was one course higher than it now is. The courses of stone still in position are each about a metre and a half high. If this supposed course were in place, the steps, according to Curtius, would be three metres below the top of the wall. Now we have seen above that there is evidence of the same character for supposing

---

[1] Curtius, *Attische Studien*, No. 1, p. 76.

that the wall was two courses higher, that there is for supposing it was one course higher. Thus the steps would be four and a half metres below the top of the circular wall at its lowest point. But the representation on Curtius's section, that the steps are below the top of the semicircular wall at *A*, is not sustained by the levellings. These show that the rock immediately above and below the steps is respectively 1.61 metres and 1.07 metres *above* the top of the semicircular wall at this point. But they show also that at the point *W* on the wall due north of the bema the top of the wall is 2.32 metres above the rock below the steps. More than this, the rock which is marked *Z* is in the line of the wall and dressed smooth on top. If the wall were built up to the level of the top of this rock, the steps would lie 4.90 metres below it. If, as has been suggested above, the smooth

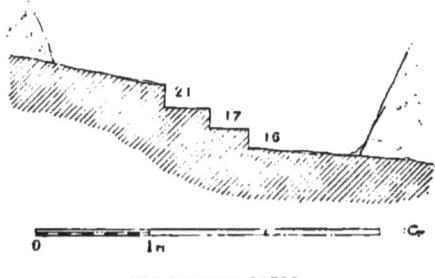

PRE-PNYXIAN STEPS.

upper surface of this rock may be taken as sufficient evidence that there was another course on the top of it, the top of the wall would be at least six metres above the level of the rock below the steps which Curtius found. One of his three supposed altars would come thus to stand on the top of the hill, one on the face of it, and the third in a kind of pit. Certainly the most capricious whim of Zeus as to the altitude of his place of worship would thus be satisfied. If we assume that there was such an altar, we must also assume that there was a floor around it on which the people stood. Curtius supposes that the rock itself was dressed smooth and constituted this floor. But this cannot have been the case, since the rock below the ledges *B* and *C* is so rough that it could not have been so used if it had been exposed. A small amount of work on either side of his trench would have convinced Curtius of this fact. His theory of the floor seems, therefore, untenable. If so, the reasonable course is to return to the old conclusion that the floor was level and at least as high as the top of the semicircular wall. This floor would be four or five metres above the three steps found by Curtius. This conclusion is very strongly supported by the nature of the three steps. As is seen from the figure on the preceding page, these steps are of a very irregular character. They are different in height, and their edges, as already stated, are much more rounded and irregular in appearance than those of the bema.[Q]

We have not a word in favor of the supposition of those who build in their imaginations a high protection against wind and weather around the lower part of the Pnyx. Had there been such a structure, the Pnyx would have been out of harmony with the ancient simplicity with which it is said to have been arranged.[1] But while we admit the improbability of such a protection, to deny that the Pnyx has some of the important features of a theatre is not possible. It might even consistently be called an embryonic stone theatre. Leake says that the floor along the foot of the back wall inclines toward the angle where the bema stands, thus showing that originally the entire plateau sloped toward this point, such being obviously the form most adapted to an assembly which stood or sat to hear an orator who stood on the bema.[2] It is more likely that the floor was level, or nearly so. That the auditors sat with their backs down a decided slope is an assumption not supported by a single well-grounded argument. It rests on another assumption, that either the earth which now covers the rock in the Pnyx or the sloping rock itself was

---

[Q]. No doubt can exist in regard to the original purpose of these steps. They were cut in the native rock, at some time anterior to the construction of the semicircular auditory, in order to facilitate the ascent to the summit of the Pnyx hill. The rock is particularly steep and slippery at this point, and some such foothold was most desirable. That this ascent was in use for a long period before being covered with the earth of the terrace, beneath which they have been buried for twenty-three centuries or more, is evident from the smoothly worn surfaces of the treads. — J. T. C.

[1] G. G. Pappadopoulos in a paper entitled Λόγος περὶ Πνυκός, published as a school programme from Τὸ Ἑλληνικὸν ἐκπαιδευτήριον in Athens in 1867, has described such a structure.

[2] Quoted by Welcker, *Der Felsaltar*, u.s.w., p. 297 (33).

the original floor, neither of which suppositions seems to be sufficiently substantiated to warrant its acceptance.

2. *The area of the enclosure is not large enough to accommodate the number of persons that attended the civic assemblies of Attica.*

Welcker says simply that the place was too small, without giving the exact area. Wordsworth gives the area as " about twelve thousand square yards."[1] Curtius has given 2586 square metres as the area. Wordsworth's estimate is too large, and Curtius's too small. The area exclusive of the bema, according to Clarke's measurement, is 6240.5 square metres. Thus we see that there was ample room to accommodate the assemblies which gathered here, which, as Leake and others think, numbered from 7000 to 8000 persons.

3. *The stone block in the angle of the back wall cannot possibly have been the bema of the Pnyx.*[2] *If it were the bema, it would need but one set of steps. As an altar it would need two, that it might be ascended by several persons at the same time. Moreover, the Attic orators moved about but little during the delivery of their orations, and indulged in few and no violent gestures. A large platform thus became entirely unnecessary. The bema was called in colloquial speech* λίθος, *a word which is not applicable to such a stage as the bema, but to a single stone in the agora or to a small platform built of several blocks. Plutarch says that the Thirty Tyrants turned the bema so as to make it look away from the sea. This block certainly was never turned.*[3]

We believe a careful study of the bema will lead to the conclusion that it can scarcely have been anything else than a tribune for a speaker. It is situated just where one would expect to find a speaker's stage in this enclosure. It is not where one would look for an altar, which would rather stand in the middle of the temenos, if this be a temenos. Such steps as we find here are no appendage of an altar.

The altar at Olympia, with which Welcker compares it, had no such steps and was unlike it in every respect. The upper part of that altar was a heap of ashes, and Pausanias tells us (v. 13, 8) that the steps leading from the lower part of it to the top of the heap were in the

---

[1] *Greece, Pictorial, Historical, and Descriptive,* p. 214.
[2] Christensen, *Athens Pnyx,* p. 95.
[3] Welcker, *Der Felsaltar des Höchsten Zeus,* u.s.w., p. (300) 36.

ashes. It stood in the open temenos, the central object in a wide space of level ground. It must have presented an appearance widely different from the bema, which is overtopped by the hill against the side of which it stands and of which it is a part. The base of this altar, which was probably circular in form, was more than 40 feet wide, and the altar was 22 feet high — more than twice the height of the bema as it now stands. The bema is 9.67 metres in front, extends out to 6.37 metres from the wall, and is 3 metres high. The upper part of the altar at Olympia was in the centre of the platform on which it stood. The people thus looked up at the offering from all points of the temenos. An offering on the bema would be lower than the feet of any one standing on the rock above the Pnyx. Around the altar of ashes at Olympia was a platform on which it stood, and this must have extended out as much as fifteen feet in all directions. On this animals were slain; on the platform in front of the bema, which is only two metres wide, the space is too narrow to permit of any such ceremonies. Certainly the argument of likeness must fail here. Altars of a similar character to that of Olympia were dedicated to Hera on the island of Samos, and to Hera, Gaia, and Apollo at Thebes. These all consisted of ashes. At Olympia altars were also constructed of unburnt tiles. Often they were built of stone, and possibly filled in with earth.[1] The argument that the bema cannot have been a stage for a speaker because it has a superfluous flight of steps seems almost trivial. Certainly no Greek would have made anything so out of harmony and homely as it would have been with a flight of steps on one side only. Again, it is unreasonable, as Bursian says, that the top of an altar should have been thus exposed to be stepped on by any one who might pass by, or that it should have been below the surface of the rock that was immediately at the rear of it. Christensen's answer to this, that the upper terrace was sacred, and that the people could not, therefore, have stepped from this terrace upon the top of the bema, is ridiculous. There is an altar on this terrace, and however sacred the terrace might have been, people must have gathered around this altar. The sacred character of the upper terrace would not prevent people from standing on its rock floor any more than the supposed sacred character of the Pnyx would

---

[1] Guhl and Koner, *Life of the Greeks and Romans*, p. 59 of Eng. transl.

prevent the people from standing on the rock floor around the bema. As to the top of the bema, nothing of any weight can be inferred from its present condition either for or against its use either as a stage or an altar. The corners are somewhat broken. Before this mishap befell it, it presented a flat top, 3.30 by 2.65 metres. A platform of this size and a metre high can scarcely justify Welcker in speaking of it as of enormous size.[1]

Professor Joseph Torrey suggests that since the bema is a block of limestone, it is scarcely possible that it could have been used for a long period as an altar without showing the effects of fire.

The passage in Plutarch about the turning of the bema by the Thirty Tyrants is difficult to understand. Some have attempted to explain it; others have rejected it as improbable. Stewart, Kinard, and some of the German archæologists think that Plutarch related a story which he found current at Athens, without inquiring whether it was true or not. Gell thinks the *upper terrace* was the old Pnyx, and the lower one the Pnyx of the Thirty Tyrants." Leake thinks there is every reason for believing " that Themistocles, by some temporary alteration, which has not lasted to the present time, turned the place to face the sea, in order to promote his design of giving the Athenians a taste for maritime affairs, contrary to their ancient prejudices; and that the Thirty Tyrants restored it to its former state. Or, supposing the existing remains to be of less ancient date, we should expect to find the bema as the last change had left it; that is to say, turned as we now find it, towards the city."[2] Goettling thinks the block of rock marked *l* on the survey was the altar of Zeus Agoraeus, which is spoken of as being in the Pnyx. This he supposes was afterwards taken for a bema, and as the sea is visible from it and not from the bema in the Pnyx, so the story of the

---

[1] "Ungeheure Grösse," *Der Felsaltar*, u.s.w., 37.

R. This view is held also by the writer of these notes. It is certainly in accordance with all the facts recognized during the survey here presented. Compare note *N*, p. 242. This does not, of course, exclude the possibility of the semicircular auditory having been constructed at some previous time. The Thirty Tyrants may not have been the first to place the speaker upon the block now called the bema, but may thereby have returned to a former custom, — as Leake supposes. — J. T. C.

[2] *Topography of Athens*, p. 42.

turning of the bema by the Thirty may have come into circulation. Ross says: "If there is any truth in the story, Plutarch can have meant no more than that the Thirty suspended the popular assemblies in the Dionysiac theatre, from which the sea could be seen, and removed them again to the Pnyx; or he repeats a popular story by which he thought to tickle the ear of the public." Curtius says that this story was at all events abroad in Athens, and could not have become so unless the bema had been movable and capable of being turned around. Forchhammer says that Plutarch's story is absurd in the highest degree, and that he has taken a joke in earnest. Christensen says Plutarch's words do not necessarily mean more than that the speaker looked from the bema in the direction of the sea. The greatest difficulty in the way of accepting his words as a statement of fact lies in the circumstance noticed by Kinard, Leake, Forchhammer, and others, that there is no place in the city except the Acropolis from which the wall of Themistocles, of which there are considerable remains on the Pnyx Hill, would not have cut off the view of the sea.[8] In the face of this fact one is embarrassed to know what Plutarch meant by intimating that a bema ever existed which looked towards the sea. It is also strange that the supporters of the altar theory use this passage to prove that the so-called Pnyx is not the true Pnyx, and yet propose locations for it still further removed from any point from which the sea is visible than the Pnyx itself. There is no possibility of seeing the sea from the site which Professor Curtius has selected for the Pnyx. As is true of many points in the topography of Athens, the Pnyx question must be discussed somewhat on the basis of cumulative evidence. When, therefore, we place this passage in the scale against the passages quoted in the first part of this paper, it is fairly outweighed.

4. *The inscriptions found by Lord Aberdeen show that this was a place of worship dedicated to Zeus Hypsistos.*

This objection is fully answered by the following points which have

---

[8]. It is by no means certain that the wall, marked *p* on the survey, would have entirely cut off the view of the sea from the higher bema: the so-called altar of the upper terrace (*l* on plan). The exact position of this wall is now uncertain; if it stood as far down on the precipitous slope of the south-west as it is drawn on the present survey,—or perhaps a little further,—this difficulty would be entirely obviated.—J. T. C.

already been suggested by others: these inscriptions are generally admitted to date from a late period, that of the Roman emperors; the inscriptions found by Ross north of the Acropolis indicate that the worship of Zeus Hypsistos was not confined to the Pnyx; there is a lack of evidence that the Κραναοί, who Curtius thinks inhabited the region of the Pnyx Hills, ever worshipped Zeus Hypsistos; it is unsafe to assume that *Hypsistos* is the same as *Hypatos;* there is no evidence that the tablets found by Lord Aberdeen were arranged with any reference to the statue which is supposed to have stood in the large niche in the back wall of the Pnyx, as one of the small niches has been destroyed in making the large one; that a tradition of an ancient worship of Zeus was preserved here through the ages, and the worship resumed in later times in consequence of the tradition, is highly improbable, as Christensen suggests; the names on the tablet found by Lord Aberdeen indicate that the tablets were set up by women of the lower classes; if the worship of Zeus as a healer in this place had had a national character, he would in all probability have been worshipped under some other name than Hypsistos.

5. *The character of the so-called Pnyx is out of harmony with the age of Attic oratory.*

This can scarcely be said of any part of the Pnyx except the semicircular wall which supports the terrace at the lower side.[7] The bema belongs manifestly to a later date than the remains of the rock-dwellings north-west of it on the Pnyx Hill. The semicircular wall is not so rude in structure as the walls of Tiryns, nor as many of the ancient walls that are to be seen in southern Italy, and would seem, therefore, to belong to a later period than several writers on the topography of Athens have supposed. Goettling, as stated above, held the opinion that the circular wall is older than the bema and the rock-wall.

After almost a month of work on the Pnyx Hill, during which time the blocks of the circular wall, the bema, and many details were measured many times, we came away with a strong impression that the work about the Pnyx has extended over a long period of time, and that while some of it was certainly done in remote antiquity, some belongs to a period much later than that of many specimens

---

7. On this point compare note *N*, p. 242. — J. T. C.

of stone work to be found in Greece. In other words, we were convinced that pre-Pnyxian work is to be found about the Pnyx itself. To this we reckon the blocks of stone which stand on top of the hill at the south-west corner of the enclosure, the steps which disappear under the circular wall, and the three steps found below the bema by Curtius, as well as the dressing of the rock which Curtius noticed in the trench which he dug. The blocks at the southwest corner have been mentioned above as similar to those of the semicircular wall; but in this place they are entirely out of harmony with their surroundings, and must have belonged to a wall such as Goettling suggests, or to something else of which we have no knowledge. The steps below the semicircular wall certainly existed before this wall was built, as they disappear under it. The steps which Curtius found, as we have seen from the description above, are lower, more rounded on the edges, and generally older in appearance, than those of the bema. In a line with the two large blocks of stone described above, near S on the survey, is another block, almost cubical in form and also marked "Wall." In a line with these three, in the "Cultivated Patch," between f and R on the survey, Goettling found another stone which has now disappeared, and which he took for a part of his supposed Pelasgic fortification. These large blocks, three of which are still in position, certainly belonged to some such wall as Goettling has supposed. Their line is out of harmony with everything about the Pnyx. They are all too far from the back wall of the Pnyx to have had any relation to it. They certainly were not put where they are to level up the irregularities of the top of this half of the back wall of the Pnyx, as some have seemed to assume. These rocks and the two sets of steps are evidence almost unmistakable that some very ancient structure has been remodelled in order to produce the Pnyx which we now see. Seen from this standpoint, the apparent lack of harmony between this structure and the general character of the age of Attic oratory may be better understood.

6. *Ulrichs and others have urged that the bema in the so-called Pnyx cannot have been the tribune of the Attic orators, because this was a λίθος, or movable stone.*

Ulrichs's thought seems to have been that the word πέτρα would more accurately describe the so-called bema, as it is a large mass of rock still undetached from the native rock of the hill; while the word λίθος, which means rather a movable block of stone, could not be applied to it. But there seems to have been no fixed usage in regard to these words in connection with the bema. πέτρα, βῆμα, and λίθος seem to have been used indifferently in speaking of it. In Aristophanes. *Pac.* v. 680, we find the words, ὅστις κρατεῖ νῦν τοῦ λίθου τοῦ 'ν τῇ Πυκνί. Again, *Eccles.* 104, ὑπὸ τῷ λίθῳ τῶν πρυτανέων καταντικρύ. In this and many other passages in Aristophanes the word λίθος is used as synonymous with βῆμα. But in the *Knights*, v. 313, are the words κἀπὸ τῶν πετρῶν ἄνωθεν τοὺς φόρους θυννοσκοπεῖς. in which Cleon is represented, as said above, as watching the incoming tributes as the tunny-fisher on the seashore watches the schools of fish. The tunny-fish are said to have been attracted by the warmth of the sun, and therefore to have appeared at the surface of the water, so as to render it possible for a fisher on a high lookout on the shore to direct others in surrounding them with the seine. This is the picture which Aristophanes has before his mind when speaking of Cleon in the Pnyx. Welcker thinks the word πετρῶν here used refers to the rocks of the Pnyx in general,[1] but this interpretation deprives the comparison of half its force. If Cleon in the Pnyx bore any likeness to a fisher on a look-out on the seashore, he must have been on some elevated object, and the prominent one in the Pnyx was the bema. Raoul-Rochette cites this passage to show that the bema was called πέτρα as well as λίθος. He also rightly refers to *Eq.* v. 780, to show that the word πέτρα was not limited in its use to large rocks, as it is here used in speaking of the seats on which the people sat. It may be noticed, too, that Dobree has τῆς πέτρας for τῶν πετρῶν in v. 313. Koch, in his note on this verse, says the bema was called indifferently βῆμα, λίθος, and πέτρα. He refers in support of this statement to v. 956, which reads λάρος κεχηνὼς ἐπὶ πέτρας δημηγορῶν. This verse is what the Sausage-Seller says of the device on the ring which Cleon gives to Demos. The "gaping cormorant," which he says was represented on the ring, is meant as a reflection on the rapacity of Cleon. Commentators generally so understand these words. If this be so, the other words, "haranguing upon a rock," will scarcely bear any other interpretation

---

[1] Welcker, *Der Felsaltar*, u.s.w., p. 301 (37).

than that they refer to Cleon haranguing the people from the bema.[1]

7. *Welcker and Curtius have also made much of the blowing of the north wind, as against the Pnyx theory.*

Curtius says that the advocates of the Pnyx theory have been so carried away with the thought of finding the place in which the popular assemblies of the ancient Greeks were held, that this and other unfavorable features of the so-called Pnyx for such assemblies have been overlooked. How severely the north wind sometimes blows over the Pnyx Hill we learned from experience, but there seems to be no solution of this difficulty. The climate has changed in some respects, but it is scarcely possible that the wind blew less hard in ancient times than now. If this be not true, the Greeks must often have held their assemblies in the wind. The site which Curtius and Welcker ascribe to the place of assembly is but little less exposed to the north wind than the so-called Pnyx. If from extant remains of structures built for purposes similar to those of the Pnyx any principle could be established as to their location or the relative position of speaker and audience, this argument would gain importance. But, judging from the theatres of which remains still exist, the Greeks seem to have had no rule about this matter. The Dionysiac theatre faces the south, the one at Argos looks toward the east, that at Nauplia toward the north-north-west, and that at Megalopolis to the north. Other theatres as well as stadia show that the Greeks constructed such places of assembly with little or no regard to wind and weather. If the Pnyx could be located on the south slope of a hill, the protection which Curtius feels is necessary for the place of assembly would be secured, but this is scarcely possible; it must have been somewhere on the north-east slope of the Pnyx Hills. These are all about equally exposed to the wind.

In conclusion, we wish to notice but two points more. The first is the use which Curtius is forced by his location of the Pnyx to make of the passage in Plutarch's Theseus in regard to the battle of the Amazons. The camp of the Amazons was on the Areopagus (Aesch. *Eumen.* 685). Before the battle began, they were so arrayed

---

[1] See note on this verse in Droysen's translation of Aristophanes, Berlin, 1838; Ribbeck's edition of the Knights, Berlin, 1867; Hickie's note on this verse in his translation of Aristophanes, London, 1881.

that their left wing extended to the Areopagus, near which the Amazoneum, a temple which commemorated the battle, also stood. Their right wing extended to the Pnyx ($\pi\rho\grave{o}s\ \tau\grave{\eta}\nu\ \Pi\nu\acute{\nu}\kappa\alpha$). The conformation of this region can be readily learned from a map. North-east of the Pnyx Hills, stretching along their foot, is a depression which separates them from the Acropolis and Areopagus, which are on the opposite side. A low ridge extends across this depression from the Acropolis to the Pnyx Hill. The camp of the Amazons was north-west of this low ridge, and the new site which Curtius assigns to the Pnyx is on the south-east of it. If the Pnyx was situated where it is usually supposed to have been, it will be seen that the battle line of the Amazons extended across the depression almost at right angles. If the Pnyx was situated where Curtius thinks it was, we stretch their line of battle inordinately, and make it extend not only along the lowest part of the depression, but also over this low ridge, a distance of between a quarter and a half a mile. Plutarch tells us, further, that the battle took place in the open ground near the so-called temple of Theseus, which was still north of where the line would stand if we locate the Pnyx in the usual place. If we accept Curtius's site of the Pnyx, we must suppose that the Athenians, who, Plutarch says, made their attack from the Museum, drove the Amazons nearly half a mile before the two armies reached the battle-field proper. But this cannot have been the case, as Plutarch tells us in the same connection that in the first onset the Amazons were victorious and drove the Athenians back to the temple of the Eumenides, which stood at the foot of the Acropolis, between it and the Areopagus. Plutarch then says that an attack was made on their right wing by persons who made the attack from the Palladium, Ardettus, and the Lyceum, and that the Amazons were driven back to their camp, many of them being killed. To this part of the passage Curtius, as has been pointed out by Bursian,[1] does violence by substituting *left wing* where Plutarch says *right wing*. If we accept the usual site of the Pnyx, the place where the line stood at first is quite near the open space in which Plutarch says the battle took place and in which the graves of the fallen were to be seen. We are also relieved of the supposition that the Amazons adopted the queer tactics of closing a valley or depression by stretching their line along the lowest part of it. Notwithstanding Curtius's view, we must

---

[1] *Literarisches Centralblatt*, No. 30, p. 712 (1863).

still retain this as one of the most valuable passages in fixing the site of Pnyx. It points plainly to the usually accepted place.

We must further disagree with Curtius, in regard to the mass of rock left in the south-east corner of the Pnyx. It bears, as we have seen above, all the marks of a piece of unfinished work. Why should not the Greeks make their "Götter Markt," as Curtius calls the Pnyx, uniform in shape in the two corners? What reason can be given for putting the official persons, whom he supposes to have stood on it, away here in the corner, more than a hundred and seventy feet away from the supposed altar and a hundred feet from the large niche in which the statue of Zeus is supposed to have stood? If this is a stage for officials to stand on, why cut it loose from the rock of the hill? If this precaution were taken with a stage for men to stand on, why not bestow the same attention on the altar of Zeus the Highest, for the so-called bema which Curtius takes for an altar is still attached to the hill? Further, how does it happen that the cut or trench by which this supposed stage is separated from the common rock is cut down to the level of the lower step of the bema? This cut is just wide enough for a man to work in, and is in some places six or seven feet deep. It is cut in with a manifest view to the saving of labor. The sides of it are left perfectly smooth. Thus when the mass of rock was removed, the back wall would present a smooth surface, and the blocks into which the mass might be broken would on one side need no further dressing before being laid up in the wall, if they were to be used for such a purpose. Why so deep, if the intention was to produce a simple line of separation?[v]

Several other points of more or less interest in regard to the Pnyx will be omitted, as they do not materially affect the principal point under consideration.

We have tried to present the question fairly; and we have found that, while we cannot say with absolute certainty that the so-called Pnyx is the real Pnyx, the evidence taken collectively is strongly in favor of this conclusion.

---

*V. On the constructive character of these masses of rock remaining in the south-eastern corner of the auditory, see note N, p. 242, and note O, p. 244. — J. T. C.

NOTES

ON

ATTIC VOCALISM.

BY

J. McKEEN LEWIS.

NOTES ON ATTIC VOCALISM.

IN these notes I have considered the most important questions relating to the pronunciation of the vowels and diphthongs in Attic, and the changes they underwent during the Attic period. The chief, almost the only, testimony to be profitably consulted in these questions is that of inscriptions of good date, principally those of Attica. I have been able to examine the bulk of those which are of service, including those contained in the *C. I. A.*, those in Kaibel's collection, and many which have appeared in the *Bulletin de Correspondance Hellénique*, in the 'Αθήναιον, in *Hermes*, and in a few other collections. For nearly all statistics, however, I am indebted to the *Grammatik der Attischen Inschriften* of Meisterhans (Berlin, 1885). I have also made free use of Blass, *Aussprache des Griechischen;* Herwerden, *Lapidum de Dialecto Attica Testimonia;* Dittenberger, in *Hermes*, VI., XV., and XVII.; Saalfeld, *Lautgesetze der Griechischen Lehnwörter im Lateinischen;* and G. Meyer, *Griechische Grammatik* (Leipzig, 1886); besides authorities not bearing directly on questions of phonetics. This paper, it is hoped, may contribute something toward the settlement of certain disputed points, and possibly suggest one or two new theories worth consideration.

1. THE E-GROUP.

The early Attic alphabet had five vowel-signs, — A, E, I, O, Y. Thus all the *e*-vowels were represented by E, and all the *o*-vowels by O. The Ionians of Asia Minor, who in literary development were in advance of the other Greek tribes, and may have enjoyed a keener grammatical sense, were the first to feel the need of a further distinction, and to employ the Phoenician symbol *Chet* or ἧτα[1] (H) as a vowel. It had served to represent the "rough breathing"; it

---

[1] Not until post-classical times written for ἦτα with smooth breathing.

now stood for the long *e*-vowel, heard *e.g.* in δῆμος, οἰκίη, which had arisen in Ionic from original *a* :[1] it stood usually, moreover, for the ab-original *ē*, heard *e.g.* in μή, τίθημι, ἀποθάνητε. The latter vowel belongs purely to the *e*-group, and we may suppose, on etymological grounds alone, that it did not in any degree incline toward *ā* in sound. This supposition is made a certainty by the evidence of inscriptions of Keos and Naxos graphically distinguishing this *e*-sound from its younger cousin. In these inscriptions the Ionic η, equivalent to a modified *ā*, is found represented by the Chet (H); the universal and aboriginal η by its old sign E. Thus we find on monuments of Keos KHΔ[ον], MHTEPA, TPIHKOΣ[τεῖα]; but ME (= μή), [ἐ]ΠΙ-BΛEMATI (ἐπιβλήματι), KΛEN[ο]ΓENEΣ (Κλεινογένης), ANE-ΘEKEN (ἀνέθηκεν). The distinction is consistently carried through with hardly an exception. On a stone of Naxos we have, perhaps, a corresponding distinction between the aboriginal ε common to all dialects, and the presumably broader or more guttural ε arising, only in the Ionic branches of the language, from *ā*. While the aboriginal ε has its usual sign, the Ionic ε is written with the same symbol (Θ) which is used for the Ionic η, and we encounter the forms ΔEINO-ΔIKΘO (Δεινοδίκεω), AΛΘON (ἀλ[λ]έων).[2] Thus the fact is established, that from the prehistoric date of its origin, at least until some time during the classical period, the Ionic η did not diverge so widely from its parent-sound *ā* as to become totally identified with the aboriginal η. That the *ē*-sound arising in the various dialects from contracted αε and εα was of the same character, lying between *a* and *ē* proper, is suggested by a comparison of such contractions as ὁρᾶσθαι, ἀργός, with ἐνίκη (ᾱε); or, to show that the same relation held good in the formation of Attic, compare ὦττᾱ, ἐνδεᾶ, with ἀληθῆ (εᾱ), and ἀλέᾱ with χρυστῇ (εᾱ).[3] It is worthy of notice in this discussion that, while there is no positive evidence of the continuance of this distinction between a broad and a narrow η during the Attic period,

---

[1] The sound was probably identical with that arising from contraction of εα and, in new Ionic Greek, of αε.

[2] Dittenberger, in *Hermes*, XV. p. 225 seqq. Perhaps, however, we should read Δεινοδίκηω, ἀλλήων. The inscriptions are of an early period.

[3] So adjectives like εὐφυής, ἀκλεής, ὑγιής, probably underwent, during the fourth century, a gradual change of neut. pl. from -ᾱ to -ῆ. On a stone of 357-354 B.C. are found both ὑγιᾶ and ὑγιῆ (as neut. pl.).

there are yet some indications of this even in the later phases of the dialect. I am inclined to regard the now authentic forms ἱείς, τιθείς, ἵεις, ἐτίθεις, etc., as a proof that aboriginal η held a slightly different place in the vowel-series from Ionic η, which was at no time confused with ē (ει). The form ἐτίθης slipped into ἐτίθεις in the new Attic orthography as naturally as βασιλῆς, on the lips of later Athenians, became βασιλεῖς, or as τέθηκα was changed, at a still later time, to τέθεικα. The laws of analogy, than which no formative principle is more marked in the development of the Attic dialect, would as surely have produced ἵστεις, ἵστει, had the Ionic η of ἵστημι been identical in sound with the vowel heard in τίθημι, ἵημι, βασιλῆς, etc.[1] These indications, together with the facts that Attic was a direct outcome of Ionic, and that the distinction was so marked in the latter dialect as to call, in some localities, for graphical representation, leave little doubt that it continued to exist at least into the fourth century B.C. To define exactly the pronunciation of the Ionic η would, of course, be impossible. We may assume with much plausibility that it lay between the *a* of English *bad* and the German *ä*. The other η, which in nearly all cases is grammatically related to ε and belongs purely to the *e*-group of vowels, was not essentially different from the long Italian *ē* as pronounced at the present time. It should be kept in mind that whatever may have been its origin, an η was always an open vowel:[2] in other words, no vanishing or *i*-sound was heard after it,

---

[1] Though these changes were all *occasioned* by analogy, they could not have occurred but for a close resemblance between the vowel-sounds interchanged. Thus ὀστᾶ, χρυσῆ, σιδηρᾶ, were shaped after the corresponding uncontracted inflections; ἐποίεις suggested ἐτίθεις just as πόλεις suggested βασιλεῖς, and as εἶκα (Meyer, *Gr.* 71) supplied a reason for writing τέθεικα. This principle could not, however, effect violent phonetic changes; it worked by stealth, not by force, and practised its deception only with such nearly equivalent sounds as ā and Ionic η, or ε and aboriginal η.

[2] The sound produced by the lengthening of ε and contraction of εε was at first written universally E: the designation EI appears first among the Ionians, the Corcyreans, and Locrians; while the mass of the Dorians wrote E, and afterwards H. That the vowel was sounded differently in Doric and Ionic appears not to have been proved. The same may be said of Old-Doric ω for ου. (So also Doric τὡμόν for τοὐμόν, etc.) The difference was, perhaps, only an orthographic one, and the Dorians kept, for the most part, the spellings with η, ω, until Ionian influence caused them gradually to disappear. This seems to me a simpler explanation

except, of course, where this is added, as in the diphthong ηι. This is demonstrated by the entire absence of any confusion between η and ηι in inscriptions of good date. The character of the η is conveniently illustrated by the well-known verse : ὁ δ' ἠλίθιος ὡς προβάτων βῆ βῆ λέγων βαδίζει (Cratinus), on which the E. M. has the gloss : βῆ· τὸ μιμητικὸν τῆς τῶν προβάτων φωνῆς· οὐχὶ βαὶ λέγεται Ἀττικῶς. The form βαί is the natural rendering of the same sound in later times, when αι had usurped the pronunciation originally belonging to η. Thus also before the beginning of the fourth century, the Boeotians, with whom the process of vowel-degeneration was more than a century in advance of that of the other dialects, borrowed the new vowel-sign η from their Ionian neighbors to serve in place of αι, which in Boeotia had already ceased to be a diphthong. The αι, as is well known, has continued to the present day to be sounded in Greece as it was at that time in the most corrupt of the dialects.

Two of the *e*-sounds long continued to be represented by E after η began to be used as a vowel-sign in Attica, — namely, ε, and the long vowel arising from its " compensative" lengthening, or from the contraction of εε. This will be called, for convenience, ē or long ε. That it had a narrower sound than η, and was in fact a closed or quasi-diphthongal vowel, is indicated by its graphical confusion, soon after the year of Eucleides, with the diphthong ει. It was felt to be (as its functions show) qualitatively equivalent to ē, and was thus during a long period written with the same symbol. From this it may be inferred that ē had also a sharp or closed sound, rather like the *e* of Italian *venti* than like the short *e* of our own language.

We are thus able to distinguish, in the Ionic dialects, four or five *e*-vowels, with three degrees of divergence from α : a broad η arising from ā (as in οἰκίη, νικήσω), perhaps its corresponding short (as in ἀλλέων, νεώς); an aboriginal and narrower η (as in βέβληκα, ἀτελής);

---

than to suppose (with G. Meyer, *Gr.* 69) an actual phonetic modification of an open *ē*-vowel to *ē* first consummated in Ionic and afterwards in Doric. Had such a thing occurred in these dialects (as it certainly did in Thessalian), it should have affected all the *ē*-sounds of this class, and resulted in forms like χρείσιμος for χρήσιμος, ἔθεινε for ἔθηκε, etc.

and, finally, the closed $\bar{\epsilon}$ and $\bar{\epsilon}$ (as in θέντος, θείς). Until the year of Eucleides these vowels were all generally written in Attica with the one symbol E. After that year the H came into general use for the long open e-sounds. By the year 380 the long ε was nearly always written ει; the vowel and the diphthong gradually ceased to be distinguished. Two opposite theories have been advanced in explanation of this orthographical change: the first, that the long ε slowly approached the diphthong in sound (the latter remaining the same), becoming more and more closed, until finally the i-element became so prominent as to give the vowel a diphthongal character. This was the first and apparently simplest explanation;[1] it will be shown, however, that the converse change was in reality what took place, — the diphthong, namely, became simplified until its pronunciation scarcely differed from that of $\bar{\epsilon}$.[2] It is not necessary to believe that the diphthong became absolutely identical with the vowel during the Attic period: it certainly did not become so at the time of their earliest graphical confusion in the fifth century. Were this the case, we should expect to find it, during its transition, written frequently with the simple vowel-sign E. The rarity of this indicates that ει did not entirely lose its diphthongal character, — rather that it approached so near the simple vowel in pronunciation as to make the Attic ear conscious, as it were by involuntary comparison, of a slight vanish or i-sound which had always existed in the $\bar{\epsilon}$ itself, and thus cause this to be written diphthongally. To establish this conclusion it is necessary to show that $\bar{\epsilon}$ did not vary in sound during the classical time.

Nearly all evidence as to the relations of $\bar{\epsilon}$ and ει must, of course, be sought in the post-Euclidean inscriptions. In these we find many indications that ει no longer necessarily represents a diphthongal sound, and that $\bar{\epsilon}$, on the other hand, is as much a monophthong as in earlier time.

A. Confusion of $\bar{\epsilon}$ and ει. When ει begins to be generally written for $\bar{\epsilon}$, we find it written also frequently for $\check{\epsilon}$ before another vowel. The true explanation of this is a most simple one: a slight i-sound will naturally insert itself after an e-sound followed by a vowel, the

---

[1] Proposed by Dietrich, who was the first to treat the subject. Cf. also Blass, *Aussprache*, pp. 26 seqq.

[2] This is the view now generally taken. Cf. G. Meyer, *Gr.* 69, 115.

result being an ĕ with a more or less perceptible vanish, but not a diphthongal sound, this being impossible to a short vowel. Thus, in this case at least, ει must stand for a simple sound which had long been written ε, the change being easily accounted for by the increasingly monophthongal character of the genuine ει; so that ε, ē, ει now meant much the same vowel-sound,—a narrow *e*-sound with a slight vanish.[1] The change undergone by the diphthong consisted in the comparative suppression of its second element.[2] The same thing will be shown to have happened in the case of ου. Examples[3] of ει for ε before vowels are: δεῶνται, 119 (about 340); ἱδρύσεως twice, 168 (330); Κιτιείων, ibid.;[4] ἀξιόχρειῳ, 578 (after 340);[5] ἑαυτόν, 115, p. 13 (after 350); εἰῶν, 14, p. 11 (387); Πλωθει[ᾶς] (originally with diphthongal ει, but cf. Πλωθῆς, etc., ibid.), or Πλωθείας, for -θέας, 570; etc. These spellings are discussed by Herwerden,[6] who remarks that they are not found in inscriptions later than the early part of the third century B.C. The cause of this is obvious: ει was after that time no longer qualitatively equivalent to ε, but had begun to feel the influence of itacism.[7]

---

[1] It is remarkable that no sooner had graphical distinctions between the various *e*- and *i*-vowels begun to be thought necessary by the Athenians than the real distinctions began to be obliterated by phonetic decay.

[2] The simplification of the diphthongs in Latin was nearly complete at the date of the earliest literary monuments we possess in that language. That ē could have taken the contrary course, and been diphthongized, is against all analogies presented by the history of phonetic decay. It has been supposed by Blass and others that the itacism of ει resulted from an increasing preponderance of its *i*-element. This, however, seems quite incompatible with the confusion of ει and ε, ē, ηι.

[3] All of a good time (between 387 and 329). Nearly all will be found in Meisterhans, *Gr.* pp. 21 seqq. Those here cited are from *C. I. A.*, II. 1.

[4] As gen. pl. of Κιτιεύς. We should, of course, expect Κιτιῶν, but the rule is not absolute even in the best time. Cf. Meisterh., *Gr.* pp. 56 seq.

[5] ἀξιοχρείῳ, Köhler. But this is perfectly analogous to the other cases of ει written for ε, and the accent should therefore not be changed. So in II. 872, Κολλυτείες must be read, not Κολλυτεῖες. In Λειωγόρου, 553 (circa Eucl. ann.), perhaps the earliest instance of this inaccuracy, we have ει written for an Ionic ε.

[6] *Lapidum de Dial. Att. Testimonia*, pp. 10, 11.

[7] The forms ἐνείγκῃ for ἐνέγκῃ, etc., frequent between 373 and 332 (v. Meisterh., p. 89), apparently on the analogy of Ion. ἐνείκῃ, show that the same confusion could exist before a double consonant when, as before vowels, quantity could not be affected by the interchange.

On the other hand, E continues to be written occasionally for ε until the latter part of the fourth century,[1] — an improbable orthographical survival, had ε become in any degree diphthongal. This occurs most frequently in the word εἰς, which is equally written ἐς when a consonant follows; the prosodial treatment of the preposition in Comedy makes it certain that in mature Attic the longer form had entirely superseded the shorter. The spellings ἐ στήλῃ and εἰ στήλῃ for ἐν στήλῃ[2] are interesting as showing that the syllable -ενς became -ἐς in rapid utterance as well in Attic of the fourth century as at far earlier periods of the Greek language.

B. Confusion of ε with η. That ε had in no degree become diphthongal in the fourth century is further testified by its interchangeableness, in certain cases, with the open e-vowel. Thus between 378 and 324 the nominative plural ending of nouns in -εύς was suffering a gradual change from -ῆς to -εῖς: during this time we find both spellings even in the same inscription.[3] Perhaps the difference in these cases is a merely orthographic one; for the frequent spellings -έες, -έης,[4] -εες,[5] of this same termination show clearly enough how easy to an Athenian ear was the confusion, at this time, between ε̄, ε, and the narrow (or aboriginal) η. The augmented forms of ἐργάζομαι furnish another example of this, beginning interchangeably with εἰ- or ἠ- during the fourth century. Here, again, the difference was probably only in the spelling. It should be kept in mind, however, that in Attic this confusion of ε and η is only occasional, — the two vowels were at no time properly equivalents, and the contractions producing them are quite different. Plurals in -ῆς are, of course, not from contracted -έες, but from -ῆες; for the dual of γένος, γένη is as much a violation of Attic as γένεε.[6] Yet, were we in possession

---

[1] The latest examples are perhaps II. 804 A, 13, 33, ἐς τὸ and ἀποδώσεν.

[2] II. 86 (376–365); 553 (403).

[3] Διεῖς, Καρθαιεῖς, Ἑστιαιῆς, Χαλκιδῆς], II. 17 (378); Κυδαθηναιεῖς, Παιανιῆς, 865 (after 400); ['Αμαξ]αντειεῖ[ς], 'Ανακαιῆς, et al., 1006 (bef. 350); v. Meisterh., p. 56.

[4] Cf. -κλέης for -κλῆς, even in the fourth century, Meisterh., p. 57. 'Αγρυλέης, I. 338 (408); ['Αλα]ιέες, Κολλ[υ]τέες, Φηγαιέες, beside Βατῆς, II. 870 (circa 350).

[5] Κολλυτεες, beside 'Αλαιεῖς, etc., II. 872 (341), etc. Cf. Meisterh., p. 55.

[6] σκέλε, II. 652 A, 24; ζεύγε, id. B, 26. πόλη (Isoc. 8, 116), φύση (Plat. Rep. 410 E), and similar forms, if genuine, are the result of a desire to differentiate the dual from the dat. sing. when the diphthong ει had become identical in sound

of all Attic inscriptions of the fourth century, we might well find that stonecutters had, in the absence of any orthographic standard, here and there written σκέλη and σκέλεε for σκέλε̄, just as they wrote Χολλῄδης for Χολλῄδης, and 'Αλαιέες for 'Αλαῆς. As it is, however, in view of the unparalleled elaborateness of the Greek vowel-system, the comparative infrequency of such errors bears witness to the marvellous accuracy of the Attic ear.

It is thus evident from the interchangeableness of ε̄, ει, with ε̆, εε, η, in the fourth century, that ε̄ was not changed, in pronunciation as in writing, to ει, but that, conversely, the diphthong must have become simplified until its symbol could represent both sounds. This degradation began earlier, and was more quickly consummated, where ει was followed by a vowel — a well-known instance is the word δωρειά, later Attic δωρεά.[1] This change is only a manifestation of one of the most important laws of Attic speech, — that law by which a semivocal ι is avoided through the dropping of ι between almost any pair of vowels. As ει before vowels becomes ε at a very early date,[2] so words like ἐλαία, κλαίω, Πειραιεύς, στοιά, ποιεῖ, υἱός, γεγονυῖα, lose their ι by the best Attic usage. The same principle is observed in all crases where final ι occurs, as in κἀμοί, οὑπιχώριοι, χὤπως, τῇκκλησίᾳ, τὠπιόντι.[3] But the degradation of diphthongal ει, independently of this law, is illustrated by the equal corruption of ῃ to ει or ε̄ during the fourth century.

Confusion of ῃ with ε̄ and ει. Not long after the year of Eucleides, and simultaneously with the falling together of ε̄ and ει, the diphthong ῃ becomes interchangeable with these. After 375, such forms as πύλῃ for πύλει, βουλεῖ for βουλῇ, grow frequent; for ᾑρέθη is found

with έ. Probably the dual of πόλις in Attic was πόλε̄ (πόλει); if πόλη arose by contraction, its parent form was not πόλεε, but πόληε.

[1] Older and newer forms are sometimes found side by side, as δωρείαν, δωρεάν, II. 1 b (circa Eucl. ann.), ἱερίας, ἱερείας, 573 b (circa 350?); the difference in these cases is, of course, merely orthographic, ει and ε standing alike for a simple closed ε-sound. Cf. Meisterh., p. 19 and notes.

[2] Cf. Αἰνέο, I. 478 (sixth century); Πελεᾶται, 230 (450), Αἰνεῶται, 234 (446); τέλεος, IV. 3 (before 444); Νεάνδρεα, I. 240 (440); Βρυλλεανοί, 247 (432); Ἀλωπεκεεῖ, 184 (412); Ἀνδρέᾳ, 324 (408); πρυτανέον twice, II. 1 b (c. Eucl. ann.), ἱέρεα, IV. 553 a, 3 (fourth century).

[3] So there is every reason to write in Attic τουτωΐ, ἐκεινοΐ, etc., in place of the unpronounceable τουτῳΐ, ἐκεινοιΐ

εἱρέθη, and εἶπει for εἴπῃ. Tribal names like Οἰνῆς, -νῆδος (not Οἰνηίς, -νηίδος, as commonly edited), are equally spelt -εῖς, -εῖδος. Heteroclitic datives from proper nouns in -ης occur, as Πεισιθείδει for -δῃ.[1] The inscriptions of various dialects give indications that the *i*-element was weaker and sooner lost in the case of ῃ than of the other like diphthongs. Moreover, the pronunciation of ῃ was facilitated by the shortening of η before ι; thus it became a simple closed *ē*-sound not widely different from *ē*.[2] Indeed, E can be written for ῃ; thus χαλκ[οθή]κε αὐτέ (-θήκῃ αὐτῇ, II. 61, c. 358). Conversely, μηνύσες (nom. pl.) is spelt μηνύσῃς in 572 (circa Eucl. ann.).[3] In short, we have examples of ει put for ῃ, ῃ for ει and for *ē*, and ε for ῃ. The two diphthongs ει and ῃ had become almost indistinguishable from each other and from *ē*. Two important inferences can be drawn from this: first, that the phonetic decay of ει did not, as has been generally assumed (and as was the case in Latin), consist in a gradually increasing preponderance of its *i*-element, but in a gradual loss of the distinctness of each separate element, so that *ei* became a close *ē* not more diphthongal than *ē*. Second, that this change had been nearly, if not quite, consummated before the end of the Attic period.[4]

---

[1] Wecklein, *Cur. Epigr.*, p. 63; Herwerden, *Lap. Test.*, pp. 5, 6. Perhaps the confusion of datives hastened that of accusatives, and finally that of genitives. By the beginning of the third century the false analogy has given the declension of *a*-stems to *s*-stems of proper nouns throughout. Perhaps in this, as in many things, Xenophon's usage anticipated the common dialect, and we should, with the manuscripts, give him such forms as Σωκράτην for Attic Σωκράτη, etc.

[2] The shortening of η before ι (cf. Dittenberger in *Hermes*, XVII. 37) is confirmed by the analogy of other diphthongs; ναῖς, *e.g.*, became ναῦς, as otherwise the Attic form must have remained νηῦς. (G. Meyer, *Gr.* 118, 298.) Cf. κωμοιδία for κωμῳδία, Kaibel, *Ep. Gr.* 38.

[3] Other examples are: πόλῃ, II. 25 (before 376?); βουλεῖ, 38; πραχθε[ῖ], δόξει (subj.), 49; Οἰνεῖς, 55; χαλκοθήκει, four times, beside -θήκε, 61; ἀ̓νοιχθεῖ, παρασκ[ευα σθεῖ, id.; [γραμμ]ασῇ, ε[ῖ] for ῇ, 90; τεῖ, αυτεῖ, etc.; τιμήσει, στεφανώσει (subj.); so δοκεῖ, twice; εἱρέθη, 114; [ἔ]νει, 125; στήλει λιθίνει, 147; συντελεσθεῖ, παραλάβει, πτωματίσει, 167; Αἰγεῖδος, 168 (and Ἀριστείδης, etc., for ηίδης after 400); τριακοστεῖ, 180; ἑορτεῖ, 577; εἶ, passim (= ῇ); ἑβδόμει, ἐνάτει, id.; ἀγαθεῖ τύχει, τεῖ φυλεῖ, 564; ἕκτει καὶ δεκάτει, 175*b* (Add. et Corrig.); ἀφιεῖ, 573*b* (id.). The list may be easily extended by reference to the *C. I. A.*, II. These citations are enough to show that analogy, in this case, has nothing to do with the changed spelling.

[4] In the fourth century, ῃι is found (in *C. I. A.*, II. 1; v. Meisterh., *Gr.* p. 18)

2. THE O-GROUP.

The history of this class of vowels presents a close analogy to that of the *e*-group; and with the advance of epigraphical study, this analogy will probably be found more complete than it has heretofore been deemed. In the relations of ο, ō, ω, ου to one another, the changes which took place during the Attic period were similar and, in general, synchronous with those undergone by the vowels already discussed. Thus, in the earlier Attic monuments, the character O does duty for ο, ō, ω,[1] while the labial diphthong corresponding to ει is consistently distinguished from those sounds by the sign OY.[2] The vowel ō is related etymologically to ο precisely as ē to ε; that is, it is produced by the doubling, or the "compensative" lengthening, of ο, also (in the Ionic dialects) by the contraction of οε, and in Attic of εο. The diphthong ου, on the other hand, can arise only by contraction of ο + υ (or ο + ϝ). From the Attic inscriptions we can prove its existence in the words ἀκόλουθος, σπουδή (*ablaut* from κελευθ-, σπευδ-), βοῦς (βοϝ-ς), Σούνιον; perhaps in οἱ, οὗτος.[3] So long as it continued diphthongal, its sound must have been equivalent to ο + υ, each vowel being distinctly pronounced, but coalescing with the other in so far that the combination was monosyllabic. The vowel ō must originally have had a closed ō-sound (like English *o* in *rose*), the labial counterpart of ē. About the same time that ē begins to be written ει, the writing ου for ō also becomes common.[4] ω, like η, comes into general use after the year of Eucleides. The treatment of ō in Doric is quite analogous to that of ē; so ω becomes ō in Thessalian as η becomes ē.[5] As ē and ει were finally merged in an

---

written HI 391 times; EI, 118 times: but in the third, ηι, ῃ, and ει are, for the most part, represented by the same symbol EI. Afterwards the confusion becomes less common, as ηι loses its iota, and ει begins to suffer itacism.

[1] Ω for ω, however, sometimes appears during the fifth century.

[2] With a few exceptions. Cf. Meisterh., *Gr.* p. 30.

[3] So in their compounds and derivatives, and in words formed like οὗτος, τοιοῦτος, τηλικοῦτος, etc. Also (as shown by inscriptions in other dialects) in βροῦκος, θοῦρος, κοῦφος, ζουθός, στροῦθος. Another *ablaut* ου is seen in the epic εἰλήλουθα (ἐλευθ-), while ἀπούρας = ἀπό-ϝρας.

[4] In the case of ō the change is completed somewhat later than with ē. Cf. Meisterh., *Gr.* p. 3.

[5] See note 2, page 5. ἐδίδου for ἐδίδω is in like manner comparable with ἐτίθει, ἵει for ἐτίθη, ἵη. In each case an open vowel becomes closed by the unconscious action of analogy.

i-sound in the decadence of the language, thus ō and ου became alike = ū.

That ō and ου were not yet, in the fourth century, identical sounds, is strongly indicated by this fact,—that while ου is written diphthongally (with a few scattered exceptions; v. Meisterh., *Gr.* p. 30), ō continues often represented by the simple O : preferentially so, indeed, until about 360. This is exactly what might be expected when ου is still diphthongal, but weakening toward a simple closed ō-sound, so that the vowel having this sound will begin to be written as the diphthong. Were ου = ū at this time, ō remaining a closed ō-sound, then ō would surely not be so frequently written ου; whereas, on the very simple hypothesis that the case of ō ου is just like that of ἰ ε, the exceptions (ο for ου and ου for ο) serve only to illustrate and vindicate the main facts. In spite of this it has been generally supposed that the degradation of these sounds to a simple ū took place as early as the end of the fifth century. This is inferred chiefly from the Boeotian inscriptions, which present ου for υ from this time on. The vowel-system was, of course, hopelessly corrupt in Boeotia already; and it is instructive that most of the changes it had suffered exactly anticipate those which occur later throughout the dialects. ου had, in Boeotia, already become = ū, while υ retained this same sound; clearly, in Attic the *nearest approach* to the pure ū-sound must in any case have been ου, since Attic υ was becoming = ü; thus the desire to write each vowel-sound as the Athenians wrote it, led to ου for υ in Boeotia. This new orthography had obtained at a time when, in Attica, O was still generally used for ο, ō, ω, and occasionally even for ου. Indeed, in one or two cases ω is found for ου and ō.[1] Crases like μού (μοι ὁ), προὐβούλευσεν are a yet clearer indication that ō, ου were, in Attic, still ō-sounds.[2]

That ō ever approximated to an ü-sound, even in post-classical times, is more than doubtful. It has been assumed partly to account

---

[1] I. 358, Λευκολοφίδω (before 444), 93 a, 8; θεῶ (after 444); II. 572, τοιῶτον (after Eucl.).

[2] μού, Ar. *Eq.*, 1237; προὐβούλευσεν, II. 57 b. Cf. also οὗτου (for ὅτου), II. 578, 30. There can be little doubt that throughout the Attic period ου, υε, εο commonly ran into ō in daily utterance, whether by contraction or crasis, and that the Athenians did not care to distinguish the four sounds. Cf. also Meisterh., *Gr.* p. 33, on Θεο- and Θου-.

for the continued representation of ου, ō by the simple O when these sounds had by supposition become = ū.[1] Blass infers this change in the ο by its frequent transliteration with Latin *u*. It is most uncommon to find it confounded with ου in inscriptions of the Roman period, and the vowel has at this day in Greece the same sound which, so far as we can gather, it had at the time of Pericles and at that of Homer. We find in contemporary Greek and Latin inscriptions a continual interchange of Latin *o*, *u*, and Greek ου; if Latin *u* is found for *o*, so is late Greek ου (ū), used to represent Latin *o* (*e.g.* φούλλικλος = *folliculus*). The Latin *-us* for *-ος* doubtless helped the confusion of the two vowels; the change is often attributable to the working of a special analogy (as in *paenula* = φαινόλης) which may equally change any other vowel to *u* (as *crapula* = κραιπάλη, *purpura* = πορφύρα). The examples collected by Saalfeld[2] make clear the Roman preference for *u*, whether to stand for an original ου, α, ε, ο, ω, η, or even to separate consonants whose collocation was unwonted in Latin.[3] But where analogy or some more obscure causes of perversion are not at work, the Latin *o* is the recognized equivalent of Greek ο. The Latin *ŭ* is transliterated by Greek ο from a different cause; this is discussed with much good sense by Dittenberger (*Hermes*, VI. p. 281), who observes that no similarity of sound is indicated by the transliteration, as the Greeks of the Roman period, having no short *u* represented in their alphabet, were obliged to resort either to ο or ου, the one in violation of vowel-quality, the other of vowel-quantity. And, in any case, the vagaries of ignorant lapicides at a time when the instincts of language were in a universal decline, and the changed and changing relations of the Roman phonetic system to that of the Greeks were an added source of confusion and misrepresentation, are not of such authority as to justify us in supposing a temporary divergence from the normal pronunciation of a vowel, standing in no relation to the general progress of

---

[1] Cf. Blass, *Ausspr. des Gr.*, p. 31, etc. Nothing can be inferred from such rare orthographical caprices as Δάμωνους, Νίκωνους.

[2] *Lautgesetze d. Gr. Lehnwörter im Latein.*, pp. 74 seqq.

[3] In the case of ἐπιστολή the process of analogy betrays itself, *epistola* becoming *epistula*. The history of Ἑκάβη in Latin is similar, and instances of the kind can be easily multiplied by any one familiar with early Latin literature and epigraphy.

phonetic decay, and leaving no trace of its existence in the later history of the language. The fact is that o, with α, ε, and ι alone of the Greek vowels and diphthongs, has never changed; and it seems highly improbable that its sign O could have been used during much of the fourth century, interchangeably with ου to represent an ū-sound. Had this been the sound to be indicated, the sign ου would have supervened entirely,[1] and ο would have been limited to its proper province. Moreover, as already pointed out, a slight difference was felt between ō and ου, even in the fourth century. This would, of course, be impossible, had the phonetic change under discussion been complete at that time. After the Attic period the two sounds are invariably written ου, and it may well have been during the third century that they were entirely merged in ū. It may be added here that ŏ, like ĕ, was clearly of a closed or narrow pronunciation, being qualitatively distinct (as shown by long ō) from the open ω, just as ĕ and ē differed from η. The spellings αο, εο, for αυ, ευ[2] are a confirmation of this. The close ŏ-sound of modern French (as in *fautif*) may be compared.

The pronunciation of ω is well understood; it corresponds to that of η, ω being the most open of the labial vowels, as η of the palatal. Very possibly the ω arising by *ablaut* from ā, η (as in πέπτωκα, ζωρός) may have kept in classical times a broader sound than that existing in connection with ο (as in λύω, δῶρον). That it was always an *open* vowel (*i.e.*, without a vanish) is evidenced by its consistent discrimination from ō after the year of Eucleides, as well as by the various contractions which give rise to it. These are all, as it would be superfluous to point out in detail, quite analogous to those producing η.

3. THE VOWEL Υ.

The confusion of υ with ι, the first indication of its change of sound from *u* to *ü*, occurs, though rarely, in inscriptions of the fourth century. Ἀμφικτίονες becomes Ἀμφικτύονες; ἥμισυς is Old-Attic, ἥμισυς New-Attic; Κινδυῆς and Κινδυῆς appear interchangeably as early as the fifth century. The spelling Μουνυχιών is found once in

---

[1] Supposing υ to have become = ü at this time in Attica.
[2] Cf. G. Meyer, *Gr.* 119, 120.

the fourth, but after the Attic period (306)[1]. In the case of ἥμισυς, Κινδῦης, the change might arise from vowel-attraction. The transition was presumably a gradual one, as the degradation of υ was not complete until the Byzantine period, when υ = ι. The *ü*-sound must have been well established by the time of Plautus, although he and his contemporaries rendered υ by Latin *u*, in the absence of an appropriate symbol.[2] That it was equally established in Attic speech, and that by the end of the fifth century, as Meyer concludes,[3] is far from certain, since, as already pointed out, the use of ου for υ in Boeotia scarcely proves anything for the other dialects.

The so-called diphthong υι hardly existed in Attic of the fourth century, unless in the dative singular of the few occurring υ-stems. It was equivalent, in sound, to ü + ι, and its degradation must have kept pace with that of υ; so that, like οι, though much earlier, it took the successive forms *ü* and *i*.[4]

4. THE DIPHTHONGS ἄι, ᾶι, ἄυ, ᾶυ, ευ, ηυ, οι, ωι, ωυ.

In the diphthongs ἄι, ἄυ, ευ, οι (and in ει, ου, so long as these continued diphthongal), the two elements were probably pronounced with equal length and distinctness. This is indicated by their consistent discrimination from the corresponding diphthongs having the first element long, and in the case of ει, ου, by their equal discrimination, during the early Attic period, from ē, ō.

ᾰι = ᾰ + ι, with no inclination toward the sound of ε, η, as in later times. This is shown by crasis (αι + ε = ᾱ, αι + ο = ω, etc. Cf. θαἰμάτια = τὰ ἱμάτια, Ar. *Vesp.* 408), and by the Attic history of words like Ἀθηναία (Ἀθηνᾶ), Πειραιεύς (Πειραεύς), etc. The earliest examples of ε written for αι on stones of Attica belong to the second century A.D. — more than four hundred years after the Attic ceased to be a distinct dialect.

---

[1] Meisterh., *Gr.* p. 12.
[2] Cf. G. Meyer, *Gr.* 85, who adduces the spellings *lunter* and *linter* = Greek πλυντήρ.   [3] *Gr.* 86.
[4] In words like υἱός, ὀργυιά, γεγονυῖα, the ι was entirely lost in Attic before the end of the fifth century (cf. Meisterh., *Gr.* p. 29), having become semi-vocal, as in the other ι-diphthongs before vowels. This shows that υι cannot have been like French *ni* of *lui* (as according to Meyer, *Gr.* 130); its first element must have been a pure vowel, as in the case of the other diphthongs.

ᾱι = ᾱ + ι. It was never confounded with ᾰι, as is shown by the divergence of their phonetic changes in post-classical times, αι becoming ultimately = ε and ᾱι = ᾱ. An instance of the omission of ι will hardly be found in inscriptions of Attica earlier than the first century B.C.

ᾰυ = ᾰ + υ. In many Ionic inscriptions αυ is written αο; so once in Attic (v. G. Meyer, *Gr.* 120). In Roman times it was transliterated by Latin *au*, and its pronunciation in Greece has changed, up to the present time, only in the devocalization of its second element (*av* or *af* for *av*).

ᾱυ existed in Attic in crases like αὐτός, ταὐτά; perhaps also in the word γραῦς.

ευ = ε + υ. In Ionic it was often written εο, and, conversely, εο could always be pronounced as one syllable = ευ. This illustrates with sufficient clearness its classical pronunciation. It has now suffered the same change as αυ, and = *ev* or *ef*. There is no indication that it had at any place or period either of the sounds given it in the ordinary English and German pronunciations of Greek; namely, *yu* and *oi*.

ηυ = η + υ. It occurs in Attic as the augment of αυ, ευ. Cf. Meisterh., *Gr.* p. 78, 5; Rutherford, *New Phrynichus*, CXXXI.

οι = ο + ι. It continued diphthongal until long after the Christian era, when ᾰι, ᾱι, ει, ηι, ου, ωι had assumed the simple *a, e, i, o, u* sounds.

ωι = ω + ι. The omission of ι scarcely occurs until the first century B.C., except before a vowel, as in λῷον, σῷῶ,[1] according to an Attic law already noticed. It is kept distinct from οι, however, becoming ultimately = ω, while οι in Byzantine times = υ (*ü*) and later = ī.

ωυ = ω + υ. Attic only in crasis, as πρωυδᾶν, Ar. *Av.* 556.[2]

It will be observed that until the end of the fifth century all the diphthongs were pronounced as they are written.

---

[1] Better than σώω, *C. I. A.*, I. 2 *b*, 7.

[2] There is only one verb in Attic beginning with ου, and the imperfect of οὐρῶ is ἐούρουν.

ARCHÆOLOGICAL INSTITUTE OF AMERICA.

AMERICAN SCHOOL OF CLASSICAL STUDIES AT ATHENS.

January, 1888.

AMERICAN SCHOOL OF CLASSICAL STUDIES AT ATHENS.

1887-1888.

TRUSTEES.

A corporation was formed in March, 1886, under the statutes of the Commonwealth of Massachusetts, with the name of "The Trustees of the American School of Classical Studies at Athens," to hold the title to the land and building in Athens belonging to the School, and to hold and invest all permanent funds which may be received for its maintenance.

The Board consists of the following gentlemen : —

    JAMES RUSSELL LOWELL, Cambridge, *President.*
    MARTIN BRIMMER, Boston.
    HENRY DRISLER, New York.
    BASIL L. GILDERSLEEVE, Baltimore.
    WILLIAM W. GOODWIN, Cambridge, *Secretary.*
    HENRY G. MARQUAND, New York.
    CHARLES ELIOT NORTON, Cambridge.
    FREDERIC J. DE PEYSTER, New York.
    HENRY C. POTTER, New York.
    WILLIAM M. SLOANE, Princeton.
    SAMUEL D. WARREN, Boston, *Treasurer.*
    JOHN WILLIAMS WHITE, Cambridge.
    THEODORE D. WOOLSEY, New Haven.

EXECUTIVE COMMITTEE OF THE TRUSTEES.

JAMES RUSSELL LOWELL.	CHARLES ELIOT NORTON.
WILLIAM W. GOODWIN.	SAMUEL D. WARREN.

MANAGING COMMITTEE.

THOMAS D. SEYMOUR, Yale University, New Haven, Conn., *Chairman*.
H. M. BAIRD, University of the City of New York, New York.
I. T. BECKWITH, Trinity College, Hartford, Conn.
FRANCIS BROWN, Union Theological Seminary, 1200 Park Ave., New York.
MISS A. C. CHAPIN, Wellesley College, Wellesley, Mass.
MARTIN L. D'OOGE, University of Michigan, Ann Arbor, Mich.
HENRY DRISLER, Columbia College, 48 West 46th St., New York.
O. M. FERNALD, Williams College, Williamstown, Mass.
A. F. FLEET, University of Missouri, Columbia, Mo.
BASIL L. GILDERSLEEVE, Johns Hopkins University, Baltimore.
WILLIAM W. GOODWIN, Harvard University, Cambridge, Mass., *Chairman of Committee on Publications*.
WILLIAM G. HALE, Cornell University, Ithaca, N. Y.
ALBERT HARKNESS, Brown University, Providence, R. I.
THOMAS W. LUDLOW, Yonkers, N. Y., *Secretary*.
AUGUSTUS C. MERRIAM, Columbia College, New York; *Director of the School* (1877-1888), Athens, Greece.
CHARLES ELIOT Norton (*ex officio*), Harvard University, Cambridge, Mass., *President of the Archæological Institute of America*.
FRANCIS W. PALFREY, 255 Beacon St., Boston.
WILLIAM PEPPER, University of Pennsylvania, 1811 Spruce St., Philadelphia.
FREDERIC J. DE PEYSTER, 7 East 42d St., New York, *Treasurer*.
WILLIAM M. SLOANE, College of New Jersey, Princeton, N. J.
FITZGERALD TISDALE, College of the City of New York, New York.
WILLIAM S. TYLER, Amherst College, Amherst, Mass.
JAMES C. VAN BENSCHOTEN, Wesleyan University, Middletown, Conn.
WILLIAM R. WARE, Columbia College, School of Mines, New York.
JOHN WILLIAMS WHITE, Harvard University, Cambridge, Mass.

EXECUTIVE COMMITTEE.

THOMAS D. SEYMOUR, *Chairman*. CHARLES ELIOT NORTON.
WILLIAM W. GOODWIN. FREDERIC J. DE PEYSTER, *Treasurer*.
THOMAS W. LUDLOW, *Secretary*. WILLIAM R. WARE.
JOHN WILLIAMS WHITE.

ANNUAL DIRECTORS.

1882-1888.

WILLIAM WATSON GOODWIN, Ph.D., LL.D., Eliot Professor of Greek Literature in Harvard University. 1882-83.

LEWIS R. PACKARD, Ph.D., Hillhouse Professor of Greek in Yale University. 1883-84.

JAMES COOKE VAN BENSCHOTEN, LL.D., Seney Professor of the Greek Language and Literature in Wesleyan University. 1884-85.

FREDERIC DE FOREST ALLEN, Ph.D., Professor of Classical Philology in Harvard University. 1885-86.

MARTIN L. D'OOGE, Ph.D., Professor of Greek in the University of Michigan. 1886-87.

AUGUSTUS C. MERRIAM, Ph.D., Professor of Greek in Columbia College. 1887-88.

CO-OPERATING COLLEGES.

1887-1888.

AMHERST COLLEGE.
BROWN UNIVERSITY.
COLLEGE OF THE CITY OF NEW YORK.
COLLEGE OF NEW JERSEY.
COLUMBIA COLLEGE.
CORNELL UNIVERSITY.
DARTMOUTH COLLEGE.
HARVARD UNIVERSITY.
JOHNS HOPKINS UNIVERSITY.

TRINITY COLLEGE.
UNIVERSITY OF THE CITY OF NEW YORK.
UNIVERSITY OF MICHIGAN.
UNIVERSITY OF MISSOURI.
UNIVERSITY OF PENNSYLVANIA.
WESLEYAN UNIVERSITY.
WELLESLEY COLLEGE.
WILLIAMS COLLEGE.
YALE UNIVERSITY.

THE AMERICAN SCHOOL OF CLASSICAL STUDIES AT ATHENS.

The American School of Classical Studies at Athens, founded by the Archæological Institute of America, and organized under the auspices of some of the leading American Colleges, was opened October 2, 1882. During the first five years of its existence it occupied a hired house on the Ὁδὸς Ἀμαλίας in Athens, near the ruins of the Olympieum. A large and convenient building has now been erected for the School on a piece of land, granted by the generous liberality of the Government of Greece, on the southeastern slope of Mount Lycabettus, adjoining the ground already occupied by the English School. This permanent home of the School, built by the subscriptions of its friends in the United States, will be ready for occupation early in 1888. During the first months of 1887–88, the School has been accommodated in temporary quarters in the city.

The new building contains the apartments to be occupied by the Director and his family, and a large room which will be used as a library and also as a general reading-room and place of meeting for the whole School. A few rooms in the house are intended for the use of students. These will be assigned by the Director, under such regulations as he may establish, to as many members of the School as they will accommodate. Each student admitted to the privilege of a room in the house will be expected to undertake the performance of some service to the School, to be determined by the Director; such, for example, as keeping the accounts of the School, taking charge of the delivery of books from the Library and their return, and keeping up the catalogue of the Library.

The Library now contains about 1,500 volumes, exclusive of sets of periodicals. It includes a complete set of the Greek classics, and the most necessary books of reference for philological, archæological, and architectural study in Greece.

The advantages of the School are offered free of expense for tuition to graduates of the Colleges co-operating in its support, and to other American students who are deemed by the Committee of sufficient promise to warrant the extension to them of the privilege of membership. It is hoped that the Archæological Institute may in time be supplied with the means of establishing scholarships, which will aid some members in defraying their expenses at the School. In the mean time, students must rely upon their own resources, or upon scholarships which may be granted them by the Colleges to which they belong. The amount needed for the expenses of an eight months' residence in Athens differs little from that required in other European capitals, and depends chiefly on the economy of the individual.

A peculiar feature of the temporary organization of the School during its first six years, which has distinguished it from the older German and French schools at Athens, has been the yearly change of Director. This arrangement, by which a new Director has been sent out each year by one of the co-operating Colleges, was never looked upon as permanent; and it has now been decided to begin the next year (1888–89) with a new organization. A Director will henceforth be chosen for a term of five years, while an Annual Director will also be sent out each year by one of the Colleges to assist in the conduct of the School. (See Regulation V.) Dr. CHARLES WALDSTEIN, of New York, now Director of the Fitzwilliam Museum of Art at the University of Cambridge, England, has been chosen Director of the School for five years beginning in October, 1888; and he has accepted the appointment on the condition that a sufficient permanent fund be raised before that time to support the School under its new organization. It is therefore earnestly hoped and confidently expected that the School will henceforth be under the control of a permanent Director, who by continuous residence at Athens will accumulate that body of local and special knowledge without which the highest purpose of such a school cannot be fulfilled. In the mean time the School has been able, even under its temporary organization, to meet a most pressing want, and to be of some service to classical scholarship in America. It has sought at first, and it must continue to seek for the present, rather to arouse a lively interest in classical archæology in American Colleges than to accomplish distinguished achievements. The lack of this interest has heretofore been conspicuous;

but without it the School at Athens, however well endowed, can never accomplish the best results. A decided improvement in this respect is already apparent; and it is beyond question that the presence in many American Colleges of professors who have been resident a year at Athens under favorable circumstances, as annual directors or as students of the School, has done much, and will do still more, to stimulate intelligent interest in classic antiquity.

REGULATIONS OF THE AMERICAN SCHOOL OF CLASSICAL STUDIES AT ATHENS.

I. The object of the American School of Classical Studies is to furnish an opportunity to study classical Literature, Art, and Antiquities in Athens, under suitable guidance, to graduates of American Colleges and to other qualified students; to prosecute and to aid original research in these subjects; and to co-operate with the Archæological Institute of America, so far as it may be able, in conducting the exploration and excavation of classic sites.

II. The School is in charge of a Managing Committee. This Committee, which was originally appointed by the Archæological Institute, disburses the annual income of the School, and has power to add to its membership and to make such regulations for the government of the School as it may deem proper. The President of the Archæological Institute and the Director and the Annual Director of the School are *ex officio* members of the Managing Committee.

III. The Managing Committee meets semi-annually, in New York on the third Friday in November, and in Boston on the third Friday in May. Special meetings may be called at any time by the Chairman.

IV. The Chairman of the Committee is the official representative of the interests of the School in America. He presents a report annually to the Archæological Institute concerning the affairs of the School.

V. 1. The School is under the superintendence of a Director. The Director is chosen and his salary is fixed by the Committee.

The term for which he is chosen is five years. The Committee provide him with a house in Athens, containing apartments for himself and his family, and suitable rooms for the meetings of the members of the School, its collections, and its library.

2. Each year the Committee appoints from the instructors of the Colleges uniting in the support of the School an Annual Director, who resides in Athens during the ensuing year and co-operates in the conduct of the School. In case of the illness or absence of the Director, the Annual Director acts as Director for the time being.

VI. The Director superintends personally the work of each member of the School, advising him in what direction to turn his studies, and assisting him in their prosecution. He conducts no regular courses of instruction, but holds meetings of the members of the School at stated times for consultation and discussion. He makes a full report annually to the Managing Committee of the work accomplished by the School.

VII. The school year extends from the first of October to the 1st of June. Members are required to prosecute their studies during the whole of this time in Greek lands under the supervision of the Director. The studies of the remaining four months necessary to complete a full year (the shortest time for which a certificate is given) may be carried on in Greece or elsewhere, as the student prefers.

VIII. Bachelors of Arts of co-operating Colleges, and all Bachelors of Arts who have studied at one of these Colleges as candidates for a higher degree, are admitted to membership in the School on presenting to the Committee a certificate from the instructors in Classics of the College at which they have last studied, stating that they are competent to pursue an independent course of study at Athens under the advice of the Director. All other persons desiring to become members of the School must make application to the Committee. Members of the School are subject to no charge for instruction. The Committee reserves the right to modify the conditions of membership.

IX. Each member of the School must pursue some definite subject of study or research in classical Literature, Art, or Antiquities, and must present a thesis or report, embodying the results of some important part of his year's work. These theses, if approved by the Director, are sent to the Managing Committee, by which each thesis is referred to a sub-committee of three members, of whom two are appointed by the Chairman, and the third is always the Director under whose supervision the thesis was prepared. If recommended for publication by this sub-committee, the thesis or report may be issued in the Papers of the School.

X. When any member of the School has completed one or more full years of study, the results of which have been approved by the Director, he receives a certificate stating the work accomplished by him, signed by the Director of the School, the President of the Archæological Institute, and the Chairman and the Secretary of the Managing Committee.

XI. American students resident or travelling in Greece who are not regular members of the School may, at the discretion of the Director, be enrolled as special students and enjoy the privileges of the School.

PUBLICATIONS OF THE AMERICAN SCHOOL OF CLASSICAL STUDIES AT ATHENS. 1882–1888.

The Annual Reports of the Committee may be had gratis on application to the Secretary of the Managing Committee. The other publications are for sale by Messrs. Damrell & Upham, 283 Washington Street, Boston.

First, Second, and Third Annual Reports of the Managing Committee, 1881–84. pp. 30.

Fourth Annual Report of the Committee, 1884–85. pp. 30.

Fifth and Sixth Annual Reports of the Committee, 1885–87. pp. 56.

Bulletin I. Report of William W. Goodwin, Director of the School in 1882–83. pp. 33. Price 25 cents.

Bulletin II. Memoir of Lewis R. Packard, Director of the School in 1883–84, with Resolutions of the Committee and the Report for 1883–84. pp. 34. Price 25 cents.

Preliminary Report of an Archæological Journey made in Asia Minor during the Summer of 1884. By J. R. S. Sterrett. pp. 45. Price 25 cents.

PAPERS OF THE SCHOOL.

Volume I. 1882–83. Published in 1885. 8vo. pp. viii. and 262. Illustrated. Price $2.00.

CONTENTS: —
1. Inscriptions of Assos, edited by J. R. S. Sterrett.
2. Inscriptions of Tralleis, edited by J. R. S. Sterrett.
3. The Theatre of Dionysus, by James R. Wheeler.
4. The Olympicion at Athens, by Louis Bevier.
5. The Erechtheion at Athens, by Harold N. Fowler.
6. The Battle of Salamis, by William W. Goodwin.

Volume III. 1884–85. Published in 1888. The Wolfe Expedition to Asia Minor in 1885, with 651 Inscriptions, mostly hitherto unpublished. By J. R. Sitlington Sterrett, Ph.D. With two Maps, made for this volume by Professor H. Kiepert. 8vo. pp. vii. and 448. Price $2.50.

Volume IV. 1885–86. Published in 1888. 8vo. pp. 277. Illustrated. Price $2.00.

CONTENTS: —
1. The Theatre of Thoricus, Preliminary Report by Walter Miller.
2. The Theatre of Thoricus, Supplementary Report by William L. Cushing.
3. On Greek Versification in Inscriptions, by Frederic D. Allen.
4. The Athenian Pnyx, by John M. Crow; with a Survey of the Pnyx and Notes by Joseph Thacher Clarke.
5. Notes on Attic Vocalism, by J. McKeen Lewis.

Volume II., 1883–84, containing Professor Sterrett's Report of his Epigraphical Journey in Asia Minor in 1884, with Inscriptions (as in Vol. III.), and with two new Maps by Professor Kiepert, will be published, it is hoped, during the year 1888.

www.ingramcontent.com/pod-product-compliance
Lightning Source LLC
Chambersburg PA
CBHW022115230426
43672CB00008B/1397